SPATIAL INEQUALITY AND DEVELOPMENT

UNU WORLD INSTITUTE FOR DEVELOPMENT ECONOMICS RESEARCH (UNU-WIDER)

was established by the United Nations University as its first research and training centre and started work in Helsinki, Finland, in 1985. The purpose of the Institute is to undertake applied research and policy analysis on structural changes affecting the developing and transitional economies, to provide a forum for the advocacy of policies leading to robust, equitable, and environmentally sustainable growth, and to promote capacity strengthening and training in the field of economic and social policy-making. Its work is carried out by staff researchers and visiting scholars in Helsinki and through networks of collaborating scholars and institutions around the world.

UNU World Institute for Development Economics Research (UNU-WIDER)
Katajanokanlaituri 6B, FIN-00160 Helsinki, Finland

Spatial Inequality and Development

Edited by
RAVI KANBUR AND ANTHONY J. VENABLES

*A study prepared by the World Institute for Development Economics
Research of the United Nations University (UNU-WIDER)*

OXFORD
UNIVERSITY PRESS

HD
75
.S69
2005

OXFORD
UNIVERSITY PRESS

Great Clarendon Street, Oxford OX2 6DP

Oxford University Press is a department of the University of Oxford.
It furthers the University's objective of excellence in research, scholarship,
and education by publishing worldwide in

Oxford New York

Auckland Cape Town Dar es Salaam Hong Kong Karachi Kuala Lumpur
Madrid Melbourne Mexico City Nairobi New Delhi Shanghai Taipei Toronto
With offices in

Argentina Austria Brazil Chile Czech Republic France Greece
Guatemala Hungary Italy Japan South Korea Poland Portugal
Singapore Switzerland Thailand Turkey Ukraine Vietnam

Oxford is a registered trade mark of Oxford University Press
in the UK and in certain other countries

Published in the United States
by Oxford University Press Inc., New York

© United Nations University World Institute
for Development Economics Research
(UNU-WIDER), 2005

British Library Cataloguing in Publication Data
Data available

Library of Congress Cataloging in Publication Data
Data available

ISBN 0-19-927863-6

Typeset by Newgen Imaging Systems (P) Ltd., Chennai, India
Printed in Great Britain
on acid-free paper by
Biddles Ltd., King's Lynn, Norfolk

Contents

Part I. Introduction

Part II. Measurement of Spatial Inequality

Part III. Location, Externalities, and Unequal Development

List of Figures

List of Maps

List of Tables

List of Acronyms and Abbreviations

ACCRA	American Chamber of Commerce Researchers Association
BLS	Bureau of Labor Statistics (USA)
BNPP	Bank Netherlands Partnership Programme
CASE	Centre for Analysis of Social Exclusion (LSE)
CDF	Cumulative distribution function
CEE	Central and Eastern Europe
CIS	Commonwealth of Independent States
COLA	Cost of Living Adjustment programme (USA)
CPD	country product dummy method
CPI	consumer price index
DFID	Department for International Development (UK)
EBRD	European Bank for Reconstruction and Development
EGI	National Statistical and Geographical Institute (Mexico)
ELI	entry-level item
ECV	Encuesta de Condiciones de Vida (Ecuador)
EPM	Enquête Permanente Auprès des Ménages (Madagascar)
FDI	foreign direct investment
FGLS	feasible generalized least squares
FGT	Foster–Greer–Thorbecke
FIPE	Fundação Instituto de Pesquisas Econômicas (Brazil)
f.o.b.	free on board
GATT	General Agreement on Tariffs and Trade
GIS	Geographical Information Systems
GLS	generalized least squares
GMM	generalized method of moments
HBS	Household Budget Survey
IAF	Inquérito Nacional aos Agregados Familiares sobre as Condições de Vida (Mozambique)
IBGE	Instituto Brasileiro de Geografia e Estatistica
ICP	International Comparison Programme
INEC	Instituto Nacional de Estadistica y Census (Ecuador)
INEGI	Instituto Nacional de Estadística Geografía e Informática (Mexico)
INSTAT	Institut National de la Statistique (Madagascar)
ISI	import substitution industrialization
LFS	Labour Force Survey
LIS	Luxembourg Income Study
LISA	local indicator of spatial association
LSE	London School of Economics and Political Science

LSMS	Living Standards Measurement Study
MAR	Marshall–Allyn–Romer
MSI	minimum subsistence income
NAFTA	North American Free Trade Agreement
NEG	new economic geography
NBS	National Bureau of Statistics (China)
OECD	Organisation for Economic Co-operation and Development
OLS	ordinary least squares
PCE	per capita expenditure
PCSE	panel corrected standard error
PNAD	Pesquisa Nacional por Amostra de Domicílios (IBGE, Brazil)
PPP	purchasing power parity
RHS	Rural Household Survey (China)
RLMS	Russian Longitudinal Monitoring Survey
RPED	Regional Programme on Enterprise Development
SMEs	small- and medium-sized enterprises
SUSENAS	Indonesian National Socioeconomic Survey
TVE	township and village enterprise
UDHS	Uganda Demographic and Health Survey
UNICP	United Nations International Comparison Programme
WHO	World Health Organization
WIDER	World Institute for Development Economics Research

List of Contributors

Bettina Aten is in the Regional Economics Division of the Bureau of Economic Analysis in Washington DC, on leave from Bridgewater State College. Her research interests include the estimation of spatial purchasing power parities and their applications at various geographic levels for income, housing, and transportation studies.

Carlos R. Azzoni is Associate Dean of the School of Economics, Administration and Accounting and a professor of economics at the University of São Paulo. His area of research is economic inequality in general, with focus on regional inequality.

Luc Christiaensen is a poverty economist at the World Bank working on East Africa and the Horn of Africa countries, currently based in Addis Ababa. He is an applied researcher with an active interest in vulnerability, poverty, and nutrition-related issues in sub-Saharan Africa.

Donald Davis is a professor of economics at Columbia University and a research associate at the National Bureau of Economic Research. His research interests span international trade, economic geography, and economic development in the open economy.

Lionel Demery is an independent consultant economist specializing in development policy, policy reform, inequality, and poverty. He was formerly with the Africa Region of the World Bank, leading its work on economic policy and poverty reduction. He has taught at the University of Warwick, has served as an adviser to the International Labour Organization in Bangkok, and was a research fellow at the Overseas Development Institute in London.

Chris Elbers teaches development economics and international economics at Vrije University, Amsterdam. His research focuses on applied microeconomics and statistics, in particular poverty mapping and the econometric analysis of household data from developing countries.

Javier Escobal is a research director and senior researcher at the Group for the Analysis of Development (GRADE) in Lima. His main research interests are rural poverty, the impact of the macroeconomic policies in rural development and rural markets in developing countries.

Michael F. Förster is a research fellow at the European Centre for Social Welfare Policy and Research, and an administrator at the Non-Member Economies and International Migration Division of OECD. His main research interests are income distribution, inequalities, poverty and social exclusion, as well as social policy development in transitional economies.

Jed Friedman is with the World Bank, Washington DC. Previously, he was an associate economist at RAND in Santa Monica, USA, where the work for this chapter was completed. His main research interests concern poverty dynamics as well as the interrelationship between poverty and health.

Alan Heston is a professor of economics at the University of Pennsylvania. His main research interests have been in economic history of India, economic development with particular reference to Asia, and in international comparisons of output and purchasing power parities.

David Jesuit is an assistant professor of political science at Central Michigan University. Exploring connections between politics, policy, and inequality at the subnational level is his main research interest.

Ravi Kanbur is the T.H. Lee Professor of World Affairs and professor of economics at Cornell University. He has taught previously at Oxford, Cambridge, Princeton, Essex, and Warwick Universities, and has served on the staff of the World Bank, including as Chief Economist for Africa.

Peter Lanjouw is a lead economist with the World Bank Development Research Group, Washington DC. Previously, he was at Vrije University, Amsterdam, and the University of Namur. His main research interests are welfare measurement and rural development.

Songhua Lin is an assistant professor at Denison University. Her main research interests are the effect of trade policy in developing countries.

Tatiane Almeida de Menezes is an assistant professor at the University of São Paulo. She is also a researcher at Fundação Instituto de Pesquisas Econômicas (FIPE), where her main research interests are regional inequality, poverty, and consumption demand.

Naercio Menezes-Filho is an assistant professor at the University of São Paulo. He is also an international research associate at the Institute for Fiscal Studies. His main interests are inequality, education, and economic development.

Johan Mistiaen is with the World Bank Development Research Group, Washington DC. His current research focuses on poverty measurement issues, the geography of poverty, targeting and policy impact, particularly in sub-Saharan Africa.

Oliver Morrissey is Director of the Centre for Research in Economic Development and International Trade (CREDIT), School of Economics, University of Nottingham, and a research fellow in the Overseas Development Institute (ODI), London. His principal research interests are on aid effectiveness, aid and government behaviour, and trade policy reform in Africa.

Berk Özler is an economist in the World Bank Development Research Group, Washington DC. His current research interests include poverty measurement, inequality, effectiveness of targeting for poverty alleviation, and the impact of inequality on various outcomes, such as crime, health, or targeting efficiency.

Stefano Paternostro is a senior economist in the World Bank Poverty Reduction Group, Washington DC. His current research interests are in the distributional impact of policy reforms and poverty issues in sub-Saharan Africa.

Martin Ravallion is a senior manager at the World Bank's Research Department. His main research interests concern poverty and policies for fighting it, and has written extensively and advised numerous governments on this topic. He has also taught economics at several universities.

Andrés Rodríguez-Pose is a reader in economic geography and a Royal Society-Wolfson Research Merit Award holder at the London School of Economics and Political Science, where he also directs the M.Sc. programme in local economic development. His main research interests lie in the social, political, and institutional factors behind the evolution of regional disparities in developed and developing countries.

Javier Sánchez-Reaza is with CIDE (Centro de Investigación y Docencia Económicas) in Mexico City. Previously, he was at the University of Texas at El Paso undertaking research on border regions and economic development. His main research interests are in trade, economic growth, and spatial analysis.

Kenneth Simler is a research fellow in the Food Consumption and Nutrition Division at the International Food Policy Research Institute (IFPRI) in Washington DC. His areas of research include the measurement of poverty, policies for poverty reduction, and the economics of investment in children's education and nutrition.

Timothy Smeeding is the Maxwell Professor of Public Policy at Syracuse University. He is also project director and founder of the Luxembourg Income Study. His work focuses on cross-national comparisons of poverty and social policy for vulnerable populations, such as children and the elderly.

Dirk Willem te Velde is a research fellow at the Overseas Development Institute, London. He specializes in trade and investment policy and international public goods, and has published considerably on these topics.

Máximo Torero is a senior researcher at the Group for the Analysis of Development (GRADE) in Lima. His research work lies mostly in analysing poverty, the economics of geography, labour economics, and regulation of public utilities.

Anthony Venables is a professor of international economics at the London School of Economics, Director of the globalization programme at the LSE Centre for Economic Performance, and research fellow at the Centre for Economic Policy Research. He works in the areas of international trade, economic integration, and economic geography.

David Weinstein is the Carl S. Shoup Professor of the Japanese Economy. He has held professorial positions at Harvard and the University of Michigan, as well as serving as a senior economist at the Federal Reserve Bank of New York. His research interests cover international trade, geography, and the Japanese economy.

Ruslan Yemtsov is a senior economist in the Poverty Reduction and Economic
Management Unit, Europe and Central Asia Region (ECSPE) of the World Bank,
Washington DC. Prior to this he was a professor at Moscow State University. His
main area of responsibility is work on poverty monitoring in CIS and Balkan
countries, and his research interests are labour markets in transition economies and
welfare and income distribution analysis.

Book Title: 420

Foreword

Many developing and transition countries exhibit significant regional disparities in average incomes, the incidence and depth of poverty, health indicators, education status, and other correlates of living standards and human development. Spatial variations are particularly high in large countries like Brazil, China, Russia, and South Africa. But they are also evident in smaller developing nations, especially in Africa, and they continue to be an important social concern in developed countries—for example, with regard to US poverty rates and UK health indices.

Variations in living standards within countries have a number of underlying causes. They reflect historical differences in the pace of development (São Paulo versus northeast Brazil), the uneven impact of economic reform (Guangdong versus Qinhai), discrimination in the provision of economic and social infrastructure (South Africa during apartheid), and impediments to labour migration (China and Russia). Unfavourable agricultural conditions and geographical remoteness from principal markets also play a role. Whatever the original source, there is a widespread perception that spatial disparities in human development have recently become more visible and that they are increasing over time.

Despite the recognition of the problem and its policy significance, there has been very little systematic scholarly analysis into the causes of growing inequalities within countries and their cumulative detrimental impact on human development. Under the direction of Ravi Kanbur and Tony Venables, the UNU-WIDER project on *Spatial Disparities in Human Development* drew together expertise from all regions of the globe in order to better understand the incidence, significance, and causes of spatial variations within countries, and to contribute to the global policy debate. This book is a collection of country, regional, and comparative studies presented and discussed at a conference at the London School of Economics in June 2002. It is the first serious attempt to examine spatial inequality in a global context from multiple perspectives and disciplines, and will be essential reading for academics and students interested in this research topic. It also provides valuable background information and advice with policymakers and policytakers, and will be useful reading material for lay readers in learning more about a topic of growing national and international significance.

Tony Shorrocks
Director, UNU-WIDER, Helsinki
May 2004

Acknowledgments

We are thankful for the administrative support received from Joyce Knuutila at Cornell University, Nigel Rogers, and Emma Taverner at the London School of Economics, and finally Lorraine Telfer-Taivainen, the project secretary at WIDER, for helping to run the whole process—submissions to the conference, the conference itself, and finally the editing of the volume—smoothly and efficiently. We could not have done our job without them.

Some of Chapter 9 previously appeared in the *World Bank Economic Review* 17(3) 2003: 317–47. It is reproduced here with the kind permission of Oxford University Press.

UNU-WIDER gratefully acknowledges the financial contributions to the research programme by the governments of Denmark (Royal Ministry of Foreign Affairs), Finland (Ministry for Foreign Affairs), Norway (Royal Ministry of Foreign Affairs), Sweden (Swedish International Development Cooperation Agency—Sida), and the United Kingdom (Department for International Development). These agencies are not responsible for any information provided or views expressed, which remain those of the contributors alone.

Ithaca and London   Ravi Kanbur
May 2004   Tony Venables

PART I

INTRODUCTION

Spatial Inequality and Development

RAVI KANBUR AND ANTHONY J. VENABLES

1.1. FIVE QUESTIONS

What exactly is spatial inequality? What are its determinants? How has it been evolving? Why does it matter? And what, if any, should be the policy response to spatial inequality?

These questions have become important in recent years as, amidst a growing concern about increasing inequality, the spatial dimensions of inequality have begun to attract considerable policy interest. In China, Mexico, Russia, India, and South Africa, as well as most other developing and transition economies, there is a sense that spatial and regional inequality, of economic activity, incomes, and social indicators, is on the increase. To some extent this may be a normal feature of economic growth, as new activities develop around coasts or border regions. But are such patterns transient or permanent? What factors are conducive to the spread of activity from booming to backward regions? Also important in the policy debate is a perceived sense that increasing internal spatial inequality is related to greater openness of economies, and to globalization in general.

Spatial inequality matters for a number of reasons. Market failures, and the positive and negative externalities associated with clustering and congestion, mean that outcomes are likely to be inefficient. The growth of megacities may be one aspect of this, but policy responses are far from clear. Should infrastructure expenditure be concentrated or dispersed? Should internal migration flows be restricted, or facilitated in order to narrow spatial wage gaps? Spatial inequality is a dimension of overall inequality, but it has added significance when spatial and regional divisions align with political and ethnic tensions to undermine social and political stability.

But despite these important popular and policy concerns, there is remarkably little systematic documentation of the facts of what has happened to spatial and regional inequality over the past ten to twenty years. Correspondingly, there is insufficient understanding of the determinants of internal spatial inequality in a globalizing world. As a result, the policy discussion tends to take place in something of an analytical and empirical vacuum. This volume of studies is the result of the first in a series of general and region-specific conferences on spatial inequality and development, which are in turn part of a project organized by the United Nations University's World Institute for Development Economics Research (UNU-WIDER) in Helsinki.

Collectively, the studies in this volume represent an attempt to answer the questions posed above, based on data from some twenty-five countries covering all regions of the world. They bring together perspectives and expertise in development economics and in economic geography. They form a well-researched entry point into an area of growing analytical and policy importance. This introduction provides an outline of the volume and brief descriptions of the chapters, and ends by highlighting key issues and areas for further research.

1.2. OVERVIEW OF THE VOLUME

The volume begins with chapters on measurement issues. An essential first step in measuring spatial inequality in a country is to develop accurate measures of real income disparities across regions within countries. The recent spurt of interest in economic geography has led to a greater focus on regional-level estimates of output within a country, but Chapter 2 by Aten and Heston addresses head-on the important question of accounting for regional price differences in making these calculations. While the Purchasing Power Parity (PPP) project has been invaluable in generating data on price variations across countries, there is very little comparable data on price variations across regions within countries. Given this limitation, the authors develop indirect methods, by modelling the variation in prices for the regional units in the world for which there is indeed regional price data, as a function of variables for which data is more generally available. The preferred estimated relationship can then be used to generate price indices for other regions of the world, and these prices can in turn be used to convert nominal output data into real output. The technique developed by Aten and Heston will prove indispensable to empirical researchers working on spatial inequality, whether in developing or developed countries.

Data availability is equally a problem in terms of household surveys which form the basis of much of the empirical work on interpersonal inequality, and the measurement of poverty in developing countries. The problem here is that while household surveys collect detailed information on income, consumption, and social indicators, their sample sizes are not large enough to allow adequate disaggregation to regional or subregional levels within a country. On the other hand, census data do not have much of the detailed information at the household level needed for inequality and poverty analysis. The obvious answer is to combine these data sources, and Chapter 3 by Elbers *et al.* does just that. Their approach is similar in some ways to that of Aten and Heston in Chapter 2. The variable of interest which is available only in the household survey, in this case some measure of household well-being, is modelled as a function of explanatory variables in the household survey that are also available in the census (or a survey with a much larger sample survey). The relationship estimated on the household survey is then applied to the census to generate an effectively larger sample of household well-being, which can then be disaggregated at the regional and subregional levels to study spatial inequality in household well-being. Elbers *et al.* illustrate the power of the technique by applying it to Ecuador, Madagascar, and Mozambique, decomposing national inequality into inequality within and between spatial units at successively finer levels of disaggregation. A major conclusion, consistent with the general inequality decomposition literature, is that the within-group component of inequality stays high (in excess of 75 per cent) even at what seem to be very high levels of disaggregation (in Ecuador, for example, down to the level of 915 local units with an average of just over 1,000 households). Thus, the contribution of average variations across spatial units, to total interpersonal inequality, seems to be no greater than 25 per cent. Does this mean that spatial inequality is not a phenomenon of great policy interest? In fact, the studies in this volume suggest otherwise, and this point will be taken up towards the end of this introductory chapter.

A further measurement issue is raised by the fact that regional per capita income is a blend of demographic and economic factors—for example, a combination of the age–income relationship and the age structure for a region. Chapter 4 by Azzoni *et al.* shows that recognizing this fact has important implications for the interpretation of studies of regional convergence. Using microage-income-level data across Brazilian regions, they demonstrate that the rate of convergence differs across age cohorts, and the aggregate results on convergence thus reflect the age composition of different regions, and changes in this age composition. The aggregate data suggest a speed of convergence which is much slower than the convergence for specific age cohorts. This opens up a new line of research, opening up the convergence black box as the title of the chapter suggests, which should become more prevalent as more extensive microlevel data become available for developing countries.

The second section of the volume moves from the perspective of measurement of income inequality to the perspective of economic geography. Chapter 5 by Escobal and Torero looks at the microlevel and investigates the determinants of the spatial variation in household-level well-being in Peru, using household survey data for 1991, 1994, 1996, and 1997. They first of all show the high level of spatial inequality in Peru. But, they also argue that these geographical differences can be accounted for by variation in private and, especially, public assets. Once these are accounted for, pure geography in the sense of altitude or temperature does not influence measures of household well-being. However, as they recognize and highlight, this simply pushes the question back one stage—the effect of geography on the provision of such an uneven distribution of public infrastructure, and the concentration of economic activity over and above the influence of physical geographical constraints.

The recent theoretical literature has suggested the importance of location and agglomeration externalities as key determinants of spatial concentration of economic activity and income. The empirical literature has lagged behind the theoretical developments, and the two studies in this section are attempts to identify and quantify these factors in the data. The chapter by Davis and Weinstein investigates the effect of region size on regional productivity, allowing for possible spillover effects across neighbouring regions, and other more standard explanatory factors. Using data from forty Japanese regions, they find that own size does matter in explaining regional total factor productivity—doubling own size raises productivity by 3.5 per cent. Moreover, the nature of neighbouring regions matters too for a region's own productivity. The uneven pattern of activity in Japan contributes to overall efficiency—if aggregate activity were to be spread evenly across the regions of Japan, output would be lower by 5 per cent.

Chapter 7 is Ravallion's contribution to this volume, looking at the issue of externalities from the microlevel of household survey data. Starting with panel data on 5,600 farm households from 111 counties in four provinces of China, he seeks an explanation of household consumption growth over the period 1985–90. He estimates a model of consumption growth that has household- and locality-level explanatory variables, allowing for time-variant fixed effects. There is strong evidence of geographical externalities, in the sense that locality level variables have an effect on consumption growth over and above household-level attributes. The explanation is that the level and nature of local economic activity, in the aggregate, affects household-level returns to human capital and infrastructure.

The next two chapters investigate the importance of the regional linkage between national growth and microlevel poverty reduction. Friedman, in Chapter 8, uses six household surveys over the fifteen-year period 1984–99 to analyse the impact of growth on poverty. He finds a very close connection between national growth and poverty reduction. But he finds rural poverty reduction that was more responsive to growth in the central locations of Java and Bali than it was in the more remote regions like Kalimantan. He suggests that, once again, public infrastructure such as transport networks can explain this variation.

In their chapter, Christiaensen *et al.* investigate the relationship between growth and poverty reduction using household survey data for eight African countries. Their conclusions are similar to those of Friedman for Indonesia. While economic growth is a key correlate of poverty reduction, its impact on poverty depends crucially on how remote poor households are from the centres of economic activity, and how well-served they are to infrastructure services. During a period of strong economic growth in Uganda between 1992 and 2000, for example, the incidence of poverty fell by a half in the Central Province, but by only 9 per cent in the remote Northern Province. In Ghana between 1992 and 1998, poverty in the capital city Accra fell sharply, but not so sharply in other, less well-connected, urban areas, and indeed it increased in the remote northern Savannah zone. Further detailed analysis highlights the importance of infrastructure in explaining these variations in the extent to which national growth is translated into poverty reduction across space.

As noted at the start of this introduction, one of the areas of concern in spatial inequality is the extent to which the increases seen in the last decade or two have been connected with the opening up that many economies have experienced, to trade and to foreign direct investment. The next section of the volume takes up this important question. The findings of Rodríguez-Pose and Sánchez-Reaza in Chapter 10 are consistent with a growing literature on regional inequality in Mexico post-NAFTA (North American Free Trade Agreement). The authors find unmistakable trends towards greater regional inequality and polarization. The earlier trend towards regional convergence has been reversed, and there is growing polarization between the North and the South. Clearly, proximity to the US market has been a determinant in the concentration of economic activity, and these forces have interacted with uneven distribution of infrastructure and public services to create very different opportunities for the different regions of Mexico.

Many studies take the spatial inequality of wage rates as the relevant object of study. The next two chapters in this section of the volume investigate spatial variation in wage rates in China and in Africa, respectively. Growing regional inequalities in China over the last two decades are much discussed in the literature, and in Chapter 11, Lin takes up the interregional wage inequality dimension of this question. Specifically, she focuses on the effects on wages of differential access to international markets. Defining 'market access' and 'supplier access' variables, she finds that about a quarter of the wage difference in the coastal provinces and about 15 per cent of the differences in the interior provinces can be explained by a province's market access and supplier access. Since China's provinces are as large as many individual countries (like Mexico), this is further support for the proposition that greater openness to trade can lead to greater spatial inequality in living standards, even when such opening up increases overall efficiency and growth, as it has done in China.

The chapter by te Velde and Morrissey is a comprehensive study of wage differentials in five African countries. Not surprisingly, wages are higher in the capital city compared to the rest of the country. This is partly because workers in the capital city have more years of formal education, which is shown to be a key individual-level determinant of wages. It is also partly due to the fact that foreign-owned firms are more likely to be located in the capital city, and it is also shown that these firms are more likely to pay higher wages than indigenously owned firms. If these foreign firms are also more productive, then the efficiency gains will have to be taken into account in assessing the consequences for distribution of opening up the economy to foreign firms. Finally, correcting for individual worker characteristics like education and tenure, and firm characteristics like size and foreign ownership, they find that workers in the capital city earn a substantial premium, compared to the rest of the country, of as much as 28 per cent. One problem with interpreting this goes back to Chapter 2 in this volume, by Aten and Heston. Since te Velde and Morrissey do not have data on price variations within a country, they cannot determine definitively that the nominal wage premium they establish in fact survives in real terms. In general, since the cost of living is higher in capital cities, the real wage differentials would be far less.

Economies in transition are a particularly interesting setting in which to study spatial inequality. Their rapid liberalizations and opening up to the external world are known to have increased inequality, and in some cases poverty. What exactly are the spatial dimensions of this increase in inequality? The last two chapters in this volume take up this issue, paying particular attention to data quality and interpretation. In their study of the Czech Republic, Hungary, Poland, and Russia, Förster *et al.* present a finding that is consistent with the outcome in many other countries—the capital city and well-connected urban areas closer to Western markets in the European Union have gained from overall economic growth, while remote regions have not done as well or actually lost out from the process of transition so far. These gaps, and relatedly the rural–urban gap, have increased.

Yemtsov conducts an in-depth study of the evolution of inequality and poverty in the Russian regions over the period 1994–2000, based on the Household Budget Survey. He finds that the contribution of between-region inequality to total interpersonal inequality is 33 per cent, a little higher than in the African and Latin American studies by Elbers *et al.* But it has been growing. In fact, most of the increase in interpersonal inequality in Russia is accounted for by the increase in the between-regional component. Not surprisingly, standard convergence tests show no convergence between Russian regions. If these trends continue, Yemtsov calculates that within a decade the majority of Russia's poor will be concentrated in a few impoverished regions, a picture of poverty concentration that bears similarity to a number of other countries such as Peru, also studied in this volume.

1.3. THE FIVE QUESTIONS AGAIN

Let us return to the five questions posed at the start. First, what exactly is spatial inequality? The dominant perspective on inequality in economics comes from considerations of interpersonal inequality—how individuals differ from each other along dimensions such as income, consumption, education, and health (in what follows, we will use income/consumption as the representative dimension). One way of approaching spatial inequality is to start from interpersonal inequality and consider its spatial dimensions. For any given delineation of individuals into mutually exclusive and exhaustive spatial units, each unit can be characterized by its per capita income and its population share. With this set-up there are several possible characterizations of spatial inequality:

 (i) Unweighted variation in per capita income across spatial units.
 (ii) Population share weighted variation in per capita income across spatial units.
(iii) Contribution of variation in per capita income across spatial units to income variation across all individuals.

All of these conceptualizations of spatial inequality are present in the literature, and in this volume. The first of them is the effective object of interest in the large number of studies on regional convergence (although they should all pay heed to the difficulties of taking into account regional price variations, as highlighted by Aten and Heston in Chapter 2). But it is the last two conceptualizations that come closest to the instinct of mainstream economics to treat interpersonal inequality as being the fundamental object of interest. Spatial inequality is clearly related to variation across spatial units and per capita income of a spatial unit is the analogue of individual income. The question can then be asked: what would have been the inequality among individuals if all individuals within a spatial unit had the per capita income of that unit, so that the only variation across individuals was that attributable to space? This is essentially the population share weighted variation in per capita income across spatial units. From this perspective, therefore, (ii) has claim to be a measure of spatial inequality. But if the ultimate object is overall interpersonal inequality, then we are led to (iii), the percentage of total interpersonal inequality 'accounted for' by (ii). As shown in this volume, taking (iii) as the concept of spatial inequality leads empirically to the conclusion that spatial inequality accounts for, at most, one-third of total interpersonal inequality. Most of the variation with individuals is within spatial units, not across them, even for quite fine disaggregations, as shown by Elbers *et al.* in Chapter 3, and by Yemtsov in Chapter 14.

What are the determinants of spatial inequality? If all economic activity were to take place on a 'featureless plane', and if economic activity had the standard neoclassical properties, economic activity would be evenly distributed across space and there would be no spatial dimension to inequality. But the world does not satisfy either of these two assumptions. There are real geographical features such as mountains and coasts and forests and rivers that can affect the distribution of economic activity and spatial inequality in well-being. But one conclusion from the studies in this volume—such as the chapters by Escobal and Torero, Friedman, and Christiaensen *et al.*—and the literature more broadly, is that the impact of these natural features is not as important as the geographical distribution of other features—specifically, infrastructure and public services. As shown in a number of chapters in this volume, a key determinant of household well-being in a region, over and above household specific characteristics, is the quantity and quality of infrastructure in that region.

However, even without variations in physical features, or infrastructure variations across regions, once the standard assumptions of neoclassical economics are dropped a number of possibilities arise for the propagation of spatial inequality. The new economic geography has highlighted, in particular, location and agglomeration externalities. These can arise because of knowledge spillovers, thick market effects, or input–output linkages between firms. They operate at various spatial levels; within regions of dense economic activity, within cities, and within narrowly specialized industrial districts of cities. Evidence has slowly begun to accumulate on the magnitude of the agglomeration externalities that create these disparities. The chapters by Davis and Weinstein and by Ravallion in this volume are an important contribution to this literature, and highlight the importance of agglomeration effects and location externalities.

How has spatial inequality been evolving over the past two decades? If the evidence presented in this volume is anything to go by, it has been on the increase. Its relationship to greater openness in trade and investment is investigated by Rodríguez-Pose and Sánchez-Reaza for Mexico and by Lin for China. Even where the last two decades have brought overall growth and poverty reduction, the benefits of this growth have not flowed evenly across space. Spatial inequality has grown—especially in transition economies, as documented in the chapters by Förster *et al.* and by Yemtsov—with the result that poverty reduction has been uneven across regions within countries, as documented in the chapters for Africa by Christiaensen *et al.* and for Indonesia by Friedman. However, a number of key questions remain. To what extent is some increase in spatial inequality a natural feature of development, as growth is initially concentrated in a few regions? Is this increase temporary, and how long is it likely to take for growth to spread from region to region? Some existing research suggests a pattern of increasing then decreasing spatial inequality, but further research is needed to identify factors that are conducive to the dispersion of activity.

Why does spatial inequality matter, and is a policy response appropriate? We have seen that spatial inequality accounts for only around one-third of total inequality, and part of this may be transient rather than permanent. Does this mean that spatial inequality is unimportant, as some might be tempted to argue? One argument in favour of doing nothing, or very little, is that if our ultimate objective is total interpersonal inequality, and if spatial inequality is at most one-third of this total, surely policy should focus on inequality *within* spatial units (which accounts for two-thirds of the total) rather than between. There are several responses to this. First, one-third is smaller than two-thirds, but is still quite big. Eliminating spatial inequality would have an impact on inequality far larger than some cross-country variations in inequality. And, as in the case of Russia, there are periods when even though spatial inequality is relatively small, much of the increase in total inequality is in fact increase in spatial inequality. However, the real question here is what policy instruments are available to address within- and between-group inequalities, and what the cost benefit of each instrument is. It may well turn out that 'per unit of inequality reduction' the instrument that addresses between-group inequality is cost-effective. This will depend on the specifics of the case—addressing between-group inequality cannot be simply dismissed because it is smaller than within-group inequality.

Furthermore, it might be the case that the distribution of individual attributes, such as ability, is the same in all regions. Spatial inequality is then particularly inequitable and—especially when aligned with political, religious, or ethnic tensions— may be dangerous to social and political stability. If spatial divisions align with ethnic, religious, or language splits, as so often happens, then the between-group component of inequality takes on a greater significance than its contribution to interpersonal inequality. In such cases, we ignore growing spatial inequality at our peril. Even when spatial units do not represent ethnic or other cleavages, but command the allegiance of the population as political entities, increasing disparities in group averages may lead to tensions and conflict.

Additional arguments derive from the real income losses that may be associated with spatial inequality. Spatial location decisions are associated with multiple market failures, particularly when agglomeration forces are present. These market failures depress real income, and may also retard growth as they depress the returns to job creation. For example, it is often suggested that prime cities are excessively large. There may be negative externalities arising from congestion costs in large cities. In addition, the presence of agglomeration economies and increasing returns to city formation gives rise to coordination failure, as it is not profitable for a single firm to relocate and establish a new centre of activity. What is needed, if new centres are to be established, is a collective or policy coordinated movement.

Complex policy choices also arise with migration and infrastructure. According to one view, there is too little migration and part of the problem of lagging regions arises because of individuals' reluctance to emigrate from such regions. The reason for the reluctance to migrate may be attachment to the area of birth, or may be that individuals are locked into declining regions by location-specific human capital. However, in neither of these cases is there a market failure. Failures, and consequent arguments for policy, arise if migrating individuals exert positive or negative externalities on other individuals in the locations that they are leaving or that they are joining. It is then far from clear that there is too little migration—there may well be too much, particularly into established urban centres. Similarly with infrastructure; as Escobal and Torero (Chapter 5) show, provision of public infrastructure is an important determinant of household well-being. Such investments may allow individuals to increase the return to their general and location-specific human capital and be a powerful instrument in favour of greater spatial equality. However, the benefits of such an allocation need to be weighed against the costs, particularly as urban infrastructure needs are often pressing.

The case for policy interventions to ensure a more spatially equitable and efficient allocation of infrastructure and public services has been powerfully made in this volume. But the specifics of this policy conclusion still need to be developed. The benefits of such an allocation need to be weighed against the costs, so both will have to be quantified. In order to do this we will need a deeper and more detailed understanding of the determinants of spatial inequality, and how exactly policy interventions in infrastructure and other areas will impinge on it. The studies in this volume have made a start. A full research agenda lies ahead.

PART II

MEASUREMENT OF SPATIAL
INEQUALITY

2

Regional Output Differences in
International Perspective

BETTINA ATEN AND ALAN HESTON

(US, Related
Countries)

2.1. INTRODUCTION

The political economy of countries revolves upon leaders gaining support from
different constituencies within an administrative boundary, be it a city ward, a province,
or a regional configuration in larger countries. Conflicts within countries frequently
centre on differences in income between regions and the extent to which these represent
one area receiving more public expenditures, projects, or subsidies than another. Within
and between countries, resources are often allocated inversely to a small degree to the
level of per capita income, for example, the social fund in the European Union (EU).
Since perceptions of regional neglect are partly based on objective estimates of income,
it is important to have good estimates. To understand the distribution of world income,
and concentrations of the very poor, it is important to have regional income estimates
that can be compared within and between countries, and this is the focus of our chapter.
We make a first step towards developing a comparable set of interarea real income comparisons for a world of about 800 subnational administrative units and countries. Some
of the subunits are larger than most countries, such as Uttar Pradesh in India with
159 million, or Sichuan in China with 115 million. We use the smallest administrative
unit that is available from official sources (see sources of regional data in the Appendix
to this chapter), except in the case of Chile, where we used the second smallest unit
since their smallest units totalled 300 plus areas. Geographically, more disaggregation
is desirable for many of the large countries.

What distinguishes this study from others such as Gallup *et al.* (1998) is that we also
ask what difference it makes to take into account price differences within countries.
We begin with nominal estimates of regional incomes based on production or other
methods of estimation, aware that the concept of income and quality of estimates
of nominal levels and growth vary widely across countries.[1] Clearly, there is much
work to be done to get good nominal income estimates, important research that is
not attempted in this chapter. As a first step we correct the nominal incomes for

---

[1] For example the *China Statistical Yearbook* for 2000 reports growth in income in all provinces but one
as higher than reported for all of China.

differences in purchasing power parities (PPPs)[2] across countries and, as a second step, across regions within countries. Unfortunately, there is only limited direct data on price differences within countries so much of the chapter addresses the problem of finding an indirect way to satisfactorily estimate differences in regional price levels. We undertake this estimation because we believe these regional price differences are important, and after going through the exercise we ask whether this correction would alter our perception of the world compared to what we obtain from step one above.

The preferred method of directly estimating regional price differences is discussed in Section 2.2. Because few countries collect price data appropriate for directly estimating regional price levels, we discuss in Section 2.3 indirect methods that might be used to estimate price levels and real incomes within countries. Models are developed of how location and trade may influence price levels. We estimate two versions of this model, one that assumes spatial heterogeneity among countries or regions and a second that explicitly includes spatial autocorrelation effects from neighbouring and nearby units.

2.2. REGIONAL PRICE LEVELS

2.2.1. *Methodology*

Just as national PPPs are used to convert GDPs in national currencies to a common unit, it is desirable for making quantity comparisons to take account of price differences across regions of a country using the same currency. The creation of a euro area or the use of the US dollar in Ecuador does not lessen the need for price comparisons. Many commercial enterprises in the United States and Europe sell information on regional price levels to employers setting salaries or employees considering relocation—American Chamber of Commerce Researchers Association (ACCRA) in the United States and Employment Conditions Abroad in the United Kingdom are two such organizations. The methods used in most commercial ventures grew out of the binary comparisons between countries, especially those carried out by Gilbert and Kravis (1954: 22–3), who used the United States as the centre of a star involving the United Kingdom, France, Germany, and Italy. Direct binary comparisons among the European countries were not carried out. The direct method is used by governments and international organizations such as the United States State Department and the International Civil Service Commission.

Multilateral comparisons grew out of binary beginnings, as methods were developed to deal with the fact that binary comparisons between A/B, A/C, and B/C do not lead to transitive results; the direct comparison of B/C does not generally equal the indirect comparison obtained by dividing A/C by A/B. The International Comparison Programme (ICP), formed in 1968 at the United Nations Statistical Office, has experimented with several different multilateral methods (Kravis *et al.* 1975). Many investigations of multilateral methods resulted; commonly used methods are discussed by Diewert (1999) and Rao (2001). The broad results of all the methods support the

---

[2] Authors' estimates available from PWT 6.1 at www.pwt.econ.upenn.edu.

most important finding of the ICP, namely that the price level (purchasing power divided by the exchange rate) of GDP rises systematically with per capita GDP; this is sometimes referred to as the Balassa–Samuelson effect (Heston *et al.* 1994).

This basic finding, when extended to regions within a country, implies that higher income regions would have higher prices than low-income regions. Whether one is making purchasing power comparisons between or within countries, the information required to carry out a full benchmark comparison are prices of comparable goods and services. In many countries substantial price information is available, especially for foods.[3] In the 1960s, the consumer price index (CPI) in the United States had enough common items across cities, collected each month within each city, to put together spatial price comparisons. However, the US Bureau of Labor Statistics (BLS) did not believe these spatial comparisons were of very good quality, and neither business nor labour was keen on having official estimates of regional price levels within the United States. Official intercity comparisons were discontinued in 1968.

The framework for the CPI that the BLS introduced in the 1970s also did not seem to readily lend itself to comparisons across space because collectors were not asked to price the same item in different outlets. The sampling frame is such that the price collector checks off, for each entry-level item (ELI), the outlet, size, packaging, and other information about the volume seller as indicated by an outlet employee. Since the CPI only required the price change for the same item from the previous period, it was not known whether the same items were priced the same in Los Angeles and Minneapolis, for instance. However, it turned out that the ELI approach to the CPI may be the model of what price data should be for making regional or international comparisons. A short discussion of the BLS experiments for the United States illustrates this point. Regional price differences remained a research subject for the BLS, and a hedonic approach was examined in the work of Kokoski *et al.* (1994) and Kokoski *et al.* (1999: 123–66).

In fact, Kokoski *et al.* began experimenting with the hedonic approach that had also been part of the early international PPP comparison work. In the ICP the method was termed the country product dummy method (CPD) by Summers (1973) to deal with the fact that not all countries collected prices for all items. The version that Summers used was a very straightforward hedonic regression model akin to those used for temporal studies—Griliches (1990. 185–206), Triplett (1990), Berndt *et al.* (1995). In eqn (2.1), $j = 1, 2, \ldots, m$ countries, $i = 1, 2, \ldots, n$ items in a basic heading, and p_{ij} is the price of item i in country j, and ε_{ij} is the error term. The prices are regressed against two sets of dummy variables, D_j for each country other than the numeraire country (country 1), and the second set with a dummy for each item specification, z_i.

$$p_{ij} = \sum_{i=1}^{n} \beta_i z_i + \sum_{j=2}^{m} \alpha_j D_j + \varepsilon_{ij}. \tag{2.1}$$

---

[3] Aten (1999) found that in Brazil some of the poorest metropolitan areas had the highest food price levels, possibly due to higher transport costs and the lack of spatial interaction among some regions of Brazil.

The transitive price parity, α_j, is the logarithm of the estimated country parity for the heading relative to the numeraire country. The item coefficient, β_i, is the logarithm of the estimates of the average item price in the currency of the numeraire country (which could be a regional currency).

The innovation of Kokoski and colleagues was to apply this data to the estimation of internal price parities by BLS city using the ELI characteristics of the prices being collected. The basic idea was similar to the CPD procedure. For example, if 'apple' is the ELI, we may not be able to match the specific apple(s) priced in Philadelphia with those priced in Los Angeles. But across all the BLS cities, as long as there is overlap of specific apples priced in some cities, then a parity can be obtained for all apples between any pair of cities. Given the unit of measurement of a kilogram, there would be a code for outlet type, city, and dummies for Fuji, Rome, Granny Smith, Delicious, McIntosh, and so forth. In the CPD equation, the β_i's would provide an average price per kilogram for types of apples, and the α_j's yield the price level of apples in each city.

A formulation of this hedonic framework that seems appropriate for regional comparisons is set out in eqn (2.2), where the subscript (j) refers to regions within a country, the subscript (i) refers to item characteristics, such as brand or product identification, and (k) refers to the outlet type. The brand characteristics (B_i) and outlets (O_k) are expressed as dummy variables, so that one characteristic or outlet must be omitted to avoid perfect multicollinearity in the estimating equation. This omitted characteristic becomes the base, and β or γ is the (log) price parity relative to this base. As in eqn (2.1), the α yield the price level relative to each region.

$$\ln p_{ikj} = \sum_{i=1}^{n} \beta_i B_i + \sum_{k=2}^{l} \gamma_k O_k + \sum_{j=2}^{m} \alpha_j D_j + \varepsilon_{ijk}. \qquad (2.2)$$

In the example below, the regions are districts into which São Paulo is divided for the purpose of collecting prices for the city CPI.[4] Although the geographical dispersion of São Paulo is not as great as in a typical country, there are significant differences in prices across its districts, so the example simulates how the framework might be applied across regions at the country level. The three items used for illustration are dentists' charges for a filling, milk, and lightbulbs. For all three items there are different characteristics, namely type of outlet and brand or product, as well as various districts where the prices are collected.

Table 2.1 presents the results of the estimated equations for the three items. For lightbulbs and milk, a base price in a supermarket is provided in Brazilian reais (R$) for a particular brand. Some further remarks will be made about the districts below. The factors to modify the base price are indicated for the highest and lowest districts for that item, for the different outlets, and for different types of fillings (dentist) or brands

    [4] We thank Professor Heron do Carmo, coordinator of the CPI for the Fundação Instituto de Pesquisas Economicas (FIPE), who was kind enough to provide illustrative prices for several items that could be readily collated from the December 2001 survey. FIPE estimates a weekly CPI for São Paulo, as do several other institutions in Brazil. This survey covers over eighty districts with a range of outlets, brands, and varieties of goods and services.

Table 2.1. *Price levels within São Paulo (eqn (2.2) results)*

Item: lightbulb		
Base price	60 W GE transparent bulb (1 unit)	R$1.04
Price level relative to base		
Outlet type	Supermarket	1.00
	Hardware	0.90
Brand/product	60 W Phillips	1.17
	100 W GE	1.33
	100 W Phillips	1.50
	Fluorescent 15 W 3-pack	16.83
District		
Highest	Vila Prado	1.48
Lowest	Aricanduva	0.65
	$N = 247, R^2 = 98.5$, RMSE $= 0.133$	
Item: dentist		
Base price	Porcelain filling 1-face	R$32.24
Brand/product type	Amalgama type B	1.31
	Amalgama type C	0.42
	Resin type B	1.48
	Resin type C	0.47
	Silicate type C	0.27
District		
Highest	Jabaquara	2.39
Lowest	Saude	0.70
	$N = 72, R^2 = 97.1$, RMSE $= 0.138$	
Item: milk		
Base price	Grade A milk 1l	R$1.57
Outlet type	Supermarket	1.00
	Bakery	1.18
Brand/product type	Skimmed	
	Special	0.60
	Paulista	0.69
	Parmalat	0.66
	Grade B milk	
	Special	0.72
	Paulista	0.82
	Parmalat	0.81
	Long-life milk	
	Parmalat	0.69
	Paulista	0.72
	Leco	0.70
District		
Highest	Raposo Tavares	1.11
Lowest	Vila Formosa	0.86
	$N = 524, R^2 = 79.7$, RMSE $= 0.162$	

Source: FIPE (São Paulo) and calculations by the authors.

(milk and lightbulbs). The value of hedonic estimation is that it holds constant price-determining characteristics of the markets for products, such as outlet type, allowing the estimation of the regional or district effects in this example. This point is made especially clear in Table 2.1 by the wide variety of prices that are observed for what is thought to be a fairly homogeneous item, namely a litre of milk. In terms of the main purpose of this illustration, an analysis of variance suggests there is a statistically significant district effect for all three items. The price in the highest district is 240 per cent above the lowest for dentists, 30 per cent for milk, and 27 per cent for lightbulbs. So it certainly makes sense to take district into account for a large city, and certainly for larger geographical units, such as countries.

2.2.2. *The European Union*

The European Union publishes nominal income differences by subnational units of their member countries. Income differences have been converted to euros by use of PPPs, but within each country the relative incomes of regions have simply been scaled to the average GDP per capita in euros on a PPP basis. The Economic Commission of the European Union has made it an action item to also adjust these nominal regional incomes to real regional incomes by taking account of the differing price levels within countries. Clearly, real regional incomes are an important statistic for the European Union because of the social funds made available for poorer regions. Eurostat, which would have responsibility for such estimates, has not been able to carry out the task because it would require a significant expenditure of resources. However, with increasing pressures from the Commission, Eurostat is considering a method that would build upon existing price collection within countries, perhaps augmented by some special collection. For example, across the departments of France, comparisons would be made of CPI item prices of comparable items in Paris and Lyon to obtain price levels to put department nominal incomes on a real income basis.

2.2.3. *Other Experiences*

Japan carries out a special survey every five years using the same survey framework as the CPI. The purpose of these quinquennial surveys is to obtain prefecture price levels for the purpose of adjustment of government salaries for regional cost of living differences. Korea carries out a similar survey. In connection with the early ICP estimates for India, an attempt was made to use prices from city and rural temporal price indexes to estimate regional differences in price levels by expenditure groups. India has a price index for rural workers, additional urban indexes for industrial workers and white-collar workers (Heston 1971). These indexes provide enough overlap to allow estimates of price level differences by rural–urban and various states of India. Deaton and Tarozzi (2000) used the national sample survey in India to investigate regional price levels based upon unit values, not transactions prices.

The United States has a Cost of Living Adjustment (COLA) programme aimed at adjusting salaries for federal employees working outside the continental US for differences in cost of living compared to Washington DC. This adjustment is done each year based upon special surveys and has become a matter of considerable litigation. Much criticism has also been attached to the US poverty line because it does not take into account regional price differences. When just regional price differences are taken into account in the United States, Aten (1996*a*) found that the cost of the poverty bundle was 40 per cent less in the Dakotas than in New York or San Francisco. It can be quantitatively important to systematically take into account regional differences in purchasing power.

For most purposes we want real regional incomes. At least one of the conference papers has moved in this direction, namely Azzoni, do Carmo, and Menezes (2001) who are working on convergence of state incomes in Brazil. There is not enough information in this study to generate real regional incomes for our world using preferred methods of estimation based on detailed price comparisons. This has led us to consider alternative methods that we believe have considerable interest, especially for those interested in how geographical factors and trade enter into the formulation.

2.3. A MODEL OF REGIONAL PRICE LEVELS

2.3.1. *Penn World Table Estimates*

We begin with the estimates of real GDP per capita for 1996 for 167 countries in PWT (Penn World Table) 6.1 (Heston *et al.* 2002). As a first step, for each subnational unit with available data, the nominal national currency income estimate is converted to 1996 international dollars (I\$) at the PPP for the country from PWT 6.1.[5] This procedure provides us with a set of nominal regional incomes that are quite interesting per se, suggesting wide geographical variation around the world. Altogether there are 36 countries with 740 subnational units and an additional 131 countries[6] with no subnational breakdown, for a total of 871 observations. Table 2.2 provides the list of countries with regional breakdowns. Where possible, per capita personal income data were used, such as those computed by the Department of Commerce and published in the Survey of Current Business for the United States. In a few countries—Brazil, Chile,

---

[5] An I\$ has the purchasing power of a US\$ over all of GDP, but not its components.

[6] Albania, Armenia, Antigua, Australia, Azerbaijan, Burundi, Benin, Burkina Faso, Bulgaria, Bahrain, Bahamas, Belarus, Belize, Bermuda, Barbados, Bhutan, Botswana, Central African, Switzerland, Côte d'Ivoire, Cameroon, Congo, Republic, Comoros, Cape Verde, Costa Rica, Cyprus, Czech Republic, Djibouti, Dominica, Denmark, Dominican Republic, Algeria, Ecuador, Eritrea, Estonia, Ethiopia, Fiji, Gabon, Georgia, Ghana, Guinea, Gambia, The Guinea-Bissau, Equatorial Guinea, Grenada, Guatemala, Guyana, Hong Kong, Honduras, Croatia, Haiti, Hungary, Ireland, Iran, Iceland, Israel, Jamaica, Jordan, Kenya, Kyrgyzstan, Cambodia, St Kitts & Nevis, Kuwait, Laos, Lebanon, St Lucia, Sri Lanka, Lesotho, Lithuania, Luxembourg, Latvia, Macao, Morocco, Moldova, Madagascar, Mexico, Macedonia, Mali, Malta, Mongolia, Mozambique, Mauritania, Mauritius, Malawi, Namibia, Niger, Nicaragua, Nepal, New Zealand, Oman, Panama, Peru, Papua New Guinea, Poland, Puerto Rico, Paraguay, Qatar, Romania, Russia, Rwanda, Saudi Arabia, Sudan, Senegal, Singapore, Sierra Leone, El Salvador, Sao Tome and Principe, Slovak Republic, Slovenia, Swaziland, Seychelles, Syria, Chad, Togo, Thailand, Tajikistan, Turkmenistan, Trinidad, Tobago, Tunisia, Taiwan, Tanzania, Uganda, Uruguay, Uzbekistan, St Vincent & Grenadines, Vietnam, Yemen, Congo, Dem. Republic, Zambia, Zimbabwe.

B. Aten and A. Heston

Table 2.2. *Units of observation for countries with regional data*

Code	Country	Units	P/I	Year
ARG	Argentina	24	*I*	1991
AUT	Austria	9	*I*	1993
BEL	Belgium	9	*I*	1993
BGD	Bangladesh	5	*I*	1991
BOL	Bolivia	9	*I*	1992
BRA	Brazil	27	*P*	1991
CAN	Canada	12	*I*	1996
CHL	Chile	12	*P*	1992
CHN	China	30	*I*	1994
COL	Colombia	23	*I*	1990
DEU	Germany	37	*I*	1993
EGY	Egypt	21	*I*	1990
ESP	Spain	17	*I*	1993
FIN	Finland	3	*I*	1992
FRA	France	22	*I*	1993
GBR	United Kingdom	35	*I*	1993
GRC	Greece	12	*I*	1993
IDN	Indonesia	27	*P*	1996
IND	India	25	*I*	1991
ITA	Italy	20	*I*	1993
JPN	Japan	47	*I*	1993
KAZ	Kazakstan	18	*I*	1994
KOR	Korea South	14	*P*	1995
MYS	Malaysia	13	*I*	1991
NGA	Nigeria	17	*I*	1992
NLD	Netherlands	12	*I*	1993
NOR	Norway	19	*I*	1992
PAK	Pakistan	4	*I*	1988
PHL	Philippine	13	*I*	1991
PRT	Portugal	7	*I*	1993
SWE	Sweden	21	*I*	1993
TUR	Turkey	69	*I*	1995
UKR	Ukraine	24	*I*	1994
USA	United States	51	*I*	1996
VEN	Venezuela	22	*I*	1994
ZAF	South Africa	9	*I*	1985

Source: See Appendix.

Indonesia, and South Korea—only gross regional product data were available for recent years, and these are labelled 'P' in Table 2.2.[7]

---

[7] We included a dummy variable for these four countries, but it was not significant in the models that we tested.

How should we think about the relationship of these nominal regional incomes to real incomes? We develop two approaches that take into account geographic and trade variables. In the first, we test whether the relationship between income and price levels is stable or whether it changes based on the latitude or the level of openness of a region. The second approach explicitly takes into account the spatial autocorrelation or 'spillover' effects that neighbouring regions or countries might have on one another.

2.3.2. *The Usual Suspects*

Income

Much work has been done on the determinants of price levels at the country-level using structural and non-structural factors as explanatory variables (Balassa 1964; Clague and Tanzi 1972; Kravis and Lipsey 1983; Heston *et al.* 1994) including the explicit modelling of a spatial component (Aten 1996*b*). Clearly, the first variable to come to mind is income. Any explanation of the variation of price levels across countries begins with income, and nominal income is where one would begin in moving from national to regional price levels.

Openness and human capital

Openness of the economy, as measured by the sum of exports and imports to total GDP, is a commonly used variable in explaining how price levels differ across countries. One view is that PPPs will be closer to the exchange rate, everything else the same, the more open is the economy. Our dependent variable, price level, is the ratio of the PPP to the exchange rate, and is generally greater than one for high-income countries and less than one for low-income countries. If openness brings PPPs closer to the exchange rate, we would expect its sign to be negative for high-income countries and positive for low-income countries, but factors other than the level of per capita income appear to interact with openness so that its effect is less straightforward.

A number of researchers have also used a human capital variable to explain price levels. The idea is that where human capital is scarce, the price of non tradables, particularly professional services in health, education, and general government will be high. Thus, a negative correlation between human capital and price levels across countries is expected. This relationship is not examined in this chapter but will be a subject of future research.

Geographic variables

Gallup *et al.* (1998), among others, explored the role of geographical factors in socioeconomic progress across countries. Similar geographical variables such as proximity to water are examined here. We classified each geographical unit into a climate zone, following the modified Koppen classification system described in McKnight and Hess (2002: 207–11). Latitude was used to 'explain' income differences

(Gavin and Haussman 1998; Haussman 2001), an approach that has revived a debate on the relationship between economic development and geographical and cultural factors. While our emphasis is on geographical factors, note should be made of a literature of dissent as illustrated by Rodrick *et al.* (2002). The debate expanded to the realm of physioeconomics; 'the economics of physics-based physiology, as affected by physiography (climate and terrain)' in Parker (2000: 33). Parker's starting point is the strong positive correlation between income levels and latitude, but he conjectures that countries in colder climates require a higher level of consumption than warmer countries to maintain the same 'homeostatic utility level' (p. 198). Thus, a single measure of per capita income can be interpreted as endogenous to climatic variation as manifested in latitude differences. That is, the relationship between income levels and latitude may exist, but it tells us more about physiological and psychological balance (homeostasis) than about economic well-being and performance (p. 198).

In recent work, Aten (2001) considered two models that contrast the significance of latitude as a direct explanatory variable for price level differences versus an indirect measure that captures income variations and only indirectly explains price level differences.[8] In either case, the interpretation of latitude is that it is a proxy for a host of unknown geographic variables such as climate, topology, and soil productivity. We find that when climate is taken into account, the role of latitude in explaining variations declines significantly.

In addition, Aten (1997) found that international prices are spatially autocorrelated at given income levels, particularly when trade flows rather than distances represent the interaction among countries. Parker (2000) argued that measures of distance across the sphere are asymmetric—neighbouring countries may be more similar across latitudes than by longitude—and a measure of climate distance would be more meaningful. Since trade flows across regions within countries are difficult to obtain, and climate distance is not a well-defined measure, we use instead nineteen climate zones dummy variables as well as a matrix of proximity weights between each possible pair of regions and countries. This matrix representing the degree of spatial interaction enables us to test for residual variation that may persist after latitude, proximity to water, and climate are taken into account.

2.3.3. *Model With Expansion Variables*

In this first specification outlined in eqn (2.3), the price levels of countries and regions are assumed to be spatially independent. That is, there is no a priori expectation that values in one geographic unit are more similar (or dissimilar) to another because

---

[8] The two models used by Aten followed Casetti's (1997) grouping of conventional versus expansion equations. The initial specification was conventional, using income, openness of the economy, and latitude as independent variables in the model. The second approach hypothesizes that the economic variables are primary, but their coefficients vary geographically. In other words, the parameters of the economic variables are allowed to drift in geographic space. This approach emphasized the two-stage structure of the model and suggests that 'the variables in the initial model carry a higher priority than the expansion variables' (Casetti 1997: 15).

of their spatial proximity.

$$PL_j = \alpha_1 Y_j + \sum_{i=1}^{n} \beta_i C_{ij} + \sum_{i=1}^{m} \gamma_i D_{ij} + \varepsilon_j, \qquad (2.3)$$

where PL_j is the price level in country or region (j), relative to the United States, Y_j is the per capita GDP in I\$, C_j is a continuous variable such as latitude, or openness, and D_j is a dummy variable such as climate zone. The dummy variables include indicators of spatial heterogeneity, such as access to water, or a political–economic grouping like former Soviet republics, or Caribbean islands. Non-linear versions of the model are also tested. The error terms (ε) are assumed to be uncorrelated, with mean zero and constant variance. As a variation of eqn (2.3), we relax the assumption of an invariant income parameter, suggesting instead that it may change with latitude or openness. That is described in eqn (2.4), where we hypothesize that the parameter α_1 is determined by the variable(s) C_i.

$$PL_j = \alpha_{1j} Y_j + \sum_{i=1}^{m} \gamma_i D_{ij} + \varepsilon_j \qquad (2.4a)$$

and

$$\alpha_{1j} = \delta_0 + \sum_{i=1}^{n} \delta_i C_{ij}. \qquad (2.4b)$$

Substituting eqn (2.4b) into eqn (2.4a) yields:

$$PL_j = \delta_0 Y_j + \sum_{i=1}^{n} \delta_i C_{ij} Y_j + \sum_{i=1}^{m} \gamma_i D_{ij} + \varepsilon_j. \qquad (2.4c)$$

In other words, we assume that latitude and/or openness may affect price levels, but their effect depends on the per capita income levels. The coefficients on the dummy variables represent the intercept or initial level of the dependent variable, and each one is tested alone and in combination with other dummy variables such as climate, water access, regional grouping, and data type. Data type refers to the fact that four out of the thirty-six countries with regional data had regional product rather than income data. We also try to capture differences that may arise because countries have participated in the 1996 benchmark study that is the basis for the PPP estimates of PWT 6.1. There are 115 countries in the 1996 benchmark, and out of the remaining fifty-two non-benchmark countries in PWT, only China, Colombia, India, Malaysia, and South Africa had subnational data. The regional groupings consist of fifteen world regions (West, Central, Eastern, and Southern Africa; North Africa and the Middle East; North, and South America; the Caribbean, Central, Eastern, Southeastern, and Southwestern Asia, East and West Europe, and Oceania).

2.3.4. *Model With Spatial Interaction*

The expansion model in (2.4c) and the various geographic dummy variables capture the effects of levels of income, openness, and geography on the price levels, that is the spatial heterogeneity of the data, but do not tell us anything about the pairwise relationships between geographic units. For example, is there a ripple or spillover effect such that regions with high price levels can be expected to be closer to each other, even after latitude, region, and climate are taken into account? We look at the residual maps and also test for autocorrelation[9] and try to specify the nature of this autocorrelation in the models below. The weights matrix W is added to our previous equations as a spatial autoregressive error term, so that the original error term ε in specification (2.3 and 2.4c) is no longer homoskedastic and uncorrelated:

$$\varepsilon_j = \lambda W \varepsilon_j + \xi_j. \tag{2.5a}$$

ξ now has mean zero and constant variance (if our specification of the weights matrix does indeed capture the residual autocorrelation). Substituting into eqn (2.3) we obtain the spatial error model (2.5b):

$$PL_j = \alpha_1 Y_j + \sum_{i=1}^{n} \beta_i C_{ij} + \sum_{i=1}^{m} \gamma_i D_{ij} + \lambda W \varepsilon_j + \xi_j. \tag{2.5b}$$

Similarly, substituting into eqn (2.4c) we obtain the expansion model with a spatially autoregressive term (2.6):

$$PL_j = \delta_0 Y_j + \sum_{i=1}^{n} \delta_i C_{ij} Y_j + \sum_{i=1}^{m} \gamma_i D_{ij} + \lambda W \varepsilon_j + \xi_j. \tag{2.6}$$

Spatial interaction is represented by the W matrix of bilateral weights representing the arc distance (great circle distance, in miles) between each possible pair of geographic units defined by the latitude and longitude of the capital city of each region. The weights are inversely proportional to the square of the distance. In other words, units that are near have a greater weight than those that are far apart. There is a growing literature on the choice of weights and the sensitivity of the chosen matrix to capturing spatial interaction, and we test a set of contiguity and nearest neighbour matrices in addition to the distance matrices.[10] Contiguity is equivalent to a dummy weight—that is, the weight between a pair of units is one if the units are within a certain distance (ranging from 100 miles to 5,000 miles) of each other and equal to zero otherwise. Nearest neighbour matrices also contain zeroes if an observation is not a k-nearest neighbour (with k ranging from 1 to 15), and one otherwise.

---

[9] Spatial autocorrelation diagnostics include Moran's I, the Lagrange Multiplier test, and the Kelejian–Robinson statistic, implemented in SpaceStat™v.1.90©1999.

[10] Two inverse distance matrices (the linear and quadratic versions), nine contiguity matrices (based on distances of 100, 200, 300, 400, 500, 1,000, 2,000, 3,000, and 5,000 miles) and eleven nearest neighbour matrices ($k = 1$–10 and 15) were tested.

Table 2.3. *Results using eqns (2.4) and (2.6)*

Model results ($N = 871$) (dependent = ln of price level)	Expansion (2.4c)	Spatial error (2.6)
ln Y	0.16* (0.06)	0.29** (0.04)
ln latitude	−0.53* (0.17)	0.15 (0.12)
ln open	−0.88** (0.24)	−0.57* (0.20)
ln latitude * ln Y	0.06* (0.02)	−0.01 (0.01)
ln open * ln Y	0.08* (0.03)	0.05* (0.02)
$W\varepsilon$ (autoregressive term)	—	0.83** (0.02)
Dummy variables[a]		
Bsh-0-1-1	1.87** (0.41)	3.65** (0.52)
Aw-0-1-1	1.97** (0.41)	3.89** (0.50)
Cfa-1-1-8	2.09** (0.43)	3.19** (0.59)
Adjusted R^2	0.89	0.81
Mean square error ML (σ^2)	0.039	0.023
Log likelihood	175	407

[a] Shows only the largest three coefficients that are common to both specifications. Detailed model results are available from the authors.

Note: *$p < 0.005$; **$p < 0.001$ (standard errors in parentheses).

Source: Calculations by the authors.

2.4. RESULTS

We report results for the expansion eqn (2.4c) and the expansion with a spatial autoregressive term (2.6) in log form. Table 2.3 shows the estimated coefficients and some diagnostics.[11] The traditional R^2 is not a good measure of fit for the spatial lag models, although a pseudo R^2 based on the ratio of the variance of the predicted values to the variance of the observed values of the dependent variable is shown. The correct measure of fit is the log likelihood, and the models with the highest log likelihood are preferred (Anselin 1999). The independent variable is the price level (PL), with the United States equal to 100. Y is the nominal per capita GDP in dollars at purchasing power parities (or I$), *open* is the sum of exports and imports as a percentage of GDP, and *latitude* is the absolute latitude in decimal degrees. The log transformation of each variable is denoted by the prefix ln. The set of dummy variables are for climate, benchmark, water proximity, and regional grouping.

Both models imply that price levels rise with income as expected. Openness has an apparent dampening effect but at given income levels it raises the price level. Similarly, the latitude coefficient is significantly negative but its effect is positive when expanded from the income variable. The significance of the expansion variables suggests that there is an intermediate influence of trade and geography on the relationship between income levels and price levels. Casetti (1992) describes a Bayesian

[11] Model results are obtained from SpaceStat™v1.90©1999, Luc Anselin.

regression to determine the stability of the initial income parameter but such an exercise is not attempted here. An interesting interpretation of the expansion variables is that they indicate how geography and trade (as measured by latitude and openness) change the effects of income levels on the price levels, and alternatively, how the effectiveness of income levels as determinants of price levels depends on geography and trade.

When we divide the data into two groups (above and below median per capita GDP) the coefficients on the low-income group change signs but are much less significant. One interpretation of the changing sign on the openness variable is that it does bring the PPPs closer to the exchange rate, and hence is negative for high-income countries that have a price level above one (PPP greater than exchange rate) and positive for low-income countries with price levels below one (PPPs less than the exchange rate). Due to the instability of the coefficients for the low-income grouping, and an analysis of the pooled versus separate model variances, the pooled model is preferred.

The dummy variables combine climate, water proximity, benchmark participation, and regional grouping. For example, the Bsh-0-1-1 dummy indicates regions in the hot, dry, low-latitude steppe (semi-arid) climate classification, without water access, with participation in the 1996 benchmark comparison and located in West Africa. In the spatial error model, the latitude coefficients are no longer significant but the coefficient on the W matrix is large, positive, and very significant (0.83). This result suggests that the spatial variation that was previously attributed to latitude is now captured by the spatial proximity matrix. Various W matrices were tested, and the one reported here (because it resulted in the highest likelihood function) is the k-nearest neighbour matrix with $k = 5$. That is, for each observation, only the five nearest observations, measured by the arc distance between them in miles, are considered neighbours. Another difference between the spatial error (2.6) and the simple expansion (2.4c) model results is that the income coefficient is higher (0.29 versus 0.16), and openness has less of a dampening effect (-0.57 versus -0.88). The dummy variable levels are also higher, and the residuals tend to be smaller for the low-income countries.

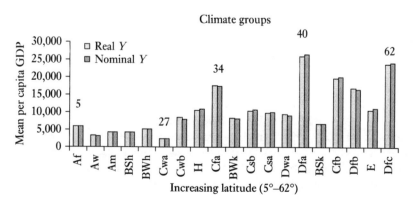

Figure 2.1. *Per capita GDP by climate and latitude*

Figure 2.1 is the breakdown of mean nominal and predicted real per capita GDPs by the climate groups. The groups are ordered by increasing latitude, and it can be seen that the distribution of incomes is not simple, with clusters of low-income regions in mid-latitude climates (BWk, Csb, Csa, Dwa, and Bsk) and a downward trend between 40° and 60° latitude.

A description of the climate types and the observed and predicted price levels and estimated real incomes (based on eqn (2.6)) are shown in Table 2.4. The highest price levels are found in Cfa, Cfb, Dfa, and Dfc, representing mid-latitude and severe mid-latitude climates, a pattern that follows the one shown in Fig. 2.1 for income levels. Climates Cfa and Cfb have the highest number of observations (110 and 139, respectively), corresponding to 34° and 51° of latitude on average. Also, the subtropical latitudes below 22° of latitude (Af, Aw, Am, BSh, BWh) have lower incomes than the higher latitude regions, but latitude per se does not appear to be the determining factor. The relationship between latitude and price levels disappears altogether when we take into account proximity (as measured by their interaction with their nearest neighbours), and more detailed geographic variables such as climate.

Tables 2.5 and 2.6 look at what difference regional price levels make for estimates of regional incomes. We take estimates of real income based on eqn (2.6), and compare them with nominal incomes. First, for countries without regional data, we take the real estimates of per capita GDP at PPPs from PWT 6.1 as the measure of income. For countries with regional data we also introduce the constraint as follows. From eqn (2.6) we take the estimated value using the country inputs as a ratio to the PWT 6.1 value of the price level. This factor is used to adjust the estimated real income value for each region of a country to the level that is consistent with nominal income for the country. There are other ways this can be done, but the method chosen is fairly simple and makes the levels of the nominal and real estimates comparable.

Table 2.5 compares the range and variability of nominal and real incomes for a selected group of countries. Brazil and Italy are included in Table 2.5 because they are both noted for having large north–south differences in income, and the United Kingdom is included because within the European Union it is noted for relative smaller regional variation. Pakistan and Italy illustrate that the income effect on price levels does not dominate in all countries. The range between lowest and highest real incomes increases for these two countries and does so for six out of the thirty-six countries with regional breakdowns (Nigeria, Pakistan, South Africa, Argentina, Spain, and Italy). In contrast, the range decreases by over 10 per cent for the United Kingdom, the United States, and Brazil, and by 9 per cent for the world (from 51,567 to 46,802). Taking account of the price variability in this indirect way is suggestive of interesting relationships, but it does not lead us to radically different views of the world. Table 2.5 is interesting with respect to within-country relationships, such as the conventional story that the spread of incomes in Italy is much higher than in the United Kingdom. At least for 1996, this is true in real terms but not true in nominal terms. In terms of the coefficient of variation Italy and Brazil have the largest variability and the United States has more variability in real terms than the United Kingdom.

Table 2.4. *Estimated price levels by climate type*

Climate group	Subtype	N	PL	Predicted PL	Real Y (I$)	Koppen
Tropical humid	Af	62	47.6	45.8	5,938	Tropical rainforest
	Am	42	36.5	36.2	4,297	Tropical monsoon
	Aw	67	50.4	50.9	3,258	Tropical savanna
Dry	BSh	51	48.2	49.2	4,183	Steppe, low-latitude, hot
	BSk	68	42.8	42.2	6,602	Steppe, mid-latitude, cold
	BWh	41	35.6	35.8	5,148	Desert, low-latitude, hot
	BWk	13	41.1	39.5	8,378	Desert, mid-latitude, cold
Mid-latitude	Cfa	110	103.4	102.3	17,679	Humid subtropical w/o dry season, hot summers
	Cfb	139	118.7	120.2	19,694	Marine west coast w/o dry season, warm–cool summers
	Cfc	N/A	—	—	—	Marine west coast w/o dry season, warm–cool summers
	Csa	95	67.8	68.8	9,725	Mediterranean, dry, hot summers
	Csb	14	74.9	76.5	10,435	Mediterranean, dry, warm summers
	Cwa	16	20.5	19.5	2,370	Humid subtropical, dry winters, hot summers
	Cwb	3	38.4	35.7	8,499	Humid subtropical, dry winter, warm summers
Severe mid-latitude	Dfa	18	123.6	127.2	25,952	Humid continental w/o dry season, hot summers
	Dfb	70	87.1	84	16,907	Humid continental w/o dry season, warm summers
	Dfc	7	109.3	108.7	23,765	Sub-Arctic w/o dry season, cool summers
	Dfd	N/A	—	—	—	Sub-Arctic w/o dry season, very cold winters
	Dwa	8	51.4	49.5	9,370	Humid continental, dry winters, hot summers
	Dwb	N/A	—	—	—	Humid continental, dry winters, warm summers
	Dwc	N/A	—	—	—	Sub-Arctic, dry winters, cool summers
	Dwd	N/A	—	—	—	Sub-Arctic, dry winters, very cold winters

1

Table 2.4. (*Continued*)

Climate group	Subtype	N	PL	Predicted PL	Real Y (I$)	Koppen
Polar	E	1	71.5	75.2	10,501	Polar
Highland	H	46	68.6	70.5	10,644	Highland, cold due to elevation

Obs.		871	PL		Real Y (I$)	Open (%)	Latitude (absolute)
Means			73.2		11,422	58.1	33.4

Source: McKnight and Hess (2002), and calculations by the authors.

Table 2.5. *Range of nominal and real incomes for selected countries*

Nominal versus real income	I$ 1996	Mean	Range	CV (%)
World	Nominal Y	11,468	51,567	79
	Real Y	11,422	46,802	78
Pakistan	Nominal Y	2,081	166	4
	Real Y	2,090	439	10
Brazil	Nominal Y	5,185	5,367	34
	Real Y	5,095	4,931	29
UK	Nominal Y	18,980	14,132	15
	Real Y	19,923	10,999	12
Italy	Nominal Y	19,777	14,008	24
	Real Y	20,098	18,464	30
USA	Nominal Y	27,993	20,193	16
	Real Y	27,937	17,435	15

Source: Calculations by the authors.

Finally there are shifts among cities, with Milano being highest in nominal terms but Trieste highest in real terms in Italy. Catanzaro in Calabria is lowest in nominal and real terms, 11,896 and 12,380, respectively. Low honours in the United Kingdom go to Liverpool at just under 15,000 in nominal and 15,800 in real terms. In the United States, Connecticut is higher in real terms and the District of Columbia in nominal terms; Mississippi takes low place in nominal terms and West Virginia in real terms. Since a great deal of political interest attaches to such figures, it is worth stressing that if our method of correction has merit, there is good reason to use real measures.

In Table 2.6, our predicted price level estimates are compared to the ACCRA (previously American Chamber of Commerce Researchers Association)[12] estimates for 1996. Their index is based on expenditure weights for upper-level white-collar

[12] ACCRA's methodology and cost of living indexes are available on the web at www.coli.org.

Table 2.6. *Estimated price levels for the United States*

ACCRA	Predicted eqn (2.6)	United States	
		State	City
93	97	Alabama	Montgomery
126	102	Alaska	Juneau
106	101	Arizona	Phoenix
87	98	Arkansas	Little Rock
103	107	California	Sacramento
104	102	Colorado	Denver
125	104	Connecticut	Hartford
104	103	Delaware	Dover
127	107	District of Columbia	Washington DC
108	100	Florida	Tallahassee
94	100	Georgia	Atlanta
—	93	Hawaii	Honolulu
97	101	Idaho	Boise
101	103	Illinois	Springfield
97	100	Indiana	Indianapolis
99	100	Iowa	Des Moines
96	101	Kansas	Topeka
90	98	Kentucky	Frankfort
100	97	Louisiana	Baton Rouge
—	98	Maine	Augusta
105	103	Maryland	Annapolis
144	101	Massachusetts	Boston
106	102	Michigan	Lansing
100	103	Minnesota	Saint Paul
92	95	Mississippi	Jackson
94	101	Missouri	Jefferson City
102	97	Montana	Helena
90	100	Nebraska	Lincoln
103	102	Nevada	Carson City
104	102	New Hampshire	Concord
—	102	New Jersey	Trenton
113	99	New Mexico	Santa Fe
113	101	New York	Albany
100	99	North Carolina	Raleigh
97	99	North Dakota	Bismark
104	100	Ohio	Columbus
92	98	Oklahoma	Oklahoma City
105	100	Oregon	Salem
101	101	Pennsylvania	Harrisburg
107	98	Rhode Island	Providence
96	97	South Carolina	Columbia
102	99	South Dakota	Pierre

Table 2.6. (*Continued*)

ACCRA	Predicted eqn (2.6)	United States	
		State	City
94	100	Tennessee	Nashville
101	99	Texas	Austin
104	97	Utah	Salt Lake City
107	100	Vermont	Montpelier
103	101	Virginia	Richmond
107	102	Washington	Olympia
99	99	West Virginia	Charleston
112	101	Wisconsin	Madison
95	99	Wyoming	Cheyenne

Source: ACCRA, and calculations by the authors.

workers, and collates price reports only for metropolitan areas. Nonetheless, ACCRA estimates give us some idea of the variation within the United States, and may expose some of our weaker estimates, for example, Nebraska seems high with a price level of 100 (equal to the US average). Our estimate for Hawaii appears to be too low (93), although there is no comparable ACCRA estimate for that year.

Two comments about Table 2.6 relate to the underlying ACCRA data and to our estimates. ACCRA data gives a reasonable weight to housing, 20 per cent, but 90 per cent of that is applied to homeowners' rent as built-up from prices of houses and their costs. Because house price variability is high and comparability is very hard to hold constant across space, the ACCRA index probably overstates the variability of prices across US states. However, the variability of our estimates across states is probably low, given the studies of Kokoski *et al.* (1994).

2.5. CONCLUSIONS

This study argues for the importance of knowing regional differences in prices within countries. While the type of price comparisons needed is analogous to those used in international comparisons, such price data are available for very few countries. Some illustrations make clear that these differences can be quite significant. Further we argue that there are ways to use price data collected for time-to-time price indexes in a way that can allow such estimates.

In terms of regional incomes, we presented models of price level determination that permit price levels to differ between and within countries. The preferred estimating equation takes account of spatial interaction among all possible pairs of the 871 geographical units in our world, using a *k*-nearest neighbour matrix of weights as a measure of interaction, in addition to climate and regional characteristics. We find that latitude is not a significant variable because it fails to take into account the spatial autocorrelation and spatial spillover effects of the relationship among prices, incomes, and openness of the economy. When the resulting real income differences between regions are compared with nominal differences, there is some plausible compression of the distribution overall, but a dispersion of incomes for six relatively large countries. The relative ordering within countries may also change. Examples include Mississippi in the United States, which is the poorest in nominal terms, but richer than West Virginia in real terms.

We believe this chapter reinforces the value of having direct regional price information and the need in the future to consider other variables that might better proxy price variations within countries. Another test of our results will be the relative performance of the nominal and real incomes as explanatory variables of other relationships not involved in the construction of our real income measures. Some of this testing will be undertaken by the authors in the future, but we hope also by other researchers.[13]

Appendix: Sources of Regional Income Data

Austria, Belgium, Germany, Spain, France, Italy, Luxembourg, Portugal, Finland, United Kingdom: *Eurostat.*

India: *The Madhya Pradesh Human Development Report (1995), Pauls Press, New Delhi. Statistical Pocket Book: India (1993), National Council of Applied Economic Research, (1993).*

Japan: *Statistics Bureau Management and Coordination Agency, Government of Japan (1996).*

South Africa: *Development Bank of Southern Africa (1994).*

South Korea: *1995 Gross Regional Domestic Product, National Statistical Office, Republic of Korea (1997).*

Pakistan: *Population Census Organization Yearbook (1993).*

United States: *Survey of Current Business (May 2000).*

United Nations Human Development Report: *Argentina (1995), Bangladesh (1994), Bolivia (1994), Brazil (1996), Chile (1994), Colombia (1994), Egypt (1994), India (1996), Indonesia (1996), Kazakstan (1996), Nigeria (1997), Pacific Islands, Philippines (1994), Turkey (1996), Ukraine (1996), Venezuela (1994).*

REFERENCES

Anselin, L. (1999). *SpaceStat*, a software programme for the analysis of spatial data, version 1.90.
Aten, B. (1996*a*). 'Some Poverty Measures are More Equal than Others', paper presented at the Western Regional Science Association Annual Meeting, February, Napa, CA.
——— (1996*b*). 'Evidence of Spatial Autocorrelation in International Prices', *Review of Income and Wealth*, 42(2): 149–63.

[13] The regional data series is available at www.pwt.econ.upenn.edu.

—— (1997). 'Does Space Matter? International Comparisons of the Prices of Tradable and Nontradables', *International Regional Science Review*, 20: 35–52.

—— (1999). 'Cities in Brazil: An Interarea Price Comparison', *National Bureau of Economic Research Studies in Income and Wealth*, Vol. 61, University of Chicago Press: Chicago, IL.

—— (2001). 'An Application of the Spatial Expansion Method to Regional Price Level Estimates', paper presented at the North American Regional Science Association International Conference, 15–17 November, Charleston, SC.

Azzoni, C., H. do Carmo, and T. Menezes (2001). 'Metropolitan Cost of Living Indexes: Methodological Aspects and Empirical Comparisons', paper presented at the North American Regional Science Association International Conference, 15–17 November, Charleston, SC.

Balassa, B. (1964). 'The Purchasing Power Doctrine: a Reappraisal', *Journal of Political Economy*, 72: 584–96.

Berndt, E. R., Z. Griliches, and N. Rappaport (1995). 'Econometric Estimates of Price Indices For Personal Computers in the 1990s', *Journal of Econometrics*, 68: 243–68.

Casetti, E. (1992). 'Bayesian Regression and the Expansion Method', *Geographical Analysis*, 24(1): 58–74.

—— (1997). 'The Expansion Method, Mathematical Modeling, and Spatial Econometrics', *International Regional Science Review*, 20: 9–33.

Clague, C. and V. Tanzi (1972). 'Human Capital, Natural Resources and the Purchasing Power Parity Doctrine: Some Empirical Results', *Economia Internazionale*, 25: 3–18.

Deaton, A. and A. Tarozzi (2000). *Prices and Poverty in India*, Princeton University Press: New Jersey.

Diewert, I. (1999). 'Axiomatic and Economic Approaches to International Comparisons', in A. Heston and R. Lipsey (eds) *International and Interarea Comparisons of Income, Output and Prices*, University of Chicago Press: Chicago; *NBER and CRIW Studies in Income and Wealth*, 61: 13–87.

Gallup, J., J. Sachs, and A. Mellinger (1998). *Geography and Economic Growth*, Annual World Bank Conference on Development Economics, World Bank: Washington DC.

Gavin, M. and R. Haussman (1998). 'Nature, Development, and Distribution in Latin America: Evidence on the Role of Geography, Climate, and Natural Resources', *Inter-American Development Bank Working Papers* 378, IADB: Washington DC.

Gilbert, M. and I. Kravis (1954). *An International Comparison of National Products and the Purchasing Power of Currencies*, Organisation for European Economic Co-operation: Paris.

Griliches, Z. (1990). 'Hedonic Price Indices and the Measurement of Capital and Productivity: Some Historical Reflections', in E. R. Berndt and J. E. Triplett (eds) *Fifty Years of Economic Measurement: The Jubilee Conference of Research in Income and Wealth, Studies in Income and Wealth*, University of Chicago Press: Chicago, IL.

Haussman, R. (2001). 'Prisoners of Geography', *Foreign Policy*, 122: 45–53.

Heston, A. (1971). 'The Purchasing Power of the Rupee in Rural and Urban Areas of the States of India: a Report on Some Exploratory Estimates for 1969', paper presented at Seminar on Income Distribution in India, 25 26 February, India International Centre, New Delhi.

——, R. Summers, and D. Nuxoll (1994). 'The Differential Productivity Hypothesis and Purchasing Power Parities: Some New Evidence', *Review of International Economics*, 2: 227–43.

——, ——, and B. Aten (2002). Penn World Table, version 6.1, Center for International Comparisons at the University of Pennsylvania (CICUP), October. Available at www.pwt.econ.upenn.edu.

Kokoski, M., P. Cardiff, and B. Moulton (1994). 'Interarea Price Indeces for Consumer Goods and Services: An Hedonic Approach using CPI data', *US Bureau of Labor Statistics Working Paper* 256, Washington DC.

——, B. Moulton, and K. Zieschang (1999). 'Interarea Price Comparisons for Heterogeneous Goods', in A. Heston and R. Lipsey (eds) *International and Interarea Comparisons of Income, Output and Prices*, University of Chicago Press: Chicago, IL.

Kravis, I. B. and R. Lipsey (1983). 'Towards an Explanation of National Price Levels', *Princeton Studies in International Finance*, 52: 1–31.

——, Z. Kenessey, A. Heston, and R. Summers (1975). *A System of International Comparisons of Gross Product and Purchasing Power*, Johns Hopkins University Press: Baltimore, MD.

McKnight, T. and D. Hess (2002). *Physical Geography*, 7th edition, Prentice Hall: New Jersey.

Parker, P. (2000). *Physioeconomics: The Basis for Long-Run Economic Growth*, MIT Press: Cambridge, MA and London.

Rao, P. D. S. (2001). 'Weighted EKS and Generalized CPD Methods for Aggregation at Basic Heading Level and Above Basic Heading Level', Joint World Bank–OECD Seminar on Purchasing Power Applications, 30 January–2 February, Washington DC. Available at www.oecd.org/std/ppp/MTG2001.

Rodrik, D., A. Subramanian, and F. Trebbi (2002). 'Institutions Rule: The Primacy of Institutions over Geography and Integration in Economic Development', *NBER Working Papers* 9305, National Bureau of Economic Research: Cambridge, MA.

Summers, R. (1973). 'International Comparisons with Incomplete Data', *Review of Income and Wealth*, 19: 1–16.

Triplett, J. E. (1990). 'Hedonic Methods in a Statistical Agency Environment: An Intellectual Biopsy', in E. R. Berndt and J. E. Triplett (eds) *Fifty Years of Economic Measurement: The Jubilee Conference of Research in Income and Wealth, Studies in Income and Wealth*, University of Chicago Press: Chicago, IL.

3

Are Neighbours Equal? Estimating Local Inequality in Three Developing Countries

CHRIS ELBERS, PETER LANJOUW, JOHAN MISTIAEN, BERK ÖZLER, AND KENNETH R. SIMLER

3.1. INTRODUCTION

The 1990s witnessed a resurgence in theoretical and empirical attention by economists to the distribution of income and wealth.[1] One important strand of research in the area of political economy and public policy has focused on the appropriate level of government to which can be devolved financial and decisionmaking power regarding public service provisioning and financing. The advantage of decentralization to make use of better community-level information about priorities and the characteristics of residents may be offset by a greater likelihood that the local governing body is controlled by elites, to the detriment of weaker community members. In a recent paper, Bardhan and Mookherjee (1999) highlight the roles of both the level and heterogeneity of local inequality as a determinant of the relative likelihood of capture at different levels of government. As most of the theoretical predictions are ambiguous, they stress the need for empirical research into the causes of political capture—analysis which to date remains relatively scarce.[2]

Detailed information on local-level inequality has traditionally been available only from case studies which focus on one or two specific localities.[3] Such studies do not

We are grateful to the Instituto Nacional de Estadistical y Censo (INEC), Ecuador; Institut National de la Statistique (INSTAT), Madagascar; and the Instituto Nacional de Estatistica, Mozambique, for access to their unit record census data and the Bank Netherlands Partnership Program (BNPP) for financial support. Helpful comments were received from Jenny Lanjouw and participants at a PREM Inequality Thematic Group seminar at the World Bank. The views in this chapter are our own and should not be taken to reflect those of the World Bank or any of its affiliates. All errors are our own.

[1] In their introductory chapter to the *Handbook of Income Distribution*, Atkinson and Bourguignon (2000) welcome the marked expansion of research on income distribution during the 1990s, but underscore that much ground remains to be covered.   [2] Although, see Ravallion (1999, 2000) and Tendler (1997).

[3] Lanjouw and Stern (1998) report on a detailed analysis of the evolution of poverty and inequality in a north Indian village over five decades. As their study covered the entire population of the village in all survey years, their measures of income inequality describe the true distribution of income in the village.

provide a basis for generalizations about local-level inequality across large numbers of communities. Construction of comprehensive 'geographic profiles' of inequality across localities has been held back by limitations with conventional distributional data. Detailed household surveys which include reasonable measures of income or consumption are samples, and thus are rarely representative or of sufficient size at low levels of disaggregation to yield statistically reliable estimates. In the three developing countries studied here—Ecuador, Madagascar, and Mozambique—the lowest level of disaggregation possible using sample survey data is to regions that encompass hundreds of thousands of households. At the same time, census (or large sample) data of sufficient size to allow disaggregation either have no information about income or consumption, or measure these variables poorly.

This chapter provides, in the next section, a description of our data and estimates of inequality at a finely disaggregated level for Ecuador, Madagascar, and Mozambique. To accomplish this, we make use of a recently developed statistical procedure to combine data sources so as to take advantage of the detailed information available in household sample surveys and the comprehensive coverage of a census. This procedure is discussed in some detail in the Appendix to this chapter. We examine how well our census-based estimates match estimates from the corresponding household surveys at the level of disaggregation at which the households surveys are representative. Whenever necessary, we also draw from previous work by some of the authors of this chapter, such as Elbers *et al.* (2002, 2003a, b), Demombynes *et al.* (2004), among others. Despite the variation in levels of development, geographical context, quality, and organization of data, we find that the method seems to work well in all three countries we examine.

In Section 3.3, we turn to a detailed examination of local-level inequality in our three countries under study. We first examine the importance of local-level inequality by decomposing national inequality in all three countries into a within-community and between-community component, where we successively redefine community to correspond to lower levels of disaggregation. We find that in all countries the within-community share of overall inequality remains dominant even after we have disaggregated the country into a very large number of small communities (corresponding to the third administrative level—often representing an average of no more than 1,000–2,000 households). These results might be construed to suggest that there is no basis for expecting communities to exhibit a greater degree of homogeneity than larger units of aggregation. To the extent that local-level inequality is correlated with factors, such as elite-capture, that might threaten the success of local-level policy initiatives such as decentralization and community-driven development, this finding sends a cautioning note where initiatives in local-level decisionmaking are being explored.

However, it is important to carefully probe these decomposition results. Decomposing inequality into a within-group and between-group component effectively produces a summary statistic that can mask important differences. Upon closer examination of

Such studies are rare. More common are village or community studies which estimate inequality across (often small) samples of households within the village.

the distribution of communities in our datasets, we find that in all three countries considered, a very high percentage share of within-community inequality is perfectly consistent with a large majority of communities having levels of inequality well *below* the national level of inequality. We illustrate how this seemingly paradoxical finding is in fact fully consistent with the decomposition procedure.

Given that in our three countries we observe a significant degree of heterogeneity in inequality levels across communities, we explore in Section 3.4 some simple correlates. Our aim is not so much to explain local inequality (in a causal sense) but rather to explore the extent to which inequality is correlated with geographic characteristics, and whether this correlation survives the inclusion of some basic economic and demographic controls. In Section 3.5, we offer some concluding remarks.

3.2. DATA AND ESTIMATES OF LOCAL INEQUALITY IN THREE COUNTRIES

In this section, we examine how our census-based estimates compare with estimates from the countries' respective surveys at the level at which those surveys are representative.[4] If the methodology we employ is applied properly, with proper attention to data comparability issues, 'first-stage' regression models and the error structures used in simulating the inequality measures, then stratum-level estimates should naturally correspond closely to those in the household survey.

The data used in this study consists of a household survey and a population census from each of the three countries. Table 3.1 presents the basics on each of the data sources, such as year, sample size, stratification, etc. For more detail on the data, please refer to the studies listed in the references row in Table 3.1.

Table 3.2 presents estimates of average per capita consumption for each country from both the household survey and census at the stratum level, for which the household survey is representative. Indeed, in nearly every case we cannot reject that estimates of average per capita consumption across the two data sources are the same (at the 95 per cent confidence level). With few exceptions, point estimates match closely. Note that the standard errors of the per capita consumption estimates in the census are almost always smaller than those in the household survey. While the census estimates are predicted with error mainly due to the imprecision of the first-stage regressions, they are free of sampling error, making them more precise than their counterparts from the household survey.

Comparing stratum-level estimates of inequality across the census and survey is less straightforward. Inequality measures tend to be sensitive to the tails in the distribution of expenditure. Since far-off portions of the tails are typically not observed in the survey (because of its small sample size), the survey estimates of inequality will often be below the true level of inequality. Perhaps more importantly, non-response may be of some importance in a household survey, and to the extent that non-response can be

---

[4] For a similar analysis, focusing specifically on poverty, see Demombynes *et al.* (2004).

Table 3.1. *Data summary*

	Ecuador	Madagascar	Mozambique
Household survey			
Year	1994	1993–4	1996–7
Source	Encuesta de Condiciones de Vida (ECV)	Enquête Permanente Auprès des Ménages (EPM)	Inquérito Nacional aos Agregados Familiares sobre as Condições de Vida (IAF96)
Sample size (households)	4,500	4,508	8,250
References	Hentschel and Lanjouw (1996), Hentschel *et al.* (2000)	Mistiaen *et al.* (2001)	Simler and Nhate (2002)
Population census			
Year	1990	1993	1997
Coverage	About 10 million individuals in 2 million households	About 11.9 million individuals in 2.4 million households	About 16 million individuals in 3.6 million households

Source: See text.

expected to be more prevalent among rich households, the resulting selection bias can lead to further downward bias of survey-based estimates.[5] To the extent that a census suffers less from such problems of observation, and assuming that the expenditure model is correct, the expenditure of rich households will be better represented in the census-based estimates of inequality. These considerations lead one to expect higher inequality estimates from census-based imputation.

Table 3.3 presents estimates of the Gini coefficient in our three countries. Standard errors are presented for all estimates—reflecting the complex sample design of the household survey for the survey-based estimates, and our imputation procedure for the census-based estimates. For Ecuador and Mozambique, we can see that the census estimates of consumption inequality tend to be higher than the survey-based estimates, although not generally to such an extent that one can reject that they are the same (Table 3.3).[6] Note that for some provinces in Mozambique, such as Sofala, Maputo Province, and Maputo City, the estimates from the census are not only higher than those in the survey, but also happen to be quite imprecisely estimated.[7]

---

[5] On this, see also Mistiaen and Ravallion (2003).

[6] These issues are subjects of current research. If anything we expect the true difference between census-based and survey-based inequality estimates to be even larger, since in the simulations underlying poverty maps we regularly discard extreme draws of the error terms. Again, this might lead to an under-representation of high-expenditure cases.

[7] Fortunately, as we shall see below, there is no evidence that the census-based estimates become even noisier at lower levels of aggregation in Mozambique.

Table 3.2. *Comparison of survey and census-based average per capita consumption estimates at the stratum level*

Ecuador			Madagascar			Mozambique		
Stratum	Sucres per capita		Stratum	Francs per capita		Stratum	Meticais per capita	
	Survey	Census		Survey	Census		Survey	Census
Quito	126,098 (11,344)	125,702 (8,026)	Antananarivo urban	513,818 (48,455)	576,470 (23,944)	Niassa	4,660 (355)	5,512 (484)
Sierra urban	121,797 (8,425)	122,415 (4,642)	Fianarantsoa urban	360,635 (42,613)	372,438 (21,878)	Cabo Delgado	6,392 (416)	6,586 (433)
Sierra rural	66,531 (4,067)	63,666 (2,213)	Toamasina urban	445,514 (73,099)	417,823 (15,406)	Nampula	5,315 (287)	5,547 (279)
Guayaquil	89,601 (5,597)	77,432 (2,508)	Mahajanga urban	613,867 (74,092)	580,775 (31,025)	Zambezia	5,090 (208)	5,316 (274)
Costa urban	86,956 (3,603)	90,209 (2,391)	Toliara urban	343,111 (76,621)	321,602 (32,193)	Tete	3,848 (267)	4,404 (176)
Costa rural	57,619 (4,477)	61,618 (2,894)	Antsiranana urban	504,841 (46,148)	693,161 (93,437)	Manica	6,299 (741)	6,334 (527)
Oriente urban	110,064 (9,078)	174,529 (56,115)	Antananarivo rural	312,553 (23,174)	324,814 (14,378)	Sofala	3,218 (191)	4,497 (379)
Oriente rural	47,072 (4,420)	59,549 (3,051)	Fianarantsoa rural	319,870 (45,215)	251,312 (18,091)	Inhambane	4,215 (359)	4,177 (134)
			Toamasina rural	275,943 (22,832)	279,239 (15,838)	Gaza	6,024 (356)	6,521 (355)
			Mahajanga rural	325,872 (30,209)	321,398 (19,385)	Maputo Province	5,844 (613)	8,559 (745)
			Toliara rural	233,801 (22,174)	259,537 (16,222)	Maputo City	8,321 (701)	11,442 (4,956)
			Antsiranana rural	486,781 (91,181)	442,431 (54,869)			

Note: All household survey estimates are computed using weights that are the product of household survey weights and household size. The census-based estimates are calculated weighting by household size. Standard errors are in parentheses.

Source: See text.

Table 3.3. *Comparison of survey and census-based inequality estimates (Gini) at the stratum level*

Ecuador			Madagascar			Mozambique		
Stratum	Gini (s.e.) survey-based	Gini (s.e.) census-based	Stratum	Gini (s.e.) survey-based	Gini (s.e.) census-based	Stratum	Gini (s.e.) survey-based	Gini (s.e.) census-based
Quito	0.490 (0.023)	0.465 (0.012)	Antananarivo urban	0.492 (0.027)	0.469 (0.012)	Niassa	0.355 (0.020)	0.402 (0.025)
Sierra urban	0.436 (0.020)	0.434 (0.011)	Fianarantsoa urban	0.430 (0.038)	0.426 (0.015)	Cabo Delgado	0.370 (0.025)	0.413 (0.021)
Sierra rural	0.393 (0.034)	0.457 (0.013)	Toamasina urban	0.434 (0.042)	0.402 (0.015)	Nampula	0.391 (0.026)	0.400 (0.020)
Guayaquil	0.378 (0.014)	0.416 (0.011)	Mahajanga urban	0.371 (0.027)	0.392 (0.016)	Zambezia	0.324 (0.017)	0.366 (0.012)
Costa urban	0.359 (0.015)	0.382 (0.011)	Toliara urban	0.514 (0.052)	0.504 (0.030)	Tete	0.346 (0.019)	0.394 (0.018)
Costa rural	0.346 (0.036)	0.400 (0.015)	Antsiranana urban	0.362 (0.025)	0.433 (0.039)	Manica	0.413 (0.036)	0.449 (0.020)
Oriente urban	0.398 (0.035)	0.563 (0.104)	Antananarivo rural	0.376 (0.023)	0.404 (0.015)	Sofala	0.405 (0.031)	0.529 (0.032)
Oriente rural	0.431 (0.034)	0.478 (0.014)	Fianarantsoa rural	0.470 (0.050)	0.437 (0.018)	Inhambane	0.382 (0.037)	0.398 (0.012)
			Toamasina rural	0.352 (0.036)	0.362 (0.017)	Gaza	0.380 (0.024)	0.421 (0.023)
			Mahajanga rural	0.320 (0.026)	0.306 (0.015)	Maputo Province	0.424 (0.029)	0.518 (0.029)
			Toliara rural	0.383 (0.029)	0.377 (0.017)	Maputo City	0.444 (0.033)	0.560 (0.108)
			Antsiranana rural	0.518 (0.110)	0.453 (0.048)			

Note: All household survey estimates are computed using weights that are the product of household survey weights and household size. The census-based estimates are calculated weighting by household size. Standard errors are in parentheses.

Source: See text.

In Madagascar, it is the standard errors on the survey estimates of inequality that are quite high (Table 3.3). This serves as a reminder that although stratum-level estimates of welfare in household surveys are often referred to as 'representative', the sample size in these strata can be rather small so that the accompanying welfare estimates are not always terribly precise. Nonetheless, for our purposes it is encouraging to note that point estimates of the Gini coefficient between the survey and the census in Madagascar are often quite close.

Elbers *et al.* (2002, 2003*a*) demonstrate that standard errors on census-based estimates are inversely correlated with the size of the target population. Thus, although they may look good at the stratum level, estimates of inequality for smaller localities could become quite imprecise. Does this imply that at fine levels of disaggregation—such as 'firaisana' in Madagascar, or 'parroquia' or 'zona' in Ecuador—our inequality estimates are too noisy to be useful? In the three countries we are working with here, we have produced estimates of inequality at the third administrative level (the firaisana in Madagascar, the parroquia in rural Ecuador, the administrative post in Mozambique). In Section 3.3, we show that the standard errors we calculate correspond to about 5–15 per cent of point estimates of inequality for these localities. This is in the same range of what is generally judged to be acceptable at the stratum level in household surveys. We also show, in Section 3.4 (Tables 3.5–3.9), that the explanatory power of simple descriptive ordinary least squares (OLS) regressions of inequality at the smallest administrative level on a set of simple community characteristics is quite high in these three countries, with R^2s ranging between 0.57 and 0.78 in urban areas and between 0.38 and 0.55 in rural areas. If the inequality estimates produced with this methodology were just noise, one would expect the explanatory power of these regressions to be much lower.[8]

Based on the evidence presented in this section, we conclude that the estimation technique used here can yield meaningful estimates of inequality for small areas. Next, we focus our attention on inequality decompositions by administrative units and the heterogeneity of inequality across communities.

3.3. DECOMPOSING INEQUALITY BY GEOGRAPHIC SUBGROUPS

We turn in this section to the important question of how much of overall inequality in a given country is attributable to differences in average consumption across localities as opposed to inequality within localities. Decomposing inequality by subgroups enjoys a long tradition in the empirical analysis of inequality, in both developed and developing countries. It is clear that where national inequality is largely due to differences in mean income across regions, the policy implications are very different from the situation where subregions themselves are unequal and national inequality is simply

---

[8] Elbers *et al.* (2003*b*) argue that although the inequality measures included in these regressions have been estimated, this does not invalidate their use for these purposes (although they do advocate correcting standard errors for model error).

an expression at the country-level of a degree of heterogeneity that already exists at the more local level. We decompose inequality using the general entropy class of inequality measures, a class of measures which is particularly well-suited to this exercise.[9] This class of measures takes the following form:

$$I_c = \frac{1}{c(c-1)} \sum_i f_i \left[\left(\frac{y_i}{\mu} \right)^c - 1 \right] \quad \text{for } c \neq 0, 1$$

$$I_c = -\sum_i f_i \log \left(\frac{y_i}{\mu} \right) \quad\quad\quad \text{for } c = 0$$

$$I_c = \sum_i f_i \frac{y_i}{\mu} \log \left(\frac{y_i}{\mu} \right), \quad\quad\quad \text{for } c = 1$$

where f_i is the population share of household i, y_i is per capita consumption of household i, μ is average per capita consumption, and c is a parameter that is to be selected by the user.[10] This class of inequality measures can be decomposed into a between- and within-group component along the following lines:

$$I_c = \frac{1}{c(c-1)} \left[1 - \sum_j g_j \left[\left(\frac{\mu_j}{\mu} \right)^c \right] \right] + \sum_j I_j g_j \left(\frac{\mu_j}{\mu} \right)^c \quad \text{for } c \neq 0, 1$$

$$I_c = \left[\sum_j g_j \log \left(\frac{\mu}{\mu_j} \right) \right] + \sum_j I_j g_j \quad\quad\quad \text{for } c = 0$$

$$I_c = \left[\sum_j g_j \left(\frac{\mu_j}{\mu} \right) \log \left(\frac{\mu_j}{\mu} \right) \right] + \sum_j I_j g_j \left(\frac{\mu_j}{\mu} \right) \quad\quad\quad \text{for } c = 1$$

where j refers to subgroups, g_j refers to the population share of group j, and I_j refers to inequality in group j. The between-group component of inequality is captured by the first term to the right of the equality sign. It can be interpreted as measuring what would be the level of inequality in the population if everyone within the group had the same (the group-average) consumption level μ_j. The second term on the right reflects what would be the overall inequality level if there were no differences in mean consumption across groups but each group had its actual within-group inequality I_j. Ratios of the respective components with the overall inequality level provide a measure

---

[9] Following Bourguignon (1979), Shorrocks (1980), and Cowell (1980). Cowell (2000) provides a useful recent survey of methods of inequality measurement, including a discussion of the various approaches to subgroup decomposition. Sen and Foster (1997) and Kanbur (2000) discuss some of the difficulties in interpreting results from such decompositions.

[10] Lower values of c are associated with greater sensitivity to inequality among the poor, and higher values of c place more weight to inequality among the rich. A c value of 1 yields the well-known Theil entropy measure, a value of 0 provides the Theil L or mean log deviation, and a value of 2 is ordinally equivalent to the squared coefficient of variation.

Table 3.4. *Decomposition of inequality by regional subgroup (GE(0))*

Level of decomposition	Number of subgroups	Within-group (%)	Between-group (%)
Ecuador			
Rural			
National	1	100	0
Region	3	100	0
Province	21	98.7	1.3
Canton	195	94.1	5.9
Parroquia	915	85.9	14.1
Household	960,529	0	100
Urban			
National	1	100	0
Region	5	100	6.6
Province	19	98.7	7.3
Canton	87	94.1	8.6
Zonas	664	85.9	23.3
Household	880,001	0	100
Madagascar			
Urban	1	100	0
Faritany	6	92.3	7.7
Fivondrona	103	78.3	21.7
Firaisana	131	76.7	23.2
Rural	1	100	0
Faritany	6	95.2	4.8
Fivondrona	104	84.6	15.4
Firaisana	1,117	81.9	18.1
Mozambique			
National	1	100	0
Province	11	90.7	9.3
District	146	81.6	18.4
Administrative post	424	78.0	22.0

Note: Quito and Guayaquil are treated as independent geographic areas.

Source: See text.

of the percentage contribution of between-group and within-group inequality to total inequality.

In Table 3.4, we examine how within-group inequality evolves at progressively lower levels of regional disaggregation in our three countries. At one extreme, when a country-level perspective is taken, all inequality is, by definition, within-group. At the other extreme, when each individual household is taken as a separate group, the within-group contribution to overall inequality is zero. But how rapidly does the within-group share fall? Is it reasonable to suppose that at a sufficiently low level of disaggregation, such as the third administrative level in our three countries (with about 1,000–10,000 households), differences within groups are small and most of overall inequality is due to differences between groups?

We decompose inequality in our three countries on the basis of the GE(0) measure.[11] In rural Ecuador we see that when we have disaggregated down to the level of 915 parroquias (with an average number of households of a little over 1,000) some 86 per cent of overall inequality remains within-group. In urban areas of Ecuador, the within-group share across 664 urban zonas (with 1,300 households on average) is only slightly lower at 77 per cent. The same pattern is observed in Madagascar and Mozambique (Table 3.4). In all three countries no less than three-quarters of all inequality is attributable to within-community differences, even after one has disaggregated down to a very low level (corresponding, in our countries, to the lowest level of central government administration). At first glance, one might understand these results as suggesting that even within local communities there exists a considerable heterogeneity of living standards. Such a conclusion might have implications regarding the likelihood of political capture, the feasibility of raising revenues locally, and the extent to which residents in these localities can be viewed as having similar demands and priorities.

However, a blanket statement about the degree of inequality within communities does not follow directly from the above decomposition results. It is important to recognize that the decomposition exercise indicates that *on average* inequality does not fall much with aggregation level. In other words, it is very well possible that at low levels of aggregation the population is characterized by both highly equal and highly unequal communities. A simple example can illustrate this. Consider a population of eight individuals with consumption values (1,1,2,2,4,4,5,5). This population could be divided into two communities as (1,2,4,5) and (1,2,4,5); or as (1,1,5,5) and (2,2,4,4). In both cases the two communities have the same average consumption. As a result the between-group component from the decomposition exercise is always zero (and thus the within-group share is 100 per cent in both cases). However, in the first case inequality in the two communities is exactly equal to national inequality, whereas in the second case one community has higher and the other lower inequality than at the national level. As can be readily seen from the expressions for decomposing the general entropy class of inequality measures provided above, when average consumption levels are the same for all communities, overall inequality is calculated by taking a population-weighted average of community-level inequality rates. Finding a high within-group share from a decomposition exercise across a large number of communities is, thus, perfectly consistent with great heterogeneity in inequality levels across communities.

In a situation such as ours, where the decomposition exercise is carried out across a very large number of communities, it is important to check for variation in the degree of inequality across communities. Are all communities as unequal as a whole? Such a finding would certainly generate a large within-group contribution in a decomposition exercise. Or do communities vary widely in their degree of inequality? That could also yield a high within-group share. In Figs 3.1–3.5 we plot community-level

---

[11] Results remain virtually identical for other values of c.

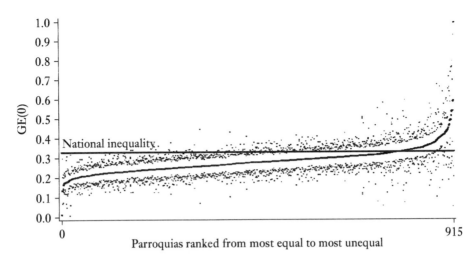

Figure 3.1. *Rural Ecuador: distribution across parroquias of parroquia-level inequality*

Note: (915 parroquias; average number of households per parroquia: 1050) (Scatter plot of 95% confidence intervals).

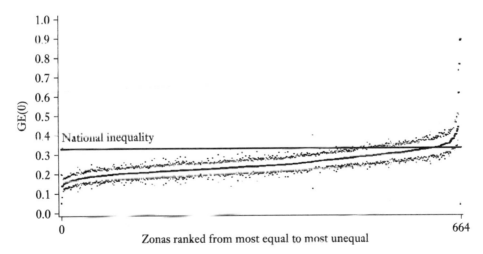

Figure 3.2. *Urban Ecuador: distribution across zonas of zona-level inequality*

Note: (664 zonas; average number of households per zona: 1325) (Scatter plot of 95% confidence intervals).

inequality estimates and compare these against national-level inequality. Communities are ranked from most equal to most unequal, and 95 per cent confidence intervals on each community level estimate are included as scatter plots.

Figure 3.1 compares parroquia-level inequality in rural Ecuador against the overall inequality level in rural areas. We see that although the within-group share from

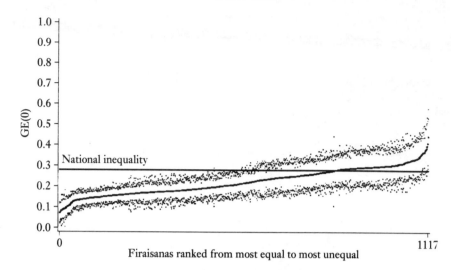

Figure 3.3. *Rural Madagascar: distribution across firaisanas of firaisana-level inequality*

Note: (1,117 firaisanas; average number of households per firaisana: 1,684) (Scatter plot of 95% confidence intervals).

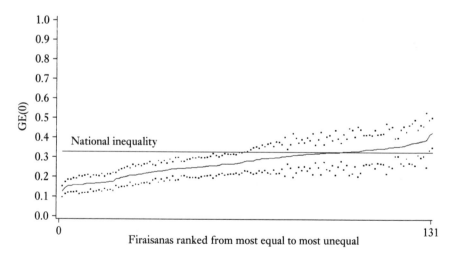

Figure 3.4. *Urban Madagascar: distribution across firaisanas of firaisana-level inequality*

Note: (131 firaisanas; average number of households per firaisana: 4,190) (Scatter plot of 95% confidence intervals).

the decomposition exercise was as high as 86 per cent, this summary statistic masks considerable variation in parroquia inequality levels. A large majority of parroquia-level point estimates are well below the national level in rural Ecuador. Even allowing for the imprecision around the parroquia-level estimates (which are typically 5–15 per cent of the point estimate), a sizeable proportion of parroquias are unambiguously more

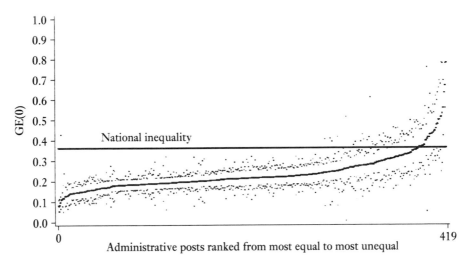

Figure 3.5. *Mozambique: distribution across administrative posts of post-level inequality*

Note: (419 administrative posts; average number of households per post: 7,978) (Scatter plot of 95% confidence intervals).

equal than the picture at the national level. The proportion of zonas that have lower inequality than the national-level inequality rate is even higher in urban than in rural areas (Fig. 3.2). The precision of point estimates in urban areas of Ecuador is somewhat higher than in rural areas; accordingly, more zonas lie unambiguously below the national inequality level.

In rural and urban Madagascar (Figs 3.3 and 3.4) and in Mozambique (Fig. 3.5) the picture is very similar. In all of the countries considered in this study, there is a clear and sizeable subset of communities with lower inequality than the country as a whole; another large group for which inequality is not significantly different from inequality in the country as a whole; and a small third group of communities with inequality higher than the national level.

3.4. CORRELATES OF LOCAL INEQUALITY: DOES GEOGRAPHY MATTER?

We have found empirical support for both the view that at the local level communities are more homogeneous than society as a whole, and the view that local communities are as heterogeneous as society as a whole. The question then arises as to whether it is possible to readily distinguish between communities on the basis of some simple indicators. In particular, we are interested to know whether there are discernible geographic patterns of inequality.

In Tables 3.5–3.9 we provide results from OLS regressions of inequality on a set of simple community characteristics. We ask whether inequality levels are correlated with location, controlling for both demographic characteristics of the communities (population size and demographic composition), and mean per capita consumption. Table 3.5 for rural Ecuador, finds strong evidence that inequality in the parroquias of the eastern Oriente region is significantly higher than the province of Pichincha in the central mountainous Sierra region. Communities located in provinces in the western coastal Costa region tend to be more equal, significantly so in the provinces of Manabi, Los Rios, Guayas, and El Oro. Relatively few differences are discernible across provinces within the Sierra region.[12] Understanding these geographic patterns of inequality is beyond the scope of this chapter, but the evidence is consistent with historical and anecdotal accounts of a very divergent evolution of society and economic structures in the mountainous Sierra vis-à-vis the Costa and Oriente.[13]

In rural Ecuador, there is evidence that larger parroquias tend to be more unequal. An interesting finding is that parroquias with a larger proportion of elderly, relative to the population share of 20–40-year-olds, are more unequal. This pattern is consistent with the findings of Deaton and Paxson (1995) regarding the positive association between an ageing population and inequality. The quantitative importance and statistical significance of both geographic and demographic characteristics remains broadly unchanged when mean per capita consumption (and its square) are added to the model. In rural Ecuador inequality is positively associated with higher consumption levels. While there is some suggestion of a turning point (at around US$2,800 per capita per month)—the well-known 'inverted U-curve'—the statistical support for this is weak. The correlation between inequality and the population share of young children, relative to 20–40-year-olds, switches in sign from negative to positive, depending on whether per capita consumption is included in the specification. It seems clear that the share of young children is likely to be (negatively) correlated with per capita consumption so that the coefficient on this variable is capturing the consumption effect, when average expenditures are excluded from the specification. Once consumption expenditures are controlled for, the correlation between inequality and the share of children in the population becomes positive. Possibly, there exists greater heterogeneity in household size in those parroquias with large population shares of young children and that this translates into greater inequality of per capita consumption.

In urban Ecuador (Table 3.6) the relatively low inequality in the Costa region is again observed. Relative to the zonas in the capital Quito, inequality in all zonas of the Costa region tends to be significantly lower. Other urban areas in the Sierra are again not noticeably less or more equal than Quito. In urban areas, in contrast to rural areas, population size of the zona does not appear to be significantly correlated with its inequality level.[14] Also in contrast to rural areas, conditioning on mean consumption

[12] We can reject with 95% confidence, for both rural and urban Ecuador, the null hypothesis that parameter estimates on province dummies within their respective regions are all equal.

[13] See, for example, 'Under the Volcano', *The Economist*, 27 November 1999 (p. 66).

[14] Although zonas vary less in population size than parroquias, they still range between 800 and 1,900 households.

Table 3.5. *Correlates of mean log deviation (GE(0)) in rural Ecuador: parroquia-level regression (915 parroquias)*

	Basic regression	+Expenditure
Log population	0.0169 (0.002)***	0.010 (0.002)***
% aged 0–10	−0.139 (0.079)*	0.321 (0.080)***
% aged 10–20	−0.375 (0.104)***	−0.084 (0.096)
% aged 40–60	−0.246 (0.130)*	0.053 (0.120)
% aged 61+	0.269 (0.123)***	0.392 (0.112)***
Log mean per capita expenditure		0.222 (0.085)***
(Log mean per capita expenditure)^2		−0.014 (0.010)
Oriente		
Sucumbios	0.036 (0.013)***	0.036 (0.012)***
Napo	0.051 (0.012)***	0.056 (0.011)***
Pastaza	0.071 (0.015)***	0.077 (0.013)***
Morona-Santiago	0.040 (0.011)***	0.036 (0.010)***
Zamora-Chinchipe	0.034 (0.013)**	0.037 (0.012)***
Costa		
Esmeraldas	−0.012 (0.010)	−0.036 (0.010)***
Manabi	−0.060 (0.010)***	−0.057 (0.009)***
Los Rios	−0.041 (0.013)***	−0.025 (0.012)**
Guayas	−0.050 (0.010)***	−0.035 (0.009)***
El Oro	−0.022 (0.010)**	−0.020 (0.009)**
Galápagos	0.027 (0.023)	−0.000 (0.021)
Sierra		
Carchi	−0.002 (0.012)	0.014 (0.010)
Imbabura	0.024 (0.010)**	0.037 (0.011)***
Cotopaxi	−0.013 (0.011)	−0.001 (0.010)
Tungurahua	−0.025 (0.010)**	−0.010 (0.009)
Bolivar	−0.0002 (0.012)	0.002 (0.011)
Chimborazo	−0.010 (0.010)	0.006 (0.010)
Canar	0.003 (0.012)	0.007 (0.011)
Azuay	0.011 (0.010)	0.014 (0.009)
Loja	0.024 (0.009)**	0.036 (0.008)***
Constant	0.296 (0.060)	−0.571 (0.192)
Observations	915	915
R^2	0.24	0.38

Notes: Standard errors in parentheses. *Significant at 10%; **significant at 5%; ***significant at 1%. Excluded groups are Pichincha and percentage of population aged 20–40.

Source: See text.

C. *Elbers* et al.

Table 3.6. *Correlates of mean log deviation (GE(0)) in urban Ecuador: zona-level regression (660 zonas)*

	Basic regression	+Expenditure
Log population	−0.013 (0.015)	−0.003 (0.014)
% aged 0–10	0.231 (0.118)*	0.253 (0.119)**
% aged 10–20	0.283 (0.098)***	0.791 (0.112)***
% aged 40–60	0.001 (0.141)	−0.673 (0.162)***
% aged 61+	0.704 (0.162)***	1.084 (0.161)***
Log mean per capita expenditure		0.025 (0.075)
(Log mean per capita expenditure)²		0.005 (0.008)
Oriente		
Pastaza	0.052 (0.033)	0.049 (0.031)
Morona-Santiago	0.457 (0.046)***	0.381 (0.045)***
Zamora-Chinchipe	0.031 (0.046)	0.004 (0.044)
Costa		
Esmeraldas	−0.073 (0.013)***	−0.066 (0.012)***
Manabi	−0.084 (0.007)***	−0.069 (0.007)***
Los Rios	−0.077 (0.010)***	−0.049 (0.011)***
Guayas	−0.097 (0.008)***	−0.064 (0.008)***
El Oro	−0.094 (0.009)***	−0.081 (0.009)***
Guayaquil	−0.087 (0.005)***	−0.054 (0.007)***
Sierra		
Carchi	−0.009 (0.017)	0.012 (0.017)
Imbabura	0.022 (0.014)	−0.008 (0.013)
Cotopaxi	0.007 (0.016)	0.006 (0.015)
Tungurahua	−0.008 (0.014)	−0.003 (0.013)
Pichincha	−0.011 (0.010)	−0.000 (0.010)
Chimborazo	−0.025 (0.015)*	−0.026 (0.014)*
Canar	−0.012 (0.024)	−0.018 (0.022)
Azuay	−0.013 (0.010)	−0.018 (0.010)*
Loja	−0.003 (0.013)	−0.010 (0.012)
Constant	0.272 (0.140)	−0.076 (0.242)
Observations	660	660
R^2	0.52	0.57

Notes: Standard errors in parentheses. *Significant at 10%; **significant at 5%; ***significant at 1%. Excluded groups are Quito and percentage of population aged 20–40.

Source: See text.

Table 3.7. *Correlates of mean log deviation (GE(0)) in rural Madagascar: firaisana-level regression (1,117 firaisanas)*

	Basic regression	+Expenditure
Log population	0.010 (0.002)***	0.012 (0.002)***
% aged 0–5	−0.768 (0.085)***	−0.700 (0.086)***
% aged 6–11	−0.226 (0.127)*	−0.091 (0.126)
% aged 12–14	0.193 (0.241)	0.236 (0.242)
% aged 50–59	−1.757 (0.292)***	−1.747 (0.286)***
% aged 60+	0.462 (0.152)**	0.696 (0.152)***
Log mean per capita expenditure		0.886 (0.118)***
(Log mean per capita expenditure)^2		−0.034 (0.005)***
Provinces		
Antananarivo	−0.068 (0.006)***	−0.065 (0.006)***
Fianarantsoa	0.011 (0.005)**	0.020 (0.006)***
Toamasina	−0.059 (0.006)***	−0.054 (0.006)***
Mahajanga	−0.115 (0.006)***	−0.116 (0.006)***
Toliara	−0.046 (0.005)***	−0.042 (0.006)***
Constant	0.430 (0.041)***	−5.356 (0.765)***
Observations	1,117	1,117
R^2	0.53	0.55

Notes: Standard errors in parentheses. *Significant at 10%; **significant at 5%; ***significant at 1%. Excluded groups are Antsiranana and percentage of population aged 15–49.

Source: See text.

levels does not add much explanatory power—there is no evidence that poorer zonas are also more equal. Zonas with large dependency ratios (irrespective of whether these are due to large numbers of young children or of a large proportion of elderly persons) are associated with higher inequality levels, irrespective of controlling for consumption.

Tables 3.7 and 3.8 provide analogous results for Madagascar. The broad conclusions are quite similar to those found in Ecuador. As in rural Ecuador, in rural Madagascar population size is positively associated with inequality, and the larger the percentage of elderly in the firaisana the more unequal the community. As in Ecuador, inequality rises with mean consumption (in the Madagascar case the inverted U-curve is more clearly discernible) and geography is strongly and independently significant. Relative to the population share aged 15–50, the higher the share of children and the share of population aged 50–59 the more equal the community, whether or not one controls for consumption. In Madagascar it seems that communities with large population shares of children are not markedly more heterogeneous in household size. For rural

Table 3.8. *Correlates of mean log deviation (GE(0)) in urban Madagascar: firaisana-level regression (131 firaisanas)*

	Basic regression	+Expenditure
Log population	−0.014 (0.005)***	−0.011 (0.005)**
% aged 0–5	−1.253 (0.202)***	−1.053 (0.243)***
% aged 6–11	0.166 (0.464)	0.147 (0.465)
% aged 12–14	−0.965 (0.777)	−0.551 (0.826)
% aged 50–59	−2.602 (0.882)***	−2.543 (0.882)***
% aged 60+	1.183 (0.396)***	1.355 (0.417)***
Log mean per capita expenditure		0.117 (0.143)
(Log mean per capita expenditure)^2		−0.004 (0.013)
Provinces		
Antananarivo	0.079 (0.015)***	0.080 (0.015)***
Fianarantsoa	0.059 (0.014)***	0.065 (0.015)***
Toamasina	−0.012 (0.014)	−0.007 (0.015)
Mahajanga	−0.025 (0.014)*	−0.027 (0.014)*
Toliara	0.117 (0.013)***	0.125 (0.014)***
Constant	0.717 (0.106)	−0.270 (2.245)
Observations	131	131
R^2	0.78	0.79

Notes: Standard errors in parentheses. *Significant at 10%; **significant at 5%; ***significant at 1%. Excluded groups are Antsiranana and percentage of population aged 15–49.

Source: See text.

Madagascar, the simple specification employed here yields an R^2 as high as 0.55 when all variables are included.

In urban Madagascar the explanatory power is even greater (Table 3.8). Here, unlike rural areas, population size is significantly negatively associated with inequality. As in rural areas, the larger the percentage of children the lower is inequality. As in urban Ecuador, mean per capita consumption is not significantly associated with inequality—there is no presumption that a poorer urban firaisana is more homogeneous than a rich one. Geographic variables remain independently significant, with urban areas in Antananarivo (the capital province), Fianarantsoa, and Toliara more unequal than the urban areas in the rest of the country. Table 3.9 confirms that in Mozambique also, geographic variables are key indicators of local-level inequality controlling for population characteristics, mean expenditure levels, and urban–rural differences. Compared with Maputo City, the rest of the country has significantly less inequality. There is more inequality in urban areas, an increasing association with mean consumption (but no Kuznet's curve), and areas with higher percentage of 17–30-year-olds seem to have higher inequality.

Table 3.9. *Correlates of mean log deviation (GE(0)) in Mozambique: administrative post-level regression (464 administrative posts)*

	Basic regression	+Expenditure	+Urban
% aged 0–5	−0.002 (0.004)	0.000 (0.003)	0.001 (0.003)
% aged 6–10	0.017 (0.005)**	0.015 (0.004)**	0.014 (0.004)**
% females aged 11–16	0.027 (0.009)**	0.020 (0.008)**	0.015 (0.008)
% males aged 11–16	−0.000 (0.009)	0.001 (0.008)	0.002 (0.008)
% females aged 17–30	0.016** (0.004)	0.012 (0.003)**	0.011 (0.003)**
% males aged 17–30	0.015 (0.005)**	0.010 (0.004)*	0.009 (0.004)*
% females aged 31–60	0.005 (0.006)	0.005 (0.006)	0.007 (0.006)
% males aged 31–60	0.007 (0.004)	0.005 (0.004)	0.004 (0.004)
Log (population of post)	0.001 (0.004)	−0.003 (0.003)	−0.005 (0.004)
Niassa	−0.200 (0.036)**	−0.138 (0.034)**	−0.136 (0.033)**
Cabo Delgado	−0.204 (0.034)**	−0.163 (0.031)**	−0.158 (0.031)**
Nampula	−0.204 (0.035)**	−0.143 (0.032)**	−0.143 (0.032)**
Zambézia	−0.215 (0.035)**	−0.154 (0.032)**	−0.149 (0.032)**
Tete	−0.212 (0.036)**	−0.133 (0.033)**	−0.127 (0.033)**
Manica	−0.135 (0.035)**	−0.095 (0.032)**	−0.089 (0.032)**
Sofala	−0.118 (0.035)**	−0.005 (0.032)	−0.006 (0.032)
Inhambane	−0.178 (0.035)**	−0.088 (0.032)**	−0.090 (0.032)**
Gaza	−0.189 (0.035)**	−0.136 (0.032)**	−0.135 (0.031)**
Maputo Province	−0.088 (0.036)*	−0.045 (0.032)	−0.044 (0.032)
Log (mean expenditure)		−0.406 (0.216)	−0.324 (0.217)
Log (mean expenditure)^2		0.031 (0.013)*	0.025 (0.013)*
Urban			0.037 (0.014)**
Constant	−0.504 (0.321)	0.856 (0.962)	0.605 (0.960)
Observations	424	424	424
R^2	0.465	0.595	0.601

Notes: Standard errors in parentheses. *Significant at 5%; **significant at 1%. Excluded groups are Maputo City and percentage of persons older than 60 years.

Source: See text.

We have not attempted here to identify the best possible set of correlates of local inequality for each of the three countries we are examining. We have chosen to employ a parsimonious and broadly similar specification in the three countries in order to ask whether there are any common patterns across countries which, in other respects, resemble each other very little (particularly the comparison between Ecuador and the two sub-Saharan African countries). We have indeed found that in all three countries, in both rural and urban areas, geographic location is a good predictor of local-level inequality even after controlling for some basic demographic and economic characteristics of the communities. With respect to other characteristics, there appear to be clear differences between urban and rural areas (best seen in the models for Ecuador and Madagascar). In rural areas, inequality tends to be higher in communities with larger populations, a higher share of the elderly in the total population, and in communities with higher mean consumption levels. In urban areas, mean consumption is not independently correlated with inequality and inequality is not typically higher in communities with larger populations. High population shares of elderly are clearly associated with higher inequality, but the correlation with population shares of children depends on the country.

3.5. CONCLUSIONS

This chapter has taken three developing countries, Ecuador, Madagascar, and Mozambique, and has implemented in each a methodology to produce disaggregated estimates of inequality. The countries are quite dissimilar, with different geographies, stages of development, quality and types of data, and so on. The methodology works well in all three settings and produces valuable information about the spatial distribution of poverty and inequality within those countries—information that was not previously available.

The methodology is based on a statistical procedure to combine household survey data with population census data, by imputing into the latter a measure of economic welfare (consumption expenditure in our examples) from the former. Like the usual sample-based estimates, the inequality measures produced here are also *estimates* and subject to statistical error. The chapter has demonstrated that the mean consumption and inequality estimates produced from census data match well the estimates calculated directly from the country's surveys (at levels of disaggregation that the survey can bear). The precision of the inequality estimates produced with this methodology depends on the degree of disaggregation. In all three countries our inequality estimators allow one to work at a level of disaggregation far below that allowed by surveys.

We have decomposed inequality in our three countries into progressively more disaggregated spatial units to show that even at a very high level of spatial disaggregation the contribution to overall inequality of within–community inequality is very high (75 per cent or more). However, such a high within-group component does not necessarily imply that there are no between-group differences and that all communities in a given country are as unequal as the country as a whole. We have shown that in all three countries, there is a considerable amount of variation in inequality across communities. Many communities are rather more equal than their respective country as a whole, but there are also many communities that are not clearly more homogeneous than society as a whole, and may even be considerably more unequal.

We have explored some basic correlates of local-level inequality in our three countries and found consistent patterns across all three countries. Geographic characteristics are strongly correlated with inequality, even after controlling for demographic and economic conditions. The correlation with geography is observed in both rural and urban areas. In rural areas, population size and mean consumption at the community level are positively associated with inequality, while in urban areas that is not the case. In both rural and urban areas, populations with large shares of the elderly tend to be more unequal. In Madagascar, populations with large shares of children and large shares of individuals aged 50–59 are consistently more equal. In Ecuador this is true only in rural areas.

Appendix: Brief Methodological Description on Small Area Estimation of Welfare Indicators

What follows is an overview of the methodology we employ to construct welfare indicators for small geographical areas, such as firaisanas in Madagascar, or parroquias in Ecuador. We provide this section so that the reader is clear about the source of the welfare measures we utilize throughout this chapter. Please see Elbers *et al.* (2002) for a fuller discussion of the methodology, and Mistiaen *et al.* (2001) and Simler and Nhate (2002) for details regarding the specific application to the Ecuador, Madagascar, and Mozambique data, respectively.

The basic methodology applied in linking surveys and census-type datasets is very similar to that of synthetic estimation used in small-area geography. Prediction models are derived for consumption or income as the endogenous variable, on the basis of the survey. The selection of right-hand side variables is restricted to those variables that can also be found in the census (or some other large dataset). The parameter estimates are then applied to the census data and poverty and inequality statistics derived. Simple performance tests can be conducted which compare basic poverty statistics across the two datasets (at representative levels for the household survey). For Ecuador, Madagascar, and South Africa, Demombynes *et al.* (2004) show that stratum-level poverty estimates derived from consumption measured directly in the household survey are very similar to those calculated on the basis of imputed household consumption in the census.

The calculation of poverty and inequality statistics using predicted income or consumption has to take into account that each individual household income or consumption value has been predicted and has standard errors associated with it. Elbers *et al.* (2002) show that the approach yields estimates of the incidence of poverty and of inequality that are consistent, and that the standard errors are reasonably precise for small geographic units, such as parroquias in Ecuador. Furthermore, Mistiaen *et al.* (2001) demonstrate that these estimates are precise enough to permit meaningful pairwise comparisons across second and third levels of administration in Madagascar.

As described above, the concept of imputing expenditures for each household in the census is simple to grasp, yet it requires great attention to detail, especially regarding the computation of standard errors. This also makes the exercise computationally quite intensive. For each country, it involves constructing an association model between per capita household expenditure and household characteristics that are common to both the census and the household survey. After carefully constructing the variables in the exact same manner in each dataset, we estimate a regression model of logarithmic per capita household expenditure on the other constructed variables that consist of household composition, education, primary occupation, quality of housing, and access to services.

The basis of the approach is that per capita household expenditure for a household h in cluster c can be explained using a set of observable characteristics. These observable characteristics must be found as variables in both the survey and the census:[15]

$$\ln y_{ch} = E[\ln y_{ch}|x_{ch}] + u_{ch}. \qquad (3.A1)$$

Using a linear approximation to the conditional expectation, the household's logarithmic per capita expenditure is modelled as

$$\ln y_{ch} = x'_{ch}\beta + u_{ch}. \qquad (3.A2)$$

More explicitly, we model the disturbance term as

$$u_{ch} = \eta_c + \varepsilon_{ch},$$

where η_c is the cluster component and ε_{ch} is the household component. This complex error structure will not only allow for spatial autocorrelation—that is, a 'location effect' for households in the same area—but also for heteroskedasticity in the household component of the error. The two error components are independent of one another and uncorrelated with observable characteristics.

The model in (3.A2) is estimated by generalized least squares (GLS) using the household survey data. The results from this first stage of the analysis are a set of estimated model parameters, including the beta vector, an associated variance–covariance matrix, and parameters describing the distribution of the disturbances.

To avoid forcing the parameter estimates to be the same for all areas in each of the three countries, we run the first-stage regressions separately for each stratum. The explanatory power ($\bar{R}^2$) of the nine regressions ranged from 0.45 to 0.77 in Ecuador, 0.29 to 0.63 in Madagascar, and 0.27 to 0.55 in Mozambique.[16]

In the second-stage analysis, we combine these parameter estimates based on the *survey data* with household characteristics from the *census data* to estimate welfare measures for subgroups of the census population. It is possible to produce these estimates for any subgroups that can be identified in the census. Specifically, we combine the estimated first-stage parameters with the observable characteristics of each household in the census to generate predicted log expenditures and relevant disturbances. We simulate a value of expenditure for each household, $\hat{y}_{ch}$, based on both predicted log expenditure, $x'_{ch}\tilde{\beta}$, and the disturbance terms, $\tilde{\eta}_c$ and $\tilde{\varepsilon}_{ch}$ using bootstrap methods:

$$\hat{y}_{ch} = \exp(x'_{ch}\tilde{\beta} + \tilde{\eta}_c + \tilde{\varepsilon}_{ch}). \qquad (3.A3)$$

---

[15] The explanatory variables are observed values and thus need to have the same definitions and the same degree of accuracy across data sources. Finally, note that from a methodological standpoint it does not matter if these variables are exogenous.

[16] Again, see Elbers *et al.* (2002), Mistiaen *et al.* (2001), and Simler and Nhate (2002) for details.

For each household, the two disturbance terms are drawn from distributions described by parameters estimated in the first stage.[17] The beta coefficients, $\tilde{\beta}$, are drawn from the multivariate normal distribution described by the first-stage beta estimates and their associated variance–covariance matrix. We then use the full set of simulated $\hat{y}_{ch}$ values to calculate expected values of the average expenditure, poverty, and inequality measures for various administrative units in each country. We repeat this procedure 100 times, drawing a new set of beta coefficients and disturbances for each set of simulations. For each subgroup, we take the mean and standard deviation of the welfare indicators over all 100 simulations. For any given location, these means constitute the point estimates of the welfare indicators, while the standard deviations are the standard errors of these estimates.

There are two principal sources of error in the welfare measure estimates produced by this method.[18] The first component, referred to as 'model error' in Elbers *et al.* (2002), is due to the fact that the parameters from the first-stage model in eqn (3.A2) are estimated. The second component, described as 'idiosyncratic error', is associated with the disturbance term in the same model, which implies that households' actual expenditures deviate from their expected values. While population size in a location does not affect the model error, the idiosyncratic error increases as the number of households in a target population decreases.

REFERENCES

Atkinson, A. B. and F. Bourguignon (2000). 'Introduction: Income Distribution and Economics', in A. B. Atkinson and F. Bourguignon (eds) *Handbook of Income Distribution*, Vol. 1, North Holland: Amsterdam.

Bardhan, P. and D. Mookherjee (1999). 'Relative Capture of Local and Central Governments' (mimeo), Boston University: Boston.

Bourguignon, F. (1979). 'Decomposable Income Inequality Measures', *Econometrica*, 47: 901–20.

Cowell, F. (1980). 'On the Structure of Additive Inequality Measures', *Review of Economic Studies*, 47: 521–31.

—— (2000). 'Measurement of Inequality' in A. B. Atkinson and F. Bourguignon (eds) *Handbook of Income Distribution*, Vol. 1, North Holland: Amsterdam.

Deaton, A. and C. Paxson (1995). 'Savings, Inequality and Ageing: an East Asian Perspective', *Asia-Pacific Economic Review*, 1(1): 7–19.

Demombynes, G., C. Elbers, and J. O. Lanjouw, *et al.* (2004). 'Producing an Improved Geographic Profile of Poverty: Methodology and Evidence from Three Developing Countries', in A. Shorrocks and R. van der Hoeven (eds) *Growth, Inequality, and Poverty: Prospects for Pro-poor Economic Development*, Oxford University Press for UNU-WIDER: Oxford.

[17] Please note that these errors are not necessarily drawn from a normal distribution. Again, refer to Elbers *et al.* (2002), Mistiaen *et al.* (2001), and Simler and Nhate (2002) for details.

[18] A third potential source of error is associated with computation methods. Elbers *et al.* (2002) found this component to be negligible with a sufficiently high number of simulation draws.

Elbers, C., J. O. Lanjouw, and P. Lanjouw (2002). 'Micro–Level Estimation of Welfare', *World Bank Policy Research Working Papers* 2911, Development Research Group, World Bank: Washington DC.

——, ——, and —— (2003*a*). 'Micro–Level Estimation of Poverty and Inequality', *Econometrica*, 71(1): 355–64.

——, ——, and —— (2003*b*) 'Imputed Welfare Estimates in Regression Analysis', *Journal of Economic Geography* (forthcoming).

Hentschel, J. and P. Lanjouw (1996). 'Constructing an Indicator of Consumption for the Analysis of Poverty: Principles and Illustrations with Reference to Ecuador', *LSMS Working Papers* 124, DECRG-World Bank: Washington DC.

——, J. O. Lanjouw, P. Lanjouw, and J. Poggi (2000). 'Combining Census and Survey Data to Trace the Spatial Dimensions of Poverty: A Case Study of Ecuador', *World Bank Economic Review*, 14(1): 147–65.

Kanbur, R. (2000). 'Income Distribution and Development' in A. B. Atkinson and F. Bourguignon (eds) *Handbook of Income Distribution*, Vol. 1, North Holland: Amsterdam.

Lanjouw, P. and N. Stern (1998). *Economic Development in Palanpur Over Five Decades*, Oxford University Press: Oxford.

Mistiaen, J. and M. Ravallion (2003). 'Survey Compliance and the Distribution of Income', *World Bank Policy Research Working Papers* 2956, Development Research Group, World Bank: Washington DC.

——, B. Özler, T. Razafimanantena, and J. Razafindravonona (2001). 'Putting Welfare on the Map in Madagascar', *Africa Region Working Paper Series* No. 34, World Bank: Washington DC.

Ravallion, M. (1999). 'Is More Targeting Consistent with Less Spending?', *International Tax and Public Finance*, 6: 411–19.

—— (2000). 'Monitoring Targeting Performance when Decentralized Allocations to the Poor are Unobserved', *World Bank Economic Review*, 14(2): 331–45.

Sen, A. and J. Foster (1997). 'Technical Appendix', in A. Sen (ed.) *On Economic Inequality*, Clarendon Press: Oxford.

Shorrocks, A. (1980). 'The Class of Additively Decomposable Inequality Measures', *Econometrica*, 48: 613–25.

Simler, K. and V. Nhate (2002). 'Poverty, Inequality and Geographic Targeting: Evidence from Small-Area Estimates in Mozambique' (mimeo), International Food Policy Research Institute: Washington DC.

Tendler, J. (1997). *Good Government in the Tropics*. The Johns Hopkins University Press: Baltimore, MD.

4

Opening the Convergence Black Box: Measurement Problems and Demographic Aspects

CARLOS AZZONI, NAERCIO MENEZES-FILHO,
AND TATIANE MENEZES

4.1. INTRODUCTION

The problem of comparing economic growth across regions or countries is on the forefront of economic analysis nowadays (e.g. Bils and Klenow 2000; Hanushek and Kimko 2000). However, most of the papers in the literature use real per capita GDP as the variable whose growth will be analysed. To the best of our knowledge, no study so far has addressed the issue of convergence using individual level data, that is, comparing the growth of income of individuals that live in different regions.[1] Introducing the concept of convergence with microdata means that we should now be concerned with factors that are correlated with individual income growth and vary systematically across regions. In this chapter we concentrate on the effects of demography.

The use of microdata to test economic models has been applied in other fields of economics, especially in consumption and labour supply (e.g. Browning et al. 1985; Attanasio and Browning 1995). According to Attanasio and Browning (1995: 1,119) life cycle models are rejected, under the assumption of a representative consumer, on aggregate time series because of 'aggregation bias and insufficient allowance for the dependence of consumption on demographics'. It is our belief that the conclusions reached by several empirical studies of convergence among countries, like those of Mankiw et al. (1992), Barro and Sala-i-Martin (1995), and Islam (1995), to cite only a few, are also dependent on the demographic structures of the countries under study, and that introducing demography may provoke substantial changes in the results obtained so far.

The authors would like to thank the Inter-American Development Bank, FIPE (Fundação Instituto de Pesquisas Econômicas), and Finep-Pronex, for different forms of support for this research.

[1] The study that uses a methodology closest to ours is Jalan and Ravallion (2002) that discusses the effect of geographic variables on household consumption growth in China.

The relationship between demography and income has a long tradition in economic literature, starting with the works of Freeman (1979) and Welch (1979), investigating the effect of the baby boom cohort on inequality in the United States. This literature has been recently extended by Higgins and Williamson (1997: 37) who look at cross-country evidence to find that 'large mature working age cohorts are associated with lower aggregate inequality and large young adult cohorts are associated with higher aggregate inequality'. In this chapter we intend to further extend the analysis to look at the effect of demography on income dynamics, that is, we use microdata to examine whether the age structure and returns to experience of different regions has any impact on the convergence of their income.

To investigate these factors we use repeated cross-sections of a Brazilian household survey and compare income patterns of individuals living in different states. The use of microdata raises several interesting questions regarding the comparison between individual and aggregate income. First of all, it seems important to compare state GDP with individual income aggregated up to state level, to check how much of what is produced is returned to individuals and is declared in the household surveys. Moreover, it is important to check whether using the arithmetic or the geometric means make a difference when comparing the levels and the growth of income across states— this we do in Section 4.2. In Section 4.3 we compare the results of the traditional cross-regions Barro regressions with the results using microdata. Section 4.4 confirms that income convergence varies across birth cohorts and explains that this is due to differences in returns to experience across states. The final section concludes and proposes future extensions of this research.

4.2. COMPARING GDP WITH INCOME

Brazil is well known for its high levels of regional inequality. Being a country with a large territory, that should not be surprising. The northeast region of Brazil was home to 28 per cent of Brazilian population in the year 2000 and produced only 13 per cent of Brazilian GDP in the year 1998; the rich southeast region presented 43 per cent of population and produced 58 per cent of GDP. Per capita income in the northeast was 54 per cent below the national average, while in the southeast it was 36 per cent above that level. The poorest state, Piauí, in the northeast region, had a per capita income level 5.6 times lower than the richest state, São Paulo, in the southeast region.[2] The above relative figures are not too different from the situation half a century ago, for in 1947 the per capita income relation between Piauí and São Paulo states was five to one. Regional income convergence in Brazil using macrodata has been the object of study by some authors, such as Ferreira and Diniz (1995), Schwartsman (1996), Zini (1998), Ferreira (2000), and Azzoni (2001). Microdata were only used in Azzoni et al. (2000) and Azzoni and Servo (2002), with different interests to the ones in this chapter.

---

[2] See www.ibge.gov.br/ibge/estatistica/economia/contasregionais, for information on regional income for Brazil, and www.ibge.gov.br/ibge/estatistica/populacao/censo2000 for information on population.

We now compare the official state GDP figures provided by the Brazilian Census Bureau (macrodata) with the income data available in the household surveys conducted by the same Bureau (microdata), using sampling weights to aggregate individual income to state level. Since the first dataset is comparable to data used in convergence studies everywhere, we want to check whether or not our aggregated microdata provides the same results as the standard macrodata for Brazilian states.

We deal with nineteen of the twenty-five Brazilian states, since survey data is not available for the unpopulated states of the Amazon Region; Brasília (the Federal District) was also dropped, since the economic dynamics in that area is strongly determined by the federal government salary policy, and thus is not driven by economic factors such as in other areas. In total, only 9 per cent of the Brazilian population of 170 million in 2000 is not included in the study. Table 4.1 presents a summary of the available data: column (1) shows the traditional GDP macrodata, as provided by Instituto Brasileiro de Geografia e Estatistica (IBGE); column (2) presents income obtained from the

Table 4.1. *Comparing GDP with microdata aggregate income (Brazilian R$ million)*

States	GDP macrodata	Rank	Income aggregated microdata	Rank	Ratio (2)/(1)
	(1)		(2)		
São Paulo	306,569	1	143.000	1	0.47
Rio de Janeiro	96,947	2	50.000	2	0.52
Minas Gerais	86,527	3	42.000	3	0.49
Rio Grande do Sul	68,689	4	31.000	4	0.45
Paraná	52,438	5	26.000	5	0.50
Bahia	36,735	6	18.900	6	0.51
Santa Catarina	31,633	7	15.800	7	0.50
Pernambuco	23,261	8	11.500	8	0.49
Ceará	17,453	9	9.900	10	0.57
Espirito Santo	16,087	10	6.940	11	0.43
Goiás	15,906	11	10.900	9	0.69
Mato Grosso do Sul	9,219	12	5.020	15	0.54
Mato Grosso	9,086	13	6.400	12	0.70
Maranhão	7,353	14	5.510	14	0.75
Paraíba	6,936	15	5.530	13	0.80
Rio Grande do Norte	6,617	16	4.330	16	0.65
Alagoas	5,711	17	4.300	17	0.75
Sergipe	4,805	18	2.600	19	0.54
Piauí	4,192	19	3.050	18	0.73
Global	806,163		400.680		0.50

Source: See text.

Table 4.2. *Per capita GDP and income, 1997 (Brazilian R$/year)*

States	Macrodata log of GDP per capita	Rank	Microdata log of per capita income	Rank	Average of the log of microdata per capita income	Rank
	(1)		(2)		(3)	
São Paulo	8,940	1	9.150	1	8.624	1
Rio de Janeiro	8,730	2	8.890	7	8.131	8
Rio Grande do Sul	8,713	3	8.773	2	8.395	3
Santa Catarina	8,615	4	8.889	6	8.280	4
Paraná	8,509	5	8.814	4	8.219	6
Espírito Santo	8,491	6	8.651	3	8.424	2
Minas Gerais	8,395	7	8.588	5	8.240	5
Mato Grosso do Sul	8,311	8	8.677	10	8.063	9
Mato Grosso	8,140	9	8.868	9	8.059	10
Pernambuco	7,898	10	8.291	8	8.149	7
Goiás	7,888	11	8.557	12	7.766	14
Sergipe	7,834	12	8.342	16	7.702	15
Bahia	7,823	13	8.265	15	7.787	13
Rio Grande do Norte	7,704	14	8.277	11	7.814	11
Ceará	7,688	15	8.184	13	7.791	12
Alagoas	7,524	16	8.419	17	7.591	17
Paraíba	7,492	17	8.254	14	7.666	16
Piauí	7,214	18	7.891	19	7.308	19
Maranhão	7,090	19	7.926	18	7.426	18

Source: See text.

aggregation of microdata. In general, the aggregate income numbers correspond to about 50 per cent of GDP, though for the poorer states (Alagoas, Paraíba, Piauí, and Maranhão) it can get close to 80 per cent. A possible reason for this discrepancy is the under-reporting of income, especially from other sources than labour. For the eight states with the highest GDP, the ranking is the same in both columns; the four lower GDP numbers belong to the same states; some minor modifications in ranking are present for the other middle-size states.

Income and GDP per capita are displayed in Table 4.2. Again, column (1) presents GDP per capita figures (macrodata) and column (2) displays per capita income figures based on the aggregation of individual data. Here we introduce an important modification in the way we calculate income, for we exclude all zero-income cases, and work only with people with positive income. This was necessary because we intend to run all regressions below using a logarithmic specification. As can be seen in Table 4.2, income values are larger than GDP values, although the numbers are not too far away from each other. That is expected, since our income data includes only households with non-zero-income and GDP per capita includes all households.

It is interesting to notice that the ten richest states are the same in both columns, although some modifications in rank are present, the largest being for Rio de Janeiro, with a jump of five positions. However, in percentage terms, the change in Rio de Janeiro was the second smallest. As a whole, poorer states present a higher percentual difference between the two figures, indicating that zero-income cases are more important for those cases than for richer states. Column (3) shows the average of the logarithms of microdata per capita income. These values will be used ahead in the chapter to state the importance of the right measurement of per capita values for convergence studies. As numbers show, the figures are always lower (between 2 and 10 per cent) than those in column (2).

In Table 4.3 the rates of growth over the period 1981–97 of the different measured state incomes are presented. Again, column (1) refers to macrodata GDP per capita, and columns (2) and (3) are our microdata per capita income. Differences in rankings

Table 4.3. *Rates of growth in GDP and income per capita, 1981–97*

State	Macrodata		Microdata			
	Growth in the log of GDP per capita	Rank	Growth in the log of per capita income	Rank	Growth in the average of the log of per capita income	Rank
	(1)		(2)		(3)	
Alagoas	0.0240	19	0.5169	1	0.4770	2
Paraíba	0.2567	10	0.5140	2	0.3583	5
Maranhão	0.1778	17	0.5057	3	0.5407	1
Ceará	0.4848	1	0.5044	4	0.3646	4
Goiás	0.3201	8	0.4774	5	0.3087	8
Rio Grande do Norte	0.2754	9	0.4428	6	0.2534	13
Paraná	0.4422	2	0.4399	7	0.1662	18
Minas Gerais	0.4388	3	0.4311	8	0.3531	6
São Paulo	0.2167	12	0.4114	9	0.3915	3
Mato Grosso	0.1918	15	0.4038	10	0.2995	11
Rio de Janeiro	0.2099	13	0.3829	11	0.1954	16
Piauí	0.3959	6	0.3746	12	0.2751	12
Espírito Santo	0.4206	4	0.3705	13	0.3061	9
Mato Grosso do Sul	0.2519	11	0.3437	14	0.3008	10
Santa Catarina	0.3884	7	0.3218	15	0.3421	7
Pernambuco	0.0641	18	0.2584	16	0.2015	15
Rio Grande do Sul	0.4012	5	0.2502	17	0.2351	14
Bahia	0.1791	16	0.2417	18	0.1954	17
Sergipe	0.1992	14	0.1449	19	0.0538	19

Source: See text.

based on growth rates are more pronounced than rankings based on total and per capita income values.[3] In general, the above tables indicate that our set of income and per capita income figures reproduce reasonably well the official GDP per capita figures. Although some differences are present, the numbers as a whole are sufficiently good to be used in the following calculations of regional income convergence in Brazil.

4.3. MACRODATA TRADITIONAL CONVERGENCE REGRESSIONS

In this section we use the macrodata for GDP and the income aggregated up to state level presented in the previous section, to estimate the traditional Barro–type convergence regressions, in which income growth over a period of time is regressed against the initial level of income. The objective here is to verify if the two sets of macrodata will lead to similar results. We will also verify if using the average of the logarithms will lead to similar results as for the logarithms of the average. Based on the Barro and Sala-i-Martin (1995) approach, we estimate the equation:

$$(\ln y_T - \ln y_0) = \alpha + \lambda \ln y_0, \tag{4.1}$$

in which y_0 is income in the beginning of the period, and $\lambda = (1 - e^{-\beta T})$. The time necessary to reduce inequality by half is given by $e^{-\beta t} = \frac{1}{2}$.

Regression results are presented in Table 4.4. In column (1), traditional GDP (macrodata) is used; column (2) presents results obtained with microdata per capita income. In both regressions absolute convergence is present, and at similar speeds: the calculated speed of convergence is only 13 per cent higher with microdata, with seventy-one years to half convergence, while eighty-one years would be needed with traditional GDP data. A better fit, as shown by the R^2, is obtained with microdata. Thus, this first set of results indicates that the microdata we use, when transformed into macrodata, lead to quite similar convergence results as the traditional macrodata, GDP, dataset. This is an important point to stress, for we will argue further in the chapter that macrodata type results might be misleading. And we will do that by exploring the richness of information present in the microdata available. Thus, it is important to show that the available microdata is equivalent to the available macrodata, so that the observed differences in results will be due to factors to be stressed in the appropriate sections of the chapter, and not to differences in the datasets.

We now move to the last point to make in this section, which is the form of calculation of average income. When one thinks in terms of using household-level income aggregated over cohorts to try and replicate the usual cross-country GDP per capita regressions, one has to address the issue of how to construct cohort income averages. As Attanasio and Weber (1993) point out, while national accounts data are only available

---

[3] This may happen because of changes over time in the proportion of young non-working people (excluded from the microsample) across states, because of changes in the misreporting of income in our surveys, or because of specific factors that affected GDP but not income for some states in 1981.

Table 4.4. *Traditional macrodata convergence regressions*

	Macrodata	Microdata	
	Log of per capita GDP (1)	Log of per capita income (2)	Average of the logs of per capita income (3)
Constant	1.269 (0.3614)	1.556 (0.406)	1.271 (0.537)
λ	−0.127* (0.048)	−0.144* (0.050)	−0.127** (0.070)
β	0.00854	0.0097	0.0085
Years to half convergence	81	71	81
R^2	0.15	0.23	0.19
Sample size	19	19	19

Note: *significant at 5%; **significant at 10%.

Source: See text.

as the arithmetic mean, we can aggregate the household income data in different ways. For example, we can use the logarithm of the arithmetic mean and the mean of the logarithm (i.e. the logarithm of the geometric mean). The difference between the two is Theil's entropy measure. If this measure differs across states and over time, the results of the usual cross-country regressions will depend on the way cohort income is generated. As column (3) indicates, results differ slightly, for the significance of the estimated coefficient for the initial income level is only marginally significant, suggesting that this is an immaterial practical point. The coefficient of the initial income in this case is almost the same as the one in the first column. In the remainder of this chapter, the properly calculated average of the logarithms will be used.[4]

4.4. EXPLORING THE RICHNESS OF MICRODATA USING BIRTH COHORTS

4.4.1. *Constructing Birth Cohorts*

Microdata have not been used so far in the literature to examine issues of convergence. It is well known in the consumption and labour supply literature that with repeated cross sections it is possible to construct demographic cohorts based on date of birth, and calculate cohort-year means for all variables of interest, including income, education, labour force participation, and living conditions; see Browning, Deaton, and Irish (1985) and Attanasio and Browning (1995). We propose to extend this methodology

---

[4] That is another important reason for not using zero-income cases in our study.

to include the state of residence as another grouping variable and derive state–cohort-year means for the variables of interest. For example, income for a cohort c in state s in year t is

$$\bar{y}_{cst} = \frac{\sum_{i}^{n_{cst}} \ln y_i}{n_{cst}}, \tag{4.2}$$

where n_{cst} is the number of household heads born in an interval of determined years (e.g. 1940–5), living in state s in period t. Ten cohorts were constructed for each state in each year. The same procedure was applied to all variables included in the analysis, so that we have, for example, the average number of years of education for the household heads included in each cohort. The same holds for all other variables.

The microdata we use come from the rich yearly household survey PNAD (Pesquisa Nacional por Amostra de Domicílios, carried out by the Brazilian Census Bureau, IBGE). This data can be used as a pseudopanel, by constructing a model that looks like an individual-level model but is for cohorts (see Ravallion 1998). For each state, in each year, we have a sample of households based on the head's year of birth. The youngest cohort is the one with the household heads born in the five-year period centred in 1972, while the oldest is formed by the household whose heads were born around the year 1922. For each cohort we calculated average levels of income, age, education, public infrastructure, etc. We can then follow these cohorts over time (as they grow older) and analyse the influence of household variables on income growth. Although these are in fact different households, they can be considered as a good representation of their cohort, provided the samples are big enough.

The average number of households per cohort is 269. Due to the small number of observations in some cohorts, only 2,470 of them were considered in the analysis, instead of the 3,040 possible cases (10 cohorts × 19 states × 16 years). Only cohorts with at least twenty-six households were included in the sample. The small cohorts were located among the youngest in the first years of the period and among the oldest in the more recent years. This means that we are dealing in fact with an unbalanced panel. The total number of households considered in different years ranged from 49,514 to 90,776, with an average of 58,328. Table 4.5 provides descriptive information about the cohorts.

The advantages of using cohort level data are manifold. First and most importantly, the use of microdata allows us to control for changes in the composition of population in each state, something that cannot be done with aggregate data. Second, we can control for life cycle and generation effects, which means that we are really analysing income growth within generations, or for a population with the same age. Third, it is possible to identify state-fixed effects without having to rely only on the time component of the series, since we have various observations for a given state in a given year (ten in our case). Finally, one can rely on the differences across generations within a state–year group to identify the effects of human capital on growth, for example, which are not readily identified using aggregate data.

Table 4.5. *Cohort description*

Cohort	Date of birth	Average age		Number of households per cohort	
		1981	1996	Minimum	Maximum
1	1922	59	75	26	1,715
2	1927	54	70	70	2,298
3	1932	49	65	80	2,646
4	1937	44	60	99	3,171
5	1942	39	55	132	3,569
6	1947	34	50	144	4,409
7	1952	29	45	182	5,439
8	1957	24	40	237	6,317
9	1962	19	35	293	6,681
10	1967	14	30	317	7,126

Source: See text.

The main disadvantage of using cohort level data is that if there are measurement errors at the household level they are likely to be carried out to the cohort means, unless the cell sizes are big. Another possible problem with this methodology is related to migration across states, for it may cause the composition of the cohorts to change over time. If this change is driven by observed variables (e.g. education), then by including these variables in the convergence equation we avoid the problem. If it is driven by unobserved components, however, it may mean that we are not in effect controlling for household fixed effect. It should be said, however, that during the period analysed migration flows were not strong in Brazil. The period involves the so-called 'lost decade', for the very bad macroeconomic performance of the country's economy, when unemployment rates rose in the country as a whole but especially in the rich areas, providing very few incentives to potential migrants.[5] Macroeconomic stabilization came in 1994 but even this could not provide enough incentives to migration for, at first, recovery was spread across the country as a whole, and second, recovery was not stable over time, with important oscillations in GDP growth and unemployment rates. Finally, the period under stabilization is short (late 1994 7) compared to the years of almost stagnation that preceded it.

4.5. REGRESSION RESULTS

Using the cohort data described above, we ran cross-section and panel convergence regressions, with results presented in Table 4.6. Column (1) repeats column (3) from Table 4.4, for easy of comparison. Column (2) presents the results for a regression relating per capita income growth in a cohort/state against the initial level of

---

[5] See Baer (2002) for more details on the Brazilian economy during the period considered in this study.

Table 4.6. *Microdata convergence regressions*

	Macrodata	Complete period (1981–97)		Thirteen four-year rolling periods			
	(1)	(2)	(3)	(4)	(5)	(6)	(7)
Constant	1.271	5.511	2.534	2.454	1.656	3,208	5,494
	(0.537)	(0.347)	(0.317)	(0.099)	(0.067)	(0.096)	(0.127)
λ	−0.127	−0.684	−0.306	−0.291	−0.170	−0.443	−0.737
	(0.070)	(0.044)	(0.039)	(0.014)	(0.009)	(0.013)	(0.017)
β	0.0085	0.0720	0.0228	0.0215	0.0116	0.0366	0.0835
Years to half convergence	81	10	30	32	60	19	8
Education						0.134	0.173
	—	—	—	—	—	(0.004)	(0.008)
Cohort dummy	No	No	Yes	Yes	Yes	Yes	Yes
State dummy	No	No	No	No	No	No	Yes
Time dummy	No	No	No	No	Yes	Yes	Yes
R^2	0.197	0.60	0.88	0.27	0.72	0.80	0.85
Sample size	19	190	190	2,470	2,470	2,470	2,470

Source: See text.

income in that cohort/state, with a total number of 190 observations (cohort/states). As compared to the result presented in column (1), the speed of convergence increases by 747 per cent, leading to a half convergence period of only 10 years.

This change in speed is important enough to show what sort of difference in results could be obtained in using more appropriate microdata to study convergence. However, having cohort data allows us to control for other aspects involved in the convergence process. One important aspect to control for is the life cycle effect, for aggregate data deal equally with young and old people. Young people are in the uprising part of their income life cycle and old people are already in the declining part of it; over time, it is expected that young cohorts get richer and old cohorts get poorer, regardless of region or income level. Thus, the study of the evolution of income over a time period should control for that, and we do that by including cohort dummies into the regressions. Results are shown in column (3). Comparing to column (2), we observe that convergence occurs at a speed 68 per cent lower, although still higher (168 per cent) than in the case of macrodata in column (1). Thus, the control for life cycle effects is important and changes significantly the calculated speed of convergence. When considering convergence within the same age range, what is in fact done in column (3), absolute convergence is still present, but at a much lower speed, around one-third of the previous calculated speed.

In columns (4)–(7) we present results of panel regressions, with four-year rolling periods (e.g. 1981–4), leading to 2,470 observations. Column (4) is similar to column (3) and the results are quite similar, with a small decrease (5.7 per cent) in the speed of

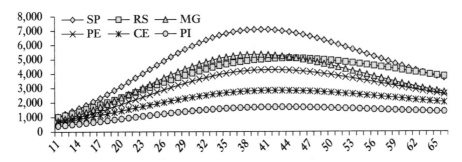

Figure 4.1. *Returns to experience, 1997*

convergence. In column (5) we include time dummies to the previous regression, to control for shocks occurring in different years. The estimated speed of convergence decreases by 46 per cent in relation to column (4), indicating that controlling for time-related shocks is also important for convergence results.[6]

In the last two columns we move into conditional convergence, introducing education as another explanatory variable in the regressions. Thus, we are not any more considering that states are converging to a common steady-state level of per capita income but, instead, that each state is converging to its own steady-state level. In column (6) we control for cohort and time dummies, as in column (5), and observe, as expected, a much higher speed of convergence (215 per cent). Education appears as positive and significant, as expected. Finally, in column (7) we introduce state dummies, to control for their specific characteristics, obtaining an additional 128 per cent increase in the speed of convergence.

4.6. INTERPRETATION OF THE RESULTS

Why do the results look so different when we use micro instead of aggregate data? One possible explanation is that the aggregated results are affected by a compositional bias. It is well known from the labour literature that earnings tend to rise over the life cycle, at a decreasing rate. Figure 4.1 shows that this is also the case in Brazil, but that the earnings profile differs markedly across states. Returns to experience are more pronounced in São Paulo than in Rio Grande do Sul, Minas Gerais, and Pernambuco, and much higher than in Ceará, for example. This means that those living in São Paulo throughout their life will experience a rise in relative earnings in the early phases of their life cycle (as compared to those living in Ceará, for example), followed by a drop in relative earnings later on.

The results of Fig. 4.1 imply that if we follow a generation over time (and therefore over its life cycle) and compare mean earnings of those living in states with high returns to experience to those living in states with flat age–earnings profiles, we will

---

[6] This point was made by Temple (1999) in his thorough review of convergence studies.

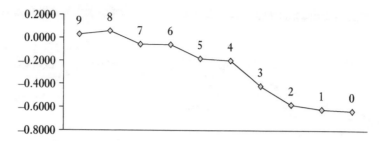

Figure 4.2. *Convergence across cohorts*

first observe a divergence in their mean earnings, until both reach the peak of their earnings profile, and then a convergence process. Therefore, whether we will observe income convergence or divergence among cohorts living in different states will depend on the stage of their life cycle.

To confirm that this is indeed the case, Fig. 4.2 presents the results of traditional convergence regressions, run separately for each cohort. The results are quite striking. One can note that for the youngest cohorts (9 and 8) we observe divergence in income, whereas for the older cohorts the opposite occurs. Moreover, the speed of convergence rises continuously across generations. As the various generations live together at any moment in time, whether we will observe convergence or not in the aggregate will depend on the relative size of each cohort in each state. For example, as the population in both São Paulo and in Ceará are predominantly young, the demographic effect will act as a force conducting to divergence of their average incomes over time, as the population grow older. This process may even out-weigh any economic tendencies leading to income convergence. Once the majority of the population reaches their forties, the reverse will occur. We expect that this effect will be even stronger when different countries are compared, for then the differences in the demographic composition will be higher, which will make the final convergence result even more dependent on the age structure and on the returns to experience prevailing in each of the countries involved in the study.

Figure 4.2 and the discussion above implies that the estimated convergence coefficients presented in Table 4.5 are in fact weighted averages of the population coefficient for each cohort, with weights given by the conditional variance of initial income at each cohort (see Angrist and Krueger 1999 for a similar discussion in the context of returns to schooling).

4.7. CONCLUSIONS AND FUTURE RESEARCH

In this chapter, we emphasized the demographic effects involved in the traditional convergence literature. We used microdata, averaged up to cohort level, to investigate the impact of returns to experience and of the age structure of the population on the estimated convergence result. We started by showing that our household-level data is compatible with the national accounts data, traditionally used in the literature, accounting for between 50 and 80 per cent of GDP per capita, depending on the state. We also showed that the cross-sectional convergence results using aggregated microdata yield similar results to using national accounts data, under different methods of aggregation.

The main results of the chapter showed that the use of microdata provokes an increase in the speed of convergence, mainly because it incorporates convergence of income across different generations within the same state. Once we controlled for cohort effects, the results approached the aggregated ones. The use of panel data did not qualitatively alter the main results, despite the rise in the speed of convergence that occurred when the more frequent data were used. Moreover, the introduction of time and state dummies raised the speed of convergence considerably, as expected.

In explaining the differences in the results using micro as compared to more aggregate data, we emphasized the fact that the speed of convergence varies considerably across cohorts, so that the aggregate results depend a great deal on the composition of the population and on the returns to experience, that differ a lot across the states of Brazil. We speculated that this dependency will be even higher when comparing income growth across countries, with very different demographic characteristics.[7]

It is our hope that this chapter will establish a new line of research in the convergence literature, and therefore there are several things we intend to do in the next steps of this research. First, we intend to simulate what would happen with the aggregate convergence results once we give different weights to each cohort within each state, to compute aggregate income, perhaps using the projections of the state population provided by the Brazilian Census Bureau. These weights can also be used directly in the microregressions. We will also try and isolate the effects of returns to experience from the overall process of economic convergence, by aggregating the residuals of state-specific regressions of earnings on age, instead of using earnings directly to compute average income at cohort and state level. We also intend to treat the returns to experience themselves as endogenous, by making them depend on the relative cohort sizes, as in Higgins and Williamson (1999) and instrument initial income. In order to do that, we will have to establish a framework to deal with migration, since it is clear that people move across states over their life cycle in a non-random way, and this affects the behaviour of the returns to experience.

REFERENCES

Angrist, J. D. and A. B. Krueger (1999). 'Empirical Strategies in Labour Economics', in O. Ashenfelter and D. Cards (eds) *Handbook of Labour Economics*, North Holland: Amsterdam.

---

[7] Although it is important to note that the key variables under study may not be compatible internationally, and that it may be difficult to control for differences in institutions and culture, that may be related to the income or growth.

Attanasio, O. and M. Browning (1995). 'Consumption over the Life Cycle and the Business Cycle', *American Economic Review*, 85: 1,118–36.

—— and G. Weber (1993). 'Consumption Growth, the Interest Rate and Aggregation', *Review of Economic Studies*, 60: 631–49.

Azzoni, C. (2001). 'Economic Growth and Regional Income Inequalities in Brazil', *Annals of Regional Science*, 35(1): 133–52.

—— and L. M. Servo (2002). 'Education, Cost of Living and Regional Labour Income Inequality in Brazil', *Papers in Regional Science*, 81(2): 57–75.

——, N. Menezes-Filho, T. Menezes, and R. Silveira-Neto (2000). 'Geography and Regional Income Inequality in Brazil', *Research Network Working Paper* R-395, Research Department, Inter-American Development Bank.

Baer, W. (2002). *The Brazilian Economy*, Praeger: Westport, CT.

Barro, R. and X. Sala-i-Martin (1995). *Economic Growth*, McGraw-Hill: New York.

Bils, M. and P. J. Klenow (2000). 'Does Schooling Cause Growth?', *American Economic Review*, 905: 1,160–83.

Browning, M., A. Deaton, and M. Irish (1985). 'A Profitable Approach to Labour Supply and Commodity Demands Over the Life Cycle', *Econometrica*, 53(3): 503–44.

Ferreira, A. (2000). 'Convergence in Brazil: Recent Trends and Long-Run Prospects', *Journal of Applied Economics*, 3(4): 479–89.

—— and C. C. Diniz (1995). 'Convergencia entre las rentas per capita estaduales en Brasil', *EURE-Revista Latioamericana de Estudios Urbano Regionales*, 21(62).

Freeman, R. (1979). 'The Effects of Demographic Factors on Age-Earnings Profiles', *Journal of Human Resources*, 14: 289–318.

Hanushek, E. A. and D. D. Kimko (2000). 'Schooling, Labour-Force Quality and the Growth of Nations', *American Economic Review*, 90(5): 1,184–208.

Higgins, M. and J. G. Williamson (1997). 'Age Structure Dynamics in Asia and Dependence on Foreign Capital', *Population Development Review*, 23(2): 261–93.

—— and —— (1999). 'Explaining Inequality the World Round: Cohort Size, Kuznetz Curves, and Openness', *NBER Working Papers* 7,224, July, National Bureau of Economic Research: Cambridge, MA.

Islam, N. (1995). 'Growth Empirics: A Panel Data Approach', *Quarterly Journal of Economics*, 110(4): 1,127–70.

Jalan, J. and M. Ravallion (2002). 'Geographic Poverty Traps? A Micro Model of Consumption Growth in Rural China', *Journal of Applied Econometrics*, 17(4): 329–46.

Mankiw, G. N., D. Romer, and D. N. Weil (1992). 'A Contribution to the Empirics of Economic Growth', *Quarterly Journal of Economics*, 107(2): 407–37.

Ravallion, M. (1998). 'Poor Areas', in A. Ullah and D. Giles (eds) *Handbook of Applied Economic Statistics*, Marcel Dekker: New York.

Schwartsman, A. (1996). 'Convergence Across Brazilian States', *IPE Discussion Papers* 02/96, IPE-Universidade de São Paulo: São Paulo.

Temple, J. (1999). 'The New Growth Evidence', *Journal of Economic Literature*, 37: 112–56.

Welch, F. (1979). 'Effects of Cohort Size on Earnings: the Baby Boom Babies Financial Boost', *Journal of Political Economy*, 87: 65–97.

Zini, A. A. (1998). 'Regional Income Convergence in Brazil and Its Socioeconomic Determinants', *Economia Aplicada*, 2(2): 383–411.

PART III

LOCATION, EXTERNALITIES, AND UNEQUAL DEVELOPMENT

5

Adverse Geography and Differences in Welfare in Peru

JAVIER ESCOBAL AND MÁXIMO TORERO

5.1. INTRODUCTION

In *The Wealth and Poverty of Nations*, David S. Landes argues that Europe's temperate climate encouraged hard work and capitalist development, while the heat of the tropics brought reliance on slaves (Eichengreen 1998). Engerman and Sokoloff (1997), trying to explain why the United States and Canada have been so much more successful over time than other New World economies suggest that the roots of these disparities lay in differences in the initial factor endowments of the respective colonies. Why do we see areas with persistently low living standards, even in growing economies? Will the legacy of these differences persist?

One view is that differences arise from persistent spatial concentrations of individuals with personal attributes inhibiting growth in their living standards. This view does not ascribe a causal role to geography per se. In other words, identical individuals will have the same growth prospects regardless of where they live. Alternatively, one might argue that geography has a causal role in determining how household welfare evolves over time, and that geographic externalities arising from natural geographic characteristics, local public assets, or local endowments of private assets, entail that living in a well endowed area means that a poor household can eventually escape poverty. Yet an otherwise identical household living in a poor area experiences stagnation or decline. If this is so, then it is important to understand which geographic factors matter for growth at the microlevel (Engerman and Sokoloff 1997; Jalan and Ravallion 1998).

Peru has an astonishing variety of ecological areas. Only a few countries offer so many climate zones and landscapes, with rainforests, mountain ranges, and deserts. Peru contains a total of 84 of the world's 104 known ecological regions and 28 different climates. This geographic diversity, its link to development, and the important

This research was supported by the IDB Research Network and the Global Development Network Award. We are greatly indebted to John Gallup, Eduardo Lora, Alejandro Gaviria, and colleagues of the 'Geography and Development' project for numerous helpful comments to the different drafts of this work. Their comments and criticism improved it substantially. We are also grateful to Jorge Aguero for excellent research assistance in this project. All errors remaining are ours.

Table 5.1. *Regional income per capita dispersion in Latin American countries (selected years)*

Country	Year	Dispersion
Colombia	1989	0.358
Brazil	1994	0.424
Chile	1994	0.470
Mexico	1993	0.502
Peru	1997	0.561
Argentina	1995	0.736

Note: Unweighted coefficient of variation.

Source: World Bank (1999) and LSMS (1997).

differences in the welfare of the different regions makes Peru a good case study in attempting to ascertain what role geographic variables—both natural and man-made—play in explaining per capita expenditure differentials across regions within Peru. As shown in Table 5.1, when comparing the income per capita and consumption per capita differences between the diverse regions of the country, it is clear that Peru has one of the highest degrees of inequality between regions in Latin America. According to the World Bank (1999) and our own estimates based on the Peruvian Living Standards Measurement Study (LSMS) of 1997, Peru has a larger dispersion of per capita income by region than Colombia, Brazil, Chile, or Mexico. Only Argentina is reported as having larger regional income disparities. Furthermore, this dispersion is also very large within the different geographical regions of Peru.

This chapter attempts to understand whether geographic externalities arising from natural geographic characteristics have a causal role in determining how household welfare evolves. The chapter is divided into six sections. Section 5.2 gives a detailed description of Peru's geography and specifically the main areas in which geography might play a fundamental role in economic development. It also makes a first attempt to analyse whether there is a correlation between geographic variables and earning levels. Additionally, it analyses whether the differences observed across the different regions in Peru are also correlated to the changes in geography and therefore to geographic externalities.

In Section 5.3 we try to formally answer whether geography is a determinant of the evolution of welfare across households over time. We developed a model of consumption growth at the province level. This model not only takes in the local effect of geographic variables but also includes spatial econometric techniques to ascertain the presence of persistent spatial concentrations forced by geography. In addition, we also analyse whether the presence of positive geographic externalities arising from local public assets, or local endowments of private assets, implies that the effect of natural geographic characteristics can be overcome and a poor household could eventually escape poverty. To be able to analyse the partial effects of each of these types of assets (geographic, private, and public assets) we also develop a methodology to break down the partial effects of each of these variables.

Section 5.4 details the main databases constructed for this chapter and the methodological issues regarding the databases. We use the National Population Census for 1972, 1981, and 1993; the LSMS surveys for 1991, 1994, 1996, and 1997; information from the district infrastructure census; geographical datasets; and information from the III National Agrarian Census of 1994. In Section 5.5, the results are presented and we detail the major conclusions of the study.

5.2. BASIC CHARACTERISTICS OF THE PERUVIAN GEOGRAPHY

Leading historians and economists have long recognized geography as having a crucial role in economic development, even though geography has been neglected in most recent empirical studies of comparative growth across countries and of comparative growth within the same country.[1] Specifically, in the case of Peru the enormous diversity of its geography makes it an extremely interesting case study to analyse the importance of these variables to economic growth within the country.[2] Peru is located in a tropical part of the globe, but because of variations in relief (particularly elevation as shown in Map 5.1) and such factors as rain shadows, bodies of water (i.e. marine currents such as El Niño and Humboldt), and wind patterns, it comprises a multitude of microclimates. Although many geographic factors interact, it can be said that throughout most of Peru the orography and the morphologic structure of the Andes have conditioned the local climate, the type and use of the land, and the agricultural activities of the country. Peru is well known for its mineral reserves. It has the world's second largest silver reserves, third largest of tin, fourth largest of lead, seventh largest of copper, and eighth largest of gold. As can be seen in Map 5.2, a large proportion of Peru's mineral surface composition is sedimentary rock where petroleum deposits are usually found. Gold, silver, and copper deposits are to be found in igneous and metamorphic rock.

The entire coastal area of Peru (around 11 per cent of its territory with 49 per cent of the total population)[3] is one of the world's driest regions. Cold waters off the coast and the proximity of the Andes, as well as high-pressure wind patterns, contribute to the virtual lack of rainfall in this region (see Map 5.3). However, this cold humid desert results in pleasant living conditions for those acclimatized to the local environment. Many separate ranges, surrounding several areas of high plateau, make up the Andes which account for 31 per cent of Peruvian territory. Passes through these mountains are usually high and difficult, especially the southern Andes, which can be considered

[1] There are few studies estimating the economic importance of geography within a region or a country, for example, Bloom and Sachs (1998) make a great contribution for the case of Africa, and Engerman and Sokoloff (1997) for Canada and the United States.

[2] There are several papers—for example, Hall and Jones (1997, 1998); Gallup *et al.* (1998); Moreno and Trehan (1997); Davies and Weinstein (1996)—that have tried to answer the question of the importance of geography in explaining the levels of economic activity across countries.

[3] Whereas the 'selva' (mountains) represents 58% of the territory but holds only 7% of the population.

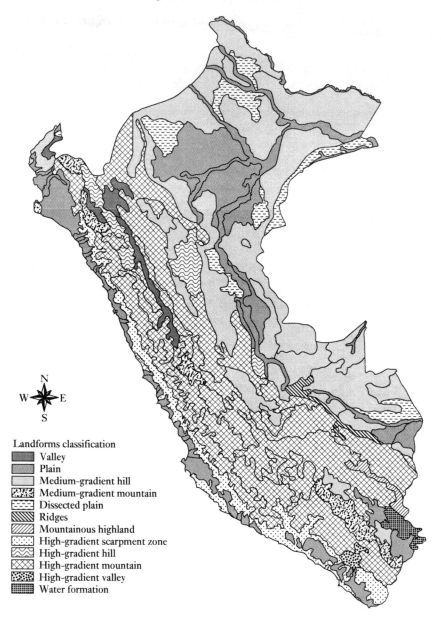

Landforms classification

- ▨ Valley
- ▧ Plain
- ☐ Medium-gradient hill
- ▨ Medium-gradient mountain
- ▨ Dissected plain
- ▨ Ridges
- ▨ Mountainous highland
- ▨ High-gradient scarpment zone
- ▨ High-gradient hill
- ▨ High-gradient mountain
- ▨ High-gradient valley
- ▨ Water formation

Map 5.1. *Major landforms in Peru*

a barrier to trade and transportation. Climatic conditions also make vast areas of the Peruvian Andes relatively inhospitable (see Maps 5.3 and 5.4).

A large part of Peruvian territory (about 58 per cent) lies in the Amazon Basin; most of this area is covered by dense forest that has slowed the development of the region.

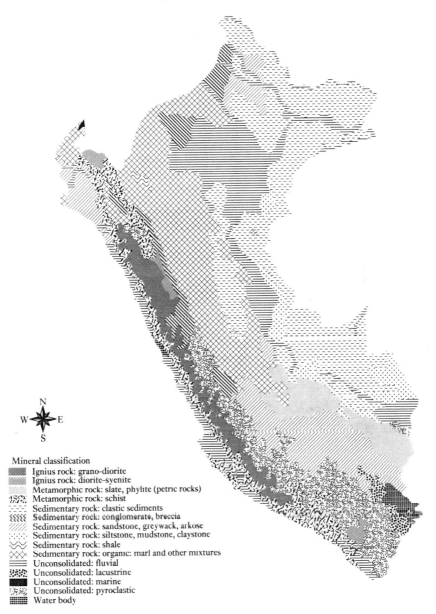

Mineral classification
- Ignius rock: grano-diorite
- Ignius rock: diorite-syenite
- Metamorphic rock: slate, phylite (petric rocks)
- Metamorphic rock: schist
- Sedimentary rock: clastic sediments
- Sedimentary rock: conglomerate, breccia
- Sedimentary rock: sandstone, greywack, arkose
- Sedimentary rock: siltstone, mudstone, claystone
- Sedimentary rock: shale
- Sedimentary rock: organic: marl and other mixtures
- Unconsolidated: fluvial
- Unconsolidated: lacustrine
- Unconsolidated: marine
- Unconsolidated: pyroclastic
- Water body

Map 5.2. *Underlying surface composition in Peru*

In some of these areas annual floods raise the water level more than 15 m (50 ft) and inundate thousands of square miles of land. These floods deposit alluvial silts that renew the soils of the flooded areas (see Map 5.3). The distribution patterns of vegetation and soils in Peru are closely related to the distribution patterns of landforms and climate.

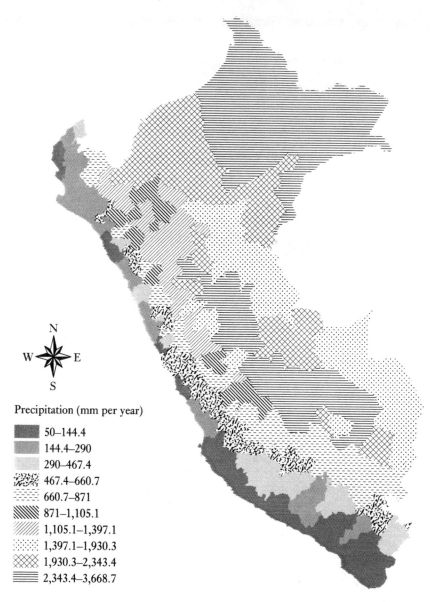

Precipitation (mm per year)

- 50–144.4
- 144.4–290
- 290–467.4
- 467.4–660.7
- 660.7–871
- 871–1,105.1
- 1,105.1–1,397.1
- 1,397.1–1,930.3
- 1,930.3–2,343.4
- 2,343.4–3,668.7

Map 5.3. *Precipitation*

Tropical forest types of vegetation and soils are found mainly in the Amazon Basin, while desert types are located mainly along the coast. Soils in most tropical forests are poorly developed and low in fertility except in areas subject to annual flooding.

Peru has a long tradition of geographic analysis and its links with development. Initially, following the Spanish tradition, the country was classified into three distinct

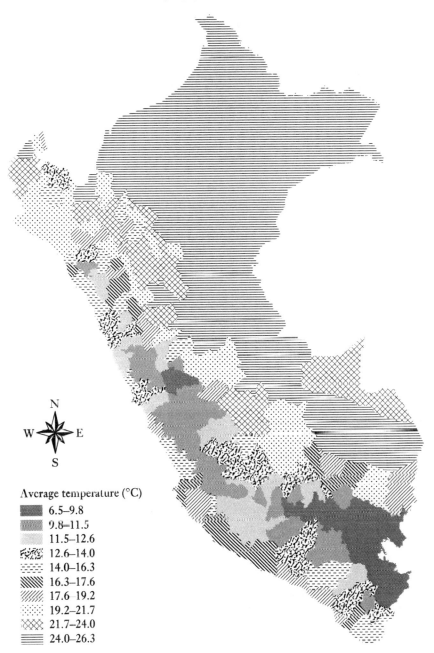

Average temperature (°C)

- 6.5–9.8
- 9.8–11.5
- 11.5–12.6
- 12.6–14.0
- 14.0–16.3
- 16.3–17.6
- 17.6–19.2
- 19.2–21.7
- 21.7–24.0
- 24.0–26.3

Map 5.4. *Temperature*

Table 5.2. *Eight natural regions of Peru*

Regions	Descriptions
Costa or Chala (coast or plain)	Territory below 500 m.a.s.l. on occidental side of Andes. Mainly desertic
Yunga (warm zone)	Both sides of Andean mountain range, located between 500 and 2,300 m.a.s.l. (occidental side) and 1,000 and 2,300 m.a.s.l. (oriental side). Typically formed by valleys
Quechua (temperate zone)	Both sides of the Andean mountain range, located between 2,300 and 3,500 m.a.s.l. Typically formed by knolls and steep hillsides
Suni or Jalca (cold lands)	Both sides of the Andean mountain range, located between 3,500 and 4,000 m.a.s.l. Typically formed by steep hills
Puna (high altitude plateau)	Both sides of the Andean mountain range, located between 4,000 and 4,800 m.a.s.l. Below snow mountains
Janca or Cordillera	At top of Andean mountain range, located between 4,800 and 6,768 m.a.s.l. Not a continuous area (only 1 district capital of 1,879 districts in Peru is located at an altitude higher than 4,800 m.a.s.l.)
Selva Alta (high altitude jungle)	On oriental side of Andean mountain range, between 400 and 1,000 m.a.s.l. Mountainous forest with valleys
Selva Baja (low altitude jungle)	On oriental side of Andes, below 400 m.a.s.l.

Note: m.a.s.l. = metres above sea level.

Source: Pulgar Vidal (1946) and Peñaherrera (1986).

zones: the costa (coast or plains), the sierra (basically the Andean mountain range), and the selva (the jungle or Amazon). However, many authors[4] have shown that this classification scheme is not sufficient to encompass Peru's geographic diversity. Peru's geographic heterogeneity is quite high and landscapes can differ widely. Based on these findings, Pulgar Vidal (1946) divided Peruvian territory into eight distinct 'natural regions' (see Table 5.2). The geographical pattern of these zones is depicted in Map 5.5.

Despite the fact that there have been many efforts to link Peruvian geographical diversity to key issues as important as settlement location or construction of administrative or political regions, very little has been done to analyse the links between this geographic diversity and development, economic growth or poverty. The only exception is the government construction of 'poverty maps' to help target social programmes. One of the most recent efforts in this regard is the construction of poverty indices at the provincial and district level by FONCODES (the public agency in charge

[4] A literature review on this topic can be found in Pulgar Vidal (1946) and in Peñaherrera (1986: 115–34).

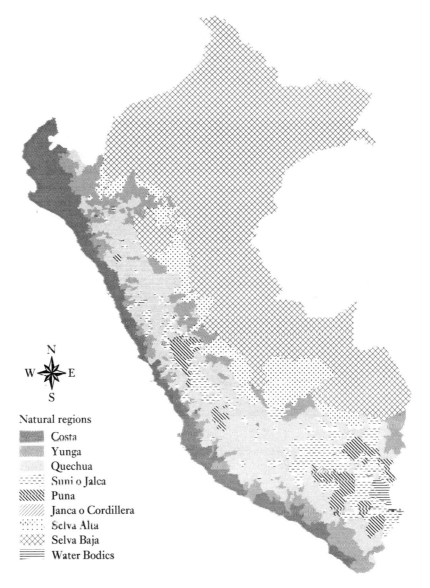

Map 5.5. *Eight natural regions of Peru*

of poverty alleviation programmes). Although these maps are geographic in nature, no effort has been made to link them to geographic variables, trying, for example, to find out whether there is any kind of poverty trap due to the negative externalities of certain 'geographic endowments'.

The next question to ask is, then, whether there is geographic concentration of poverty in Peru. Map 5.6 graphically answers this question by showing the poverty

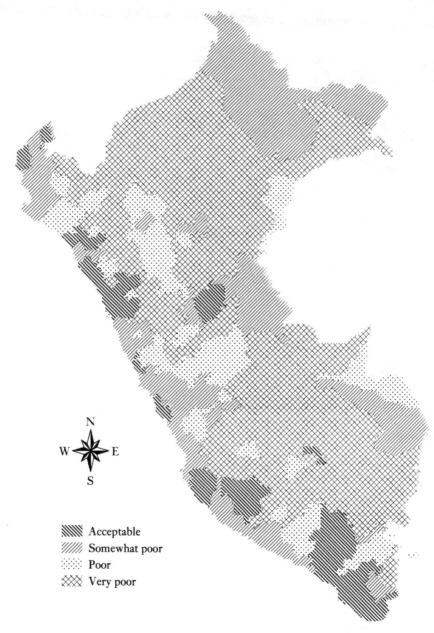

Map 5.6. *Poverty indices at the provincial level in Peru*

Table 5.3. *Geography and economic welfare (% of poor households)*

	1985	1994	1997
Altitude (m.a.s.l)			
0–500	41.4	37.5	46.1
500–1,000	43.5	38.2	48.6
1,000–2,300	51.9	37.0	53.8
2,300–3,500	57.7	43.7	59.7
>3,500	52.1	62.5	63.3
Precipitation (mm per year)			
0–100	35.3	33.2	40.7
100–200	54.0	33.4	42.8
200–400	46.0	65.3	58.7
400–600	59.4	69.8	61.9
600–1,000	51.5	49.2	63.1
1,000–1,400	67.0	42.8	59.4
1,400–2,000	63.4	43.4	58.4
2,000–2,800	60.3	70.4	55.8
>2,800	42.7	34.4	54.7
Temperature (°Celsius)			
0–5	52.7	67.6	65.4
5–10	49.1	44.2	57.8
10–15	40.6	34.4	43.1
15–20	55.1	43.0	53.1
>20	61.7	46.8	55.9

Note: Authors' calculations based on LSMS 1985/6, 1994, and 1997.

Source: Poverty line obtained from Escobal *et al.* (1998).

indices at the provincial level based on a 'poverty index' constructed by FONCODES.[5] As shown in the map there are huge welfare disparities across the country, and there is a heavy concentration of very poor people along the most geographically adverse regions, as in the sierra and selva. Table 5.3 also shows how there is a negative relation between the main geographic variables (altitude, rainfall, and temperature) and household economic welfare. The higher the altitude the larger the number of poor households in the specific region (districts). As expected, temperature shows a non-linear relationship such that poverty increases in areas with extreme temperature levels (high and low). The precipitation variable, however, does not display a clear relationship. These welfare disparities can also be attributed, at least in part, to a significant dispersion of asset

[5] This index was constructed at the district level by weighting socioeconomic indicators reflecting: extreme poverty (infant mortality, child malnutrition), indicators of education (illiteracy rate, school attendance rate), labour market indicators (proportion of working children, percentage of illiterate adults), housing indicators (percentage of overcrowded households, percentage of houses with inadequate roofing), and basic services indicators (access provided by public networks to water, sanitation, and electricity); see FONCODES (1995).

Table 5.4. *Regional differences in access to services and assets, 1997*

	Urban (%)	Rural (%)	Ratio
Family size	6.1	6.3	1.0
Years of education (head)	8.6	4.5	1.9
Years of education (adults)	8.1	5.0	1.6
Drop-out rates, secondary school	12	15	0.8
Access to electricity	97	30	3.2
Access to water, public network	89	43	2.1
Access to sanitation	84	12	7.3
Access to credit	37	23	1.6
Memo: poverty rate	40	65	

Source: LSMS (1997).

Table 5.5. *Distribution of new access to basic and social services, 1994–7*

	Urban	Rural	Ratio
Water, public network (%)	57	43	1.3
Electricity (%)	72	28	2.6
Sanitation connection (%)	78	22	3.5
Outpatient health (%)	74	26	2.8
School enrolment (%)	33	67	0.5

Source: LSMS (1994, 1997).

ownership or access. As can be seen in Tables 5.4 and 5.5, most of the access to public assets and services is at least two or three times as high in urban areas as compared to rural areas. In the case of access to sanitation connection, differences are even greater.[6] Even though access to public goods and services has increased dramatically in rural areas during the last four years, new access continues to be biased in favour of urban areas. Two-thirds of the new electricity, sanitation, and health services are placed in urban areas. Only in education does the pattern of new public goods placed in rural areas surpass that of urban areas.

Given the above evidence, the major questions this research will try to answer are: what causal role do geographic variables, both natural and man-made, play in explaining per capita expenditure differentials across regions within Peru? How have these influences changed over time, how important will they be in the future, through what channels have those influences been transmitted, and does access to private and

---

[6] Poverty maps provide a detailed description of the spatial distribution of poverty within the country and are a crucial tool for research in trying to explain the relationship between poverty or inequality and indicators of development. On the other hand, it is important to mention that they must be interpreted within their limitations given that their quality is limited by the sparseness of the desegregated data. Some improvements on these methodologies can be found in Hentschel *et al.* (1998).

public assets play a crucial role in reducing the negative effects of an adverse geography? The next section describes how we plan to formally answer these questions.

5.3. ANALYTICAL FRAMEWORK TO TEST THE EFFECTS OF GEOGRAPHY

The main question this chapter tries to answer is whether geography has any effect on living standards after controlling for observable non-geographic characteristics of the households and whether access to public and private assets compensates for an adverse geography. To address this question, we have divided the analysis into three stages.

The first stage analyses the evidence of regional income differences and to what extent these differences had been hampered (or facilitated) by local or neighbouring, natural or man-made, geographic endowments. We analyse the evolution of geographic patterns and the importance of clustering in some areas by using spatial econometric techniques, such as the Moran I statistic (Moran 1950, see Appendix I). We measure for the presence, over time, of spatial concentration of per capita expenditure and geographical, private, and public assets and test for their significance. In the second stage, to formally answer whether geography has a causal role in determining how household welfare evolves over time, we developed an estimable micromodel of consumption levels and growth.

To model changes in consumption over time we use three census databases at the province level (see Appendix II for details on how consumption is estimated for the census databases). This analysis also allows us to see what geographic factors matter to growth prospects at the microlevel (Engerman and Sokoloff 1997; Jalan and Ravallion 1998). Our explanatory variables include a set of individual characteristics such as human assets (x), a set of private assets (z), a set of public assets at the district level (r), and a set of variables comprising specific geographic characteristics such as climate, soil characteristics, and altitude (g). Specifically the change in consumption equation is:

$$\Delta c_p = a + \beta x_{p,0} + \phi z_{p,0} + \gamma r_{p,0} + \varphi g_p + \varepsilon_p \tag{5.1}$$

in which the subscript p refers to province-level averages of the respective variables, and the subscript zero refers to information of the initial period. We include each of the groups of regressors incrementally and lastly we estimate the full model. We run a set of models including, one by one, each of the groups of explanatory variables: geography (g), neighbouring public assets (r), private assets (z), and individual characteristics (x) and identify the direct externality effects of the presence of each of them. Additionally, according to the hypothesis of the presence of spatial concentration we analyse the importance of neighbouring province effects by measuring the significance of spatial autocorrelation[7] in each of our specifications and test how it decreases as we

---

[7] Spatial autocorrelation, or more generally, spatial dependence, is the situation where the dependent variable or error term at each location is correlated with observations on the dependent variable or values for the error term at other locations.

include additional groups of regressors (see Appendix I for the spatial autocorrelation tests used).

We model the spatial dependence as a nuisance (a nuisance since it only pertains to the errors). Formally, this dependence is expressed by means of a spatial process for the error terms, either of an autoregressive or a moving average form (see Anselin 1988; and Anselin *et al.* 1996). Such an autoregressive process can be expressed as:

$$\Delta c_p = \alpha + \beta x_{p,0} + \phi z_{p,0} + \gamma r_{p,0} + \varphi g_p + \varepsilon_p$$
$$\varepsilon_p = \lambda W \varepsilon_p + \xi \tag{5.2}$$

with $W\varepsilon^8$ as a spatially lagged error term, λ as the autoregressive coefficient and ξ as a well-behaved (i.e. homoskedastic uncorrelated) error term. As a consequence of the spatial dependence, the error term no longer has the usual diagonal variance matrix but instead takes the following form (Anselin 1988):

$$E[\varepsilon\varepsilon'] = \Omega = \sigma^2[(I - \lambda W)'(I - \lambda W)]^{-1}. \tag{5.3}$$

Therefore, ordinary least squares (OLS) estimates are no longer efficient but they are still unbiased. Furthermore, given that the lambda coefficient is unknown, the regression coefficients cannot be estimated using generalized least squares (GLS) and, therefore, in our last specification we estimate the lambda coefficient jointly with the regression coefficients using full maximum likelihood estimation techniques.[9]

Lastly, the results of the previous specifications are used to break down the geographic effects into their component elements. For this purpose, we compute the expected gain (or loss) in consumption from living in one geographic region (coastal, for example) against living in another geographic region (mountainous, for example) specifying how much of the gain is explained by geographical variables, location (urban/rural), infrastructure, and private assets:

$$(\overline{X}_M - \overline{X}_C)\hat{\beta}, \tag{5.4}$$

where $\overline{X}_{M,C}$ are the sample means for mountain and coastal regions, for example, and $\hat{\beta}$ is the parameter of the respective variables under analysis (i.e. geographical, location, infrastructure, and private assets). This breakdown represents the differential impact on a household's standard of all non-excluded variables in the two regions.

---

[8] For N districts observed, W_i is the ith row of an $(N \times N)$ matrix W that assigns neighbouring districts to each district. The W used can be characterized by $W = \{w_{ij}\}$ such that $w_{ij} = 1$ if i and j are neighbouring districts, $w_{ij} = 0$ otherwise, and $w_{ii} = 0$ for all i. The rows of W are then normalized such that each observation's neighbouring districts have the same amount of influence, that is $\sum_j W_{ij} = 1$, for all i. In addition it will be assumed that each neighbouring district of a given district carries equal weight, $w_{ij} = w_{ik}$ for non-zero elements (neighbours) k and j, for firm i. If more information were available about the amount of influence each district yields, this could be incorporated into the W matrix (regarding the different possible structures see Anselin 1988).

[9] For a more extensive technical discussion of the relative merits of the various estimators suggested in the literature, see Anselin (1988, 1990).

5.4. THE DATA

To be able to answer the major questions outlined in the previous section we have developed three different databases—census and household surveys (LSMS) all of which were linked to a geographical database (see data sources).

Using the population and household census of 1972, 1981, and 1993 to construct a set of variables allows us to analyse the kind of changes that have emerged in the geographical pattern of Peru's most important socioeconomic variables during the last three decades. Additionally, using the methodology of Hentschel *et al.* (1998), we estimate a household-level expenditure equation using the information from the 1985/6 and 1994 LSMS surveys which allowed us to model the determinants of per capita expenditure growth at the provincial level. This, in turn, allows us to determine what role geographic variables play in explaining per capita expenditure differentials across regions in Peru.[10] This interpolation method is basically a non-linear interpolation, and as such may be subject to the criticism that it may show the structure of the model more rather than the structure of the data. Although we fully acknowledge this, it is worthwhile mentioning that a similar model was tested against a different dataset to check whether or not the results were reasonable. The results, available in Escobal *et al.* (2001), show that when this model was fitted to the fourth quarter official household survey of 1998 (ENAHO) the results were quite good, as we were able to validate the model comparing the poverty rates it predicted with that of seven regions from which that survey was statistically representative. It should also be mentioned that in all of the seven regions, the interpolation allowed that more than 80 per cent of the household were correctly assigned as poor or not poor.

Therefore, to estimate per capita expenditure at provincial levels for census years we regress per capita expenditure on private and public assets, allowing interactions between them.[11] Table 5.A1 in Appendix II shows the results of this procedure. The endogenous variable in each equation was the per capita expenditure in constant nuevos soles of 1994. From the coefficients obtained in Table 5.A1, we simulated the province-level per capita expenditure using the province-level variables obtained from the census data, and the means of the household surveys whenever there was not a counterpart variable in the census. For 1972 and 1981 we used the parameters of LSMS 1985/6 and for 1993 the calculations of LSMS 1994 due to the proximity of the sample surveys and census dates.

The province-level variables used in all census years were household size, percentage of houses without access to potable water, without drainage, without electricity, total illiteracy rate, schooling attendance rate, percentage of child labourers, and percentage of the population living in urban areas. Additionally, for 1993 we included

---

[10] For an example, see Borjas (1995) on effects of neighbourhood on schooling and wages in the United States and Ravallion and Wodon (1997) on effects of geography on the level of poverty in Bangladesh, as well as on the importance of public and private assets in explaining regional poverty variations.

[11] A more detailed discussion of these estimations can be found in Escobal *et al.* (1998).

the percentage of the non-professional, economically active population, percentage of households headed by women, and college attendance rate. We complete the set of variables (to estimate province-level expenditure) using sample average values of the LSMS by regions. As we mentioned above, LSMS are divided in geographical regions to improve the quality of the sampling. These regions were included in the regression as dummy variables associated with location: northern coast, central highland, and Greater Lima, for example.

Per capita expenditure at the provincial level in each census year was adjusted to reproduce the aggregate consumption growth rate of national accounts within those years. Using 1981 as an anchor, we changed slightly the intercept coefficients of the other regressions to re-estimate the projected variables. Thus, we replace the OLS estimated coefficients 6.690 with 6.350, and 7.695 with 7.595, for 1993 and 1972, respectively. In this way the growth rate of the projected per capita expenditure (weighted by population in each year) is equal to the macroeconomic statistics. The coefficients reported in Table 5.A1 display the new values for the intercepts.

Finally, the number of provinces has not remained constant in the last thirty years. In 1972 the number of provinces was 150, in 1981 it was 153, and in 1993 it was 188, therefore we had to homogenize the province areas and shapes through time. With this purpose we decided to use the political–administrative division of Peru in 1993 because the Geographical Information System (GIS) was developed following the 1993 census. To impute the values in 1972 for new provinces we repeated the 'original' province information in each of its new regions or areas. For 1981 we had district-level data and since the creation of a new province is basically a new clustering of districts we aggregate those district values to create data for the new provinces.

5.5. EMPIRICAL RESULTS

5.5.1. *Peru's Geography and its Regional Differences in Expenditure*

In this section we analyse the kind of changes that have emerged in the geographical pattern of Peru's most important socioeconomic variables during the last three decades. In addition we analyse changes in expenditure estimates, at the province level, between three census years of 1972, 1981, and 1993. We analyse twenty-four variables at the provincial level for a panel of the three given census years, as well as 160 additional variables at the provincial level and 88 additional variables at the district level for variables that were available only for 1993 and beyond. The data section described these variables as well as the databases that generate them.

We have included in this section some of the maps generated with these variables. It is interesting to note that there are several types of evolution in the geographic patterns. There are cases such as the one depicted in Map 5.7 that show a dramatic reduction of illiteracy rates among women but, at the same time, the high rates are clustered in some areas (such as the southern sierra and other high altitude zones). This kind of pattern can also be found in other key socioeconomic variables, such as total illiteracy rate or household size.

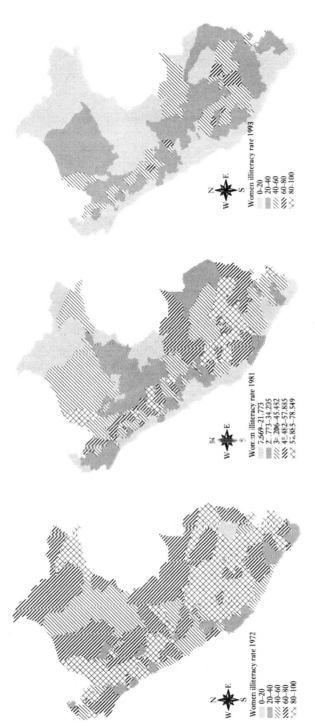

Map 5.7. *Illiteracy rate of women*

Women illiteracy rate 1993

0–20
20–40
40–60
60–80
80-100

Women illiteracy rate 1981

7.569–21.773
21.773–34.205
34.206–45.432
45.482–57.885
57.885–78.549

Women illiteracy rate 1972

0–20
20–40
40–60
60–80
80-100

There are other variables, such as percentage of households without access to potable water, percentage of households without access to sanitation services, or percentage of households without access to electricity that display during the 1972–81 period a significant reduction in the coastal areas and afterward some clustering of high values specially in the southern sierra and high altitude jungle regions and no distinguishable pattern in the rest of the country (access to potable water is depicted in Map 5.8).

In order to more comprehensively analyse the changes that occurred in these geographic patterns we have constructed a per capita expenditure variable at the provincial level. Following a procedure similar to that of Hentschel *et al.* (1998), we used household data to construct expenditure functions using the Peruvian LSMS surveys of 1985 and 1994. We used the 1985 expenditure function to construct provincial-level expenditure estimates using data taken from the 1972 and 1981 census as explanatory variables. We used the 1994 expenditure function to construct the provincial-level expenditure estimates based on data taken from the 1993 census (see data section for details).

The geographical evolution of Peru's per capita expenditures between 1972 and 1993 can be viewed in Map 5.9. Here it is evident that higher per capita expenditure is to be found along low altitude coastal regions. This pattern, which is already clear using 1972 data, is even more apparent as time passes. It is interesting to note that the Gini coefficients are extremely low (0.118 in 1972, 0.088 in 1981, and 0.187 in 1993). It must be noted, however, that interregional expenditure variance is very low, at least when compared to intraregion variance, making these Ginis perfectly consistent with a national Gini coefficient of 0.42 and 0.38 in 1985 and 1994, respectively.

Map 5.10 shows the pattern of distribution of interannual per capita expenditure growth rates between census years. Here it can be noted that the provinces whose per capita expenditures have grown faster tend to be clustered, as do those provinces showing little or even negative growth. Provinces showing high growth tend to be clustered in the higher altitude jungle. Table 5.6 confirms the graphical analysis showing high and statistically significant Moran Index and Geary Index values for all three census years. In addition, high Moran and Geary Index values can also be found for per capita expenditure growth.

Table 5.7 shows some of the most significant spatially autocorrelated variables in our dataset. Using the Moran and Geary Indexes we find, aside from some obviously spatially correlated variables such as annual precipitation or altitude of the province or district capital, critical socioeconomic variables such as household size, percentage of households headed by women, or total and female illiteracy rates to be heavily clustered, high values in high altitude zones and low values in coastal areas. A similar situation can be found in other variables such as percentage of houses with inadequate floors or overcrowded housing, malnutrition rates, and school drop-out rates and schooling years.

One summary welfare variable, per capita expenditure, for 1993 displays high and statistically significant Moran and Geary Index values. It is also interesting to note that the variable of soil depth, constructed to show agricultural land potential, also has a highly spatial autocorrelated pattern. Aside from some obvious variables, such

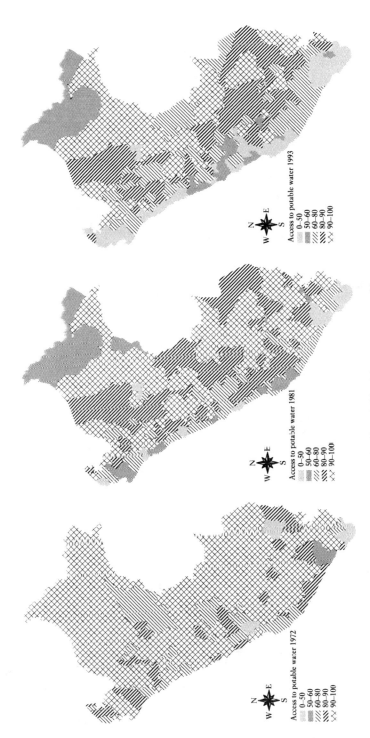

Access to potable water 1972

N
W ✦ E
S

Access to potable water
  0–50
  50–60
  60–80
  80–90
  90–100

Access to potable water 1981

N
W ✦ E
S

Access to potable water
  0–50
  50–60
  60–80
  80–90
  90–100

Access to potable water 1993

N
W ✦ E
S

Access to potable water
  0–50
  50–60
  60–80
  80–90
  90–100

Map 5.8. *Households without access to potable water*

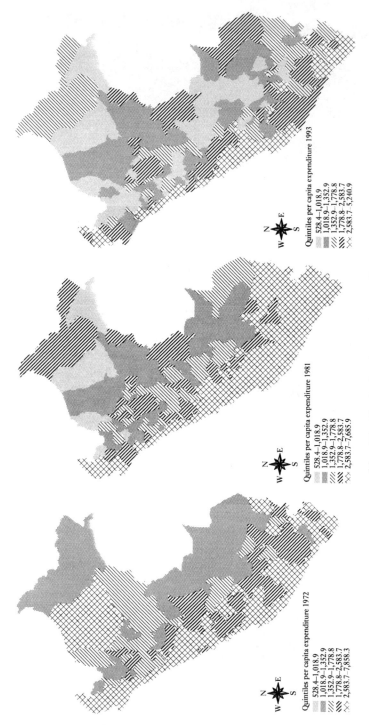

Quintiles per capita expenditure 1972

- 528.4–1,018.9
- 1,018.9–1,352.9
- 1,352.9–1,778.8
- 1,778.8–2,583.7
- 2,583.7–7,858.3

Quintiles per capita expenditure 1981

- 528.4–1,018.9
- 1,018.9–1,352.9
- 1,352.9–1,778.8
- 1,778.8–2,583.7
- 2,583.7–7,685.9

Quintiles per capita expenditure 1993

- 528.4–1,018.9
- 1,018.9–1,352.9
- 1,352.9–1,778.8
- 1,778.8–2,583.7
- 2,583.7–5,240.9

Map 5.9. *Distribution of per capita expenditure*

Map 5.10. *Change in per capita expenditures (%)*

Table 5.6. *Spatial autocorrelation of province-level expenditure variables*

Variables	Moran Index	Prob.[a]	Geary Index	Prob.[a]
Per capita expenditure				
1972	0.4131	0.00	0.6078	0.00
1981	0.5709	0.00	0.3993	0.00
1993	0.4888	0.00	0.4565	0.00
Change in per capita expenditure				
1972–81	0.3708	0.00	0.6186	0.00
1981–93	0.4990	0.00	0.4616	0.00
1972–93	0.2427	0.00	0.7308	0.00

Note: [a] Probability to reject null hypothesis (absence of spatial autocorrelation).
Source: Authors' calculations based on province estimates.

Table 5.7. *High spatial autocorrelated variable*

Variables	Moran Index	z-value	Geary Index	z-value
South latitude	0.9302	20.21*	0.057	−18.76*
North longitude	0.8870	19.27*	0.093	−18.04*
Precipitation	0.7573	16.47*	0.259	−14.73*
Household size 1993	0.7495	16.30*	0.241	−15.10*
Temperature (average)	0.7486	16.29*	0.256	−14.79*
Temperature (min.)	0.7469	16.25*	0.255	−14.83*
Temperature (max.)	0.7422	16.15*	0.265	−14.62*
Altitude of the district capital (metres above sea level)	0.6693	14.57*	0.322	−13.47*
% female-headed households 1993	0.6560	14.28*	0.325	−13.43*
Inadequate flooring	0.6518	14.19*	0.339	−13.16*
Soil depth	0.6422	13.99*	0.328	−13.37*
Total illiteracy rate 1981	0.6352	13.83*	0.356	−12.82*
Overcrowded houses 1993	0.6286	13.69*	0.339	−13.15*
Household size 1981	0.6130	13.35*	0.377	−12.39*
Per capita expenditure in 1981	0.6084	13.26*	0.399	−11.95*
Perimeter of the province	0.6032	13.14*	0.390	−12.12*

Note: *= $p < 0.01$, where p is the probability to reject null hypothesis (absence of spatial autocorrelation).
Source: Authors' calculations based on National Population Census of 1972, 1981, and 1993.

as those related to urban areas (urban density or number of towns per province, for example) there are very few variables that do not show a clear geographical pattern. Only three variables deserve some mention—change in household size between 1972 and 1981; the growth of the illiteracy rate between 1981 and 1993; and the growth in per capita expenditures between 1972 and 1981—which do not show any geographical pattern measured by the Moran spatial autocorrelation index or the Geary Index (see Appendix III).

5.5.2. *Testing the Causal Role of Geography on the Evolution of Welfare*

As we read in Section 5.3, it is possible to derive a connection between the asset endowment of an individual household and its expenditure level. Following the same reasoning we can derive a connection between the level of private and public assets that can be found at some level of spatial aggregation (here the provincial level) and the per capita expenditure level that can be found in that area.

Table 5.8 shows the econometric results of what could be called the determinants of per capita expenditure growth at the provincial level. To reduce any possible endogeneity bias in explaining 1972–93 per capita expenditure growth rates we have chosen initial asset endowments as independent right-hand side variables. To this basic dataset we have added several key geographical variables to check whether they can provide some explanation of causes of expenditure growth. Table 5.8 shows the Moran spatial autocorrelation index for the four different specifications that were evaluated: (i) only private assets; (ii) private assets plus geography variables; (iii) the previous variables plus public assets; and (iv) all the variables plus changes in access to key public assets.

We have used the log difference of per capita expenditures as a dependent variable. The reason for this choice (as opposed to using percentage changes) is related to functional form issues. If there is any misspecification in the per capita expenditure equations (which have been estimated as semi-log functions) the log difference of per capita expenditures will clean the bias, provided that these variables have similar effects over the years.

As can be seen in Table 5.8, when geographic variables are included as the only explanatory variables, altitude and longitude prove to be highly significant in explaining expenditure growth. In particular, it can be shown that the higher altitude provinces tend to have slower expenditure growth rates. When we add the variable of basic needs,[12] which encompasses the absence of critical public infrastructure (sanitation, water, telephone, and electricity) we can see that altitude remains significant but its negative impact diminishes considerably. This effect can be viewed as demonstrating the importance of public infrastructure to lower negative geographic externalities. It is important to note that when we add private assets (some of which are obviously correlated with public assets) the importance of geography almost vanishes. This effect can be seen in Map 5.11 where we have graphed the pattern of geographic residuals of each model. This initial finding will be followed up more rigorously in the next section.

It is interesting to note that despite the fact that this expenditure growth function has included all relevant geographic variables at hand, the residuals continue to show spatial

---

[12] Those defined as poor according to the unmet or unsatisfied 'basic needs' approach are those who suffer severe deprivation in one or more aspects of material well-being, such as poor housing, poor health, inadequate education, or unemployment. This approach has a long history among development practitioners and, although seldom mentioned in the literature, is being used by most statistical agencies around the world. As Hicks and Streeten (1979) and Streeten (1984) mention, this approach tends to highlight those living in chronic poverty as opposed to short-term poverty that may be captured by other measures based on income or expenditure.

Table 5.8. *Determinants of per capita expenditure growth rate, 1972–93 (OLS estimations with robust standard errors, at province level)*

Variables at initial period	Models				
	(1)	(2)	(3)	(4)	(5)
Intercept	4.8269*	4.6892*	4.3913*	−0.0277	−0.3270
	(1.631)	(1.563)	(1.585)	(1.385)	(1.706)
Altitude	−1.1081*	−0.7872~	−0.5096	0.2616	0.4580
	(0.385)	(0.377)	(0.447)	(0.385)	(0.389)
Latitude	−0.0226	−0.0308	−0.0288	−0.0231	−0.0170
	(0.017)	(0.017)	(0.017)	(0.019)	(0.019)
Longitude	−0.0561*	−0.057*	−0.0543*	−0.0182	−0.0171
	(0.018)	(0.017)	(0.018)	(0.015)	(0.015)
Soil slope	−0.0012	0.0016	0.0021	0.0033	0.0035
	(0.003)	(0.003)	(0.003)	(0.002)	(0.002)
Soil depth	−0.003	−0.0017	−0.0018	0.002	0.0023
	(0.003)	(0.002)	(0.003)	(0.002)	(0.002)
Igneous rock	−0.2143	−0.2944~	−0.3102*	−0.3197*	−0.2757*
	(0.126)	(0.123)	(0.123)	(0.100)	(0.106)
Metamorphic rock	0.0732	0.0536	0.0863	−0.1318	−0.1362
	(0.149)	(0.145)	(0.146)	(0.122)	(0.122)
Temperature	−0.0191	−0.0045	−0.0043	−0.0114	−0.0082
	(0.010)	(0.010)	(0.010)	(0.009)	(0.009)
Basic needs		−0.0561*	−0.0393~	−0.0222	−0.0225
		(0.013)	(0.020)	(0.017)	(0.016)
High × basic needs			−0.1110	0.0045	−0.0149
			(0.097)	(0.090)	(0.080)
School attendance rate				0.0143*	0.0144*
				(0.003)	(0.003)
Households headed by women (%)				−0.0109~	−0.0134~
				(0.005)	(0.005)
Working children (%)				0.0533*	0.0462~
				(0.020)	(0.018)
Household size				0.0783	0.1057
				(0.133)	(0.128)
Household size growth[a]				−0.2624	−0.2208
				(0.140)	(0.136)
Number of migrants				0.0171	0.0101
				(0.029)	(0.029)
Spatial autocorrelation					0.2305~
					(0.102)
Number of observations	190	190	190	190	190
Adjusted R^2	0.122	0.195	0.197	0.486	0.526

Notes: [a] Instrumental variables are shown in the Appendix. Standard deviation in parentheses; *=$p < 0.01$, ~=$p < 0.5$. Model 1: Geography. Model 2: Geography + infrastructure. Model 3: Geography + infrastructure + geography × infrastructure. Model 4: Geography + infrastructure + geography × infrastructure+private assets. Model 5: Geography+infrastructure+geography × infrastructure+private assets, modelling first-order spatial error autocorrelation.

Source: Authors' calculations based on Population and Household Census 1972 and 1993.

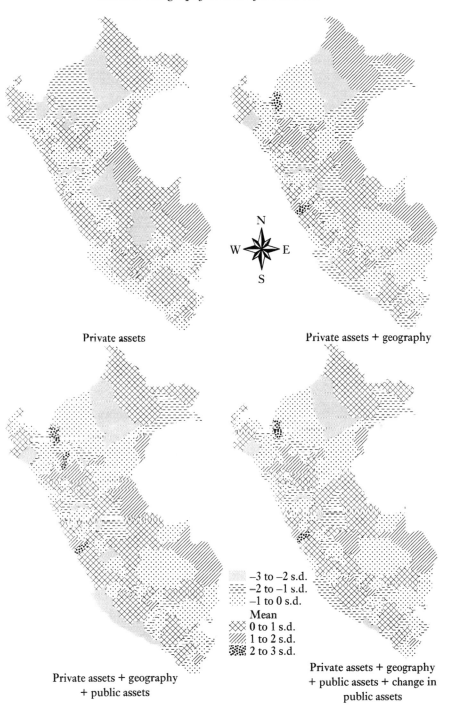

Private assets

Private assets + geography

-3 to -2 s.d.
-2 to -1 s.d.
-1 to 0 s.d.
Mean
0 to 1 s.d.
1 to 2 s.d.
2 to 3 s.d.

Private assets + geography
+ public assets

Private assets + geography
+ public assets + change in
public assets

Map 5.11. *Spatial distribution of regression residuals by model*

Table 5.9. *Spatial autocorrelation of growth regression residuals,*
by model

Type of association	Regression model residuals			
	1	2	3	4
Moran Index	0.1091	0.1005	0.0973	0.0816
z-value	3.1226	2.9658	2.9357	2.7877
Probability	0.0018	0.0030	0.0033	0.0053

Notes: Model 1: Geography. Model 2: Geography + infrastructure. Model 3: Geography + infrastructure + geography × infrastructure. Model 4: Geography + infrastructure + geography × infrastructure + private assets.

Source: Authors' calculations based on Table 5.7.

autocorrelation. As can be seen in Table 5.9, although the Moran Index diminishes as we include explanatory variables it remains significant. This fact suggests that there may be non-geographic non-observables affecting the provincial expenditure pattern. This is consistent with Ravallion and Wodon (1997) when they show that sizeable geographic differences in living standards can persist even if we take into account the spatial concentration of households with readily observable non-geographic characteristics conducive to poverty. The last column in Table 5.8 shows the estimated parameter values corrected for spatial autocorrelation.[13] The results confirm that when public and private assets, as well as household characteristics, are included in the regression the impact of geographic variables is dampened.

Finally, in Table 5.10 we can find the spatial breakdown of the regression model according to the Anselin (1995) technique (see Appendix I). Here residuals are clustered in four groups: large residual values clustered around large value areas; small residual values clustered around small value areas; large residual values located around small value areas; and, finally, small residual values located around large value areas. The results confirm that geography and public asset access variables tend to lower spatial autocorrelation, and geography variables are the ones that (at the marginal level) account most for per capita growth patterns.

5.5.3. *Breakdown of Regional Per Capita Expenditure*

To disentangle the effect of geography on regional expenditure and expenditure growth we have applied the breakdown technique described in Section 5.3 to the province per capita expenditure growth equations reported in Table 5.8. For this breakdown we have assumed that parameters are stable across the three main geographic

---

[13] The likelihood ratio test for spatial error dependence for the equation in the last column in Table 5.7 has a value of 3.67 with 1 degree of freedom, which confirms that the estimation has been properly corrected for spatial autocorrelation. For alternative methods of correcting for spatial autocorrelation see Appendix I and for the empirical results Appendix IV.

Table 5.10. *Spatial association of growth regression residuals, by model (number of provinces)*

Type of association	Regression model residuals			
	1	2	3	4
Positive association	111 (72.1)	102 (65.3)	102 (63.2)	100 (63.2)
Large values in large value areas	49 (40.5)	48 (34.2)	52 (34.2)	52 (33.7)
Small values in small value areas	62 (31.6)	54 (31.1)	50 (28.9)	48 (29.5)
Negative association	79 (27.9)	86 (34.7)	88 (36.8)	90 (36.8)
Large values in small value areas	38 (11.6)	43 (17.9)	44 (17.4)	45 (17.4)
Small values in large value areas	41 (16.3)	43 (16.8)	44 (19.5)	45 (19.5)
Total	190 (100.0)	188 (100.0)	190 (100.0)	190 (100.0)

Notes: Column percentages are shown in parentheses. Model 1: Geography. Model 2: Geography + infrastructure. Model 3: Geography + infrastructure + geography × infrastructure. Model 4: Geography + infrastructure + geography × infrastructure + private assets.

Source: Authors' calculations based on Table 5.7.

areas: coastal, highland, and jungle. This initial breakdown is shown in Table 5.11. In this case, per capita growth rate differentials between highland and coastal regions and between jungle and coastal regions can be broken down into their main determinants: geographical differences, infrastructure differences, and asset endowment differences.

Here, as was the case with the previous result, geography does not appear to significantly contribute to growth differentials, once infrastructure differences and private asset endowment differences are accounted for. In other words, once the main geographic variables are accounted for (altitude, temperature, and surface characteristics), only private assets are needed to explain regional expenditure differences. Similarly, the second column shows the breakdown of the differences in log per capita expenditure between the jungle area and the coast, showing again that once main geographic variables are accounted for most of the regional expenditure differences can be explained by private asset composition.[14]

Obviously, the fact that geography has no additional impact on regional per capita expenditure differences has to do with the fact that key infrastructure variables—such as school and medical facilities, access to electricity, water and sanitation, as well as private assets—have dampened the effect of geography on regional expenditure differentials. To see this, Table 5.12 performs the same breakdown exercise introducing each set of variables sequentially. First, geography variables are entered in the model

[14] When we carry out a similar exercise using household surveys similar results are obtained, that is, once the main geographic variables are accounted for only private assets and infrastructure endowments are needed to explain regional expenditure differences (see Escobal and Torero 2000). Although it is important to mention that given that we cannot correct for spatial autocorrelation in the household-level regressions, households could be sorted geographically on the basis of some latent characteristics, for example, earning ability and land quality, and therefore geographic characteristics could be correlated with these latent characteristics not allowing us to genuinely identify a causal effect.

Table 5.11. *Decomposition of regional per capita expenditure differences*
(growth rate differences at province level)

Group of variables	Highland–coast	Jungle–coast
Geography	*0.2126*	*0.1296*
Altitude level	0.1182	0.0055
Latitude	−0.0280	0.0471
Longitude	0.0437	0.0396
Soil slope	0.0518	−0.0159
Soil depth	−0.0020	0.0379
Igneous rock	−0.0329*	0.0222
Metamorphic rock	0.0300	0.0399
Temperature	0.0319	−0.0467
Infrastructure	*−0.0431*	*−0.0920*
Basic needs	−0.0431	−0.0920
Geography × Infrastructure	*−0.0125*	*−0.0041*
Altitude × Basic needs	−0.0125	−0.0041
Private assets	*−0.3430**	*−0.0031*
School attendance rate	−0.1335*	−0.0663
Female household head (%)	−0.0739~	0.0147
Working children (%)	0.0278~	0.0090
Household size	−0.0689	0.0580
Household size growth[a]	−0.0881+	−0.0133
Number of migrants	−0.0063	−0.0051
Total explained	−0.1860	0.0304
Residual	0.1048	0.0989
Total	*−0.0812*	*0.1293*

Notes: [a]Instrument variables are shown in the Appendix. *= $p < 0.01$, ~= $p \le 0.05$, += $p \le 0.1$.

Source: Authors' calculations based on Population and Household Census 1972 and 1993.

alone and the breakdown exercise is conducted only with these variables. In this case, geography is highly significant in explaining per capita expenditure growth differentials between the highland and coastal areas, as well as between the jungle and coastal areas. Geography remains highly significant even after we introduce location variables and their cross-products into the analysis. However, once infrastructure variables come into play in the analysis, the impact of geography disappears, as the coefficients associated with these types of variables are shown to be jointly non-significant. This could be because, in the models without infrastructure, the geography variables were choosing their effect and therefore when improving our specification the effect of these variables disappears. It must be noted that the analysis remains valid even if we correct for possible spatial autocorrelation due to possible omitted non-geographic spatially correlated variables.

Table 5.12. *Decomposition of regional per capita growth expenditure differences, by model (at province level)*

Group of variables	Highland-coast					Jungle-coast				
	(1)	(1) + (2)	(1) + (2) +(3)	(1) + (2) +(3) + (4)	(1) + (2) +(3) + (4)[a]	(1)	(1) + (2)	(1) + (2) +(3)	(1) + (2) +(3) + (4)	(1) + (2) +(3) + (4)[a]
(1) Geography	−0.163~	−0.113	−0.047	0.158	0.213	0.023~	0.154	0.136	0.126	0.130
(2) Infrastructure		−0.108*	−0.075~	−0.043	−0.043		−0.229*	−0.161~	−0.091	−0.092
(3) Geography × infrastructure			−0.093	0.004	−0.013			−0.031	0.001	−0.004
(4) Private assets				−0.327*	−0.343*				−0.025*	−0.003*
Explained	−0.163	−0.221	−0.215	−0.208	−0.186	0.023	−0.075	−0.056	0.012	0.030
Residual	0.082	0.139	0.134	0.127	0.105	0.106	0.205	0.185	0.118	0.099
Total	−0.081	−0.081	−0.081	−0.081	−0.081	0.129	0.129	0.129	0.129	0.129

Note: [a] Modelling first-order spatial error autocorrelation. * $= p < 0.01$, ~ $= p \leq 0.05$.

Source: Authors' calculations based on 1972 and 1993 Population and Household Census.

5.6. CONCLUSIONS

Peru's enormous geographic diversity makes it an extremely interesting case study to analyse whether geography has a causal role in determining how household welfare evolves over time. We know that there are huge welfare disparities across Peru, and there is a heavy concentration of very poor people throughout the most geographically adverse regions, as in the sierra and selva. Although these welfare disparities can be attributed to geography they can also be related, at least in part, to a significant dispersion in access to infrastructure and other public assets. Therefore, there is no clear evidence that regional income differences can only be explained by geography or if they had been hampered (or facilitated) by local or neighbouring natural or man-made geographical endowments.

Despite the fact that there have been many efforts to link Peru's geographical diversity to key issues as important as settlement location or construction of administrative or political regions, very little has been done to analyse the links between this geographic diversity and development, economic growth, or poverty. To reduce this gap, our research strategy consisted of describing how geography might play a fundamental role in regional economic growth and what relationship there is between geographic variables and expenditure levels and growth across regions within Peru. To formally answer whether geography is a determinant of the evolution of welfare over time, we developed a micromodel of consumption which not only took in the local effect of geographic variables but also included public and private assets as variables that could reduce the potentially adverse effect of geography. For this purpose we used national census data for 1972, 1981, and 1993, the LSMS surveys for 1991, 1994, 1996, and 1997, information from the district-level infrastructure census; geographical datasets, and information from the III National Agrarian Census of 1994. This cross-sectional analysis helped us in attempting to understand whether geographic externalities arising from local or neighbouring public assets, or local endowments of private goods, entail that living in or near a well-endowed area implies that a poor household can eventually escape poverty.

We have shown that what seem to be sizeable geographic differences in living standards in Peru can be almost fully explained when one takes into account the spatial concentration of households with readily observable non-geographic characteristics, in particular public and private assets. In other words, the same observationally equivalent household has a similar expenditure level in one place as in another with different geographic characteristics such as altitude or temperature. This does not mean, however that geography is not important, but that its influence on expenditure levels and growth differentials comes about through a spatially uneven provision of public infrastructure. Furthermore, when we measure the expected gain (or loss) in consumption from living in a geographical region (i.e. coastal) as opposed to living in another geographic region (i.e. highlands), we found that most of the difference in log per capita expenditure between the highland and the coast can be accounted for by the differences in infrastructure endowments and private assets. This could be an indication that the availability of infrastructure could be limited by the geography and therefore the more adverse geographic regions are the ones with less access to public infrastructure.

Another interesting result is that despite the fact that in our models of expenditure growth we included all relevant geographic variables, as well as infrastructure and private assets variables, the residuals continue to show spatial autocorrelation. This fact suggests the idea that there may be non-geographic non-observables that could be affecting the provincial expenditure pattern. This is consistent with Ravallion and Wodon (1997) when they show that sizeable geographic differences in living standards can persist even if we take into account the spatial concentration of households with readily observable non-geographic characteristics conducive to poverty.

It is important to note that there appear to be non-geographic, spatially correlated omitted variables that need to be taken into account in our expenditure growth model. Therefore policy programmes that use regional targeting do have a rationale even if geographic variables do not explain the bulk of the difference in regional growth, once we have taken into account differentials in access to private and public assets.

Lastly, an issue which we had not taken into account, and which could be very important for future research, is the fact that adverse geographic externalities can provide incentives to migration. This is something which we do not control for in this research. The migration effect could be twofold. On the one hand, it could be the reason why households with fewer private assets are the ones which choose to locate in the more adverse geographical regions. On the other hand, it could be very important for policymaking in developing infrastructure, in the sense that certain investments in infrastructure, such as education, are mobile with migration, while others are not. Therefore, it could be more profitable to invest in mobile infrastructure in the more adverse geographic regions, to give the individuals the necessary tools to migrate from these regions and therefore increase their probability of escaping a poverty trap.

Appendix I

Measuring Geographical Association: Theoretical Framework

The importance of the spatial relationships began in the 1970s with the works of Cliff and Ord (1972) in the United Kingdom, and Hordijk (1974), Hordijk and Pelinck (1976), and Hordijk and Nijkamp (1977). These studies created a great interest in the development of a methodology for the study of observations distributed in a specific geographical location and gave birth to what is called 'spatial econometrics'. Spatial autocorrelation says that what is observed in one place is in part determined by what is occurring in the other spatial locations. So, any observation of a variable y in i (where i is an element of a population S), is related formally through a function f to the magnitudes of the variable in other spatial units in the system.

$$y_i = f(y_1, y_2, \ldots, y_{i-1}, y_{i+1}, \ldots, y_n). \tag{5.A1}$$

There are a large number of tests to detect the presence of spatial correlation (Anselin 1988), but those that are most used are the 'Moran Statistic' (I) and the G statistics (Getis and Ord 1992).

The Moran Statistic

Formally, Moran's I is:

$$I = \frac{N}{S_0} \times \frac{\sum_i \sum_j w_{ij}(x_i - \mu) \cdot (x_j - \mu)}{\sum_i (x_i - \mu)^2}, \qquad (5.A2)$$

where N is the number of observations, x_i and x_j are observations for location i and j (with mean μ), w_{ij} is the element in the spatial weight matrix corresponding to the observation pair i, j. The W used here can be characterized $W = \{w_{ij}\}$ such that $w_{ij} = 1$ if i and j are neighbours, $w_{ij} = 0$ otherwise, and $w_{ii} = 0$ for all i. The rows of W are then normalized such that each observation's neighbours have the same amount of influence, that is $\sum_j W_{ij} = 1$, for all i. In addition, it will be assumed that each neighbour of a given farm carries equal weight, $w_{ij} = w_{ik}$ for non-zero elements (neighbours) k and j for farmer i. If more information were available about the amount of influence each household exercises, this could be incorporated into the W matrix (regarding the different structures see Anselin 1988). S_0 is a scaling constant:

$$S_0 = \sum_i \sum_j w_{ij}, \qquad (5.A3)$$

that is, the sum of all weights. For a row-standardized spatial matrix, which is the preferred way to implement the test and the way it is done in this chapter, S_0 equals N (since each row sums to 1), and the statistic simplifies to the ratio of a spatial cross-product to a variance:

$$I = \frac{\sum_i \sum_j w_{ij}(x_i - \mu) \cdot (x_j - \mu)}{\sum_i (x_i - \mu)^2}. \qquad (5.A4)$$

Moran's I is similar but not equivalent to a correlation coefficient and is not centred around 0. In fact, the theoretical mean of Moran's I is $-1/N - 1$. In other words, the expected value is negative and is only a function of the sample size (N). Note, however, that this mean will tend to zero as the sample size increases. Instead of using the I statistics by themselves, inference is typically based on a standardized z-value. This is computed by subtracting the theoretical mean and dividing the result by the theoretical standard deviation.

$$z_I = \frac{(I - E(I))}{\text{s.d.}(I)}, \qquad (5.A5)$$

where $E(I)$ is the theoretical mean and s.d.(I) is the theoretical standard deviation. For a technical discussion and detailed expressions for the moments see Cliff and Ord (1972, 1981). The most common approach is to assume that the variable in question follows a normal distribution. Based on asymptotic considerations (i.e. by assuming that the sample may became infinitely large) the z-value, using the proper measures for mean and standard deviation, follows a standard normal distribution (i.e. normal distribution with mean 0 and variance 1). Significance of the statistic can then be judged by comparing the computed z-value to its probability in a standard normal table (see Case 1992).

Deriving the G and G Statistic*

The Getis and Ord (1992) statistic is used as a validation of the Moran I. Getis and Ord introduced a family of statistics, G, that can be used as measures of spatial association in a number of circumstances. Formally, the G statistic, for a chosen critical distance d, $G(d)$, is defined as:

$$G(d) = \frac{\sum_i \sum_j w_{ij}(d)x_i x_j}{\sum_i \sum_j x_i x_j},$$ (5.A6)

where x_i is the value observed at location i, and $w_{ij}(d)$ stands for an element of the symmetric (non-standardized) spatial weights matrix for distance d. The numerator of the statistic is similar to that of Moran's I, but its denominator is different. Its significance is assessed by means of a standardized z-value, obtained in the usual fashion. The mean and variance of the $G(d)$ statistic can be derived under a randomization assumption and the z-value can be shown to tend to a standard normal variable in the limit (see Getis and Ord 1992 for detailed derivations).

For each observation i, the G_i and G_i^* statistics indicate the extent to which that location is surrounded by high values or low values for the variable under consideration, for a given distance d. Formally, the G_i and G_i^* statistics are defined as:

$$G_i = \frac{\sum_j w_{ij}(d)x_j}{\sum_j x_j}$$ (5.A7)

where $w_{ij}(d)$ are the elements from the contiguity matrix for distance d. The G_i and G_i^* measures differ with respect to the number of observations that are included in the computation of the denominator. For G_i statistic, $j \neq i$ while for the G_i^* statistic, $j = i$ is included in the sum. In other words, the G_i^* measure provides a measure of spatial clustering that includes the observation under consideration, while the G_i measure does not. Inference about the significance of the G_i and G_i^* statistics is based on a standardized z-value, which is computed by substituting the theoretical mean and dividing by the theoretical standard deviation (for more details see Getis and Ord 1992).

A positive and significant z-value for a G, G_i, or G_i^* statistic indicates spatial clustering of high values, whereas a negative and significant z-value indicates spatial clustering of low values. Note that this interpretation is different from that of the more traditional measures of spatial autocorrelation, as the Moran I, where spatial clustering of like values, either high or low, are both indicated by positive autocorrelation.

Local Indicators of Spatial Association (LISA)

In Anselin (1995), a local indicator of spatial association (LISA) is defined, and shows how they allow for the breakdown of the global indicators, such as Moran's I, into the contribution of each observation. The LISA statistics serve two purposes. On the one hand, they may be interpreted as indicators of local pockets of non-stationarity, or hot spots, similar to the G_i and G_i^* of Getis and Ord (1992). On the other hand, they may be used to assess the influence of individual locations on the magnitude of the global statistic and to identify 'outliers', as in Anselin's Moran scatterplot (1995). Both of these uses will help in determining which locations had the greatest correlation with their neighbours. The LISA for a variable y_i, observed at location i, can be expressed as a statistic L_i, such that:

$$L_i = f(y_i, y_{\mathcal{J}_i}), \qquad (5.A8)$$

where f is a function (possibly including additional parameters), and the $y_{\mathcal{J}_i}$ are the values observed in the neighbourhood $\mathcal{J}_i$ of i.

Similar to the rationale behind the significance tests for G_i and G_i^* statistics of Getis and Ord (1992), the general LISA can be used as the basis for a test on the null hypothesis of no local spatial association. However, in contrast to what holds for the G_i and G_i^* statistics, general results on the distribution of a generic LISA may be hard to obtain.

As a special case of the local Gamma,[15] a local Moran statistic for an observation I may be defined as:

$$I_i = z_i \sum_j w_{ij} z_j, \qquad (5.A9)$$

where, analogous to the global Moran's I, the observations z_i, z_j are in deviations from the mean, and the summation over j is such that only neighbouring values j element of $\mathcal{J}_i$ are included. For ease of interpretation the weights w_{ij} may be in row-standardized form, though it is not necessary, and by convention, $w_{ii} = 0$.

It can be easily seen that the corresponding global statistic is indeed the familiar Moran's I; the sum of the local Moran is:

$$\sum_i I_i = \sum_i z_i \sum_j w_{ij} z_j. \qquad (5.A10)$$

The moments of I_i under the null hypothesis of no spatial association can be derived using the principles outlined by Cliff and Ord (1981: 42–6) and a reasoning similar to the one by Getis and Ord (1992).

A test for significant local spatial association is based on these moments, although, as mentioned by Anselin (1995), the exact distribution of such a statistic is still unknown.

---

[15] See Mantel (1967) and Luc Anselin (1995).

Appendix II: Data Description

Table 5.A1. *Determinants of (log) per capita expenditure (OLS estimation with robust errors)*

Variables	Census year					
	1972[a]		1981[a]		1993[b]	
	Coeff.	s.d.	Coeff.	s.d.	Coeff.	s.d.
Intercept	7.6959	(0.1954)	7.7777	(0.3271)	6.3502	(0.1377)
Access to credit	0.1384	(0.0399)	0.1351	(0.0364)	0.0826	(0.0366)
Access to drinking water	−0.1051	(0.0589)	−0.1316	(0.0535)		
Access to electricity	0.0846	(0.0541)	0.0788	(0.0497)	0.0021	(0.0004)
Access to in-house drainage services	0.1165	(0.1455)	0.1032	(0.1030)	0.0016	(0.0009)
Cattle	0.1288	(0.0827)	0.1368	(0.0800)	0.0913	(0.0788)
Durable goods	0.0680	(0.0092)	0.0681	(0.0087)	0.0051	(0.0046)
Fertilizers usage	0.1619	(0.0436)	0.1839	(0.0414)	0.1056	(0.0327)
Hh head gender	0.0278	(0.0627)	−0.0035	(0.0523)		
Hh members with secondary education (%)			0.0031	(0.0023)		
House with inadequate floor	−0.0042	(0.0009)	−0.0038	(0.0008)	−0.0021	(0.0003)
Hh size	−0.2760	(0.0341)	−0.3361	(0.0306)	−0.3253	(0.0283)
Illiteracy rate	−0.0017	(0.0008)	−0.0012	(0.0008)	−0.0016	(0.0007)
School attendance (children)	0.0010	(0.0006)	0.0006	(0.0006)		
Land size	0.0432	(0.0503)	0.0185	(0.0413)		
Number of migrants (hh members)	−0.0061	(0.0410)	−0.0039	(0.0409)	0.1359	(0.0261)
Number of rooms in the house	0.0050	(0.0015)	0.0041	(0.0013)	0.0562	(0.0108)
Non-professional labour force			0.0002	(0.0028)		
Potential work experience	−0.0001	(0.0065)	0.0002	(0.0057)	0.0153	(0.0058)
Savings	0.0772	(0.0343)	0.0471	(0.0349)	0.0775	(0.0359)
Schooling attendance rate					0.0004	(0.0004)
Schooling years (hh head)	0.0167	(0.0119)	0.0168	(0.0114)	0.0310	(0.0073)
Schooling years (other members)	0.0372	(0.0188)	0.0388	(0.0160)	0.0326	(0.0070)
Seeds usage	0.1419	(0.0366)	0.1390	(0.0335)	0.0798	(0.0322)
Social networks	0.2282	(0.0601)	0.2197	(0.0620)	0.0862	(0.1102)
Spell of illness (hh head)	0.0153	(0.0299)	0.0268	(0.0299)	−0.0516	(0.0326)
Urban zone	0.0064	(0.0021)	0.0092	(0.0034)	0.0176	(0.1592)
Working children (%)	−0.0014	(0.0005)	−0.0013	(0.0005)		
Northern coast	−0.1374	(0.0334)	−0.1408	(0.0321)	−0.0460	(0.0257)
Central coast	−0.1991	(0.0375)	−0.2033	(0.0393)	−0.0304	(0.0332)
Southern coast	−0.0352	(0.0595)	−0.0552	(0.0642)	−0.0939	(0.0490)
Northern highlands	−0.5987	(0.0541)	−0.5789	(0.0508)	0.1185	(0.0358)
Central highlands	−0.3599	(0.0379)	−0.3670	(0.0374)	−0.0564	(0.0267)

Table 5.A1. (*Continued*)

Variables	Census year					
	1972[a]		1981[a]		1993[b]	
	Coeff.	s.d.	Coeff.	s.d.	Coeff.	s.d.
Southern highlands	−0.7135	(0.0365)	−0.0413	(0.0356)	−0.0769	(0.0287)
Northern high altitude jungle	−0.4818	(0.0579)	−0.4313	(0.0583)	−0.2987	(0.0488)
Central high altitude jungle	−0.4875	(0.0547)	−0.4324	(0.0509)	−0.2745	(0.0501)
Low altitude jungle					−0.2327	(0.0561)
Durable goods (squared)	−8.59E−04	(0.0003)	−8.07E−04	(0.0002)	−7.72E−06	(0.0000)
Hh size (squared)	0.0120	(0.0024)	0.0156	(0.0021)	0.0153	(0.0020)
Number of migrants (hh members) squared	0.0002	(0.0072)	−0.0019	(0.0073)		
Potential work experience (squared)	1.07E−05	(0.0001)	−3.00E−05	(0.0001)	−1.63E−04	(0.0001)
Savings (squared)	0.0002	(0.0003)	0.0004	(0.0003)	−0.0015	(0.0007)
Schooling years (other members, squared)	−0.0020	(0.0022)	−0.0034	(0.0021)		
Spell of illness (hh head) squared					0.0002	(0.0063)
Durable goods × social networks	−0.0060	(0.0022)	−0.0035	(0.0021)	0.0007	(0.0037)
Hh size × potential work experience	0.0001	(0.0003)	0.0004	(0.0003)	0.0001	(0.0002)
Hh size × savings	−0.0065	(0.0033)	−0.0053	(0.0036)	−0.0032	(0.0017)
Hh size × spell of illness	0.0011	(0.0078)	0.0020	(0.0084)	0.0076	(0.0135)
Number of migrants × durable goods	−0.0002	(0.0005)	−0.0003	(0.0006)	0.0005	(0.0009)
Number of migrants × land size	0.0296	(0.0319)	0.0227	(0.0354)	0.0596	(0.0506)
Number of migrants × savings	0.0043	(0.0023)	0.0040	(0.0026)	−0.0004	(0.0030)
Potential work experience × durable goods	−0.0001	(0.0001)	−0.0001	(0.0001)	0.0000	(0.0001)
Potential work experience × number of migrants	−0.0003	(0.0006)	0.0001	(0.0006)	−0.0017	(0.0006)
Potential work experience × savings	−0.0005	(0.0004)	−0.0004	(0.0004)	0.0002	(0.0004)
Potential work experience × spells of illness	−0.0001	(0.0006)	−0.0003	(0.0006)	0.0007	(0.0006)
Savings × durable goods	−5.06E−05	(0.0002)	−2.19E−05	(0.0002)	−2.12E−04	(0.0001)
Schooling years (hh head) × durable goods	−0.0001	(0.0003)	−0.0003	(0.0003)	−0.0006	(0.0003)
Schooling years (hh head) × land size	−0.0113	(0.0120)	−0.0053	(0.0102)	0.0092	(0.0089)
Schooling years (hh head) × potential work experience	−0.0001	(0.0002)	0.0000	(0.0002)	−0.0002	(0.0002)

Table 5.A1. (*Continued*)

Variables	Census year					
	1972[a]		1981[a]		1993[b]	
	Coeff.	s.d.	Coeff.	s.d.	Coeff.	s.d.
Schooling years (hh head) × potential work experience	0.0023	(0.0019)	0.0027	(0.0020)	−0.0067	(0.0016)
Schooling years (hh head) × savings	−0.0044	(0.0016)	−0.0044	(0.0017)	0.0003	(0.0013)
Schooling years (hh head) × spells of illness	−0.0026	(0.0023)	−0.0013	(0.0022)	0.0056	(0.0017)
Spell of illness × durable goods	0.0005	(0.0007)	0.0002	(0.0007)	−0.0001	(0.0006)
Spell of illness × number of migrants	−0.0024	(0.0044)	−0.0028	(0.0045)	−0.0014	(0.0057)
Spell of illness × savings	0.0042	(0.0024)	0.0024	(0.0026)	−0.0006	(0.0033)
Urban zone × hh head gender	−7.85E−05	(0.0007)	1.95E−04	(0.0006)		
Urban zone × land size	0.0007	(0.0013)	0.0001	(0.0012)		
Urban zone × savings (squared)	−6.82E−06	(0.0000)	−8.07E−06	(0.0000)	1.29E−03	(0.0006)
Urban zone × schooling years (hh head, squared)	7.18E−05	(0.0001)	4.79E−05	(0.0001)	6.57E−03	(0.0066)
Urban zone × schooling years (other member)	−0.0001	(0.0002)	−0.0002	(0.0002)	−0.0015	(0.0079)
Urban zone × schooling years (other member, squared)	2.20E−05	(0.0000)	3.07E−05	(0.0000)		
Urban zone × access to credit	0.0004	(0.0005)	0.0004	(0.0004)	0.0560	(0.0540)
Urban zone × access to drinking water	0.0009	(0.0007)	0.0010	(0.0006)		
Urban zone × access to electricity	−1.31E−04	(0.0007)	−4.18E−05	(0.0006)	−7.86E−04	(0.0006)
Urban zone × access to in-house drainage services	−0.0003	(0.0015)	−0.0001	(0.0011)	−0.0006	(0.0009)
Urban zone × cattle	−0.0009	(0.0013)	−0.0004	(0.0012)	−0.0223	(0.1018)
Urban zone × durable goods	−0.0003	(0.0001)	−0.0003	(0.0001)	0.0519	(0.0056)
Urban zone × durable goods (squared)	6.12E−06	(0.0000)	5.38E−06	(0.0000)	−3.06E−04	(0.0000)
Urban zone × fertilizers usage	−0.0011	(0.0008)	−0.0011	(0.0008)	−0.1592	(0.0816)
Urban zone × hh size	0.0009	(0.0004)	0.0013	(0.0003)	0.0609	(0.0326)
Urban zone × hh size (squared)	−0.0001	(0.0000)	−0.0001	(0.0000)	−0.0054	(0.0024)
Urban zone × illiteracy rate	7.28E−06	(0.0000)	6.38E−06	(0.0000)	7.38E−04	(0.0010)

Table 5.A1. (*Continued*)

Variables	1972[a] Coeff.	s.d.	1981[a] Coeff.	s.d.	1993[b] Coeff.	s.d.
Urban zone × number of migrants	0.0001	(0.0001)	0.0001	(0.0001)		
Urban zone × number of migrants (squared)	−0.0001	(0.0004)	−0.0003	(0.0004)		
Urban zone × number of rooms in the house	−2.31E−05	(0.0000)	−3.27E−05	(0.0000)	−0.0004	(0.0122)
Urban zone × pesticides usage	0.2702	(0.0764)	0.3074	(0.0659)	0.1272	(0.0326)
Urban zone × potential work experience	0.0001	(0.0001)	0.0001	(0.0001)	−0.0032	(0.0059)
Urban zone × potential work experience (squared)	−7.84E−07	(0.0000)	−1.12E−06	(0.0000)	0.0001	(0.0001)
Urban zone × savings	0.0006	(0.0003)	0.0008	(0.0003)	−0.0535	(0.0255)
Urban zone × schooling attendance rate					0.0006	(0.0005)
Urban zone × seeds usage	−0.0024	(0.0008)	−0.0017	(0.0007)	0.0109	(0.0830)
Urban zone × social networks	−0.0009	(0.0005)	−0.0011	(0.0005)	0.0554	(0.0770)
Urban zone × spells of illness	0.0003	(0.0002)	0.0001	(0.0002)		
Urban zone × Urban zone × inadequate floor	4.02E−05	(0.0000)	3.51E−05	(0.0000)	0.0004	(0.0005)
Urban zone × working children	2.04E−05	(0.0000)	1.62E−05	(0.0000)	−0.0989	(0.0863)
Number of observations	4,949		4,949		3,623	
R^2	0.7546		0.7612		0.8596	

Notes: Standard deviation in parentheses. [a] Based on 1985–6 LSMS. [b] Based on 1994 LSMS.
Source: Authors' calculations based on LSMS 1985/6 and 1994.

Appendix III: Results of Spatial Autocorrelation at the Province Level

Table 5.A2. *Spatial correction at province level*

Variables	Moran Index	z-value	Geary Index	z-value
South latitude	0.9302	20.21*	0.057	−18.76*
North longitude	0.8870	19.27*	0.093	−18.04*
Precipitation	0.7573	16.47*	0.259	−14.73*

Table 5.A2. (*Continued*)

Variables	Moran Index	z-value	Geary Index	z-value
Hh size 1993	0.7495	16.30*	0.241	−15.10*
Temperature (average)	0.7486	16.29*	0.256	−14.79*
Temperature (min.)	0.7469	16.25*	0.255	−14.83*
Temperature (max.)	0.7422	16.15*	0.265	−14.62*
Altitude of district capital (metres above sea level)	0.6693	14.57*	0.322	−13.47*
% female-headed hh 1993	0.6560	14.28*	0.325	−13.43*
Inadequate floor	0.6518	14.19*	0.339	−13.16*
Soil depth	0.6422	13.99*	0.328	−13.37*
Total illiteracy rate 1981	0.6352	13.83*	0.356	−12.82*
Overcrowded houses 1993	0.6286	13.69*	0.339	−13.15*
Hh size 1981	0.6130	13.35*	0.377	−12.39*
Per capita expenditure in 1981	0.6084	13.26*	0.399	−11.95*
Perimeter of the province	0.6032	13.14*	0.390	−12.12*
Female illiteracy rate 1993	0.6030	13.14*	0.389	−12.16*
Igneous rocks	0.5994	13.06*	0.389	−12.14*
Total illiteracy rate 1993	0.5977	13.02*	0.397	−11.99*
Female illiteracy rate 1981	0.5948	12.96*	0.386	−12.20*
Malnutrition rate 1993	0.5871	12.80*	0.389	−12.14*
Schooling years 1993	0.5833	12.71*	0.396	−12.02*
Potential bioclimate score	0.5798	12.64*	0.412	−11.68*
Forestry land potential score	0.5798	12.64*	0.425	−11.43*
% urban population in 1993	0.5781	12.60*	0.437	−11.19*
Soil slope	0.5750	12.53*	0.395	−12.02*
Population 1993	0.5740	12.51*	0.440	−11.13*
Forestry potential bioclimate score	0.5738	12.51*	0.432	−11.30*
Natural resources score	0.5721	12.47*	0.413	−11.67*
Total area of the province	0.5712	12.45*	0.351	−12.91*
Living standard 1993 according to FONCODES	0.5609	12.23*	0.436	−11.22*
% hh without electric appliances 1993	0.5577	12.16*	0.426	−11.41*
Male illiteracy rate 1993	0.5558	12.12*	0.441	−11.12*
Rural basic needs: hh head with low schooling 1993	0.5536	12.07*	0.419	−11.55*
Number of rooms per house 1993	0.5521	12.04*	0.424	−11.45*
Urban basic needs: hh head with low schooling 1993	0.5392	11.76*	0.464	−10.66*
Urban basic needs: inadequate housing 1993	0.5382	11.74*	0.450	−10.95*
FONCODES poverty index 1996	0.5372	11.72*	0.459	−10.75*
Total illiteracy rate 1972	0.5352	11.68*	0.453	−10.87*
Total land potential score	0.5344	11.66*	0.447	−11.01*

Table 5.A2. (*Continued*)

Variables	Moran Index	z-value	Geary Index	z-value
Change per capita expenditure 1981–93	0.5267	11.49*	0.462	−10.71*
Per capita expenditure in 1993	0.5265	11.49*	0.457	−10.81*
Hh size 1972	0.5183	11.31*	0.471	−10.52*
School attendance 1993	0.5074	11.07*	0.475	−10.44*
Child mortality rate 1993	0.5070	11.07*	0.481	−10.31*
Rate of migration 1988–93	0.5056	11.04*	0.514	−9.66*
FONCODES poverty ranking 1996	0.5023	10.96*	0.491	−10.12*
School attendance 1981	0.5004	10.92*	0.481	−10.33*
Elementary school attendance 1981	0.4940	10.78*	0.496	−10.02*
School attendance 1972	0.4861	10.61*	0.493	−10.08*
Agriculture land potential score	0.4833	10.55*	0.490	−10.15*
Agriculture potential bioclimate score	0.4825	10.54*	0.501	−9.93*
Climate II zones	0.4731	10.33*	0.511	−9.72*
Unsatisfied basic needs	0.4590	10.03*	0.546	−9.02*
Cattle potential bioclimate score	0.4446	9.72*	0.539	−9.17*
Per capita expenditure in 1972	0.4399	9.62*	0.608	−7.80*
% hh without electric appliances 1972	0.4398	9.61*	0.548	−9.00*
Access to drinking water 1993	0.4376	9.57*	0.558	−8.79*
Earthquake zone	0.4306	9.42*	0.558	−8.79*
Metamorphic rocks	0.4221	9.23*	0.564	−8.66*
Change in female-headed hh 1972–93	0.4214	9.22*	0.596	−8.04*
Climate I zones	0.4173	9.13*	0.583	−8.30*
% of child workers 1981	0.4124	9.02*	0.571	−8.53*
Total fallow crop land	0.4111	8.99*	0.639	−7.18*
Access to electricity 1993	0.4081	8.93*	0.584	−8.28*
Change in illiteracy rate 1972–93	0.3858	8.45*	0.640	−7.16*
School attendance 1972–93	0.3857	8.44*	0.614	−7.67*
Cattle land potential score	0.3842	8.41*	0.614	−7.67*
Change in illiteracy rate 1972–81	0.3814	8.35*	0.614	−7.68*
Access to electricity 1981	0.3812	8.35*	0.600	−7.95*
Access to sanitation services 1993	0.3811	8.35*	0.608	−7.79*
Types of natural resources	0.3804	8.33*	0.615	−7.65*
Change in per capita expenditure 1972–81	0.3762	8.24*	0.619	−7.59*
% of rural population 1993	0.3643	7.98*	0.658	−6.80*
Access to sanitation services 1981	0.3577	7.84*	0.625	−7.46*
% of permanent crops for own consumption	0.3540	7.76*	0.635	−7.26*

Table 5.A2. (*Continued*)

Variables	Moran Index	z-value	Geary Index	z-value
Access to drinking water 1981	0.3505	7.68*	0.622	−7.51*
Rural population 1993	0.3501	7.68*	0.658	−6.79*
Change in female illiteracy rate 1972–93	0.3486	7.65*	0.675	−6.47*
School attendance 1981–93	0.3329	7.31*	0.643	−7.11*
Non-irrigated land for temporal crops	0.3327	7.30*	0.663	−6.70*
Total fallow land	0.3285	7.21*	0.731	−5.34*
Economically active population without profession 1993	0.3281	7.20*	0.674	−6.48*
Total temporal irrigated land	0.3241	7.11*	0.680	−6.36*
% female-headed hh 1972	0.3238	7.11*	0.669	−6.59*
Annual per capita income 1981	0.3234	7.10*	0.655	−6.86*
Inadequate ceiling 1993	0.3173	6.97*	0.665	−6.67*
Total grassland	0.3148	6.91*	0.742	−5.13*
% of working children 1993	0.3050	6.70*	0.639	−7.18*
Temporal crops sold in farm	0.2984	6.56*	0.683	−6.30*
Number of medics 1993	0.2895	6.37*	0.730	−5.38*
Number of rural houses 1993	0.2883	6.34*	0.722	−5.53*
Total agricultural land	0.2880	6.34*	0.728	−5.41*
Total used land crop	0.2784	6.13*	0.718	−5.61*
Change in access to drinking water 1981–93	0.2755	6.07*	0.717	−5.63*
Total agrarian units	0.2751	6.06*	0.731	−5.36*
Change in access to sanitation services 1972 93	0.2713	5.97*	0.790	−4.17*
Change in hh size 1981–93	0.2700	5.95*	0.695	−6.06*
Change in access to drinking water 1972–93	0.2698	5.94*	0.781	−4.35*
Change in access to sanitation services 1981–93	0.2691	5.93*	0.723	−5.51*
Number of rural towns	0.2685	5.91*	0.786	−4.26*
Land of crops sold in farm	0.2677	5.90*	0.704	−5.88*
Inadequate ceiling 1981	0.2643	5.82*	0.727	−5.43*
Total harvested land	0.2639	5.81*	0.737	−5.22*
Temporal crops for own consumption	0.2622	5.78*	0.790	−4.18*
Hospital beds per 1,000 inhabitants 1981	0.2600	5.73*	0.751	−4.95*
Change in non-durable goods 1972–93	0.2557	5.64*	0.799	−4.00*
Change in women illiteracy rate 1981–93	0.2514	5.54*	0.788	−4.21*

Table 5.A2. (*Continued*)

Variables	Moran Index	z-value	Geary Index	z-value
Economically active population without profession 1981–93	0.2491	5.50*	0.711	−5.75*
Change in per capita expenditure 1972–93	0.2460	5.43*	0.731	−5.35*
Change in child workers 1981–93	0.2443	5.39*	0.716	−5.65*
Change in access to drinking water 1981–93	0.2325	5.14*	0.807	−3.84*
Land for sale	0.2313	5.11*	0.712	−5.72*
Change in child workers 1981–93	0.2306	5.10*	0.754	−4.90*
Change in hh size	0.2271	5.02*	0.750	−4.96*
Number of towns	0.2254	4.98*	0.869	−2.60*
Temporal crops sold in market	0.2184	4.83*	0.766	−4.65*
Change in access to electricity 1972–81	0.2110	4.67*	0.844	−3.10*
Permanent crop land	0.2095	4.64*	0.844	−3.09*
Change in female illiteracy rate 1972–81	0.2032	4.50*	0.818	−3.62*
% child workers 1972	0.2016	4.47*	0.794	−4.09*
Access to drinking water 1972	0.2006	4.45*	0.793	−4.11*
Access to electricity 1972	0.1955	4.34*	0.797	−4.03*
Change in school attendance 1972–81	0.1938	4.30*	0.806	−3.86*
Land used for own crops/production	0.1920	4.26*	0.878	−2.44~
Total no. agricultural land	0.1872	4.16*	0.828	−3.42*
Population with college education	0.1817	4.04*	0.835	−3.27*
Total land	0.1763	3.92*	0.837	−3.24*
Total land used	0.1711	3.81*	0.807	−3.84*
Change in access to sanitation services 1981–72	0.1709	3.81*	0.941	−1.18
Permanent crops sold in market	0.1659	3.70*	0.858	−2.82*
Permanent crops sold in farm	0.1650	3.68*	0.948	−1.03
Inadequate ceiling 1972–93	0.1620	3.61*	0.856	−2.87*
Change in access to electricity 1972–93	0.1612	3.60*	0.897	−2.05~
Economically active population without profession 1981	0.1556	3.47*	0.812	−3.73*
Hospital beds per 1,000 inhabitants 1993	0.1447	3.24*	0.870	−2.59*
% change working children 1972–81	0.1434	3.21*	0.862	−2.75*
Number of urban towns	0.1153	2.60*	1.256	5.09*
Urban population 1993	0.1127	2.55~	1.282	5.61*
Urban houses 1993	0.1122	2.54~	1.285	5.66*

Table 5.A2. (*Continued*)

Variables	Moran Index	z-value	Geary Index	z-value
Total houses 1993	0.1020	2.32~	1.291	5.78*
Total occupied houses 1993	0.1016	2.31~	1.291	5.79*
Rural town density 1993	0.0999	2.27~	0.864	−2.71*
Access to sanitation services 1972	0.0786	1.81	0.921	−1.56
Change in access to drinking water 1972–81	0.0624	1.46	1.029	0.58
Change in illiteracy rate 1981–93	−0.0688	−1.37	1.060	1.20
Rural house density 1993	0.0554	1.31	0.900	−1.98~
Hospital beds 1993	0.0395	0.97	0.933	−1.34
Temporal crops used as seeds	0.0383	0.94	0.912	−1.74
Rural population density 1993	0.0309	0.78	0.934	−1.32
Land whose main output was used as seeds	0.0281	0.72	0.918	−1.63
Change in hh size 1972–81	0.0188	0.52	0.988	−0.24
Forest land	0.0157	0.45	1.081	1.61
Permanent crop with main output used as seed	0.0036	0.19	1.026	0.51
Towns density 1993	0.0019	0.16	0.870	−2.58~
Urban towns density 1993	−0.0106	−0.12	0.825	−3.49*
Houses density 1993	−0.0094	−0.09	0.818	−3.62*
Population density 1993	−0.0093	−0.09	0.818	−3.61*
Vegetation zones typology	−0.0020	0.07	0.796	−4.06*
Urban houses density 1993	−0.0081	−0.06	0.817	−3.63*
Urban population density 1993	−0.0070	−0.04	0.816	−3.66*

Notes: $* = p < 0.01$, $\sim = p < 0.5$, where p is the probability to reject null hypothesis (absence of spatial autocorrelation); hh refers to households.

Source: Authors' calculation based on National Census of Populations 1972, 1981, and 1993.

Appendix IV: Alternative Methods for Correcting for Spatial Autocorrelation

Table 5.A3. *Comparing methods—determinants of per capita expenditure growth rates 1972–93 (OLS estimations with robust standard errors, at province level)*

Variables at initial period	Models		
	(1)	(2)	(3)
Intercept	−0.0277 (1.385)	−1.2303 (7.537)	−0.3270 (1.706)
Altitude	0.2616 (0.385)	0.1863 (0.171)	0.4580 (0.389)
Latitude	−0.0231 (0.019)	−0.0815 (0.083)	−0.0170 (0.019)
Longitude	−0.0182 (0.015)	−0.0788 (0.068)	−0.0171 (0.015)

Table 5.A3. (*Continued*)

Variables at initial period	Models		
	(1)	(2)	(3)
Soil slope	0.0033 (0.002)	0.0154 (0.010)	0.0035 (0.002)
Soil depth	0.002 (0.002)	0.0102 (0.010)	0.0023 (0.002)
Igneous rock	−0.3197* (0.100)	−1.2763* (0.463)	−0.2757* (0.106)
Metamorphic rock	−0.1318 (0.122)	−0.6157 (0.540)	−0.1362 (0.122)
Temperature	−0.0114 (0.009)	−0.0382 (0.039)	−0.0082 (0.009)
Basic needs	−0.0222 (0.017)	−0.1029 (0.073)	−0.0225 (0.016)
High × basic needs	0.0045 (0.090)	−0.0347 (0.358)	−0.0149 (0.080)
School attendance rate	0.0143* (0.003)	0.0649* (0.014)	0.0144* (0.003)
Female-headed households (%)	−0.0109~ (0.005)	−0.0574~ (0.024)	−0.0134~ (0.005)
Working children (%)	0.0533* (0.020)	0.2151* (0.082)	0.0462~ (0.018)
Household size	0.0783 (0.133)	0.4608 (0.573)	0.1057 (0.128)
Household size growth[a]	−0.2624 (0.140)	−1.0146 (0.606)	−0.2208 (0.136)
Number of migrants	0.0171 (0.029)	0.0588 (0.128)	0.0101 (0.029)
Spatial autocorrelation		0.1702* (0.000)	0.2305~ (0.102)
Number of observations	190	190	190
Adjusted R^2	0.486	0.528	0.526

Notes: Standard deviation in parentheses and *= $p < 0.01$, ~= $p < 0.5$. [a]Instrumental variables are shown in the Appendix. Model 1: Geography+infrastructure+geography×infrastructure+private assets. Model 2: Geography + infrastructure + geography × infrastructure + private assets, modelling first-order spatial error autocorrelation (GMM). Model 3: Geography+infrastructure+geography×infrastructure+private assets, modelling first-order spatial error autocorrelation (ML).

Source: Author's calculation based on Population and House Census 1972 and 1993.

DATA SOURCES

At household level

• LSMS 1985–6 and 1994, Cuanto Institute.

At province level

• Population and Household Censuses 1972, 1981, and 1994, Instituto Nacional de Estadística e Informática: population and household characteristics.
• Third National Agrarian Census 1994, Instituto Nacional de Estadística e Informática: agricultural variables, cattle, and land.
• Basic Needs Map 1994. Instituto Nacional de Estadística e Informática: basic needs and health variables.
• Social Investment Map 1994, FONCODES: poverty index and its components, living standard.

Geographic variables

- Arc data online at: www.esri.com/data/online/esri/wothphysic.html. This information was afterwards overlaid on a map of Peru at provincial and district levels. The score for each province or district was selected according to the position of its centroid on the thematic map: earthquake zones, precipitation, soils, and vegetation.
- Natural Resources in Peru 1995, Instituto Nacional de Recursos Naturales: bioclimate and land potential scores.
- Social Investment Map 1994, FONCODES: altitude and geographic location.

REFERENCES

Anselin, L. (1988). *Spatial Econometrics: Methods and Models*, Kluwer Academic Publishers: Amsterdam.

—— (1995). 'Local Indicators of Spatial Association-LISA', *Geographical Analysis*, 27(2): 93–115.

——, A. Varga, and Z. Acs (1996). 'Local Geographic Spillovers Between University Research and High Technology Innovations: A Spatial Econometric Approach', *Regional Institute and Department of Economics Research Papers* 9606, West Virginia University: Morgantown, WV.

Bloom, D. E. and J. Sachs (1998). *Geography, Demography, and Economic Growth in Africa*, Harvard Institute for International Development, Harvard University: Cambridge, MA.

Case, A. C. (1992). 'Neighbourhood Influence and Technological Change', *Regional Science and Urban Economics*, 22: 491–508.

Cliff, A. D. and J. K. Ord (1972). 'Testing for Spatial Autocorrelation Among Regression Residuals', *Geographical Analysis*, 4: 267–84.

—— and —— (1981). *Spatial Processes*, Pion: London.

Eichengreen, B. (1998). 'Geography as Destiny: A Brief History of Economic Growth', *Foreign Affairs*, 77(2): 128–33.

Engerman, S. L. and K. L. Sokoloff (1997). 'Factor Endowments, Institutions, and Differential Paths of Growth among New World Economies: A View from Economic Historians of the United States', in S. Haber (ed.) *How Latin America Fell Behind*, Stanford University Press: Palo Alto, CA.

Escobal, J. and M. Torero (2000). 'Does Geography Explain Differences in Economic Growth in Peru?', *IDB Research Network Working Papers* 404, Inter-American Development Bank: Washington DC.

——, J. Saavedra, and M. Torero (1998). 'Los Activos de los Pobres en el Perú' (mimeo), report presented to IDB Research Network.

——, M. Torero, and C. Ponce (2001). 'Focalización Geográfica del Gasto Social: Mapas de Pobreza', Red CIES de Pobreza, GRADE-APOYO, Informe Final. Available at www.grade/

Friedman, M. (1992). 'Communication: Do Old Fallacies Ever Die?', *Journal of Economic Literature*, 30(December): 2129–32.

FONCODES (1995). *El Mapa de la Inversión Social: FONCODES frente a la Pobreza 1991–94*, UNICEF: Lima.

Gallup, J. L., J. Sachs, and A. D. Mellinger (1998). *Geography and Economic Development*, Harvard Institute for International Development, Harvard University: Cambridge, MA.

Getis, A. and K. Ord (1992). 'The Analysis of Spatial Association by Use of Distance Statistics', *Geographical Analysis*, 24: 189–206.

Hall, R. E. and C. Jones (1997). 'Levels of Economic Activity Across Countries', American Economic Association Annual Meeting, 4–7 January, New Orleans.

—— and —— (1998). 'Why do Some Countries Produce So Much More Output per Worker than Others?' (mimeo), Stanford University: Stanford.

Hentschel, J., J. O. Lanjouw, P. Lanjouw, and J. Poggi (1998). 'Combining Census and Survey Data to Study Spatial Dimensions of Poverty: A Case Study of Ecuador' (mimeo), Poverty Division, World Bank: Washington DC.

Hicks, N. and P. Streeten (1979). 'Indicators of Development: The Search for a Basic Needs Yardstick', *World Development*, 7(6): 567–80.

Hordijk, L. (1974). 'Spatial Correlation in the Disturbance of a Linear Interregional Model', *Regional Science and Urban Economics*, 4: 117–40.

—— and P. Nijkamp (1977). 'Dynamic Models of Spatial Autocorrelation', *Environment and Planning*, 9: 505–19.

—— and J. Paekinck (1976). 'Some Principles and Results in Spatial Econometrics', *Recherches Economiques de Louvain*, 42: 175–97.

Jalan, J. and M. Ravallion (1998). 'Geographic Poverty Traps?', *Institute for Economic Development Discussion Papers* 86, IED, Boston University: Boston.

Moran, P. A. P. (1950). 'Notes on Continuous Stochastic Processes', *Biometrika*, 37: 17–23.

Moreno, R. and B. Trehan (1997). *Location and the Growth of Nations*, Economic Research Department, Federal Reserve Bank of San Francisco: San Francisco, CA.

Peñaherrera, C. (1986). 'El desarrollo de la geografía en el Perú', in E. Yepes (ed.) *Estudios de historia de la ciencia en el Perú*, Ciencias Sociales, Sociedad Peruana de Historia de la Ciencia y la Tecnología: Lima.

Pulgar Vidal, J. (1946). *Geografía del Perú: las ocho regiones naturales*, Décima Edición 1986, Lima Editorial Universo: Lima.

Ravallion, M. and Q. Wodon (1997). 'Poor Areas, Or Only Poor People?', *Policy Research Working Papers* 1798, World Bank. Washington DC.

Streeten, P. (1984). 'Basic Needs: Some Unsettled Questions', *World Development*, 12: 973–82.

World Bank (1999). *Poverty and Social Development in Peru: 1994–7*, World Bank Country Study, World Bank: Washington DC.

6

Market Size, Linkages, and Productivity: A Study of Japanese Regions

DONALD R. DAVIS AND DAVID E. WEINSTEIN

6.1. GEOGRAPHY AND PRODUCTIVITY

A central tenet in both the traditional and new work in economic geography is that space matters. This has found application in urban and regional economics, and in the theory of international trade, as exemplified in the monograph *The Spatial Economy*, by Fujita, Krugman, and Venables (1999). These literatures highlight the extraordinarily uneven geographical distribution of activity across space and take this as a central problem to understand. For example, in this study we will be working with regional data from Japan, across which the density of GDP per square kilometre varies by more than a factor of twenty. Such vast disparities in economic activity across space invite an explanation.

Theory provides a variety of reasons why space may matter. The one on which we will focus in this study is the possibility that space affects productivity. Directly or indirectly, this has been an important focus not only for theoretical work, but also for prior empirical applications. Classic papers in the urban and regional literature—such as Sveikauskas (1975), Henderson (1986), and Glaeser *et al.* (1992)—have contributed to the understanding of this problem. The former two papers sought directly to measure and explain productivity differences across regions within the United States. The last paper implicitly pursued the same objective by trying to explain differential rates of city growth, much of this difference believed to devolve from differential productivity growth.

These papers have been very important in focusing our attention on the magnitude of the regional productivity differences and in identifying candidate explanations. They provide a compelling account that space does indeed matter. In doing so, however, they also point to an important limitation of the studies. Each proposes that productivity or

We have benefitted from excellent research assistance by Paris Cleanthous, William Powers, and Pao-Li Chang. Gordon Hanson graciously provided us with a programme for calculating great arc distances. We gratefully acknowledge support for this project from the National Science Foundation. David Weinstein was at the Federal Reserve Bank at New York while final work was done on this study. The opinions presented here do not necessarily reflect the views of the Board of Governors of the Federal Reserve Bank.

growth within a region depends on the characteristics of that particular region. This is the manner in which space is introduced—own region versus all others. A moment's reflection, however, suggests that this distinction is likely to be too sharp. If real space is to matter, and if it does so for more than purely jurisdictional reasons, then the characteristics of regions that are quite near should likewise matter, not only the region's own characteristics. And proximate regions should likely matter more than remote regions. Thus, an important contribution of the present study will be its examination of cross-regional productivity differences while taking account of the fact that a region's productivity may depend differentially on its access to neighbouring regions.

The approach that we develop builds on prior work of Davis and Weinstein (1999, 2002) and Leamer (1997). While pursuing a different agenda, the former studies provide a strong object lesson in why it is important to introduce greater geographical realism into our empirical work to the extent possible. The Leamer study is more closely related to the present work, considering geographical determinants of cross-country growth patterns. An important advantage of the present study, though, is precisely the fact that our data is from regions within a single country. This eliminates a large number of potentially confounding variables that may differ across countries, but not across regions of a country. This difference may arise, for example, because it is much more likely that firms are the same across regions than across countries, so that the same underlying technology is more likely to be at work across regions. As well, focus on the regions eliminates a host of potential measurement problems introduced by looking at international data.

In considering the influence of space on productivity, there are two separate questions that we might consider. One considers the ultimate source of the productivity differences. For example, do they arise from Marshallian externalities, from access to a greater variety of intermediate inputs, learning from customers, or some other source? While some of our results could make one or another of these more or less plausible, and we will comment on this as appropriate, we think that these are important but difficult questions that deserve precise answers. Unfortunately, they are beyond the scope of this study. The alternative that we pursue in this study is to examine the simpler, but nonetheless important, question of the channels through which space influences productivity. Does own aggregate region size matter? Will it matter when we allow for neighbouring regions to affect your market access? Do these influences work through aggregate economic size, through access to the type of inputs your industries require, or by special access to your customers? Will variables reflecting heterogeneity of production that have been shown to affect city growth matter for productivity, particularly when controlling for these other influences?

It is precisely these questions concerning the channels by which geography and economic space influence productivity that we pursue in this study. We examine this in a sample of forty Japanese regions, utilizing the same data as Davis *et al.* (1997), Davis and Weinstein (1999), and Bernstein and Weinstein (2002). The premise for our study is that cross-regional variation in average productivity will have observable implications for the relation between the national technology, regional output, and regional factor supplies. Since theory provides many accounts, we look to the data to identify which seem most important. The results identify a few robust channels by which space affects productivity. A region's own aggregate size does contribute importantly to productivity, as does good access to the suppliers of inputs that figure importantly in a particular region's production structure. Both a more general 'market potential' variable and a variable reflecting so-called Marshall-Allyn-Romer (MAR) externalities matter when introduced alone, but not when the supplier-access variable is included. We cannot find evidence that good access to consumers of your product raises productivity. The magnitude of the effects we do identify are economically important. Doubling own region size raises productivity by 3.5 per cent. In a counterfactual in which Japanese regions were not allowed to trade with each other, output would fall at least 6.5 per cent.

In sum, our results make four contributions. They confirm earlier work that identifies own region size as mattering for productivity. Second, they allow for a richer conception of the way in which space or geography affects productivity. Third, our use of an excellent regional dataset allows us to avoid numerous confounding problems that might exist with international data. Finally, they allow us to place in contention some of the leading theories about the channels by which space affects productivity.

6.2. TOWARDS EMPIRICAL IMPLEMENTATION

6.2.1. *Study Design*

Our study investigates determinants of regional productivity. The dependent variable 'productivity' will be described below. We relate productivity to a variety of traditional variables as well as introducing new variables that stress the role of demand and cost linkages. A first set of variables consists of various measures of market size. The simplest is 'own-size', which will be represented as the regional labour force. A variety of rationalizations of why this may affect productivity may be offered. One is that local economic activity gives rise to a pure Marshallian externality. A second is that the variety link to productivity developed in the theory section is very general, so that productivity depends on the level of local activity, but not directly on its composition. An alternative to own-size is what Harris (1954) termed 'market potential'. The latter is a more general framework which allows productivity to be affected by a weighted average of GDPs of the region itself as well as its neighbours, where the weights are inverse to bilateral distance. In this sense, the own-size variable is one of market potential where all of the weight is placed on local regional output.

Two new variables may be considered which likewise emphasize issues of market access, but which focus more directly on the linkages between suppliers, users, and final consumers. The variable 'cost linkage' measures the degree of access to sources of precisely the inputs required for that particular region's output. Theory suggests that these structural input–output links between producers and their suppliers should be closely related to regional productivity. One may also consider the structural relation embodied in 'demand linkages'. One interpretation of demand linkages suggests that this may matter greatly for location decisions as producers seek to be near purchasers of their product. However, under this interpretation, there need not be any direct link to productivity. An alternative interpretation, however, might suggest that producers have a great deal to learn from consumers of their product so that strong demand linkages may also be a source of productivity advantage.

We will also consider two variables which have figured prominently in previous studies. The first is a measure of regional specialization. Glaeser *et al.* (1992) examined the role of MAR versus Jacobs externalities in city growth. In their schema, the MAR view posits that learning should be greater where there is a concentrated output structure, whereas Jacobs emphasized potential benefits of a diverse production structure. Glaeser *et al.* found evidence which they interpreted as favourable to the MAR view. Our study differs from theirs in that it considers the level of productivity rather than city growth. However, if productivity gains are believed to be the source of the differential city growth, then we should be able to find some evidence of this in the resulting productivity levels.

6.2.2. *Data Construction*

In this section we provide an overview of the data used in the study. Details on the construction of variables are in the appendix to Davis and Weinstein (1999). Our dataset contains output, investment, consumption, government expenditure, endowment, and absorption data for the forty-seven prefectures/cities of Japan. We form two aggregates: 'Kanto', out of the city of Tokyo and the prefectures of Ibaraki, Kanagawa, Chiba, and Saitama; and 'Kinki', out of the prefectures/cities of Hyogo, Kyoto, Nara, and Osaka.[1] This reduces our sample to forty observations, but reflects the high level of integration of the prefectures surrounding Tokyo and Osaka. Our distance data is derived from the Kei/Ido Ichiran Database, which provides longitude and latitude data for Japanese cities, allowing calculation of the great arc distance between points.

Define X_r as the $N \times 1$ gross output vector for region r, and [1] as an $N \times 1$ vector of ones. Let AX_r, C_r, I_r, and G_r be prefectural intermediate input demand, consumption, investment, and government expenditure vectors. Construction of these variables is described in more detail in Davis and Weinstein (1999). Define X_r^{TRAD} to be equal to X_r for all manufacturing, agricultural, and mining sectors and zero otherwise. Finally, we set $\text{DIST}_{rr'}$ equal to the distance between the prefectural capital cities when $r \neq r'$ and equal to the square root of the area of the prefecture divided by π otherwise.

We now turn to the construction of our key variables. We begin with the measure of productivity, which will be the dependent variable in our study. Previous studies, such as Sveikauskas (1975), Henderson (1986), and others, have looked at productivity

---

[1] The astute reader will realize that our definitions of Kanto and Kinki do not correspond exactly to the official definitions. The official definitions of these two regions contain several prefectures that are relatively far away from the centres of economic activity in the Tokyo and Osaka area. We therefore decided to use the aggregation described in the text.

differences by estimating regional production functions for particular industries. The standard approach involves either calculating TFP using index numbers or estimating a regional production function. One of the problems with this approach is that it is impossible to identify demand and cost linkages using a production function approach because one needs to have information about the regional availability of inputs and absorption of output. Such information is available if one turns to input–output data. In this study, we will measure factor productivity using the matrix of direct factor input requirements. Our measure of regional productivity of factor f is π_{rf} where we arbitrarily set the productivity of each factor for Japan as a whole equal to unity. For each region and factor, the following condition must hold:

$$B_f X_r \equiv \pi_{rf} V_{rf}.$$

Note here that B_f is the Japanese average input requirement, so unlike the other variables is not specific to region r. Hence, we define productivity in region r of factor f as

$$\pi_{rf} \equiv \frac{B_f X_r}{V_{rf}}.$$

We now turn to specification of our independent variables. Our own-size variable will measure aggregate regional size, and will be implemented alternatively as the regional labour force or regional GDP. An alternative measure of a region's size takes account of its proximity to other regions. Following Harris (1954), we define market potential for region r as

$$MP_r \equiv \sum_{r'} \frac{GDP_{r'}}{DIST_{rr'}}.$$

In this definition, as well as in all of our subsequent definitions of variables involving distance, we assume that a 1 per cent increase in distance causes the impact of output of demand to fall by 1 per cent. This choice is based on the typical coefficient obtained in gravity model using both regional and international data.[2] When we say that a region has strong cost linkages, we mean that it has excellent access within the region and in neighbouring regions to the investment goods and intermediate inputs used intensively by that region's producers. An empirical implementation of this concept defines cost linkage as follows:

$$COST_r = \sum_{r'} \sum_{i \in TRAD} \frac{m_{ir}}{m_r} \frac{X_{ir'}}{DIST_{rr'}},$$

where X_{ir} is output of industry i in region r, m_{ir} is industry i's use as in intermediate input by region r, and m_r is total intermediate input use in r. This variable is an input-weighted average of production across all of Japan. Hence, cost linkages are strong when the producers of our inputs are large and proximate. We sum up the intermediate input usage over all tradables (TRAD), which we define to be agriculture, mining, and

---

[2] Polenske (1970) verified that the gravity model fits Japanese regional data quite well.

manufacturing industries. This definition only allows cost linkages to occur through tradable goods sectors. The decision to focus on traded goods output was based on the Bernstein and Weinstein (2002) finding that services sectors behave as if they are non-traded in Japan.

In addition to these core variables, we define a number of other variables that have been used in previous studies. Glaeser *et al.* (1992) test for the existence of MAR or Jacobs externalities using an index of specialization based on the concentration of employment in particular industries. We will also allow for these factors by following their definition but will use output instead of employment as our measure of concentration. Let s_{ir} be the share of Japanese industry i in region r. Our measure of specialization is

$$\text{SPECIALIZATION}_r = \frac{1}{s_r^2}\left(\frac{1}{I}\sum_{i=1}^{I}s_{ir}^2\right).$$

The term in parentheses is like a Herfindahl index that would equal the square of the region's share of Japanese output if the share of output for each industry within a region equalled the region's GDP share, that is, $s_{ir} = s_{jr} = s_r$. We therefore divide this index by the square of the region's GDP to obtain an index that is independent of region size. This provides us with an index that is increasing in specialization, but independent of region size. Finally, we also define a variable that can capture demand linkages. We set demand linkage to be

$$\text{DEMAND}_r = \sum_{r'}\sum_{i\in\text{TRAD}}\frac{X_{ir}}{X_r}\frac{m_{ir'}}{\text{DIST}_{rr'}}.$$

Our demand linkage variable gives us an output-weighted average of demand across regions. Paralleling our cost linkage variable, our demand linkage variable is large when the demanders of our tradable goods are large and close. Table 6.1 presents sample statistics for all of our variables.[3] There are a number of points that are worth noticing. First, the average deviation in productivity across prefectures is not necessarily zero because small prefectures may have higher or lower factor productivity than large prefectures. This explains why the average deviation is negative for both labour factors and positive for capital. Second, there appears to be more variation in labour productivity than in capital productivity. This may reflect the relatively high degree of capital mobility across Japan. Third, all of our geographic market variables—market potential, cost linkage, and demand linkage—are highly correlated. This makes it difficult, though not impossible, to separate the effects of these variables.

6.2.3. *Estimation Issues*

When we move to a multifactor, multigood, multidistance world, analytic solutions become infeasible. Therefore, we need to abstract to some degree from the theory in

---

[3] We normalized our cost and demand linkage variables to sum to one.

Table 6.1. *Sample statistics*

Variable	Mean	S.d.	Minimum	Maximum
Productivity of non-college	−0.128	0.134	−0.341	0.206
Productivity of college	0.055	0.137	−0.298	0.379
Productivity of capital	−0.020	0.086	−0.172	0.164
Market potential	0.025	0.011	0.007	0.049
Demand linkage	0.025	0.010	0.009	0.051
Cost linkage	0.025	0.013	0.005	0.064
ln(labour force)	14.001	0.800	12.983	16.916
Specialization	2.024	1.059	0.828	5.390

Correlation matrix

	NON-COLL	COLL	CAP	MP	DEM	COST	ln(LF)	SPEC
Productivity of non-college	1.000							
Productivity of college	0.214	1.000						
Productivity of capital	0.374	0.285	1.000					
Market potential	0.607	0.167	0.324	1.000				
Demand linkage	0.648	0.170	0.377	0.970	1.000			
Cost linkage	0.658	0.261	0.395	0.956	0.976	1.000		
ln(labour force)	0.679	0.155	0.251	0.328	0.358	0.352	1.000	
Specialization	0.089	0.125	0.174	0.399	0.308	0.327	−0.230	1.000

Source: See text.

the implementation, while hoping to capture its salient insights. Using our definition of productivity, we can estimate the effects of cost linkages, demand linkages, and market potential on productivity through variants of the following equation:

$$\pi_{rf} = \alpha_f + \beta_{1f}MP_r + \beta_{2f}\ln(GDP)_r + \beta_{3f}COST_r + \varepsilon_{rf}. \qquad (6.1)$$

This gives us one equation for each factor or three equations in total. There are a number of simple estimation issues we need to address. First, the ε_{rf}'s are likely to be correlated across factors since neutral technical differences will affect all factors equally. This suggests that we should not assume that corr(ε_{rf}, $\varepsilon_{rf'}$) equals zero. We solve this by treating our equations as a system of seemingly unrelated regressions. Second, it is unlikely that the impact of market size variables should differ across factors. Rather it seems more reasonable that the economic geography variables should have common effects for all factors. We can impose this on the data by forcing $\beta_{if} = \beta_{if'}$ for each factor. Finally, we are likely to measure average productivity more accurately in larger regions than in smaller regions because mismeasurement of output and endowments is likely to fall. We therefore weight all observations by the square root of the regional labour force before estimation.

The fact that our productivity and linkage measures are both based on a region's gross output potentially introduces a simultaneity bias that makes a standard seemingly unrelated regressions procedure inappropriate. If output-per-factor is high in a prefecture then output in that prefecture may be high as well. This will tend to cause the cost and demand linkage variables to rise, creating a simultaneity bias. In order to deal with this problem, we first construct instrumental variables for COST and DEM. For COST, the instrumental variable is defined as

$$\text{COST}_r = \sum_{r'} \sum_{i \in \text{TRAD}} \frac{m_{ir}}{m_r} \frac{\hat{X}_{ir'}}{\text{DIST}_{rr'}},$$

where $\hat{X}_{r'} = X_{r'}$ when $r \neq r'$ and X_{Japan} times that region's share of Japanese labour otherwise. We define a similar instrument for DEM. These instruments are highly correlated with the linkage variables because all of the data from other prefectures is the same, however they should be uncorrelated with productivity in the prefecture. We then estimated the entire system of equations using three-stage least squares.

6.3. DATA PREVIEW AND RESULTS

6.3.1. *Data Preview*

Before proceeding to a formal data analysis, it will prove useful to preview certain features of the data. A first issue worth addressing is the level of aggregation used in the analysis. A check on this comes in the form of Zipf's law, an extremely robust feature of national datasets. Zipf's law holds that the log of city population will fall one-for-one with the log of the rank of that city's population among all cities. Here we use regional data, and so it is natural to wonder whether this relationship holds for our dataset as well. Figure 6.1 examines this for our Japanese regions. As the plot reveals, this relationship holds almost exactly for Japanese prefectures under our aggregation scheme. The slope coefficient is −0.951.[4] This reflects the fact that the size distribution of regions is quite skewed. The largest region, Kanto, is about seventy-seven times

---

[4] Zipf's law is typically applied to cities and not regions. However, in much of the theoretical literature (cf. the recent work of Gabaix), the theory is developed for regions within a country and not cities per se. Similarly, in Davis and Weinstein (2002), we demonstrate that Zipf's law can be applied to regional data.

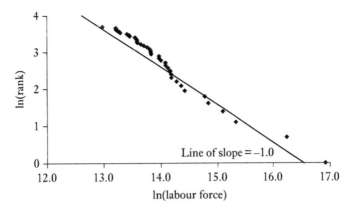

Figure 6.1. *Zipf's law*

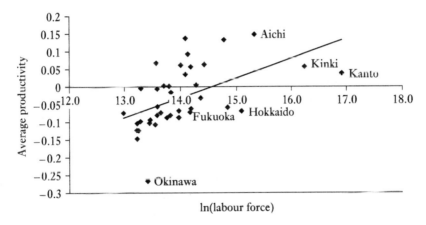

Figure 6.2. *Productivity and home market size*

larger than the smallest region, Tottori. The three largest regions—containing the cities of Tokyo, Yokohama, Osaka, and Nagoya—produce nearly half of Japanese GDP.

Japanese region size seems also to be positively correlated with our measure of productivity. In Fig. 6.2, we plot the average factor productivity in a region against region size. These variables are clearly positively related. Doubling region size is associated with productivity rising by about 5 per cent. This positive relationship between region size and productivity has been confirmed econometrically in a large number of previous studies (e.g. Sveikauskas (1975) and others).

Average productivity of Japanese regions ranges from 27 per cent below the national average in Okinawa, to as much as 15 per cent above the national average in Aichi. These extreme points are quite suggestive of the role that geography may play in regional productivity. Okinawa is not the smallest Japanese prefecture, indeed it is

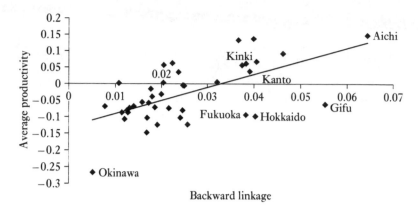

Figure 6.3. *Productivity and backward linkages*

not even in the smallest decile, but it is by far the most remote prefecture, situated about 50,000 miles southwest of the Japanese archipelago. Shimane prefecture, a more centrally located prefecture with a similar population, has a productivity gap that is only half that of Okinawa's. This is suggestive of the possibility that Okinawa may be at a disadvantage because of its distance from the mainland. Hokkaido and Fukuoka are also significant outliers. Despite being the fourth and fifth largest prefectures in Japan in terms of labour force, their productivity is significantly below average. Both of these prefectures are located off the main Japanese island at the northern and western extremes and are therefore quite remote from other sources of supply. At the other extreme is Aichi, which has the highest productivity in all of Japan. Aichi contains the moderately sized city of Nagoya and is only one-fifth the size of Kanto and less than one half the size of Kinki. However, situated almost equidistantly between the two largest Japanese regions on the major Japanese rail lines and highways, producers in Aichi have easy access to goods produced in either of these large regions.

This anecdotal evidence suggests that we also explore how market access affects productivity. In Fig. 6.3, we plot productivity against our cost linkage variable. Allowing remoteness to matter, we now find that the most productive prefecture, Aichi, has the strongest cost linkages, and the least productive prefecture, Okinawa, has the weakest. The only really troubling point in this plot is Gifu, the second point from the right. Gifu appears to have substantial market access but low productivity. One reason for this is that Gifu's population is 25 per cent below that of the average region. A second reason is that Gifu's excellent market access is an artefact of the way we construct the cost linkage variable. For almost all prefectures, the capital city lies in the centre of the prefecture. Gifu, however, lies just above Aichi, and since the city of Gifu is only about 20 km from Nagoya, in our data Gifu is closer to Aichi than it is to itself! That is, our measure overstates the strength of Gifu's market access. We could have aggregated Gifu with Aichi or recalculated the cost linkage variable to improve the fit, but we preferred not to change our data construction method in order to eliminate outliers.

Table 6.2. *Determinants of regional productivity*

	1	2	3	4	5	6
ln(labour force)	0.043		0.035		0.028	0.045
	(0.007)		(0.006)		(0.008)	(0.009)
Cost linkage		3.830	3.576			7.933
		(0.568)	(0.558)			(2.147)
Market potential				4.907	4.360	−6.063
				(0.721)	(0.922)	(2.922)
N	120	120	120	120	120	120

Note: Dependent variable is regional factor productivity. Standard errors below estimates.
Source: See text.

6.3.2. *Results*

Table 6.2 presents the results from estimating eqn (6.1). As is suggested by Figs 6.2 and 6.3, there is a strong positive relationship between region size and productivity as well as between region market access and productivity. This relationship is present regardless of whether the variables are considered separately or together. Our estimates indicate that a doubling of region size is associated with a productivity increase of about 3.5 per cent. This we attribute to a pure Marshallian externality and the tendency of factors to locate in more productive regions.

Of more interest is the role played by market access. For example, consider Okinawa. Okinawa has a population that is 10 per cent larger than Yamanashi (located adjacent to Tokyo), but while Yamanashi's level of productivity is almost exactly average, Okinawa's productivity level is 27 per cent below average. Our estimates indicate that 10 percentage points of the gap between the two prefectures is due to the greater distance between Okinawa and the mainland. Similarly, Shizuoka prefecture, located just west of Kanto, has a slightly smaller population than Hokkaido, but significantly better market access to Kanto, Kinki, and Aichi. Our estimates suggest over half of the 19 per cent productivity gap between Hokkaido and Shizuoka is due to the latter's advantage in market access. These examples suggest that market access plays an important role in Japanese productivity even after controlling for size.

The economic significance of market access can be assessed by considering a number of thought experiments. For example, suppose that all Japanese prefectures were banned from trading with each other. We can model this by rebuilding the cost linkage variable with zero-weights applied to the outputs of all other prefectures. Our estimates indicate that this would cause Japanese GNP to fall by 6.7 per cent. Of course this is simply a 'first round' effect. The full general equilibrium effect could be smaller or larger depending on what assumptions one made about the movement of factors and the impact on demand. Even so, our estimates indicate that trade within Japan has a significant impact on Japanese welfare.

We can also obtain some sense of the role played by agglomeration in Japan. Agglomeration enters into our estimation through two routes. First, not all regions are the same size, and second, large regions are often close to each other. We can see how important agglomeration is by considering the following counterfactual. Suppose that all Japanese workers were evenly distributed across Japan so that the population density of every prefecture was the same. This would change each prefecture's aggregate labour force as well as its linkages. Prefectures near Kanto would tend to see their linkages worsen while those in the hinterland would benefit. We model what happens to output by assuming that each prefecture's new output vector is equal to Japan's output vector times that region's new share of aggregate employment. Our estimates indicate that Japanese GNP would fall by 5.4 per cent. This suggests that Japan benefits from having large regions close to each other.

6.3.3. *Robustness Tests*

In Table 6.3, we conduct a number of robustness tests. Glaeser *et al.* (1992) include a variable for regional specialization in their growth regressions and find that regions that are less specialized in particular sectors have higher growth rates. They interpret this as evidence in favour of Jacobs' externalities. In the cross-section, one should also expect that specialization should have an impact on productivity. In the first column of Table 6.3, we include a variable that increases with regional specialization. When included with GDP, we obtain a positive coefficient, indicating that on the contrary regions that are more specialized have higher productivity. However, when we control for cost linkages, we find that the specialization variable ceases to be significant; this suggests that specialization is not that important if one controls for market access.

Theory is ambiguous about the role that demand linkages may play in productivity. Clearly in a world with trade costs, it is advantageous for producers to locate near important sources of demand in order to minimize trade costs. However, this need not confer on them any productivity advantage in the link between inputs and outputs. Yet this could arise if excellent access to consumers of your product yields information that allows productivity gains. This suggests adding demand linkages to the horse race over how market size matters. We see in Table 6.1 that demand and cost linkages are highly correlated with each other (as well as market potential), so it will be interesting which

Table 6.3. *Determinants of regional productivity: robustness check of alternative explanations*

	1	2
ln(labour force)	0.057 (0.008)	0.039 (0.009)
Cost linkage		3.338 (0.663)
Specialization	0.032 (0.012)	0.008 (0.011)
N	120	120

Note: Dependent variable is regional factor productivity. Standard errors in parenthesis.

Source: See text.

Table 6.4. *Determinants of regional productivity: robustness check using demand linkages as well as cost linkages*

	1	2	3	4
ln(labour force)	0.035 (0.006)		0.032 (0.007)	0.039 (0.010)
Cost linkage	3.576 (0.558)			8.507 (4.016)
Demand linkage		5.721 (0.747)	5.056 (0.883)	−7.096 (5.767)
N	120	120	120	120

Note: Dependent variable is regional factor productivity. Standard errors in parenthesis.
Source: See text.

the data identifies as key in influencing productivity. As we noted, demand linkages are highly correlated with cost linkages ($\rho = 0.95$), so multicollinearity is likely to be a major problem. As we see in Table 6.4, the addition of the demand linkage variable does increase the standard errors of the coefficient on cost linkages, but the effect that we have identified seems clearly to flow through cost and not through demand linkages. Demand linkages typically have the wrong sign in specifications with cost linkages.

6.4. CONCLUSION

This study investigates the determinants of productivity for forty regions of Japan. We look at traditional determinants, such as own–size and market potential, as well as determinants more strongly linked to the recent literature on economic geography, such as demand and cost linkages. We also consider influences that have figured prominently in recent work, such as the MAR versus Jacobs debate on the role of regional diversity of production.

The most robust relations to productivity come from the own–size and cost linkage variables. Both the MAR externality and market potential variables are significant and the correct sign in the absence of the cost linkage variable. However, they become insignificant or take on the wrong sign when it is included. While one can posit theories under which demand linkages may have a role in productivity, we do not find this in the data.

Our estimates suggest an important link between region size and productivity. *Ceteris paribus*, a doubling of region size is associated with productivity rising by about 3.5 per cent. Cost linkages are also quite economically significant in accounting for differences across regions in productivity. A simple counterfactual, premised on aggregate activity being spread evenly across the regions of Japan, would lower output by around 5 per cent. Clearly, size and geography play important roles in understanding the regional distribution of national welfare. This has implications for international integration too. For example, the European Union has a population that is just over twice that of Japan and most European nations have populations that are smaller than Kanto (approx. 35 million) or Kinki (approx. 17 million). Economic geography suggests that countries located near the major economies are likely to be the major winners from integration. Taken together, these results suggest that there are quite important direct productivity gains associated with the concentration of economic activity in Japan. We must caution, though, that while we can quantify directly the productivity gains, a full consideration of welfare effects would likewise need to quantify costs arising from congestion, which falls beyond the scope of this study.

REFERENCES

Bernstein, J. and D. E. Weinstein (2002). 'Do Endowments Predict the Location of Production? Evidence from National and International Data', *Journal of International Economics*, 56(1): 55–76.

Davis, D. R. and D. E. Weinstein (1999). 'Economic Geography and Regional Production Structure: An Empirical Investigation', *European Economic Review*, 43(2): 379–407.

—— and —— (2002). 'Bones, Bombs, and Break Points: The Geography of Economic Activity', *American Economic Review*, 92(5): 1269–89.

——, ——, S. C. Bradford, and K. Shimpo (1997). 'Using International and Japanese Regional Data to Determine When the Factor Abundance Theory of Trade Works', *American Economic Review*, 87(3): 421–46.

Fujita, M., P. Krugman, and A. Venables (1999). *The Spatial Economy*, MIT Press: Cambridge, MA.

Glaeser, E. L. *et al.* (1992). 'Growth in Cities', *Journal of Political Economy*, 100(6): 1126–52.

Harris, C. (1954). 'The Market as a Factor in the Localization of Industry in the United States', *Annals of the Association of American Geographers*, 64: 315–48.

Henderson, J. V. (1986). 'Efficiency of Resource Usage and City Size', *Journal of Urban Economics*, 19(1): 47–70.

Leamer, E. (1997). *Access to Western Markets, and Eastern Effort Levels*, Kluwer: Boston, MA.

Polenske, K. (1970). 'An Empirical Test of Interregional Input–Output Models: Estimation of 1963 Japanese Production', *American Economic Review*, 60: 76–82.

Sveikauskas, L. A. (1975). 'The Productivity of Cities', *Quarterly Journal of Economics*, 89(3): 393–413.

7

Externalities in Rural Development: Evidence for China

MARTIN RAVALLION

P25 0 18

R 11

R 12

7.1. INTRODUCTION

There is a long-standing view that externalities play an important causal role in economic development. Famously, Rosenstain-Rodan (1943) argued that the investment decisions made by one firm in a developing economy influenced the profitability of others, leading him to argue for international assistance for the industrialization of the lagging regions of Eastern and Southern Europe in the 1940s. More recently, the hypothesis that there are externalities through knowledge spillovers has been built into theoretical models of economic growth (notably Romer 1986; Lucas 1993). In the context of rural development in poor countries, similar ideas have motivated policy arguments that getting one activity going locally stimulates others, in a 'virtuous cycle' of growth; Mellor (1976) provided an influential statement of this hypothesis.[1] Hazell and Haggblade (1993) tested the hypothesis using district- and state-level data for India, and reported seemingly strong effects of agricultural growth on rural non-farm development.[2]

This chapter explores the microempirical foundations of these arguments using household panel data for a developing rural economy. Some stylized facts about the setting will help motivate the subsequent analysis. One such fact is that in a poor rural economy, the income gains that are claimed to stem from linkage will be transmitted

The data used here were kindly provided by China's National Bureau of Statistics, and I am grateful for the assistance and advice provided by NBS staff in Beijing and at various provincial and county offices. For help with setting up the panel dataset I am grateful to Shaohua Chen and Qinghua Zhao and for help with the calculations reported here I am grateful to Jyotsna Jalan. The support of the World Bank's Research Committee and a Dutch Trust Fund is also gratefully acknowledged. For their comments, I am grateful to Vernon Henderson, Jyotsna Jalan, Peter Lanjouw, Forhad Shilpi, Dominique van de Walle, participants and discussants at the WIDER-Cornell-LSE conference on spatial inequality held at the London School of Economics in June 2002, the World Bank and anonymous referees for this work. These are the views of the author, and should not be attributed to the World Bank or any affiliated organization.

[1] Building on Mellor and Lele (1972). Much earlier still, Clarke (1940) had argued that higher agricultural productivity was a crucial precondition for industrialization.

[2] Also see Haggblade et al. (1989, 2002). Lanjouw and Lanjouw (2001) provide a useful review of the arguments and evidence on the rural non-farm sector.

in large part through the farm household economy, which accounts for the bulk of rural economic activity in most developing countries. No doubt, spillover effects will also involve rural-based firms. However, it is plausible in this setting that any external impacts of local economic activity on income growth would be evident at the farm household level. A second stylized fact is that many farm households engage in multiple activities simultaneously, including non-farm activities. Casual observations do not suggest that it is commonly the case that a rural household is fully specialized in either farm or non-farm activities. Indeed, it has been argued that such income diversification is an important strategy by which rural households cope with uninsured risk (see, for example, Ellis 1998). There is a large literature pointing to the problems of incomplete credit and risk markets in underdeveloped rural economies (for an overview see Besley 1995).

It is not implausible that there are externalities in this setting. One way this happens is when farmers learn about new techniques of production from the experience of their neighbours; Feder and Slade (1985) provide survey evidence for northwest India that this is an important channel for knowledge diffusion among farmers. Foster and Rosenzweig (1995) find evidence of this type of learning externality in farm profitability from adopting new seed varieties in India. Network effects in the marketing of agricultural products can also generate externalities: a farmer can benefit from the infrastructure already in place locally. Another possible source of externalities is the presence of local non-farm industries that encourage the acquisition of knowledge and skills that also benefit local farmers or non-farm enterprises at household level, possibly through knowledge sharing within households (Basu et al. 2002). In the case of China, it has been argued that higher output from the non-farm sector has brought external benefits to the traditional farm sector, through improved technologies and management (Sengupta and Lin 1995). Or a higher density of commercial enterprises may enhance the local tax base, allowing better local public goods, and so promoting higher growth for those not actually engaged in those enterprises. Alternatively, negative externalities might result when the expansion of one activity creates congestion, or otherwise crowds out, another activity. This can happen when there are local-level fixed factors of production (including environmental assets) that are shared across activities. For example, with imperfect credit markets leading to rationing of the available credit, an expansion in one activity may crowd out growth prospects in another. With restricted migration and wage stickiness, the same could happen with regard to labour.

If the patterns found in aggregate data reflect such externalities this would provide an important insight into the causal processes creating rural underdevelopment. That depends crucially on whether markets exist for the externalities.[3] That cannot be judged on a priori grounds. However, a complete set of such markets is not inherently plausible for the sorts of externalities discussed above. Knowledge spillovers or network effects do not lend themselves to the excludability properties needed for a market. (It would clearly be difficult to define and enforce property rights for such

---

[3] On the economic theory of markets for externalities, see Dasgupta and Heal (1979: Chapter 3).

externalities.) So there must be a reasonable presumption that private decisionmakers will not typically take account of the external costs and benefits of their allocative decisions and so one will expect to see underinvestment in the activities that generate positive externalities, and overinvestment in those that have negative externalities. The externalities then impede or distort rural development. On the other hand, if the underlying linkage effects are purely internal at the farm household level then their welfare and policy significance is greatly diminished.[4] Given the stylized facts summarized above, the averaging of purely internal effects within diversified farm household units could readily generate the appearance of externalities in economic activity in aggregate data when in fact none exist at the microlevel. For example, given capital market imperfections, higher farm income for a given household may create the resources needed to finance a new non-farm activity. Farm and non-farm incomes may then co-move in a process that one might identify as intersectoral linkage in aggregate data even though there is no genuine externality involved. The causal connection is of course unclear, nor is it obvious that there would be any believable identification strategy.

The concern with geographic externalities goes beyond economic efficiency. It also raises concerns about horizontal equity. In particular, if the microgrowth process involves such externalities then the economy will reward otherwise identical individuals differently depending on where they live. This may also help understand geographic dimensions of social unrest, as has been reported in China in the 1990s.[5] Motivated by these observations, the central question addressed in this chapter is whether the signs of linkage among economic activities found in geographic data stem from externalities. From what we know about the features of a developing rural economy it is clear that one cannot conclude from the existing literature on linkages in rural development that externalities are present to any significant extent. The signs of linkage in geographically aggregated data could easily stem from a process in which there is in fact no interdependence among individual farm household units.

Testing for externalities poses a problem, even with micropanel data. Correlations between individual outcomes and geographic variables have been widely reported in the literature. However, as is well recognized, one cannot assume that the geographic placement of economic activity is exogenous at the microlevel.[6] Placement in a given locality cannot be expected to be independent of the characteristics of the households

---

[4] It is often argued that the same is true if the externalities are 'pecuniary', meaning that they are transmitted through prices. However, it is known that with incomplete markets, pecuniary externalities can still be a source of inefficiency (Greenwald and Stiglitz 1986; Hoff 1998, 2000). The externality transmitted through prices could exacerbate the pre-existing inefficiency.

[5] For example, an article on page 1 of *the New York Times* on 27 December 1995, stated: 'As China's economic miracle continues to leave millions behind, more and more Chinese are expressing anger over the economic disparities between the flourishing provinces of China's coastal plain and the impoverished inland, where 70–80 million people cannot feed or clothe themselves and hundreds of millions of others are only spectators to China's economic transformation'.

[6] For example, Foster and Rosenzweig (1996) report a significant coefficient on village placement of agricultural extension services in regressions for the adoption of high-yielding varieties in microdata for India. As they point out, this cannot be considered a causal effect since the placement of extension services may depend on geographically associated latent factors influencing adoption.

that live there—no doubt including characteristics that are unobserved by the analyst. Persistent spatial concentrations of individuals with personal attributes that inhibit growth in their living standards, and lead to a worse assignment of geographic assets, can readily entail that the cross-sectional correlations often found in the data are entirely non-causal, with little or no bearing on development policy. All one is really picking up in the data is the fact that households who are poor in terms of some latent characteristic tend to be grouped together spatially and are less able to attract infrastructure and other geographically assigned resources.

To make this argument more concrete, consider the following example. In any rural economy, the quality of farmland is likely to be important to the productivity of current and past investments and hence economic growth. Land quality tends to be spatially correlated; the quality of one farmer's land is positively correlated with the quality of his neighbour's. However, land quality is rarely captured well even in quite comprehensive surveys. At the same time, one can expect that the composition of economic activity and the placement of rural infrastructure (irrigation, roads, etc.) will be influenced by land quality. In such circumstances, one can expect to find correlations between one farmer's income growth rate over time and the attributes of the area in which he lives, even controlling for observable characteristics of the farmer, such as his capital stock. That correlation might look like an externality, but it may simply be picking up the geographically associated latent heterogeneity in land quality.

The chapter presents results of a test for geographic externalities through the composition of economic activity that is robust to such latent heterogeneity. Both household panel data and geographic data are clearly called for to have any hope of identifying geographic externalities in the growth process at the microlevel. In modelling such data, one might turn to a standard panel-data model with a time-invariant error component, as in, for example, the regressions for farm profits in Foster and Rosenzweig (1995). Allowing for latent heterogeneity in the household-level growth process will protect against spurious geographic effects due to time-invariant omitted variables. However, standard panel-data methods of eliminating the household-specific effect wipe out the time-invariant geographic variables of interest in this context, namely the initial composition of economic activity in the locality. Nor is it plausible that the latent heterogeneity in growth rates is time-invariant; macroeconomic and geoclimatic conditions might well entail that the impact of these individual effects varies from year to year.

However, by simply relaxing the assumption that the fixed effect has a time-invariant impact one can estimate the effect of geographic differences in the observed initial level of economic activity on the microgrowth process robustly to the latent heterogeneity. In particular, the analysis in this chapter allows for non-stationary individual effects, following Holtz-Eakin *et al.* (1988) and Jalan and Ravallion (2002). The analysis combines geographic data on the composition of economic activity and infrastructure endowments with longitudinal micro-observations of consumption and income growth by sector. The growth rate of household consumption is decomposed by income source to explore the income effects of geographic differences in the composition of economic activity and other geographic characteristics. This allows a reasonably flexible description of the patterns of externalities within and between sectors of the economy, as they affect the growth process. The following section outlines the econometric model. Section 7.3 describes the setting and data while Section 7.4 presents the results. Section 7.5 summarizes the conclusions.

7.2. ECONOMETRIC MODEL

The aim is to test for external effects of the local composition of economic activity on the consumption growth process at the microlevel. To provide a theoretical motivation for the empirical work, let us start with the standard assumption that households maximize an intertemporally additive utility integral, with common preferences. Since this is an agricultural setting, each household owns a production technology, and one can make the standard assumption that its output is a concave function of the household's own-capital. Add to this the (non-standard) assumption that output also depends non-separably on characteristics of the area of residence, including the composition of economic activity. If we further add restrictions on capital mobility, then marginal products of own-capital will not be equalized across farm households, but will differ geographically. The optimal rate of consumption growth will depend on the farm household's marginal product of own-capital, which in turn depends on both the farm household's capital stock and its geographic characteristics, including the composition of economic activity locally.

The key feature of this model for the present purpose is that geographic externalities can influence consumption growth rates at the farm household level, through their effects on the productivity of private investment, given capital market imperfections. (The extreme case in which markets worked perfectly would imply that one had no power to explain the growth in consumption at the farm household level.) To derive a parametric model, one can assume constant discount and time preference rates and that the marginal product of own-capital at the farm household level can be written as a linear function of observable household and geographic characteristics.[7] Thus, one can postulate the following parametric model of consumption growth for N households observed over T periods:

$$\Delta \ln C_{it} = \alpha + \beta X_{it} + \xi Z_i + \varepsilon_{it} \quad (i = 1, \dots, N; \ t = 2, \dots, T), \quad (7.1)$$

where C_{it} is consumption by household i at date t, $\Delta \ln C_{it}$ is the growth rate of consumption, X_{it} is a vector of time-varying explanatory variables, and Z_i is a vector of exogenous time-invariant explanatory variables including measures of the initial economic activity in the locality in which household i lives. (The properties of the error term, ε_{it}, are discussed later.) The variables in X_{it} and Z_i capture observable differences between households that influence the marginal product of their own-capital;

---

[7] Alternatively, one can allow for heterogeneity in discount rates or preferences, which can be taken to vary with the same characteristics. The interpretation in terms of productivity effects is then lost, since the geographic variables could in principle influence the intertemporal parameters.

these variables include indicators of the initial level (at time $t - 1$) of own–capital plus relevant geographic variables, including the composition of economic activity locally.

Notice that in this model, one is testing for significant effects of the local composition of economic activity on the consumption growth rate at the household level, controlling for predetermined household characteristics that directly influence the marginal product of own–capital. This can be thought of as a key structural equation within a more complete model that also accounted for the evolution over time of the own–capital stock, which can then also be postulated as depending on the geographic variables. Intuitively, one might expect lower rates of capital accumulation in areas for which the local composition of economic activity leads to lower productivity of private capital. Thus, one can postulate a more complex multiequation dynamic model that traces out these various direct and indirect effects of the composition of local economic activity on the evolution of household living standards. In this chapter, the concern is solely with the key structural equation, which identifies the external effect of local economic activity on the productivity of own–capital, and hence consumption growth, given the level of own–capital.

The assumptions made about the error term in eqn (7.1) are of course critical. One naturally wants to include a fixed error component that may well be correlated with the regressors of interest, as discussed in the introduction. The potential endogeneity of the explanatory variables in eqn (7.1) is assumed to be fully captured by non-zero correlations with this error component. However, it is not assumed that the impact of the heterogeneity is necessarily constant over time. For example, some farmers are more productive than others in ways that cannot be captured in the data and this matters more in a bad agricultural year than a good one. Following Holtz-Eakin *et al.* (1988), the specification of the error term allows for non-stationarity in the impacts of the individual effects:

$$\varepsilon_{it} = \theta_t \omega_i + \mu_{it}, \tag{7.2}$$

where μ_{it} is the i.i.d. random variable, with zero mean and variance σ_μ^2, and ω_i is a time-invariant effect that is not orthogonal to the regressors, that is, $E(\omega_i X_{it}) \neq 0$ and $E(\omega_i Z_i) \neq 0$, while μ_{it} is a white-noise innovation process, that is, $E(\omega_i \mu_{it}) = 0$ and $E(Z_i \mu_{it}) = 0$. The assumed error structure in eqn (7.2) facilitates quasi-differencing of the model in eqn (7.1). Substituting eqn (7.2) into eqn (7.1) and lagging by one period one obtains:

$$\Delta \ln C_{it-1} = \alpha + \beta X_{it} + \xi Z_i + \theta_{t-1} \omega_i + \mu_{it-1}. \tag{7.3}$$

Multiplying eqn (7.3) by $r_t \equiv \theta_t / \theta_{t-1}$ and subtracting from eqn (7.1), the quasi-differenced model for consumption growth is:

$$\Delta \ln C_{it} = \alpha(1 - r_t) + r_t \Delta \ln C_{it-1} + \beta(X_{it} - r_t X_{it-1}) + \xi(1 - r_t)Z_i$$
$$+ \mu_{it} - r_t \mu_{it-1}. \tag{7.4}$$

It is evident from eqn (7.4) that as long as $r_t \neq 1$ one can identify the impact of the time-invariant variables on the growth rate robustly to latent heterogeneity. The test described in Jalan and Ravallion (2002) (following Godfrey 1988) is used to test the null hypothesis that $r_t = 1$ for all t. In estimating eqn (7.4) one must allow for the fact that $\Delta \ln C_{it-1}$ is correlated with the error term, $\mu_{it} - r_t \mu_{it-1}$. One can estimate eqn (7.4) by generalized method of moments (GMM) using differences and/or levels of log consumptions lagged twice (or higher) as instruments for $\Delta \ln C_{it-1}$. (So one loses two observations over time in estimating eqn (7.1).) The essential condition to justify this choice of instruments is that the error term in eqn (7.4) is second-order serially independent, as implied by serial independence of μ_{it}. The Arellano and Bond (1991) second-order serial correlation test is performed, given that the consistency of the estimator for the quasi-differenced model depends on the assumption that the composite error term is second-order serially independent.[8] Note that there is some first-order serial correlation introduced in the model due to the quasi-differencing. This means that consumption lagged once is not a valid instrument.

Let us now see how the household-level impacts on consumption growth identified using the above model can be decomposed by income source. There are $M-1$ income sources and let Y_{jit} denote income from source j for household i at date t and (for notational convenience) let Y_{Mit} denote savings. From the identity:

$$C_{it} = \sum_{j-1}^{M} Y_{jit},\tag{7.5}$$

we have

$$\Delta \ln C_{it} \cong \frac{\Delta C_{it}}{C_{it-1}} = \sum_{j=1}^{M} \frac{\Delta Y_{jit}}{C_{it-1}}.\tag{7.6}$$

This motivates a decomposition of eqn (7.4) as follows:

$$\frac{\Delta Y_{jit}}{C_{it-1}} - \frac{r_t \Delta Y_{jit-1}}{C_{it-2}} = \alpha_j(1 - r_t) + \beta_j(X_{it} - r_t X_{it-1}) + \xi_j(1 - r_t)Z_i$$
$$+ \mu_{jit} - r_t \mu_{jit-1} \quad (j = 1, \ldots, M).\tag{7.7}$$

Summing eqn (7.7) over all j yields eqn (7.4), with $\alpha = \sum \alpha_j$, $\beta = \sum \beta_j$, and $\xi = \sum \xi_j$. Notice that for consistency with aggregation, the r_t $(t = 1, \ldots, T)$ parameters cannot vary by income source. To estimate eqn (7.7), I replace the r_t parameters by their estimates from the consumption growth model to give

$$\frac{\Delta Y_{jit}}{C_{it-1}} - \frac{\hat{r}_t \Delta Y_{jit-1}}{C_{it-2}} = \alpha_j(1 - \hat{r}_t) + \beta_j(X_{it} - \hat{r}_t X_{it-1}) + \xi_j(1 - \hat{r}_t)Z_i$$
$$+ \mu_{jit} - \hat{r}_t \mu_{jit-1} \quad (j = 1, \ldots, M).\tag{7.8}$$

---

[8] To test if the instruments are valid, the Arellano and Bond (1991) over-identification test is also used. Lack of second-order serial correlation and the non-rejection of the over-identification test support our choice of instruments. For further discussion see Jalan and Ravallion (2002).

Thus, provided the individual effect has a time-varying impact, one can identify geographic effects by income sources, which are robust to latent (individual or geographic) heterogeneity.

7.3. SETTING AND DATA

China experienced a surge in rural non-farm activity in the 1980s, in the wake of country-wide economic reforms (Byrd and Qingsong 1990). An important element of this was the emergence and rapid growth of township and village enterprises (TVEs). The fact that growth in the number of non-farm enterprises was preceded by more rapid agricultural growth (following decollectivization starting in the late 1970s) is sometimes interpreted as evidence of a strong forward linkage from agriculture to non-farm rural development in the Chinese setting. For example, Jiacheng (1990) argues that agricultural growth provided the key precondition for the rapid expansion of non-farm economic activities in the 1980s. However, there are other interpretations in the literature; for example, Haiyan (1990) argues that, while the stimulus for non-farm rural enterprise development came from agriculture, it was a *negative* stimulus, not positive—that the expansion of rural non-farm enterprises was stimulated by low agricultural productivity in certain regions.

Anti-poverty policy in China has emphasized poor area development programmes, which have traditionally emphasized the role of agriculture (Leading Group 1988; World Bank 1992). There has been debate in policy circles about this emphasis on agriculture, with some people arguing that non-farm enterprise development should be given priority instead. There has also been a debate about whether these programmes are effective in longer-term poverty reduction, or are simply short-term palliatives (with outmigration from poor areas seen by some as the only long-term solution). In previous work using these data, evidence was found of dynamic income gains from the central and provincial poor area development programmes, implying quite reasonable economic rates of return (Jalan and Ravallion 1998).

The following analysis uses household-level data from China's Rural Household Survey (RHS) done by the National Bureau of Statistics of China (NBS). A panel of 5,600 farm households spanning 111 counties over the six-year period 1985–90 was formed for four contiguous provinces in southern China, namely Guangdong, Guangxi, Guizhou, and Yunnan. The latter three provinces form southwest China, widely regarded as one of the poorest regions in the country. Guangdong on the other hand is a relatively prosperous coastal region (surrounding Hong Kong). The RHS is a well-designed and executed survey of a random sample of households in rural China, with unusual effort made to reduce non-sampling errors (Chen and Ravallion 1996). Sampled households fill in a daily diary on expenditures and are visited on average every two weeks by an interviewer to check the diaries and collect other data relevant to incomes. There is also an elaborate system of cross-checking at the local level. The consumption and income data from such an intensive survey process are almost certainly more reliable than those obtained by the common cross-sectional surveys in which the data are based on recall at a single interview. For the six-year period 1985–90 the survey was also longitudinal, returning to the same households over time. While this was done for administrative convenience (since local NBS offices were set up in each sampled county), the panel can still be formed.[9]

The income aggregate includes imputed values of revenues from own production (net of costs) valued at actual local selling prices (rather than the planning prices used in the original data; see Chen and Ravallion 1996). The consumption data include imputed values of the consumption streams from the inventory of consumer durables. Poverty lines designed to represent the cost at each year and in each province of a fixed standard of living were used as deflators. These were based on a normative food bundle set by NBS, which assures that average nutritional requirements are met with a diet that is consistent with Chinese tastes. This food bundle is then valued at province-specific prices. The food component of the poverty line is augmented with an allowance for non-food goods, consistent with the non-food spending of those households whose food spending is no more than adequate to afford the food component of the poverty line.[10] Income sources are broken down as follows:

1. *Farm income*: income from grain production and other farm crops.
2. *Non-farm income type I*: forestry, animal husbandry, fishery, gathering, and hunting.
3. *Non-farm income type II*: handicrafts, industry, material processing, construction, transportation, productive labour service, commerce, catering trade, services.
4. *Collective income*: collective production, income from TVEs, collective welfare funds, collective prizes, other collective income.

In adopting this classification, I wanted to distinguish the types of land-based non-farm income sources that are often associated with farming (type I) from others (type II). My usage is not standard in this respect; it is more common in the literature to only refer to my 'type II' as the 'non-farm sector' (see, for example, Lanjouw and Lanjouw 2001). Of course, in a literal sense, my 'type I' is not farming. And, as we will see, these three sectors behave differently, making their separation of interest. In 1985, these four income sources accounted for 58.4, 24.5, 15.0, and 2.1 per cent (respectively) of aggregate household income in the sample. Multiple sources for one household are common. Indeed, every one of the sampled households who had income from farming also recorded at least some income from a non-farm activity.

Collective income is the most problematic of the four categories. Although income gains from non-household non-farm enterprises are excluded from this analysis, the profits received from such enterprises by households are included under 'collective income'. However, the category accounts for only 2 per cent of income. And it is likely that some of this comes from outside the county. One can be justifiably sceptical as to how well the following analysis will then be able to capture external effects on local

---

[9] Constructing the panel from the annual RHS survey data proved to be more difficult than expected since the identifiers could not be relied upon. Fortunately, virtually ideal matching variables were available in the financial records, which gave both beginning and end of year balances. The relatively few ties by these criteria could easily be broken using demographic (including age) data.

[10] For further details on the poverty lines and the dataset see Chen and Ravallion (1996).

M. Ravallion

Table 7.1. *Correlation coefficients in sample mean incomes across 102 counties*

	Farm income	Non-farm income I	Non-farm income II	Collective income
Farm income	1.0000			
Non-farm income I	0.3240	1.0000		
Non-farm income II	0.1134	0.0027	1.0000	
Collective income	0.4505	0.1125	0.2171	1.0000

Source: See text.

non-household income growth. Echoing the empirical literature on linkages, one finds positive correlations across counties between farm income per capita and non-farm income of type I above, though less so for type II. Table 7.1 gives the correlation coefficients in the time means in the dataset. There is very little correlation between the two types of non-farm income.

In estimating eqn (7.8), I shall use two distinct types of data on the geographic composition of economic activity. The first uses the initial (1985) county mean of the income sources identified above. Initial values of the corresponding household variables are also included. This gives a conceptually clean representation of the four-by-four matrix of linkage effects. However, there is a potential concern that the explanatory variables are from the same survey-based data source. There are of course sampling errors in the county means, and possibly correlated measurement errors. For the second set of estimates, I draw instead on county administrative data. This has two advantages. First, the data sources are then largely independent, relieving possible concerns about correlated measurement errors when using a common data source. Second, the county administrative data encompass the rural non-household sector, including TVEs. A disadvantage is that the available county data are less complete, which reduces the sample size to 4,800 (96 counties).

From the county data, one can identify three obvious indicators of the extent of development of local agriculture, namely irrigated land area, fertilizer usage, and agricultural machinery usage. For the rural non-farm sector, I have used the county administrative data on the number of commercial enterprises in 1985 and the sector composition of gross product per capita at county level. The latter is broken down according to whether it is industry (distinguished according to whether the industrial enterprise is township, village, or household-based), construction, transport, or services. In this second model, controls are also added for geographic and household heterogeneity. The geographic variables at the county-level database include population density, average education levels, road density, health indicators, and schooling indicators. Dummy variables for the province are also included. A composite measure of household wealth can be constructed, comprising valuations of all fixed productive assets, cash, deposits, housing, grain stock, and consumer durables. Data are also used on agricultural inputs used, including landholding. These asset and farm input variables are time-varying, but are treated as endogenous, using lagged values as instruments. To allow for differences in the quality and quantity of family labour (given that labour markets are thin in this setting), initial education attainments and demographic characteristics are also included. Table 7.A1 in the Appendix provides descriptive statistics.

7.4. RESULTS

First the simpler model described above is estimated, in which consumption growth and its components by income source are regressed on the survey-based estimates of initial county mean income by source and initial own incomes. Table 7.2 gives the consumption growth regression (corresponding to eqn (7.4)), while Table 7.3 gives the decomposition by all four income sources (eqn (7.8)). (Saving is the residual, not estimated.) The diagnostic tests described in Section 7.2 passed comfortably. (This was also true of the extended model, discussed later in this section.) The results in Tables 7.2 and 7.3 are for the full sample ($n = 5,600$); the models were also estimated on the smaller sample for which county data are complete (as used in the extended

Table 7.2. *Consumption growth regressed on county-mean incomes and own incomes*

Consumption growth 1985–90	GMM estimates	
	Coeff.	*t*-ratio
Constant	−0.019034*	−3.631332
Coeff. on lagged consumption		
1987	−0.023637	−0.260700
1988	0.231193*	5.477698
1989	−0.036034	−0.974515
1990	0.192418*	4.036306
County mean household incomes by source, 1985		
Farm income	0.000195*	7.029119
Non-farm income I	6.77E−05	1.848970
Non-farm income II	6.10E−05	1.376225
Collective income	0.000148	1.925260
Household's own income by source, 1985		
Farm income	−5.07E−05*	−3.616862
Non-farm income I	−7.25E−05*	−4.473417
Non-farm income II	−7.47E−05*	−5.055279
Collective income	−2.25E−05	−0.795760

Notes: * Indicates significant at 1% level, two-tailed test; $n = 5,641$ (111 counties).

Source: See text.

Table 7.3. *Decomposition of growth by income source*

Income change 1985–90, normalized by initial consumption	Farm income		Non-farm income I		Non-farm income II		Collective income	
	Coeff.	t-ratio	Coeff.	t-ratio	Coeff.	t-ratio	Coeff.	t-ratio
Constant	−1.042776	−0.606657	0.007246	1.581473	−0.001584	−0.304262	−0.006296*	−2.776274
County mean household incomes by source, 1985								
Farm income	0.058360*	5.582170	9.02E−05*	3.587523	−1.43E−05	−0.527382	4.85E−06	0.405785
Non-farm income I	−0.019292	−1.864275	−7.72E−05*	−2.922507	9.23E−05*	2.627234	7.64E−05*	4.199318
Non-farm income II	−0.012158	−0.836240	−2.46E−05	−0.722362	0.000358*	7.216553	1.95E−06	0.156793
Collective income	0.009052	0.365210	7.86E−06	0.104518	−0.000232	−2.364964	8.38E−05	1.705881
Household's own income by source, 1985								
Farm income	−0.065339*	−7.964560	−2.23E−05	−2.032218	−2.72E−05	−2.032737	9.13E−07	0.225140
Non-farm income I	−0.009548	−2.082792	−8.46E−05*	−5.212832	8.70E−07	0.069791	−1.86E−05*	−3.288436
Non-farm income II	−0.005469	−1.357622	4.01E−06	0.394638	−4.41E−05	−1.707732	1.76E−06	0.414443
Collective income	−0.024780*	−2.654654	−1.04E−05	−0.393923	1.42E−05	0.485131	−0.000132*	−5.666340
J-statistic	0.073149		0.037610		0.020013		0.005590	

Notes: * Indicates significant at 1% level, two-tailed test; $n = 5,641$ (111 counties).

Source: See text.

specification below). The results were very similar between the two samples, suggesting that there is nothing particularly unusual about the countries with incomplete county data. I chose to use all the available data for Table 7.2 rather than to limit the sample to the counties included in the regressions in Table 7.3.

Consumption growth at the household level is significantly higher in counties with higher initial levels of farm income, non-farm income type I, and collective income. The size and significance of the effect of differences in county-mean farm income are notable; the regression coefficient in Table 7.2 implies that a 100 Yuan per month increase in mean farm income in the county of residence (equivalent to one standard deviation, or about 60 per cent of mean farm income) increases the consumption growth rate by 0.0195—about two percentage points per annum. In marked contrast to the county variables, higher *own* incomes tend to result in lower subsequent consumption growth. This pattern echoes the finding of Jalan and Ravallion (2002) that the microconsumption growth process tends to be convergent with respect to household characteristics (in that characteristics that tend to raise the current level of consumption lead to lower subsequent growth), but divergent with respect to geographic characteristics.

Turning to the decomposition of consumption growth by income source, the results in Table 7.3 indicate a significant within-sector external effect in all cases except collective income. Higher initial mean incomes from farming in the county of residence entail higher subsequent income gains from farming. This is also the case for type II non-farm incomes. For type I non-farm incomes however, one finds a negative external effect within the sector, suggestive of a crowding-out effect.

Looking at the cross-sectoral linkages in Table 7.3, one finds no significant effects of initial non-farm income in the county on farm income gains at the household level. A significant positive effect of a higher initial level of farm incomes in the county on the growth of type I non-farm incomes is found, but not for type II. Non-farm incomes of type I in turn have positive effects on the growth of type II and collective incomes. However, higher collective incomes locally tend to attenuate growth in non-farm incomes of type II. For each of the four income growth regressions in Table 7.3, one can convincingly reject the null hypothesis that the four coefficients on the county-mean income sources are equal.[11] Thus, the composition of economic activity matters. Summing the external effect of a given income component horizontally in Table 7.3, it is plain that farming is the largest generator of external effects on the growth process at microlevel. Including savings, the sum across all components is given by the coefficient in the consumption growth regression. The aggregate external effects on consumption are positive for all four income components, but farming is the largest (Table 7.2). Across the four income components (excluding savings), the aggregate impact of higher farm income per capita in a county on subsequent income

---

[11] Wald tests of the null hypothesis that the four coefficients on county-mean incomes in Table 7.3 are equal gave 44.9, 35.8, 71.7, and 19.5, respectively. For the consumption growth regression in Table 7.2, the Wald test gave 15.3. The test has a Chi-square distribution with four degrees of freedom, implying rejections of the null hypotheses at the 1 per cent level or better.

gains (normalized by lagged consumption) is 0.058, as compared to −0.019, −0.012, and 0.009 for non-farm incomes types I and II and collective incomes, respectively (Table 7.3).

And in all four cases, the bulk of the external effect is the 'own-effect' of higher income in a county on subsequent income growth. For farming, 99 per cent of the external effect is the own-effect. So, while we see signs of an external effect of higher initial agricultural development on the growth of non-farm incomes at the household level, it is quantitatively small. With regard to the effects of initial household income on income growth by source, we can see some strong signs of negative own-income effects, suggestive of convergence due to diminishing marginal products of own-capital. There are also negative effects of the other income components on farm income.

Tables 7.4 and 7.5 give the extended specification, which exploits the county administrative records on output by source and indicators of local human and physical infrastructure. The regression in Table 7.4 indicates significant positive effects of initial agricultural development on consumption growth at the household level. We also see significant positive effects of a higher density of commercial enterprises. Higher mean industrial output at village level is also associated with higher subsequent consumption growth at the farm household level, though this is not true when the enterprises are township- or household-based. On the other hand, there are indications of negative external effects of construction and transport sector development. Some of the other geographic controls are suggestive of positive externalities from better local endowments of human and physical infrastructure; in particular, higher

Table 7.4. *Consumption growth model using geographic data from county administrative records*

	Coeff.	t-statistic
Constant	−0.328076*	−3.938664
Coeff. on lagged consumption		
1987	−0.563094*	−5.580720
1988	0.226777*	6.313155
1989	−0.031837	−0.878866
1990	0.264715*	6.118230
Economic activity at county level		
Farm		
Cultivated area per 10,000 persons	0.003075*	3.424595
Fertilizer used per cultivated area	0.004131*	7.433107
Farm machinery used per cultivated area	0.000368*	2.651082
Non-farm		
Number of commercial enterprises in county per 10,000 population	0.000220*	2.768617
Rural industry gross product per 10,000 persons		
Township enterprises	−6.63E−05	−1.759901

Table 7.4. (*Continued*)

	Coeff.	*t*-statistic
Village enterprises	0.000415*	3.729650
Household enterprises	−1.77E−05	−0.173829
Rural construction gross product per 10,000 persons	−0.000154	−2.063245
Rural transportation gross product per 10,000 persons	−0.000509*	−3.639974
Rural gross product from services per 10,000 persons	0.000169	0.715551
Other geographic controls		
Guangdong (dummy)	0.037373*	4.338988
Guangxi (dummy)	0.022666*	4.345667
Yunnan (dummy)	−0.005237	−0.869316
Revolutionary base area (dummy)	0.050238*	3.248796
Border area (dummy)	0.002216	0.563537
Coastal area (dummy)	−0.012471	−1.278915
Minority area (dummy)	−0.012457*	−3.714323
Mountainous area (dummy)	−0.015838*	−4.452355
Plains (dummy)	0.005659	1.459167
Population density (log)	0.021519	2.480439
Proportion of illiterates in 15+ population	−0.000322	−1.866172
Infant mortality rate	−0.000147	−1.296671
Medical personnel per capita	0.000584	1.988495
Kilometres of roads per capita	0.000455*	3.185796
Proportion of population living in urban areas	−0.097467*	−3.199404
Household variables		
Expenditure on agricultural inputs per cultivated area	−0.001911*	−7.161740
Fixed productive assets per capita	1.27E−05	−0.883144
Cultivated land per capita	−0.008748	−1.802922
Household size (log)	0.056994*	8.967627
Age of household head	0.002086*	2.617436
Age^2 of household head	−2.57E−05*	−2.899381
Proportion of adults in the household		
Illiterate	0.007032	1.125765
With primary school education	7.77E−06	0.001468
Proportion of children		
6–11 years	0.013395	1.377193
12–14 years	0.032215*	2.502249
15–17 years	0.002467	0.158605
With primary school education	−0.002868	−0.736394
With secondary school education	0.020066	2.002172
Whether a household member works in the state sector		
(dummy)	−0.001098	−0.147539
Proportion of 60+ members in the household	0.002312	0.187774

Notes: * Indicates significant at 1% level, two-tailed test; $n = 4,778$ (96 counties).

Source: See text.

Table 7.5. *Decomposition by income source*

Income change 1985–90, normalized by initial consumption	Farm income		Non-farm income I		Non-farm income II		Collective income	
	Coeff.	t-ratio	Coeff.	t-ratio	Coeff.	t-ratio	Coeff.	t-ratio
Constant	−0.037285	−0.551930	−0.317851	−5.899826	0.017037	0.312113	0.002492	0.213991
Economic activity at county level								
Farm								
Cultivated area per 10,000 persons	0.001425	1.975995	0.004668*	7.661727	0.00096	1.694963	−5.92E−05	−0.494620
Fertilizer used per cultivated area (×100)	0.3298*	7.450607	0.1553*	4.623649	0.0775*	2.335067	0.000321	0.042174
Farm machinery used per cultivated area (×100)	0.0137	0.881606	0.00559	0.539991	−0.0262*	−2.185012	0.00757*	2.829688
Non-farm								
Number of commercial enterprises per 10,000 population	−6.40E−05	−1.012804	1.02E−05	0.192262	0.000256*	4.728632	−1.06E−06	−0.084385
Rural industry gross product per 10,000 persons								
Township enterprises	1.53E−05	0.472816	−7.68E−05*	−3.695281	−5.09E−05	−2.126782	3.83E−05*	3.920372
Village enterprises	0.000128	1.339266	−1.44E−05	−0.280215	0.000355*	4.522848	−2.83E−05	−1.738851
Enterprises owned by households	0.000207*	2.549566	0.000188*	3.230548	−9.72E−05	−1.487319	−3.74E−05	−1.336554
Rural construction gross product per 10,000 persons	−1.16E−06	−0.017589	5.40E−05	1.257481	−2.94E−05	−0.546224	1.46E−06	0.136096
Rural transportation gross product per 10,000 persons	−0.000225	−1.893099	−0.000234*	−2.760754	−0.000240	−2.109118	−3.10E−05	−1.163832
Rural gross product from services per 10,000 persons	−0.000870*	−4.433674	0.000235	1.700295	3.25E−05	0.212639	−4.47E−05	−1.095567

Other geographic controls

Guangdong (dummy)	0.040192*	5.578835	−0.039672*	−7.215861	−0.001470	−0.261715	0.001851	1.382536
Guangxi (dummy)	0.007369	1.729346	0.006060	1.656530	0.000142	1.066986	0.000817	1.080041
Yunnan (dummy)	−0.003800	−1.728530	−0.003452	−0.851059	−0.000270*	−3.355940	0.000545	0.646179
Revolutionary base area (dummy)	0.051141*	3.953926	−0.005317	−0.896477	−0.000388*	−1.856168	0.000267	0.172994
Border area (dummy)	0.015034*	4.753477	−0.006759	−2.516487	6.47E−05	0.512528	−0.000337	−0.645808
Coastal area (dummy)	−0.050290*	−5.715417	0.001306	0.172308	0.007192	0.300917	0.002023	0.869084
Minority area (dummy) (×100)	−0.2665	−1.020337	−0.6569*	−2.915940	−0.01381	−0.598987	0.0167	0.369802
Mountainous area (dummy)	−0.019013*	−6.629943	0.004989	2.179428	0.005246	2.187413	0.000247	0.478782
Plains (dummy)	0.003090	0.882888	0.009975*	3.68431	0.002272	0.751968	−0.000332	−0.527546
Population density (log)	0.003167	0.445301	0.026073*	4.853929	−0.001470	−0.261715	−0.000364	−0.297651
Proportion of illiterates in 15+ population (×100)	−0.0397*	−2.810640	0.0183	1.371223	0.0142	1.066986	0.00253	0.982911
Infant mortality rate	−3.89E−05	−0.437105	−0.000126	−1.605491	−0.000270*	−3.355940	−3.62E−05	−2.187786
Medical staff per capita (×100)	0.0368	1.435438	−0.00388	−0.148288	−0.0388*	−1.856168	0.00424	1.070008
Kilometres of roads per capita (×100)	0.0678*	5.693957	−0.0100	−0.985167	0.00647	0.512528	0.00121	0.663914
Proportion of population living in urban areas	−0.082497*	−3.331008	0.039684	1.939799	0.007192	0.300917	−0.004783	−0.796981
Household-level variables								
Expenditure on agricultural inputs per cultivated area (×100)	−0.1788*	−9.474159	−0.00532	−0.578969	−0.0199	−2.058113	9.48E−06	0.435807
Fixed productive assets per capita (×100)	−0.000515	−0.512903	8.22E−05	0.074993	0.00457*	2.566003	−0.000204	−0.867348
Cultivated land per capita	−0.008281	−1.818687	−0.007585	−2.438985	−0.008547*	−3.224610	−0.000337	−0.511164
Household size (log)	0.012321*	2.596482	0.014103*	2.919817	0.002724	0.615920	−0.000927	−1.012190
Age of household head	0.000470	0.718755	0.000379	0.635091	−0.000143	−0.251665	5.26E−05	0.476080

Table 7.5. (*Continued*)

Income change 1985–90, normalized by initial consumption	Farm income		Non-farm income I		Non-farm income II		Collective income	
	Coeff.	t-ratio	Coeff.	t-ratio	Coeff.	t-ratio	Coeff.	t-ratio
Age^2 of household head (×100)	−0.000731	−0.999952	−0.000355	−0.522368	2.45E−06	0.385523	−0.0001	−0.775087
Proportion of adults in household								
Illiterate	−0.002009	−0.373594	0.000758	0.185174	−0.001015	−0.229459	0.002438	2.292417
With primary school education	−0.002942	−0.667418	0.004343	1.223840	−0.005701	−1.464877	0.001718	1.771110
Proportion of children in household								
6–11 years	0.005990	0.711307	0.009385	1.432443	−0.006400	−0.877534	0.001215	0.583170
12–14 years	0.004234	0.378313	0.012715	1.410109	0.012735	1.341365	0.003008	0.917733
15–17 years	0.002616	0.209421	−0.005501	−0.529853	0.018894	1.796201	0.005167	1.699518
With primary school education (×100)	−0.0409	−0.121831	−0.3429	−1.283922	0.001907	0.612289	0.0189	0.220488
With secondary school education	−0.001224	−0.149337	0.010930	2.011010	−0.007282	−1.247138	0.002381	1.411268
Household member works in state sector (dummy)	−0.018599*	−3.088751	−0.004086	−0.805931	−0.003461	−0.765217	−0.000913	−0.493164
Proportion of 60+ members in the household	0.002762	0.261581	−0.005292	−0.646863	0.001195	0.151179	−0.000654	−0.363943

Notes: * Indicates significant at 1% level, two-tailed test; n = 4,778 (96 counties).

Source: See text.

levels of literacy locally and higher road density promote higher consumption growth at household level.

By allowing us to break up non-farm incomes by sector (industry, construction, transport, and services) the regressions using the county administrative data in Table 7.5 reveal that the more aggregate effects identified in Table 7.3 disguise some potentially important differences between subsectors. Indeed, while there are generally positive external effects of local industrial development, we see signs of *negative* external effects on farm and non-farm income growth of greater local activity in the transport and service subsectors. (Notice that the transport income effect is probably not picking up an effect of transport infrastructure, since I am controlling for road density.) It appears that these sectors are competing with household-level farm and non-farm activities for limited local resources that enhance the productivity of private investment and hence income growth at the farm household level.

Higher cultivated area per person in a county has a significant positive effect on the growth of non-farm type I incomes, but the (positive) effect on type II is barely significant at the 10 per cent level. These findings lead one to question the claims sometimes made (in the case of China, see Haiyan 1990) that a shortage of cultivated land in an area was an inducement to non-farm activities. One finds the opposite to be the case for non-farm activities by the household, though there is a sign of this effect on collective income (which here includes income from enterprises). Higher fertilizer usage also has an external effect on both types of non-farm income growth, though the dominant external effect is on farm incomes. The extended models in Table 7.5 also point to some diverse and in some cases surprising impacts across income sources. The positive effect of higher population density on consumption growth (Table 7.4) appears to be transmitted entirely through non-farm type I income growth. The effect of road density appears to be largely through higher farm incomes. Lower infant mortality (as an indicator of health care more generally) appears to have high returns to non-farm (type II) income growth. Higher basic education appears to spill over more into farming.

7.5. CONCLUSIONS

The literature on linkages in rural development has largely ignored what is surely the most relevant question for policy: do the signs of linkage found in geographic data reflect externalities at the level of the individual decisionmaker? The data and methods used in past empirical work cannot distinguish externalities from other factors far more benign from a policy point of view. Yet, the implications for understanding rural underdevelopment, and the implications for policy, depend crucially on whether the aggregate appearance of intersectoral linkage in rural development stems from externalities at the microlevel.

The chapter has offered a test that can identify any genuine linkage externalities, and can also test for microeffects on the growth process of differing geographic endowments of human and physical infrastructure. The chapter has implemented the test using data for rural China during the post-reform period of farm and (particularly) non-farm rural development. The aim has been to describe the patterns of linkage in a way that is robust to latent heterogeneity. Like any description, the results beg many questions. In particular, the analysis has thrown little light on the precise sources of external effects. Are we seeing the effects of knowledge spillovers, or something else such as network externalities or pecuniary externalities?

The results do suggest that the level and composition of local economic activity has non-negligible impacts on consumption and income growth at the farm household level. There are significant positive effects of the level of local economic activity in a given sector on income growth from that income source. And there are a number of significant sectoral cross-effects, notably from farming to those categories of non-farm activities that tend naturally to be more linked to agriculture (forestry, animal husbandry, fishery), but also between the latter type of non-farm activity and other types (handicrafts, industry, processing, transportation, etc.). Thus, there is a direct link from the initial level of agricultural development to the first type of non-farm activities and a more indirect link to the second. There is less sign of the reverse linkage—from initial level of non-farm economic activity to growth in farm incomes. And there are indications of negative external effects from some non-farm activities, notably involving non-industrial subsectors (construction and transport). While I do find significant cross-sector effects, they are dwarfed by the within-sector effects. The composition (as well as the level) of local economic activity matters, and the sector that clearly matters most quantitatively is agriculture.

The results of this chapter suggest that there are externalities at the farm household level underlying the signs of linkage found in more geographically aggregated data. Under the chapter's identifying assumptions, the linkages found can be interpreted as genuine externalities, suggesting that private agents in this economy are not going to take account of all the potential income gains from their actions. Thus, these results offer an explanation for rural underdevelopment, arising from underinvestment in externality-generating activities, notably agriculture and (to a lesser extent) certain non-farm activities. By the same token, the results offer a microempirical foundation for the long-standing, but poorly validated, claims in the literature about the potential for virtuous cycles whereby a well-targeted external growth stimulus in a poor area can generate positive and more widely diffused income gains over time.

Thus, these results offer support for the types of poor-area development programmes that have been pursued by the Government of China since the mid-1980s. The emphasis that these programmes have given to agricultural development is consistent with this chapter's findings that agriculture is the key externality-generating sector of the Chinese rural economy. Of course, the detailed design of such programmes is crucial, and this is not something that the results of this chapter can throw much light on. However, the present results also point to the importance of local endowments of human and physical infrastructure to the microgrowth process. When combined with data on the costs to the government's budget of alternative interventions, these empirical results will hopefully also help inform public choices on how best to balance agricultural development initiatives with infrastructure development, so as to assure maximum growth of living standards in poor areas.

Appendix

Table 7.A1. *Descriptive statistics*

	Mean	S.d.
Dependent variables		
Average growth rate of consumption, 1986–90	0.0042	0.0777
Mean change as a proportion of lagged consumption, 1986–90		
Farm income	−0.0065	0.0687
Non-farm income I	0.0027	0.0688
Non-farm income II	0.0157	0.0755
Collective income	−0.0005	0.0244
Economic activity at county level		
Farm income, 1985 (Yuan/person/month)	161.0459	100.846
Non-farm income I, 1985 (Yuan/person/month)	92.9326	98.303
Non-farm income II, 1985 (Yuan/person/month)	62.9430	100.405
Collective income, 1985 (Yuan/person/month)	9.4162	40.971
Fertilizers used per cultivated area (tonnes/km^2)	11.5402	6.6497
Farm machinery used per capita (horsepower)[a]	151.7879	110.2427
Cultivated area per 10,000 persons (km^2)	13.0447	3.2518
Number of commercial enterprises per 10,000 population	52.5922	22.003
Rural industry gross product per 10,000 persons		
Enterprises in townships (central administrative villages)	32.7465	132.874
Enterprises in villages	16.2585	45.475
Enterprises owned by households	27.5416	33.049
Rural construction gross product per 10,000 persons	32.5597	42.9291
Rural transportation gross product per 10,000 persons	13.3423	0.9594
Rural gross product from services per 10,000 persons	22.6664	23.121
Other geographic variables		
Proportion of sample in		
Guangdong	0.1618	0.3683
Guangxi	0.3414	0.4742
Yunnan	0.2285	0.4199
Proportion living in a revolutionary base area	0.0191	0.1367
Proportion of counties sharing a border with a foreign		
country	0.1712	0.3767
Proportion of villages		
Located on the coast	0.0316	0.1749
With an ethnic minority concentration	0.2978	0.4573
With a mountainous terrain	0.45563	0.498
Located in the plains	0.2292	0.4203
Population density (log)	8.20602	0.3929
Proportion of illiterates in the 15+ population (%)	36.9547	16.0225
Infant mortality rate (per 1,000 live births)	43.24006	23.8535
Medical personnel per 10,000 persons	7.816894	5.0388

Table 7.A1. (*Continued*)

	Mean	S.d.
Kilometres of roads per 10,000 persons	14.7122	10.9721
Proportion of population living in the urban areas	0.0907	0.0548
Household-level variables		
Expenditure on agricultural inputs (fertilizers and pesticides) per cultivated area (Yuan/mu)[a]	29.224	47.9954
Fixed productive assets per capita (Yuan per capita)[a]	129.8417	150.8919
Cultivated land per capita (mu per capita)[a]	1.2591	0.7802
Household size (log)	1.7086	0.3508
Age of the household head	41.8262	11.3887
Age^2 of the household head	1879.114	1015.252
Proportion of adults		
In the household who are illiterate	0.33876	0.2932
With primary school education	0.3787	0.3074
Proportion of children		
6–11 years	0.1199	0.1415
12–14 years	0.0845	0.1071
15–17 years	0.06796	0.0988
With primary school education	0.2780	0.3689
With secondary school education	0.0484	0.1709
Proportion of household members working in the state sector	0.0421	0.2008
Proportion of 60+ household members	0.06270	0.1222
Number of households		4,778
Number of counties		96

Notes: [a] Indicates time-varying variables; 1 mu = 0.000667 km^2.

Source: See text.

REFERENCES

Arellano, M. and S. Bond (1991). 'Some Tests of Specification for Panel Data: Monte-Carlo Evidence and an Application to Employment Equation', *Review of Economic Studies*, 58: 277–98.

Basu, K., A. Narayan, and M. Ravallion (2002). 'Is Literacy Shared within Households?', *Labour Economics*, 8: 649–65.

Besley, T. (1995). 'Savings, Credit and Insurance', in J. Behrman and T. N. Srinivasan (eds) *Handbook of Development Economics*, Vol. 3, North-Holland: Amsterdam.

Byrd, W. and L. Qingspong (1990). 'China's Rural Industrialization', in W. A. Byrd and L. Qingspong (eds) *China's Rural Industry: Structure, Development and Reform*, Oxford University Press: New York.

Chen, S. and M. Ravallion (1996). 'Data in Transition: Assessing Rural Living Standards in Southern China', *China Economic Review*, 7: 23–56.

Clarke, C. (1940). *The Conditions of Economic Progress*, Macmillan: London.

Dasgupta, P. S. and G. M. Heal (1979). *Economic Theory and Exhaustible Resources*. Cambridge University Press: Cambridge.

Ellis, F. (1998). 'Household Strategies and Rural Livelihood Diversification', *Journal of Development Studies*, 35: 1–38.

Feder G. and R. Slade (1985). 'The Role of Public Policy in the Diffusion of Improved Agricultural Technology', *American Journal of Agricultural Economics*, 67: 423–8.

Foster, A. D. and M. R. Rosenzweig (1995). 'Learning by Doing and Learning from Others: Human Capital and Technical Change in Agriculture', *Journal of Political Economy*, 103(6): 1176–209.

—— and —— (1996). 'Technical Change and Human-Capital Returns and Investments: Evidence from the Green Revolution', *American Economic Review*, 86: 931–53.

Godfrey, L. G. (1988). *Misspecification Tests in Econometrics*, Cambridge University Press: Cambridge.

Greenwald, B. and J. E. Stiglitz (1986). 'Externalities in Economies with Imperfect Information and Incomplete Markets', *Quarterly Journal of Economics*, 101(2): 229–64.

Haggblade, S., P. Hazell, and J. Brown (1989). 'Farm–Non-farm Linkages in Rural sub-Saharan Africa', *World Development*, 17(8): 1173–201.

——, ——, and T. Reardon (2002). 'Strategies for Stimulating Poverty-Alleviating Growth in the Rural Non-farm Economy in Developing Countries' (mimeo), International Food Policy Research Institute: Washington DC.

Haiyan, Du (1990). 'Causes of Rapid Rural Industrial Development', in W. A. Byrd and L. Qingspong (eds) *China's Rural Industry: Structure, Development and Reform*, Oxford University Press: New York.

Hazell, P. and S. Haggblade (1993). 'Farm–Non-farm Growth Linkages and the Welfare of the Poor', in M. Lipton and J. van der Gaag (eds) *Including the Poor*, World Bank: Washington DC.

Hoff, K. (1998). 'Adverse Selection and Institutional Adaptation' (mimeo), Development Research Group, World Bank: Washington DC.

—— (2000). 'Beyond Rosenstain-Rodan: The Modern Theory of Underdevelopment Traps', paper presented at the Annual Bank Conference on Development Economics, World Bank, Washington DC.

Holtz-Eakin, D., W. Newey, and H. Rosen (1988). 'Estimating Vector Autoregressions with Panel Data', *Econometrica*, 56: 1371–95.

Jalan, J. and M. Ravallion (1998). 'Are There Dynamic Gains from a Poor-Area Development Programme?', *Journal of Public Economics*, 67: 65–85.

—— and —— (2002). 'Geographic Poverty Traps? A Micro Model of Consumption Growth in Rural China', *Journal of Applied Econometrics*, 17(4): 329–46.

Jiacheng, H. (1990). 'Development Issues and Policy Choices', in W. A. Byrd and L. Qingspong (eds) *China's Rural Industry: Structure, Development and Reform*, Oxford University Press: New York.

Lanjouw, J. O. and P. Lanjouw (2001). 'The Rural Non-farm Sector: Issues and Evidence from Developing Countries', *Agricultural Economics*, 26: 1–23.

Leading Group (1988). *Outlines of Economic Development in China's Poor Areas*, Office of the Leading Group of Economic Development in Poor Areas Under the State Council, Agricultural Publishing House: Beijing.

Lucas, R. E. (1993). 'Making a Miracle', *Econometrica*, 61: 251–72.

Mellor, J. W. (1976). *The New Economics of Growth: A Strategy for India and the Developing World*, Cornell University Press: Ithaca, NY.

Mellor, J. W. and U. Lele (1972). 'Growth Linkages of the New Grain Technologies', *Indian Journal of Agricultural Economics*, 18(1): 35–55.

Romer, P. M. (1986). 'Increasing Returns and Long-Run Growth', *Journal of Political Economy*, 94: 1002–37.

Rosenstain-Rodan, P. (1943). 'Problems of Industrialization of Eastern and Southeastern Europe', *Economic Journal*, 53: 202–11.

Sengupta, J. L. and B. Q. Lin (1995). 'Recent Rural Growth in China: The Performance of the Rural Small-Scale Enterprises' (mimeo), University of California: Santa Barbara, CA.

World Bank (1992). *China: Strategies for Reducing Poverty in the 1990s*, World Bank: Washington DC.

PART V

GROWTH AND POVERTY REDUCTION—THE REGIONAL LINKAGE

8

How Responsive is Poverty to Growth? A Regional Analysis of Poverty, Inequality, and Growth in Indonesia, 1984–99

8.1. INTRODUCTION

Events such as the 1997 Asian currency crisis have focused much popular attention on increasing global integration and its consequences for the world's poor. Both sides of the debate, the pro- and anti-globalizers, promote their development strategies as pro-poor and look to recent history to support their views. This uncertainty surrounding the potential impacts of globalization on the world's poorest households has motivated several recent studies to re-examine the relationship between global integration and economic growth on the one hand and economic growth and poverty reduction on the other.[1] This chapter will offer further evidence on the second question by documenting changes in poverty in Indonesia over the period 1984–99 and then relating the observed changes to income growth and changes in inequality.

Most studies that explore the poverty reduction–growth relationship have utilized a short panel of country-level data to estimate a mean response of a particular poverty measure to population-wide gains in income. These studies have indeed typically shown that national poverty change is fairly responsive to national economic growth. For example, Dollar and Kraay (2004) find that, on average, a 1 per cent gain in mean income is associated with a 1 per cent gain in income among households in the bottom quintile. If accepted at face value, the summary estimates of poverty responses to growth convey a sense of how much growth is needed to reduce poverty to low

Many thanks are due to James Levinsohn, David Lam, and Jan Svejnar for their invaluable advice and assistance. An anonymous referee supplied very useful direction. Culpability for all remaining errors accrues solely to the author. The views expressed solely reflect those of the author and not necessarily those of the World Bank.

[1] See, for example, Ben-David (1993), Sachs and Warner (1995), Edwards (1998), and Rodriguez and Rodrik (1999) that explore the former question and Bruno et al. (1998), Dollar and Kraay (2000), and Ravallion (2001) that explore the latter.

levels. Additionally, if poverty change is largely determined by growth, then the question concerning the effects of globalization on the *poor* largely becomes a question concerning the effects of globalization on *growth*. However, just as there may very well be no single 'effect' of global integration on economic growth—growth in turn may impact the poor in different ways. These impacts can vary on a national and regional basis as well as across time due to such factors as differing initial economic conditions or differing government policy choices. The use of summary national measures necessarily ignores the potential heterogeneity in the growth–poverty relationship that may exist across countries and also exist even within a country, especially a large country with imperfectly integrated regional economies such as Indonesia.

This chapter will revisit the poverty–growth relationship but this time with a long panel of information (six repeated cross-sections over the period 1984–99) for one country and investigate how poverty change at the provincial level varies with province growth rates and province changes in inequality (while importantly controlling for time-invariant provincial characteristics). A necessary first step in this process involves the generation of successive regional poverty profiles with which to document, as carefully as possible, long-run changes in poverty. This is the first aim of this chapter. The definition of poverty adopted for analysis here follows a 'cost-of-basic-needs' approach and as such is particularly suited to measures of absolute poverty and deprivation. Typical studies of this kind need information on the prices of basic consumption commodities in order to determine a poverty line. When price information is lacking, researchers must often turn towards other definitions of poverty. Although the consumption data used here does not contain price information, it does enable computations of a price proxy, the unit value, which is simply the household's total expenditure on a given good divided by the total quantity consumed. Utilizing a simple structural model of consumer choice, this chapter argues that unit values can indeed serve as good proxies for prices.

The main body of the chapter presents a regional analysis of poverty responses to overall economic growth. This regional focus avoids three difficulties associated with the aforementioned national-level studies. The first difficulty concerns data comparability. Typically, cross-national studies employ secondary datasets that by necessity are comprised of measures derived from underlying primary data of differing design and quality. For example, poverty measures for a particular country can be estimated from either income or consumption surveys, depending on the type of data available. Atkinson and Brandolini (1999) explore various shortcomings with secondary data and identify several measurement concerns when utilizing national-level data collected from heterogeneous sources. By using the repeated cross-sections of a household consumption survey as a uniform data source, this study avoids the pitfalls of measurement heterogeneity often found in secondary data.

The cross-national studies are able to control for time-invariant country-level characteristics that may influence the poverty–growth relation. However, the potential existence of time-varying national-level variables that affect poverty and also are related to economic growth presents a second difficulty. One example of such a time-varying national-level variable is a national pro-poor welfare policy enabled by high growth. The failure to control for these unobserved variables may bias estimates of the poverty–growth relationship. By looking within a country, this study de facto controls for such national-level factors.

The final difficulty with these studies derives from the simple observation that the poor do not constitute a homogeneous group but rather differ substantially along dimensions such as region and urban/rural location. The national scope of previous studies obscures important heterogeneity *among* the poor and the failure to account for such heterogeneity may limit the applicability of the results. Friedman and Levinsohn (2002) find that the consumption impacts of the Indonesian crisis for poor households were dramatically different depending on whether the poor lived in cities or in the country as well as which particular region of the country. By looking at poverty variations within a single country, this study will more carefully account for such heterogeneity.

From a policy perspective, however, the conclusion that growth is good for the poor (or a particular group among the poor) is not especially illuminating. Most economists would expect some benefits of overall growth to accrue to the poor. A more useful question from the policy perspective might instead be posed as: which *types* of growth are better for the poor? This is a more difficult question to answer. However, for this question it is possible to push the data a little harder and look at how poverty responds to growth in different regions across Indonesia. A priori, it is quite possible that poverty differentially responds to the differing sources and structures of growth that can exist across provinces.[2] This chapter finds some evidence to support this view. Regional differences in poverty persist even after controlling for the effects of provincial income and inequality levels. Given these findings, future studies need to take a more careful look at these local determinants of poverty and attempt to identify the sources and structures of growth towards which poverty measures are particularly responsive.

The remainder of the chapter is structured as follows: the next section describes the data used in the study, summarizes the methods of poverty determination, and presents the estimated poverty trends in Indonesia over the period 1984–99 at both the national and regional level. Section 8.3 documents the degree of regional variation in growth and inequality change present in the data, examines the relation between poverty reduction and economic growth in a regression context, and explores regional heterogeneity in this relationship. Section 8.4 concludes. An Appendix then explains the methods of poverty line determination adopted herein.

8.2. DATA AND METHODS

The poverty measurements used in this study are derived from Indonesian household consumption and demographic data. This information is provided by six successive waves of the Indonesian National Socioeconomic Survey—known by its Indonesian

---

[2] In the case of India, Ravallion and Datt (2002) find that the degree of poverty reduction associated with gains in non-farm output varies across provinces.

acronym SUSENAS—which is an annual survey that includes a detailed consumption component every three years. This study utilizes the 1984, 1987, 1990, 1993, 1996, and 1999 consumption components. Every SUSENAS surveys thousands of households from each of Indonesia's twenty-seven provinces (for a total sample size of 50,000–60,000 households, depending on the survey year).[3] Population weights enable representative analysis at the provincial level and, unless otherwise noted, are used in the analysis to follow.[4]

SUSENAS gathers household consumption data at a fairly detailed level, especially for food items. For example, the 1996 SUSENAS records the total weekly consumption and expenditure for 217 individual foods such as tomatoes or rice (actually four different varieties of rice are included in the survey). The consumption component contains a large core of important individual consumption items that are recorded in every survey year, thus enabling a consistent comparison of consumption across time. SUSENAS is also fielded in January or February of each year to ensure that intertemporal comparisons are not confounded by seasonal variation in household income and consumption. For self-produced food items, SUSENAS interviewers are trained to impute the value of such consumption based on prevailing local prices. The survey itself does not report direct price observations. However, a price proxy, the unit value, can be computed by dividing total household expenditures on a particular food by total quantity consumed. These unit values play an important role in determining the poverty lines used later in the analysis.[5]

Table 8.1 gives an overview of the six SUSENAS surveys as well as some simple summary statistics. The general trend in urbanization in Indonesia is quite apparent. The percentage of rural households in the total sample declines from 78 to 61 per cent over the 15-year period. Table 8.1 also reports mean per capita household expenditures in 1984 rupiahs. It is important to note that the deflators used in this study are not the standard deflators derived from official price data but rather a food-only price deflator derived from the household consumption information in SUSENAS.[6] This deflator is a welfare consistent measure in that it represents the cost of a predetermined, culturally appropriate, and adequately nutritious basket of food goods. These issues will be explored further when we discuss poverty line determination methods but we note here that the cost of this basket is one of the poverty lines adopted by this study.

---

[3] Due to the unclear sampling frame of the data from the contested province of East Timor (urban areas were not surveyed) this province is dropped from subsequent analysis.

[4] From 1993 on, the SUSENAS sampling frame was modified to enable representative analysis at the Regency (Kabupaten) level, one administrative level lower than province. To remain consistent with the pre-1993 period, this study will use the province as the sole geographic unit.

[5] SUSENAS also collects expenditure information for approximately 100 non-food goods and aggregate goods such as electricity or male apparel. Also included are expenditures on festivities and ceremonies as well as taxes and insurance. Due to the aggregate nature of most of these non-food categories, SUSENAS does not record the quantities of the goods consumed. As such, and unlike food goods, researchers are unable to impute unit values for these goods.

[6] This price deflator is a 'democratic' deflator in the spirit of Prais (1959) in that it gives greater weight (indeed total weight) to the most basic necessities, in this case food.

Table 8.1. *Summary characteristics of the SUSENAS survey, 1984–99*

	Year	Total	Urban	Rural
Proportion of rural households	1984	0.779	—	—
	1987	0.742	—	—
	1990	0.712	—	—
	1993	0.696	—	—
	1996	0.644	—	—
	1999	0.608	—	—
Per capita monthly expenditure				
(1984 rupiahs)[a]	1984	17,307	27,427	14,436
	1987	20,555	31,213	16,852
	1990	20,619	30,025	16,819
	1993	24,248	35,963	19,130
	1996	26,262	37,861	19,856
	1999	19,021	25,276	14,984
Food share of total expenditure	1984	0.675	0.590	0.699
	1987	0.662	0.574	0.693
	1990	0.658	0.572	0.692
	1993	0.625	0.554	0.656
	1996	0.622	0.552	0.661
	1999	0.681	0.616	0.722
Unweighted no. of households	1984	50,296	15,893	34,403
	1987	51,257	15,651	35,606
	1990	46,026	11,646	34,380
	1993	58,100	22,725	35,375
	1996	61,965	24,472	37,493
	1999	62,210	25,626	36,584
Unweighted no. of individuals	1984	244,347	80,567	163,780
	1987	245,416	79,141	166,275
	1990	212,860	56,924	155,936
	1993	260,368	105,581	154,787
	1996	269,869	110,180	159,689
	1999	258,211	107,926	150,285

Note: [a] As determined from a food price deflator estimated from SUSENAS.

Source: Author's calculations from SUSENAS surveys, various rounds.

Over the period 1984–96, changes in Indonesian food prices tracked quite closely with overall inflation and so the food deflator here yields real income changes consistent with other studies of income change (Biro Pusat Statistik 1997). Household welfare, as measured by either the mean real per capita monthly household expenditure or by the average share of food expenditures, shows clear gains over the 1984–96 period of sustained national growth. Real mean per capita household expenditure (in 1984 rupiahs) increases from 17,300 rupiahs/person/month in 1984 to 26,300 in 1996. Gains of similar magnitude are found in both urban and rural areas.

As a result of the financial crisis and the lifting of price controls in late 1997, Indonesia experienced a prolonged period of high inflation where food prices rose even more rapidly than non-food prices. Because of this, the food deflator over the 1996–9 period will overstate overall inflation and the decline in real per capital expenditure (PCE) when compared with the deflators used in most other studies of the post-crisis impacts. Table 8.1 reveals a 28 per cent decline in mean PCE—from 26,260 to 19,020, 1984 rupiahs per person per month. This decline stands in comparison to a 17 per cent decline over the same period when consumption change is measured with a general price index (Suryahadi *et al.* 2000). We will not adjust our deflators so that they correspond with more commonly used ones since we are primarily concerned with the poverty–growth relationship and the approach should not lead to biases in the multivariate analysis to come once appropriate period controls are included. We also hope to exhibit in this study the types of analysis possible with only repeated consumption surveys (a point made clear in the Appendix). However, we do note that our approach will overstate the real expenditure declines as a result of the 1997 financial crisis.

Despite the use of a food price deflator, our summary findings are qualitatively similar to other studies documenting the impacts of the crisis. We observe a greater decline in consumption in urban areas as opposed to rural (33 per cent versus 26 per cent). Frankenberg *et al.* (1999) find a similar sectoral difference with a measured 34 per cent decline in PCE in urban areas and 18 per cent in rural over the single year period 1997–8. The detrimental impacts of the crisis are also apparent in the proportion of household expenditures devoted to food, another common welfare measure. The food share declines over the 1984–96 period from 68 to 62 per cent of total household expenditures. This decline is partly due to the decreasing mean food shares within urban and rural areas as well as the increasing proportion of the population living in cities. However, given the rise in relative food prices and fall in real income as a result of the crisis, the national food share returns to 68 per cent in 1999. The proportional rise in the food share is greater for urban households, from 55 to 62 per cent. Unlike real expenditures, the magnitude of change in this welfare measure is not dependent on the particular choice of price deflator.

Although Table 8.1 reports changes in summary measures of mean household welfare, we are mainly concerned with the welfare of households towards the bottom of the distribution, particularly households deemed 'poor'. The poverty determination methods adopted here define poor households as those households unable to afford a basic consumption bundle which, while also reflecting prevailing notions of taste, ensures adequate nutrition as well as a necessary amount of non-food expenditures. This cost-of-basic-needs approach and its relative merits are discussed in Ravallion and Bidani (1994). The method used here is, in many ways, a refinement and adaptation of work developed by Bidani and Ravallion (1993) and Ravallion (1994). The approach involves the estimation of the total cost for a bundle of 'basic food goods' as well as 'basic non-food goods' typically utilizing direct observations of price. The method adopted here enables poverty computations without direct information on prices but instead uses a simple model of consumer choice to impute prices from unit values.

A household is deemed poor if its per capita expenditure lies below a fixed poverty line. As a check on the robustness of any results, three different poverty lines representing different levels of welfare are in fact determined and used in the analysis. The poverty line methodology is explained in detail in the Appendix but the general approach is summarized as follows: a nutritionally adequate food bundle (with nutritional guidelines stipulated by WHO *et al.* 1985) that reflects the actual consumption choices of Indonesian households is determined and then priced. To ensure time consistent welfare comparisons the food bundle is fixed and applied to each survey year. The total cost of this bundle represents one poverty line termed the food poverty line. The food poverty line can then be scaled upwards by an econometrically estimated factor that represents the cost of essential non-food goods. Two such scale factors are utilized, one more generous than the other. Thus, these final values which we term the lower and upper poverty lines, proxy the total cost of essential food and non-food consumption needs.

Due to important differences in relative prices between urban and rural areas, poverty lines are computed separately for each area. Poverty lines can also be determined with national mean prices or with more local provincial prices. We have estimated poverty lines from both types of price data as a check on the robustness of our findings. Since the results from the subsequent analysis do not appreciably differ if local or national prices are used, we only present the results with poverty estimates based on local prices since they will more accurately reflect local conditions. After the determination of a particular poverty line we then use the class of Foster–Greer–Thorbecke (FGT) poverty measures to assess poverty In particular, we will use the headcount index, the poverty gap, and the squared gap measure. These measures are also described in the Appendix. To give some sense of the precision of the poverty estimates, bootstrapped standard errors will be reported alongside some of the poverty measures in the analysis to follow.[7]

Table 8.2 and Fig. 8.1 present national trends in the overall poverty measures. As is readily apparent, Indonesia has indeed experienced broad gains in poverty reduction over the 12-year-period 1984–96. Table 8.2 contains the values of all three poverty measures (the headcount, poverty gap, and squared gap measures) calculated at each poverty line (the food line, the lower, and the upper) for each of the six survey years. The national poverty headcount, as measured by the upper poverty line, declined 61 per cent from 1984 to 1996, while the lower poverty line national headcount posted even greater declines of 71 per cent. While Indonesia made significant gains in reducing the proportion of population living in poverty, it made even greater gains in reducing

---

[7] Since SUSENAS has a clustered survey design, the bootstrapped standard errors are calculated by drawing random samples of clusters with replacement. For each cluster selected, all households are used in the error calculation. As noted in Deaton and Paxson (1998), failure to recognize the clustered design of the survey data will result in an understatement of sampling variability.

Table 8.2. *Summary national poverty measures, 1984–99*

Poverty line	Poverty measure	1984			1987			1990		
		Total	Urban	Rural	Total	Urban	Rural	Total	Urban	Rural
Upper	Headcount	0.4151	0.1972	0.4819	0.2920	0.1282	0.3508	0.2647	0.1464	0.3160
	s.e.	0.0065	0.0068	0.0070	0.0053	0.0075	0.0071	0.0037	0.0081	0.0062
	Poverty gap	0.1165	0.0461	0.1381	0.0632	0.0244	0.0771	0.0537	0.0274	0.0651
	Squared gap	0.0459	0.0166	0.0549	0.0199	0.0071	0.0245	0.0162	0.0078	0.0198
Lower	Headcount	0.1357	0.1155	0.3771	0.1951	0.0648	0.2418	0.1671	0.0723	0.2083
	Poverty gap	0.0806	0.0250	0.0977	0.0371	0.0106	0.0466	0.0299	0.0115	0.0379
	Squared gap	0.0298	0.0085	0.0363	0.0107	0.0028	0.0135	0.0082	0.0029	0.0105
Food	Headcount	0.1684	0.0461	0.2056	0.0737	0.0150	0.0948	0.0578	0.0192	0.0745
	Poverty gap	0.0362	0.0091	0.0445	0.0114	0.0024	0.0146	0.0083	0.0024	0.0109
	Squared gap	0.0120	0.0029	0.0148	0.0028	0.0006	0.0036	0.0020	0.0005	0.0026

Poverty line	Poverty measure	1993			1996			1999		
		Total	Urban	Rural	Total	Urban	Rural	Total	Urban	Rural
Upper	Headcount	0.2013	0.0973	0.2520	0.1625	0.0843	0.2083	0.3508	0.2433	0.4223
	s.e	0.0048	0.0056	0.0073	0.0034	0.0036	0.0045	0.0046	0.0070	0.0054
	Poverty gap	0.0370	0.0169	0.0468	0.0286	0.0136	0.0373	0.0775	0.0502	0.0957
	Squared gap	0.0103	0.0043	0.0132	0.0077	0.0035	0.0102	0.0248	0.0153	0.0312
Lower	Headcount	0.1190	0.0447	0.1552	0.0913	0.0355	0.1239	0.2329	0.1338	0.2989
	Poverty gap	0.0191	0.0063	0.0254	0.0143	0.0050	0.0198	0.0449	0.0234	0.0592
	Squared gap	0.0048	0.0013	0.0065	0.0035	0.0011	0.0049	0.0130	0.0062	0.0175
Food	Headcount	0.0349	0.0088	0.0477	0.0261	0.0070	0.0373	0.0884	0.0413	0.1197
	Poverty gap	0.0045	0.0008	0.0063	0.0032	0.0008	0.0046	0.0135	0.0052	0.0191
	Squared gap	0.0009	0.0001	0.0014	0.0007	0.0002	0.0009	0.0034	0.0011	0.0049

Source: Author's calculations from SUSENAS surveys, various rounds.

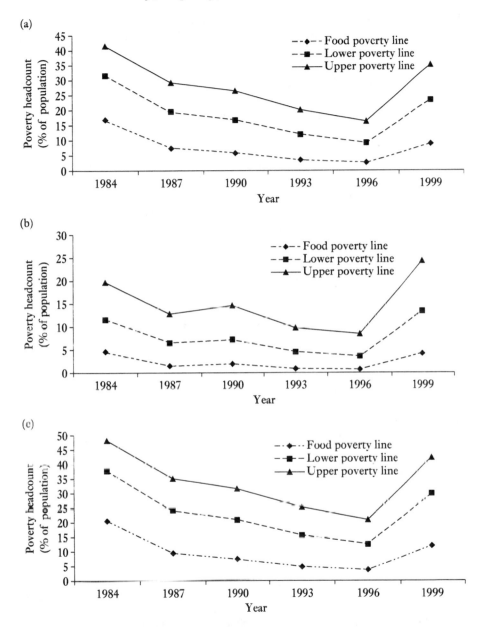

Figure 8.1. *Overall poverty trends in Indonesia, various poverty lines: (a) national poverty headcounts, (b) urban poverty headcounts, (c) rural poverty headcounts*

the severity of poverty, with the squared gap measure declining by more than 80 per cent over the period. To give some sense of the precision of these estimates, Table 8.2 also lists the estimated standard errors for the upper poverty line headcount measure. As is quite apparent by the relatively small standard errors, the headcount measures are all precisely estimated and the year-on-year changes in poverty are statistically significant at standard significance levels.

Broadbased gains in poverty reduction were found in both rural and urban areas. The greatest poverty reductions were witnessed in rural areas with the headcount measure based on the upper poverty line declining by 57 per cent and the squared gap measure falling by 81 per cent. Similar to the national figures, not only did rural Indonesia experience large declines in the incidence of poverty, but the severity of poverty, as conveyed by the squared gap measure, fell by an even greater amount. The story is slightly different in urban areas as poverty does not decline monotonically over time. Indeed most urban poverty measures pose a slight increase over the 1987–90 period.[8]

In terms of the timing of poverty reduction, the greatest gains were reported over the 1984–7 period. There is some fear that SUSENAS underreports consumption (van de Walle 1988), and this may be especially true for the 1984 wave. Inspecting the underlying consumption baskets across the years, it is clear that the reported consumption of one of the rice varieties is substantially less in 1984 than in all subsequent periods. If the 1984 SUSENAS does indeed underreport consumption then the 1984 poverty measures may be overestimated. It is not immediately clear what can be done to correct for such possible consumption underestimation without further information on survey implementation or consumption patterns. As such, we report the numbers without correction. However, subsequent multivariate analysis will include a vector of time period dummy variables that should absorb any year-to-year variation in poverty measures due to idiosyncrasies in survey implementation.

After the gains in poverty reduction from 1984–96, the increase in poverty as a result of financial crisis is severe and abrupt. We estimate increases in poverty headcounts on the order of 116 per cent when using the upper poverty line, 155 per cent with the lower poverty line, and 239 per cent with the food poverty line (albeit the food

---

[8] Even though each poverty measure determined at each poverty line records the same general decline (or increase) in poverty, we look into whether another arbitrary poverty line or poverty measure might convey a different result by estimating the successive cumulative distribution functions (CDFs) for household consumption (results not shown). These results confirm that there will be no reversals in estimated poverty change if any arbitrary poverty line is adopted. We find that the 1996 consumption CDF stochastically dominates the 1993 CDF, as 1993 dominates 1990, and so on, at any point the CDF for 1996 lies below that for 1993, as 1993 lies below 1990. That is, a combination of any arbitrary poverty line and measure will record the same general decline in poverty for 1984–96; see Foster and Shorrocks (1988) for a discussion of stochastic dominance and poverty measures. Of course these gains are reversed by the financial crisis where the CDF for 1999 almost coincides with the CDF from the earliest period, 1984. Again, a deflator with a non-food component would not have yielded quite this extreme a change in consumption even though the drop in consumption would still be severe. Similar analysis conducted separately for urban and rural areas confirms that the higher poverty rates observed in urban areas in 1990 than 1987 would have been found with any poverty line or measure.

poverty line increase starts from a low base). The gap and squared gap measures, more sensitive to distributions among the poor, show even greater increases thus indicating an increased mass of households at the very tail end of the expenditure distribution. As previously discussed, the measured magnitude of these poverty changes depends on our choice of an all-food price deflator. Since food prices rose more rapidly than non-food prices, and even the poorest of households consume some non-food items, these poverty change measures surely overstate the actual change in poverty at least to some extent. As a point of comparison, Suryahadi *et al.* (2000) calculate the increase in national poverty headcounts to be on the order of 57–129 per cent depending on the exact type of deflator used.

Regardless of the exact magnitude of the poverty increase, it is clear that the impacts of the crisis do not fall equally across urban and rural areas. For example, the headcount measure based on the upper poverty line increases 189 per cent for urban households and 103 per cent for rural households. The difference in the increase in the squared gap measure is even greater. These differential changes are consistent with other studies. Friedman and Levinsohn (2002) predict that the urban poor would be especially affected by the crisis and Frankenberg *et al.* (1999) have indeed found this to be the case. Clearly, there are important distinctions to be made among the urban and rural poor. Even within urban or rural areas, there is significant variation in the incidence of poverty across the different Indonesian regions. Table 8.3 presents the regional poverty profiles for the survey years 1987 and 1993, two years in the middle of a period of sustained high national growth. Reported in this table are both the upper poverty line headcounts for each provincial rural/urban cell, as well as the Gini coefficient, in order to give a sense of the extent of variation in regional poverty and regional inequality.

Within urban and rural areas, poverty levels are quite varied. The capital Jakarta has the lowest poverty headcount in both years whereas cities in both west and east Nusa Tenggara (a collection of islands east of Bali) tend to have the highest poverty incidence. Poverty levels overall are higher in rural areas but still varied across Indonesia. Some of the lowest rural poverty in both years is found in the Sumatran province of Jambi and some of the highest in the remote island of Irian Jaya as well as the islands of Nusa Tenggara. A cursory inspection across the two years will also confirm a good deal of heterogeneity in the change of poverty incidence. In most regions poverty decreases, with the rural areas of Java and Bali experiencing the largest reduction in poverty. Nevertheless, a handful of regions, such as rural south Sumatra actually post an increase in poverty incidence.

In regards to inequality, the regional Gini coefficient is generally lower in rural areas. Since real income is also lower in rural areas, the combination of low mean income and low inequality necessarily implies higher poverty levels in rural regions. Nevertheless, there is also a good deal of regional variation in inequality—Gini coefficients in 1987 range from 0.25 to 0.35 in urban areas and from 0.21 to 0.31 in rural areas. Temporal trends in regional inequality are harder to discern from this table, although inequality does appear to be increasing for most urban areas and decreasing for rural ones. These trends will be explored in a more comprehensive fashion in the next section.

Table 8.3. *Headcount poverty estimates at the upper poverty line and Gini coefficients, by province*

Province	Urban				Rural			
	1987		1993		1987		1993	
	Poverty count	Gini coeff.	Poverty count	Gini coeff.	Poverty count	Gini coeff.	Poverty count	Gini coeff.
Aceh	0.096	0.291	0.083	0.319	0.272	0.243	0.160	0.248
N. Sumatra	0.104	0.278	0.108	0.307	0.340	0.253	0.221	0.228
W. Sumatra	0.094	0.272	0.080	0.333	0.221	0.248	0.196	0.258
Riau	0.096	0.251	0.039	0.245	0.275	0.209	0.151	0.242
Jambi	0.082	0.211	0.089	0.242	0.219	0.234	0.130	0.227
S. Sumatra	0.128	0.295	0.064	0.296	0.231	0.250	0.291	0.238
Bengkulu	0.133	0.266	0.058	0.274	0.297	0.212	0.250	0.210
Lampung	0.136	0.281	0.156	0.282	0.366	0.270	0.310	0.251
Jakarta	0.015	0.305	0.012	0.356	—	—	—	—
W. Java	0.158	0.322	0.108	0.305	0.273	0.278	0.134	0.271
C. Java	0.203	0.290	0.166	0.307	0.409	0.256	0.307	0.269
Yogyakarta	0.108	0.320	0.068	0.339	0.275	0.287	0.107	0.270
E. Java	0.132	0.332	0.120	0.361	0.394	0.280	0.265	0.237
Bali	0.135	0.322	0.100	0.327	0.300	0.313	0.177	0.283
W. Nusa Tenggara	0.390	0.331	0.192	0.328	0.504	0.281	0.395	0.246
E. Nusa Tenggara	0.217	0.347	0.221	0.328	0.593	0.253	0.485	0.208
W. Kalimantan	0.155	0.273	0.114	0.300	0.529	0.218	0.463	0.253
C. Kalimantan	0.110	0.247	0.077	0.291	0.335	0.220	0.257	0.214
S. Kalimantan	0.071	0.284	0.036	0.275	0.293	0.249	0.176	0.262
E. Kalimantan	0.083	0.314	0.026	0.303	0.248	0.277	0.118	0.251
N. Sulawesi	0.125	0.309	0.076	0.291	0.295	0.280	0.264	0.257
C. Sulawesi	0.037	0.257	0.104	0.292	0.363	0.265	0.225	0.262
S. Sulawesi	0.159	0.291	0.104	0.259	0.414	0.238	0.205	0.258
S.E. Sulawesi	0.141	0.281	0.141	0.272	0.533	0.256	0.312	0.251
Maluku	0.064	0.251	0.050	0.246	0.488	0.280	0.426	0.263
Irian Jaya	0.171	0.311	0.126	0.290	0.669	0.310	0.515	0.360

Source: SUSENAS 1987 and 1993.

8.3. POVERTY CHANGE AND ECONOMIC GROWTH

Having documented Indonesia's gains in poverty reduction over 1984–96 and its reversal from 1996–9 we now turn to how these poverty changes covary with income growth. Several previous studies cited in the introduction have found a significant positive association between poverty reduction and growth in cross-national studies and, thus, they conclude that overall growth benefits even the very poor. This section of the chapter explores the same topic. However, instead of using national variation in poverty and income growth to trace out any association between poverty change

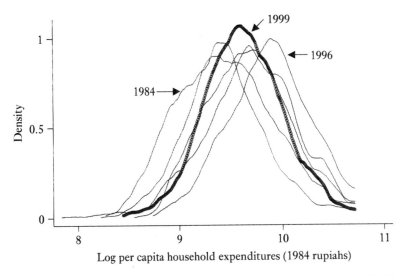

Figure 8.2. *Density plots of per capita household consumption—rural Bali, 1984–99*

and growth, this section will look within one country and utilize regional variation to identify the association between poverty change and income growth at the local level.

For a given poverty line and initial poverty level, the growth and poverty relationship will be determined by how changes in inequality and gains in overall income levels covary over time. These time paths of inequality and income can be quite different across the different regions of Indonesia, given the diversity in sectoral composition of economic activity and in initial provincial conditions. To explore in a descriptive and flexible manner how the growth–poverty relation may vary across regions, we plot kernel density estimates of the log of household PCE in each survey year separately for each provincial urban/rural cell. The resulting cell groupings of density estimates were quite varied. For expositional purposes we present the density estimates for two such cells: rural Bali and urban central Kalimantan.

Figure 8.2 presents the PCE densities for rural Bali. Each year of observation is plotted and three years are labelled: 1984, 1996, and 1999. For rural Bali, the results of high growth from 1984–96 are apparent in the rightward shift of the density plots over time. The fact that the expenditure density maintains its rough shape as it shifts to the right indicates that expenditure distributions in Bali have been fairly consistent over time. The general distributional shape is also maintained after the crisis, indicating that inequality has been left relatively unchanged by the crisis. The exact magnitude of the leftward shift of the 1999 density depends of course on the choice of deflator (which is here again a food price deflator).

The story revealed in Fig. 8.3, for urban central Kalimantan, is quite different. In this cell, growth appears to occur simultaneously with an increase in inequality as the density plots shift rightward over time from 1984 to 1996 but also flatten out, thus increasing the density in both tails. The growth that occurred in this cell has very

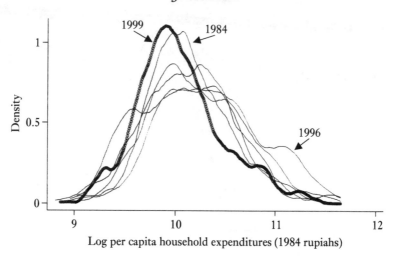

Figure 8.3. *Density plots of per capita household consumption—urban central Kalimantan, 1984–99*

different distributional implications than the type of growth observed in rural Bali. Furthermore, the financial crisis not only results in a leftward shift of the density but also a contraction of the right tail. The distribution in 1999 appears very similar to that for 1984 and so another consequence of the crisis, besides the income decline, is a decline in inequality.

The heterogeneity in regional growth and inequality change suggested by the province-specific density plots is summarized in Figs 8.4 and 8.5, which portray the magnitude of growth and inequality change for each province in the data. Figure 8.4 depicts the proportional change in mean regional PCE over two periods—the growth period of 1984–96, and the contractionary period 1996–9—for each provincial urban/rural cell. For expositional ease, provinces are ordered from west to east and the major island groups to which they belong are indicated on the horizontal axis. The regional diversity in the provincial growth experience, in either period, is very apparent. Most provincial rural–urban areas gained in mean PCE from 1984–96, especially rural areas in Java and Lampung (the southernmost Sumatran province close to Java). However, even in this period of national growth, the restive easternmost and westernmost provinces of Aceh and Irian Jaya actually experienced drops in mean PCE. The severe consequences of the financial crisis suggested by the density plots are also apparent in Fig. 8.4 where every region experiences a drop in mean PCE, often of a magnitude at least as great as the gains in PCE over the preceding twelve years. Again, the magnitude of this loss is far from uniform. Urban areas generally experienced greater declines in mean PCE than their rural counterparts although the reverse is the case for the easternmost provinces of Irian Jaya, Maluku, and southeast Sulawesi where rural areas appear to have suffered a greater proportional decline in income.

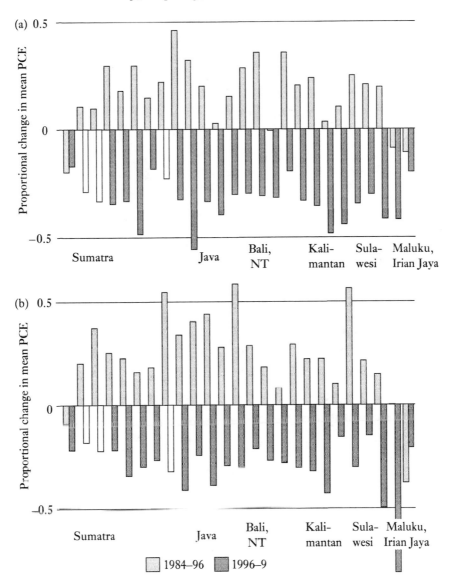

Figure 8.4. *Proportional change in real mean per capita household expenditures, by province 1984–96 and 1996–9: (a) urban areas, (b) rural areas*

Given the diversity of change in regional inequality (measured as the proportional change in the Gini coefficient) apparent in Fig. 8.5, fewer generalizations can be made for either the growth or contractionary periods. In the earlier period, a greater number of urban regions witnessed rising inequality than rural regions, with the greatest increase in inequality experienced by the capital Jakarta. Other regions, such as the rest

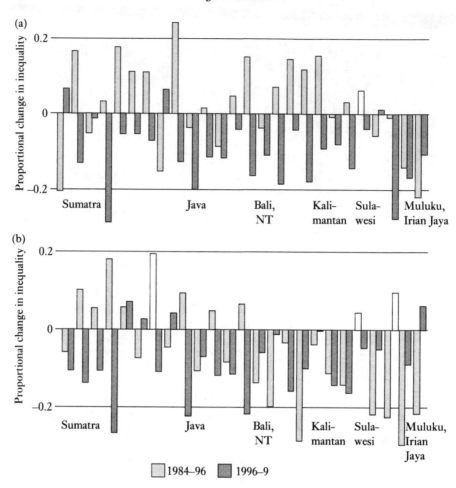

Figure 8.5. *Proportional change in inequality (Gini coefficient), by province 1984–96 and 1996:*
(a) urban areas, (b) rural areas

of urban Java, saw little change in inequality in either direction. Over the crisis period, the vast majority of regions in both rural and urban areas experienced a decline in inequality with the magnitude of this change in certain regions greater than 20 per cent. Thus, not only did the crisis negatively impact overall income, but this decline was not distributionally neutral for in most regions the crisis disproportionately affected the better off households consequently reducing inequality as well as income. In terms of income and inequality comovements, changes in regional income and inequality are positively correlated in both periods, especially over the 1984–96 period (a correlation coefficient of 0.40 compared with a coefficient of 0.14 for the 1996–9 period). As we have seen, however, these summary measures mask a great deal of underlying regional heterogeneity.

Having described how regional income and inequality vary (and covary), we turn now to parameterized estimates of the poverty–growth relationship as we look at regressions of changes in poverty on changes in various income measures. We will return to the regional heterogeneity suggested in Figs 8.3–8.6 soon after. We first estimate a simple econometric specification relating poverty change to income change with the following expression:

$$\Delta \ln P_{\alpha,i}^{t+1,t} = \gamma_0 + \gamma_1 \Delta \ln \mu_i^{t+1,t} + f_p + e_i^{t+1,t},$$

where $\Delta \ln P_\alpha$ is the change in the natural log poverty measure α for region i, $\Delta \ln \mu_i$ is the change in mean real income for region i (here nominal income is once again deflated by the food poverty line as in the previous section), and f_p a vector of time period dummies. These difference regressions are estimated separately for rural and urban areas as well as jointly on the pooled sample. The coefficient γ_1 yields what we can term the gross effect of income growth on poverty change since there is no control for changes in regional inequality. It simply conveys the association between poverty change and mean income change net of period intercept effects. A second specification specifically controlling for changes in regional inequality is given by the following:

$$\Delta \ln P_{\alpha,i}^{t+1,t} = \gamma_0' + \gamma_1' \Delta \ln \mu_i^{t+1,t} + \gamma_2' \Delta \ln G_i^{t+1,t} + f_p + e_i^{t+1,t},$$

where $\ln G_i$ is the natural log of some inequality measure, here taken to be the standard Gini coefficient used in the earlier figures and tables.[9] In this specification γ_1' yields what we will term the net effect of income growth on poverty change since it can be interpreted as the estimated association between distributionally neutral growth and poverty measures, that is, the effect of income growth net of changes in inequality. γ_2' yields the impact of inequality change on poverty while holding income constant.

We also estimate a third specification that includes the initial levels of regional inequality and regional mean income. Since the poverty–growth elasticity is determined by the magnitude of changes in mean income and the shape of the income distribution, as well as the location of the poverty line, the poverty–growth response may vary over time, or across regions, partly due to the initial conditions of the region. Unless each regional cell has the same average income and distributional shape, and the kernel density plots have shown this not to be the case, then even distributionally neutral growth will yield poverty–growth elasticities that vary across regions. Put another way, the density of the distribution around the poverty line at the start of a period may be a significant factor influencing the poverty growth elasticity. Therefore, we also adopt a third specification that includes the initial period mean income μ_i and inequality G_i of the distribution in order to investigate whether regional initial conditions impact the poverty–growth elasticity:

$$\Delta \ln P_{\alpha,i}^{t+1,t} = \gamma_0'' + \gamma_1'' \Delta \ln \mu_i^{t+1,t} + \gamma_2'' \Delta \ln G_i^{t+1,t} + \gamma_3'' \ln \mu_i^t$$
$$+ \gamma_4'' \ln G_i^t + f_p + e_i^{t+1,t}.$$

---

[9] An alternative inequality measure, the variance of log income, was also used in this analysis with little impact on the overall results. For brevity's sake, only results with the Gini coefficient will be reported.

The gross growth elasticities, the net growth elasticities, and the net effects with initial conditions were estimated on the entire sample and then separately for rural and urban areas with feasible generalized least squares (FGLS) to account for hetero-skedasticity across regions.[10] The coefficients and standard errors for all regressions are presented in Table 8.4 and some of the findings are also summarized graphically in Fig. 8.5, which depicts the gross elasticity and the net elasticity with initial conditions of the upper poverty line measures to growth. Looking at the results we see that for any combination of poverty measure and poverty line, the gross effect of growth on poverty reduction is large and significant.[11,12] For example, a 10 per cent increase in regional mean income is associated with an average reduction of 20 per cent in the upper line poverty headcount (and conversely, a 10 per cent decline in income is associated with a 20 per cent increase in poverty). The poverty headcount from the lower line is even more responsive to mean income growth. Alternative poverty measures that account for the depth or severity of poverty, the gap and squared gap measures, yield even larger estimated elasticities than the headcount measure. Not only is the incidence of poverty reduced by income growth, but also the poorest of the poor seem to gain relatively more than the poor closer to the poverty line as Indonesian regions grow.

Since increases in regional inequality are at least weakly positively correlated with gains in income, then we should expect the net response of poverty change to income

---

[10] This framework loosens the restrictions on the regression residuals and allows the within-region variance to vary by region. The point estimates from feasible generalized least squares (FGLS) are virtually identical to the point estimates from ordinary least squares (OLS) and the OLS Huber–White corrected standard errors still result in the precise estimation of each growth and inequality change coefficient. We report the FGLS results but obtain very similar results with OLS.

[11] The poverty measures and the growth measures estimated here derive from the same underlying consumption surveys. It is possible for errors in survey measurement to create a negative correlation between income measures such as the mean income and poverty measures. This spurious correlation can create an upward bias in the estimated poverty–growth elasticities. Ravallion (2001), working with a cross-national sample, explores this issue by instrumenting mean survey income with a national accounts income measure and indeed finds indications of such upward bias. In the case of Indonesia, the regional accounts data are only loosely correlated with the survey means of regional income (with a correlation coefficient near zero for many survey periods) and as such serve as weak instruments at best. Indeed the 2SLS estimates of the poverty–growth elasticities using regional per capita GDP growth as an instrument result in estimated elasticities larger in magnitude than the results in Table 8.4. This increase in the estimated elasticities more likely reflects the low correlation between survey measures and regional accounts data rather than the absence of survey measurement error.

[12] One caveat for these results concerns population migration across provinces or between urban and rural areas and the possible impact of such migration on the consistency of parameter estimates. By aggregating the household data into provincial urban/rural cells and then comparing cell level measures across time, we have created a pseudopanel of information. McKenzie (2001) shows that if the underlying cohort composition does not retain the same mean properties over time then parameters estimated from a pseudopanel may be inconsistent. The concern in the context of this study is the potential presence of differential household or individual migration by income level and its implications for estimates of the poverty–growth elasticity. Surprisingly, Frankenberg et al. (1999) find that household migration rates after the financial crisis do not vary across income quintiles. Nevertheless, possible differential migration before the crisis can pose problems and will need to be explored further in future work. Given the relatively brief time interval of three years, however, it is unlikely that differential migration would substantially affect cohort composition in this data.

Table 8.4. *Difference regressions, poverty change on mean income and inequality change, various specifications, local prices*

Poverty measure	Gross effect of growth		Net effect of growth				Net effect of growth with initial conditions							
			Growth		Inequality change		Growth		Inequality change		Base income		Base inequality	
	Coeff.	s.e.	Coeff.	s.e.	Coeff.	s.e.	Coeff.	s.e.	Coeff.	s.e.	Coeff.	s.e.	Coeff.	s.e.
Total sample														
Headcount upper	−1.959	0.110	−2.624	0.116	1.432	0.114	−2.722	0.122	1.527	0.125	−0.127	0.044	0.128	0.090
Headcount lower	−2.332	0.161	−3.111	0.155	1.797	0.147	−3.222	0.167	1.863	0.165	−0.123	0.070	0.063	0.116
Gap upper	−2.546	0.160	−3.572	0.129	2.202	0.129	−3.650	0.132	2.183	0.146	−0.117	0.050	−0.049	0.112
Gap lower	−3.025	0.216	−4.139	0.295	3.517	0.307	−4.853	0.300	3.377	0.336	−0.179	0.108	−0.381	0.269
Square gap upper	−3.150	0.209	−4.117	0.171	2.666	0.183	−4.183	0.178	2.559	0.205	−0.099	0.067	−0.226	0.159
Square gap lower	−3.488	0.264	−4.682	0.295	3.517	0.307	−4.853	0.300	3.377	0.336	−0.179	0.108	−0.381	0.269
Urban areas														
Headcount upper	−1.782	0.225	−2.890	0.213	2.223	0.232	−2.947	0.206	2.041	0.262	−0.164	0.081	−0.084	0.174
Headcount lower	−2.142	0.369	−3.665	0.363	3.179	0.351	−3.759	0.393	3.261	0.410	−0.129	0.197	0.133	0.343
Gap upper	−2.324	0.329	−3.916	0.278	3.175	0.282	−4.000	0.297	3.097	0.324	−0.113	0.142	−0.112	0.240
Gap lower	−3.040	0.457	−4.691	0.488	4.325	0.496	−4.666	0.520	4.104	0.554	−0.025	0.260	−0.294	0.328
Square gap upper	−2.639	0.421	−4.422	0.379	3.833	0.388	−4.413	0.405	3.636	0.432	−0.034	0.208	−0.305	0.274
Square gap lower	−2.284	0.618	−5.082	0.747	5.698	0.717	−5.047	0.791	5.316	0.810	−0.033	0.398	−0.551	0.541
Rural areas														
Headcount upper	−1.938	0.116	−2.122	0.108	0.795	0.111	−2.175	0.117	0.901	0.137	−0.069	0.069	0.194	0.138
Headcount lower	−2.317	0.170	−2.531	0.143	1.346	0.130	−2.582	0.159	1.347	0.169	−0.053	0.079	0.003	0.176
Gap upper	−2.689	0.169	−3.200	0.136	1.747	0.128	−3.229	0.150	1.715	0.164	−0.049	0.078	−0.062	0.160
Gap lower	−3.076	0.219	−3.322	0.177	2.120	0.163	−3.793	0.196	2.053	0.212	−0.001	0.110	−0.117	0.209
Square gap upper	−3.369	0.221	−3.954	0.175	2.132	0.173	−3.914	0.194	1.990	0.220	−0.022	0.110	−0.250	0.214
Square gap lower	−3.807	0.279	−4.486	0.260	2.402	0.277	−4.428	0.284	2.165	0.339	−0.047	0.156	−0.441	0.332

Note: Estimates from FGLS. $N = 255$ for total sample estimates; 130 for urban, and 125 for rural estimates.

Source: Author's estimates from SUSENAS surveys, various rounds.

growth to be even greater once inequality changes are controlled for. This is indeed the case. The net elasticity of the upper headcount to mean income growth is −2.62. Elasticities for the gap and squared gap measures are still greater in magnitude. When looking within urban and rural areas, the increase in magnitude from the gross to the net growth elasticity is much greater in urban areas than in rural (−1.78 to −2.89 for the upper line urban poverty headcount as opposed to −1.94 to −2.12 for the rural count), indicating that the association between rising inequality and economic growth is much greater in urban areas than rural. Of course inequality change itself is significantly and positively correlated with poverty change. A mean income preserving 10 per cent reduction in the Gini coefficient would reduce the upper line headcount measure by 14 per cent and the squared gap measure by 27 per cent. The inequality coefficients are far greater for urban areas, again attesting to the relatively inequitable growth in urban areas as opposed to rural.

When the base period conditions are included in the poverty growth regressions, the coefficients on mean income growth and inequality change are statistically indistinguishable from the net effects regressions without the initial regional conditions. This suggests that, for this data, the initial conditions of the regional expenditure distributions would add little to historical predictions of poverty change once information on the changes in those distributions are taken into account. The initial condition coefficients themselves are generally insignificant and small in magnitude. By already controlling for inequality change, base period inequality exerts no discernible influence whatsoever on poverty change. Regional mean income does exert some influence on poverty reduction, at least in the total sample estimates, where the greater the mean income, the more responsive the poverty headcounts are to overall growth. This is not the case, however, within urban or rural areas (except for the upper line poverty headcount in urban areas).

Table 8.4 and Fig. 8.6 present the association between growth in provincial mean income and poverty reduction and found that poverty responds strongly to gains in mean income. Mean income growth is, of course, only one potential measure of growth and the data enable further investigations into the elasticity of poverty to changes in other points in the income distribution in addition to this summary mean measure. Therefore, we re-estimate the above specifications using the change in income at the tenth, twenty-fifth, fiftieth, seventy-fifth, and ninetieth expenditure percentiles as alternative growth measures. Figure 8.7 summarizes the estimated gross and net elasticities of the upper line poverty gap measure using these alternative income change measures in order to give some sense of the results without presenting a large table with numerous coefficients and standard errors. All poverty growth elasticities in the tables are precisely estimated. Not surprisingly, poverty reduction responds quite strongly to gains at low levels of income. For example, the elasticity of the upper line poverty gap to an increase in the tenth income percentile is −3.6, indicating a greater poverty response to tenth percentile income growth than to mean income growth. Similar coefficients are found for the gross effect of increases in the twenty-fifth expenditure percentile. Growth in higher points in the income distribution is substantially less related to poverty reduction. A 1 per cent gain in the ninetieth income percentile translates into

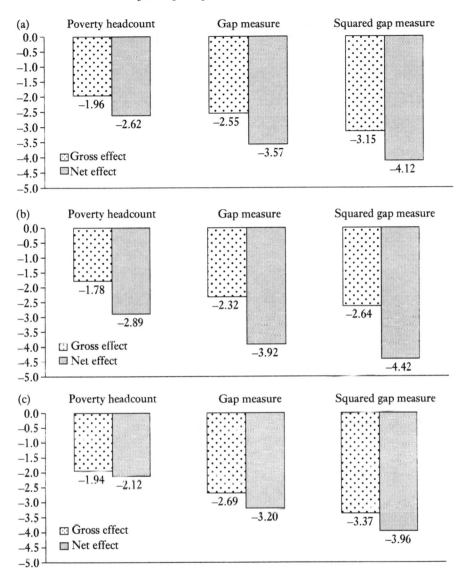

Figure 8.6. *Gross and net elasticities of upper line poverty measures to mean income growth: (a) total sample, (b) urban areas, (c) rural areas*

only a 1.5 per cent decline in the upper poverty gap. Indeed in urban areas, gains in the ninetieth income percentiles implies less than a 1 per cent decline in the gap. Clearly, growth in the upper tail of the income distribution is only weakly correlated with growth in the bottom tail, especially for urban areas. Controlling for inequality, however, the net effects of gains in income at any percentile are now much more similar.

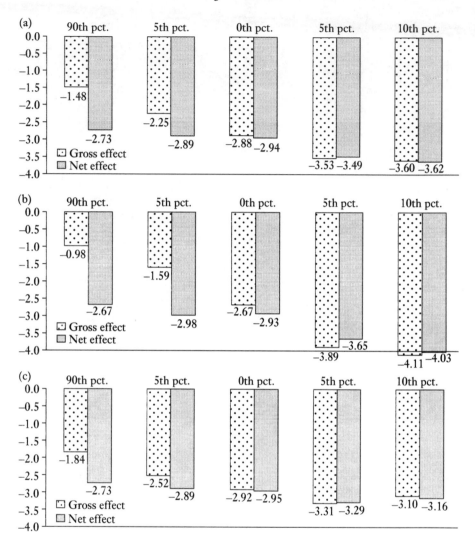

Figure 8.7. *Gross and net elasticities of upper poverty line poverty gap to growth in various percentiles of income distribution: (a) total sample, (b) urban areas, (c) rural areas*

The upper line gap elasticities for the entire sample now range from −2.7 with respect to the ninetieth income percentile to −3.6 with respect to the tenth percentile. The narrowing of differences across percentiles is not surprising, of course, since by netting out the effects of inequality change we force the entire income distribution to increase in lock step with the particular income measure.

All regression results until now have been estimated on the entire sample and, thus, implicitly constrain the poverty–growth elasticities to be the same during periods of

Table 8.5. *Net effects of growth distinguished by periods of expansion and contraction*

	Periods of positive growth				Periods of negative growth			
	Net effect of growth		Inequality change		Net effect of growth		Inequality change	
	Coeff.	s.e.	Coeff.	s.e.	Coeff.	s.e.	Coeff.	s.e.
Total sample								
Headcount upper	−3.181	0.185	1.832	0.147	−2.007	0.241	1.265	0.159
Headcount lower	−3.756	0.168	2.479	0.139	−2.461	0.302	1.582	0.145
Gap upper	−3.640	0.144	2.325	0.196	−3.075	0.259	1.950	0.195
Gap lower	−3.959	0.326	2.772	0.362	−3.777	0.379	2.743	0.261
Square gap upper	−4.056	0.241	2.762	0.299	−3.947	0.283	2.455	0.216
Square gap lower	−4.816	0.457	3.783	0.467	−4.892	0.460	3.793	0.478
Urban areas								
Headcount upper	−3.094	0.387	2.128	0.368	−2.961	0.379	2.764	0.286
Headcount lower	−2.685	0.430	3.355	0.357	−4.718	0.648	3.428	0.380
Gap upper	−3.081	0.202	2.942	0.291	−3.827	0.537	3.161	0.354
Gap lower	−2.625	0.728	3.692	0.657	−4.530	0.945	4.453	0.547
Square gap upper	−2.826	0.430	3.043	0.468	−3.990	0.680	3.671	0.423
Square gap lower	−3.626	1.126	4.235	1.081	−5.182	1.399	7.005	0.843
Rural areas								
Headcount upper	−3.212	0.216	1.532	0.158	−1.328	0.232	0.897	0.132
Headcount lower	−4.011	0.307	2.064	0.214	−1.987	0.293	1.058	0.247
Gap upper	−4.076	0.274	1.939	0.219	−2.899	0.247	1.279	0.209
Gap lower	−4.917	0.403	2.420	0.316	−3.388	0.318	1.568	0.298
Square gap upper	−4.661	0.393	2.408	0.305	−3.742	0.263	1.392	0.276
Square gap lower	−5.029	0.565	2.768	0.435	−4.684	0.297	1.414	0.403

Note: Estimates from FGLS with $N = 139$ for expansionary periods (67 in urban areas and 72 in rural areas) and 166 for contractionary periods (63 urban and 53 rural). Initial inequality and income levels included in analysis but results not shown.

Source: Author's estimates from SUSENAS surveys, various rounds

expansion and of contraction. However, the historical poverty responses to growth and contraction may very well be different given not only differences in initial conditions but also in the way expansions and contractions affect regional expenditure distributions. Remember that the contractions over the 1996–9 crisis period appear to have disproportionately affected the upper tail of the distribution. To explore these potential differences further, we estimate the net elasticity with initial conditions regressions separately for periods of growth and decline in mean regional expenditures and report the results in Table 8.5. Some differences in the poverty response during periods of expansion and contraction are readily apparent. The headcount measure from the upper and lower poverty lines exhibit a significantly greater response to gains in mean income than declines, yet this is not the case for the gap and squared gap measures. When looking within rural and urban areas, we see that these differences only arise in rural areas—the urban elasticities are the same for both expansions and contractions while the headcount elasticities in rural areas are substantially greater during periods of growth.

A clear link between income growth and poverty reduction has been established, it is fairly robust across income measure, and it is largely similar whether an Indonesian region experiences an expansion or contraction. None of the results have yet looked at potential geographic variation in poverty responses even though it is quite possible for poverty to respond to growth in a non-uniform way across different regions. This possibility is indeed suggested by the comparison of density estimates across the two provinces in Figs 8.3 and 8.4. Regional differences can arise for many reasons, for example, if the sectoral composition of growth both varies across provinces and impacts on poverty in different ways. It is also possible that regional variations in the implementation of national policy lead to different poverty outcomes. Furthermore, simple geographic differences in market integration may cause poverty to respond differently to growth. To look further into these possibilities, we return to the net effects with initial conditions regressions in Table 8.4 and plot the mean residuals of these regressions by province in order to investigate whether there is any clear spatial pattern to their distribution.

These mean residual plots are presented in Fig. 8.8. The first plot in Fig. 8.8 relays the residual from the pooled urban and rural regression of the upper line poverty gap change on income growth. The 95 per cent confidence interval band around the mean is plotted as well. From this simple inspection, little systematic variation in the residual is apparent. Although there is evidence of heteroskedasticity across the various regions, none of the mean residuals are significantly different from zero. The point estimates for the mean residual are all very close to zero as well. The following two graphs in Fig. 8.8 plot the mean residuals derived from the separate urban and rural regressions. An inspection of these plots draws the same conclusions. The poverty response to income change in any particular province does not appear to deviate from the nationally estimated mean response in a systematic geographic fashion.[13]

These preliminary investigations find no evidence of systematic variation across regions in the response of poverty to growth. One potential reason for the failure to find such variation, if it does indeed exist, is a problem common to all difference estimators measurement error. If the underlying dataset contains measurement error then differenced data will tend to exacerbate measurement error problems (see, for example, Card 1996) and there surely must be some error in the poverty and income measures. One approach to increase the signal to noise ratio is to return to the levels data and investigate how deviations from mean income and inequality covary with poverty rates within a time period.

Similar specifications to the difference regressions above were estimated on the pooled level data of provincial poverty measures and income. Specifically, the poverty

---

[13] The conclusions are the same regardless of the poverty measure and also do not change if instead we investigate the residuals from the gross elasticity regressions.

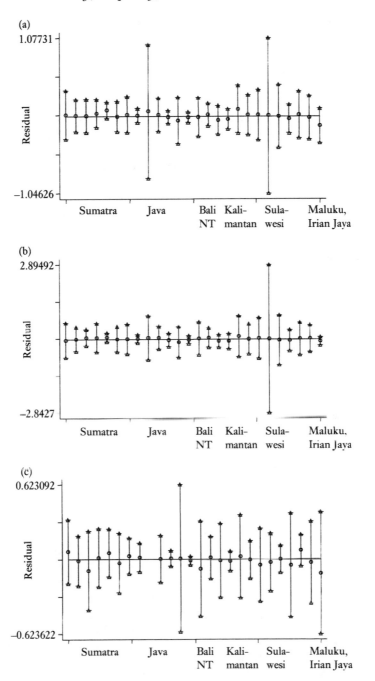

Figure 8.8. *Mean residual plots (and 95% confidence interval) from upper line poverty gap difference regressions, by province: (a) total sample, (b) urban only, (c) rural only*

measure P_α was regressed on income according to the following gross and net specifications:

$$\ln P^t_{\alpha,i} = \gamma_0 + \gamma_1 \ln \mu_{it} + f_c + f_t + e_{it},$$
$$\ln P^t_{\alpha,i} = \gamma'_0 + \gamma'_1 \ln \mu_{it} + \gamma'_2 \ln G_{it} + f_c + f_t + e_{it},$$

where f_c is a vector of cell dummies and f_t is a vector of survey year dummies. The results from these fixed effect generalized least squares (GLS) estimates are given in Table 8.6.

Similar to the findings with the difference regressions, deviations of provincial income from its mean are highly and significantly associated with reduced poverty. In addition, the gap and squared gap measures are even more responsive to income deviations as in the difference regressions. The estimated coefficients for both the

Table 8.6. *Levels regressions, growth, and inequality elasticities of poverty measures*

Poverty measure	Gross effect of growth		Net effect of growth			
			Growth		Inequality change	
	Coeff.	s.e.	Coeff.	s.e.	Coeff.	s.e.
Total sample						
Headcount upper	−2.072	0.103	−2.592	0.105	1.317	0.112
Headcount lower	−2.444	0.146	−3.129	0.131	1.857	0.144
Gap upper	−2.639	0.134	−3.491	0.118	2.152	0.130
Gap lower	−3.038	0.171	−4.056	0.178	2.654	0.211
Square gap upper	−3.178	0.150	−4.139	0.157	2.650	0.186
Square gap lower	−3.472	0.199	−4.678	0.247	3.431	0.296
Urban areas						
Headcount upper	−1.960	0.225	−3.244	0.209	2.518	0.216
Headcount lower	−2.318	0.334	−3.946	0.311	3.467	0.333
Gap upper	−2.520	0.287	−4.071	0.256	3.343	0.278
Gap lower	−3.300	0.347	−4.996	0.432	4.663	0.465
Square gap upper	−2.936	0.336	−4.716	0.348	4.054	0.38
Square gap lower	−2.883	0.484	−5.794	0.620	6.300	0.644
Rural areas						
Headcount upper	−1.957	0.106	−2.185	0.106	0.739	0.122
Headcount lower	−2.383	0.156	−2.612	0.143	1.348	0.139
Gap upper	−2.721	0.151	−3.244	0.123	1.756	0.120
Gap lower	−3.079	0.194	−3.831	0.155	2.220	0.158
Square gap upper	−3.296	0.175	−4.061	0.151	2.231	0.169
Square gap lower	−3.762	0.207	−4.660	0.209	2.552	0.264

Note: Estimates for fixed effect GLS with $N = 306$ for total sample (156 for urban, and 150 for rural areas).

Source: Author's estimates from SUSENAS surveys, various rounds.

gross and net effect of growth, as well as the coefficient on inequality, are all similar to the coefficients in the difference regressions and few deviate in any statistically significant manner. For example, the gross effect of mean income growth on the upper line headcount has an estimated elasticity of -2.07 from the fixed effect estimator and -1.96 from the difference estimator. The difference in these two estimates is not statistically significant. The response of poverty to growth and inequality change, already found to be quite robust over various specifications of difference regressions, is also robust across the use of differenced or level data.[14]

Turning to potential geographic variation in the relation between levels of poverty and income and inequality, we plot the mean residuals from the net effect levels regressions by province. The residual plots for the upper line gap measure, analogous to the Fig. 8.8 plots, are given in Fig. 8.9. Several differences from Fig. 8.8 are readily apparent. The plots of the mean residual for the overall sample appear to follow systematic geographical regularities. Residuals from provinces in the island of Sumatra tend to all be centred on zero. Provinces from Java and Bali generally appear to have residuals falling below zero (although some of these mean residuals are not significantly different from zero). Thus, a researcher would tend to overpredict the incidence of poverty in Java given the regression coefficients estimated on the national sample. Provinces from the east of Indonesia (Irian Jaya, Maluku) have residuals above the zero axis. Poverty in those regions would be systematically underpredicted given the nationally estimated relation between income, inequality, and growth.

Looking at the residuals from the split sample regressions within urban or rural areas, it is quite apparent that, while there is indeed spatial variation in urban area residuals and several residuals are significantly different from zero, it is the regional differences in rural areas that are most pronounced with numerous mean residuals significantly different from zero. This contrasts sharply with the mean residuals from the difference regressions where no clear regional pattern was observed. Based on the levels regressions, poverty levels in rural Java, Bali, and parts of Sulawesi would be systematically overestimated. Poverty in Irian Jaya, Maluku, Kalimantan, and some Sumatran provinces would be systematically underestimated. These residual plots make clear that regional factors have an important impact on poverty determination independent of the effects of within-region income change.

While suggestive, it would be premature to conclude that the regional variation in the fixed effect GLS residuals is necessarily a result of regional-specific differential responses to growth. Since we are now analysing levels data, these residual patterns may be generated by differing regional poverty–growth elasticities. Alternatively, they may instead simply reflect the persistence of high poverty regions and low poverty regions over time. The poverty reduction record of Indonesia casts some doubt on this second alternative since, for example, rural Java began the 1984–96 period with relatively high poverty and witnessed the greatest reduction in poverty by 1996. It is indeed rural Java that has significantly negative residuals in Fig. 8.9.

---

[14] If the true poverty–growth relation is linear then the fixed effect and difference specifications are functionally equivalent. The fixed effect estimator is efficient when the e_{it} are serially uncorrelated. Standard tests for serial correlation fail to reject the null of the absence of serial correlation.

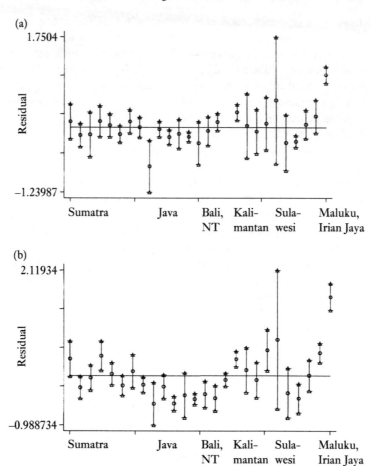

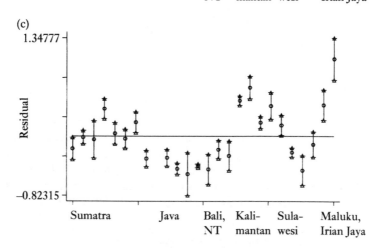

Figure 8.9. *Mean residual plots (and 95% confidence interval) from upper line poverty gap levels regressions, by province: (a) total sample, (b) urban only, (c) rural only*

We can try to distinguish between these two possibilities by returning to the difference data and this time adopting a random coefficients regression framework that allows the growth coefficient to vary by major island group. To control for the potentially confounding effects of base period inequality (a high level of inequality can stifle poverty reducing growth), instead of regressing poverty change on the rate of growth, we now regress it on the distribution corrected rate of growth in mean regional income. Following Ravallion (1997) we define the distribution corrected rate of growth as $(1 - G_i)(\Delta \ln \mu_i)$ and estimate the following:

$$\Delta \ln P_{\alpha,i}^{t+1,t} = \gamma_0 + \gamma_{1j}(1 - G_i^t)\Delta \ln \mu_i^{t+1,t} + f_p + e_i^{t+1,t},$$

where j indexes six major island groups: Sumatra, Java and Bali, Nusa Tenggara, Kalimantan, Sulawesi, Maluku, and Irian Jaya. Figure 8.10 presents the results from the above specification with both the upper line headcount and gap poverty change measures. The set of γ_{1j} is plotted for both the total sample and for only rural areas and the point estimates are bracketed by 95 per cent confidence bands. Since we are utilizing differenced data, measurement error is again a major concern, especially now as we are multiplying a noisy rate of growth measure with a Gini coefficient also measured with noise. Nevertheless, the results are suggestive, especially when considered in conjunction with the residual plots of Fig. 8.9.

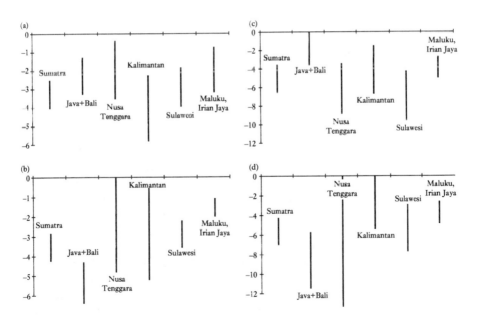

Figure 8.10. *Estimated response of upper line poverty measures to growth in distribution corrected mean income, with 95% confidence band: (a) poverty headcount, total sample, (b) poverty headcount, rural only, (c) poverty gap, total sample, (d) poverty gap, rural only*

The island group-specific point estimates for both the headcount and the gap measure suggest the presence of regional differences in the poverty response to distribution corrected growth for the total sample, however, the large standard errors of the residuals rule out any statistically significant deviations. This is not the case in the rural estimates where poverty responses are statistically distinct across regions. The poverty responses for Java and Bali are greatest in magnitude and significantly different from Sumatra, Sulawesi, and Maluku and Irian Jaya for the headcount measure and different from Kalimantan and Maluku and Irian Jaya for the gap measure. The estimated poverty responses for Maluku and Irian Jaya, Nusa Tenggara, and Kalimantan (in the case of the gap measure) are relatively low in magnitude and some are significantly different from the more responsive regions of Java, Bali, and Sumatra. Nusa Tenggara in particular is estimated with a great deal of imprecision indicating a wide diversity of responses within that small region. Ignoring that island group, the plots in Fig. 8.10 highlight the regional diversity of poverty responses and suggest a spatial pattern very similar to the residual patterns of Fig. 8.9. We conclude from the analysis that there are indeed identifiable regional deviations from nationally estimated growth–poverty elasticities in Indonesia over the 1984–99 period. Although growth in every region has reduced poverty, growth in certain regions has reduced poverty at a significantly faster rate than in other regions.

8.4. CONCLUSIONS

Motivated by recent discussion concerning the impacts of globalization on the world's poor, this chapter utilized successive waves of a large-scale household consumption survey to investigate poverty change in Indonesia. Any attempt to measure the impact of increased international integration on the poor would first require consistent estimates of poverty change over a relatively long period. The creation of such estimates was the first goal of this study.

This chapter extends poverty measurement methods with a simple structural model of consumer choice in order to estimate the cost-of-basic-needs method in the absence of price information. This method was used to generate repeated poverty profiles of Indonesia over the 1984–99 period. These profiles reveal first substantial reductions in poverty, in both urban and rural areas and as measured by numerous poverty lines and poverty measures, and then a dramatic reversal after the 1997 financial crisis. The second goal of this chapter was to investigate how regional poverty measures covary with economic growth. For the case of Indonesia over the period studied, all poverty measures are found to be highly responsive to the growth or decline in mean income or other points of the income distribution. This is certainly true for the net results, but even when provincial changes in inequality are ignored (income growth and increasing inequality are positively related over this period), poverty is found to strongly respond to mean income growth.

The spatial distribution of poverty responses to growth was investigated and little regional variation in these responses was observed with the first differences estimator.

However, the increased detrimental effects of measurement error in differenced data may obscure any such variation. Looking into this further we found that levels regressions with fixed effects generated very similar elasticities of poverty reduction to income growth as found with the difference regressions. However, the residuals from the level regressions do appear to vary systematically by region. This suggests the presence of persistent provincial level characteristics that affect poverty, even after controlling for income and inequality, especially in rural areas. These findings are further confirmed by a random coefficients framework that found significant differences in the poverty response to distribution corrected growth rate across rural regions.

Both the residual plots and the random coefficients framework indicate that poverty has been much more responsive to growth in rural Java and Bali than in the more remote areas of Kalimantan, Maluku, and Irian Jaya with other regions such as Sumatra and Sulawesi falling somewhere in between these two extremes. Future work will need to explore why this is the case, and also why there appears to be relatively little variation in the urban poverty–growth elasticities across regions. Nevertheless, we can speculate over the cause for these rural regional differences. Huppi and Ravallion (1991) analyse Indonesian household data from the 1980s and illustrate the importance of off-farm employment opportunities for poverty reduction in rural households, with members employed in rural industry significantly better off than otherwise observationally equivalent households. Opportunities for off-farm employment, especially in rural industry, are not randomly distributed across regions but tend to cluster in areas with well-developed transport networks and ease of access to large urban and export markets (Krugman 1991). These conditions apply to Java and Bali but not to the more remote areas and the ability for rural areas to take advantage of these conditions when present offers one potential explanation for the observed differences, but certainly not the only one.

Unlike Java, regions such as Kalimantan, Maluku, and Irian Jaya are more ethnically diverse and at points over the 1984–99 period suffered from ethnic conflict. If ethnic conflict limits the ability of a region to invest in public goods, as has been argued by Easterly and Levine (1997), this in turn may impact on the ability of the poor to benefit from overall growth processes, especially poor households facing social exclusion, and thus stands as another potential cause of regional differences.

The empirical findings in this chapter point to the importance of future work, with additional data sources, to better understand why the poor in some regions appear to benefit from growth opportunities while the poor in other regions do not. First, causes of the observed persistent regional differences in poverty can be investigated with the inclusion of further provincial level information. This information can include, but is not limited to, provincial level data on sectoral economic activity, measures of market integration (such as population density or quality of transport networks), provincial level measures of social programme coverage and efficacy, and so on. In addition, household-level information can be utilized to better explore the covariates of poverty change at the household level and investigate how these covariates, and the relation between them and poverty reduction, vary spatially across Indonesia.

Appendix: Generating Poverty Lines from SUSENAS Data

This Appendix summarizes the approach to poverty measurement used in the analysis, an approach derived from Ravallion (1994) and Bidani and Ravallion (1993).[15] The method begins with a look at household food consumption.

Determining the Food Bundle

Although human nutritional requirements form an important basis for determining basic food needs, food consumption choices are also determined by national (or local) cultural and dietary practices. Numerous different bundles of food goods can achieve the necessary caloric and other nutritional requirements for healthful living, but only certain bundles are actually consumed by the target population. It would be unfair to the locality studied to have the chosen food bundle simply be determined from calculations of the cheapest aggregate source of calories if this bundle is not a realistic consumption choice given local dietary practices. As such, the food bundle in this study is chosen to reflect the existing food choices of lower-income households in Indonesia. Lower-income households are here defined as the bottom quintile of per capita household expenditure. The mean food consumption levels of this quintile will constitute the initial food bundle under consideration (this initial bundle will be modified as described below).

Within a large and diverse country such as Indonesia, the possibility of wide variation in local food choices is quite high. A staple in one area may not be consumed at all in another. Ideally, these regional differences should be incorporated in a national poverty study. However, regional differences in income and living standards are often conflated with regional taste differences and it is difficult to determine food consumption differences that should be attributed to regional differences in income and consumption differences due to regional differences in taste. Hence the chosen food bundle in this study includes only relatively common food items that are universally or near universally consumed in every Indonesian province. In practice this translates into a basket only containing food goods that are consumed by at least 10 per cent of all households in at least 80 per cent of all Indonesian provinces. This selection

---

[15] It is important to mention, at least in passing, two factors in poverty analysis that this method is unable to address. The first factor concerns the intrahousehold allocation of resources. SUSENAS data contain no information on the within-household distribution of consumption. If a relatively well off household allocates resources in such an unequal fashion that certain members should be deemed poor, this method will fail to identify those individuals. Another factor concerns access to non-market goods such as clean water or non-market healthcare that may not be fully captured by an income or expenditure based measure of poverty. Clearly, a low-income household located near a public health clinic or source of clean water is better off than an otherwise identical household lacking such access. This study will not be able to identify differential access to such goods across households, although biases due to this second factor may not be such a problem. Previous research with SUSENAS and other Indonesian data (Wiebe 1994) finds that lack of access to non-market health care, education, and clean water is highly correlated with poverty measures similar to those used in this study.

Table 8.A1. *Food consumption bundle and mean monthly per capita consumption levels for the lowest expenditure quintile (scaled to ensure adequate average calorie intake)*

Item	Item (Bahasa Indonesia)	Unit	Quantity
Local rice	Beras lokal	kg	5.7236
Hybrid rice	Beras kualitas ungg	kg	7.1405
Cassava	Ketela pohon	kg	2.3595
Mackerel	Ikan tonggol	kg	0.0431
Preserved anchovies	Ikan tering - Teri	ons	0.784
Beef	Daging sapi	kg	0.0067
Chicken	Daging ayam	kg	0.034
Chicken eggs	Telur ayam	kg	0.1181
Spinach	Bayam	kg	0.6226
Water lilies	Kangkung	kg	0.5044
String beans	Kacang panjang	kg	0.5004
Tomatoes	Tomat sayur	ons	0.5192
Eggplant	Terong	kg	0.3334
Red onions	Bawang merah	ons	1.8232
Garlic	Bawang putih	ons	0.2728
Red pepper	Cabe merah	ons	0.5242
Cayenne pepper	Cabe rawit	ons	1.6607
Peanuts	Kacangtanah	kg	0.0403
Soft soybean cake	Tahu	kg	0.3383
Dried soybean cake	Tempe	kg	0.4785
Other bananas	Pisang lainnya	kg	0.755
Coconut oil	Minyak kelapa	l	0.3235
Other cooking oil	Minyak goreng lainr	l	0.2571
Coconut	Kelapa	Number	1.9228
Sugar	Gula pasir	ons	6.4074
Tea	Te-h	ons	0.561
Ground coffee	Kopi bubuk	ons	0.5094
Salt	Garam	ons	3.2254
Coriander seeds	Ketumbar/Jinten	ons	0.1218
Red peppers	Merica/Lada	ons	0.0695
Tamarind	Asam	ons	0.2814
Fish paste	Terasi/Petis	ons	0.5468
Soy sauce	Kecap	10 ml	1.0929
Noodles (dried)	Mie	kg	0.0337

Note: 1 ons = 100 g.

Source: SUSENAS, various rounds.

rule results in a food basket of thirty-four main food items.[16] Appendix Table 8.A1 lists each of these thirty-four foods contained in the basic needs food basket. Note

[16] These thirty-four food items constituted 79 per cent of mean household food expenditures for the bottom expenditure quintile in 1993.

that this basket includes the two most important staples—rice (actually two varieties) and cassava—as well as a wide range of meat, fish, vegetables, and seasonings. Also included are packaged noodles, the only prepared food in this basket.

Before discussing how the various goods in the food bundle are priced, problems with intertemporal comparisons of welfare need to be highlighted. Since this study attempts to measure poverty over repeated cross-sectional surveys, the choice of the base year food bundle will impact the estimated poverty levels. If relative prices or expenditure patterns change over time then the results for years relatively far from the base period will not reflect the actual consumption patterns in those years. The choice of base period and resulting problems are well documented in discussions of Laspeyres (where the base time period is the initial period) and Paasche (base period is final period) price indices. Most importantly, the two indices fail to account for demand substitutions due to changes in relative prices. This can be a concern with the SUSENAS consumption data. For example, the per capita weekly consumption of local rice increased from 0.80 to 0.99 kg over the six-year period 1987–93, while the consumption of hybrid rice declined from 1.01 to 0.98 kg in the same period. The adoption of either the initial period or final period consumption levels as the base of comparison would not account for this potentially important substitution.

The Fisher Ideal Index, a hybrid index defined as the geometric mean of the quantities in the various periods studied, does account for the substitution patterns over time. The Fisher Ideal Index is a superlative index in that it is exactly equal to a true cost-of-living index if preferences are homothetic (Diewert 1976), and it can better account for the problems presented by intertemporal substitution effects. Changes in consumption patterns due to income effects are not accounted for as nicely in the Fisher Index (nor in the other indices as well), and of course if preferences are not homothetic then the level of living suggested by the Fisher Index is only an approximation of the true level of living. Nevertheless, the Fisher Index is at least a marginal improvement over the Laspeyres and Paasche indices. As such, the food bundle used in this study is calculated from the geometric mean of the consumption quantities determined in each of the first five survey years studied.

To ensure that the consumption bundle achieves the necessary food energy requirements, the quantities actually consumed by the lowest expenditure quintile are then scaled so that the total bundle ensures 2,100 daily calories per person—the standard mean daily caloric requirement (see WHO *et al.* 1985). These scaled quantities are listed alongside the food items in Appendix Table 8.A1. The total cost of this food bundle yields the first of the three poverty lines employed in this study; the food poverty line, z^f. This poverty line represents the cost of an adequately nutritious and nationally representative personal food bundle. Higher poverty lines, to be discussed shortly, are based on z^f but also make some allowance for non-food expenditures.

Pricing the Food Bundle: Unit Values as Proxies for Price

In pricing the food bundle derived in the previous subsection, there are two main conceptual issues to resolve. The first concerns regional variation in price and the question of which prices to adopt: national or local prices. The second issue concerns the absence of direct price observation in the data. Instead of prices, the survey data allows for the imputation of unit values, and this use of unit values instead of observed prices presents some important concerns.

With regards to regional price variation, many developing countries with only partially integrated markets exhibit significant price differences across regions. This is especially true for price difference between rural and urban areas. For this reason the food bundle costs for rural and urban areas are computed separately. Likewise, there may be significant variation in rural or urban prices across different provinces or regions. This problem may be especially pertinent for Indonesia, which has approximately 200 million people spread out over a large archipelago. Indeed the impact of the 1997 currency crisis on price changes has exhibited a high degree of heterogeneity across Indonesian provinces—for further details see Levinsohn *et al.* (2003). Because SUSENAS is a large nationally representative sample the data enable the food bundle to be priced at both a national level and priced separately for each province. Since there are twenty-six Indonesian provinces (not including East Timor) this enables the computation of fifty-two separate food poverty lines (one rural and one urban food poverty line for each province). Subsequent analysis will contrast poverty measurements obtained with both national and regional prices.

Another conceptual problem arises due to the lack of information on actual market prices. In lieu of market prices, SUSENAS data records the weekly consumption quantity of various disaggregate food goods as well as the total weekly expenditure on each of those goods. Although the imputed unit values are related to the prices paid by the household, they are not identical because consumers not only choose the quantity but also the *quality* of the good consumed. Since we do not directly observe prices we must rely on the unit values to serve as proxies for prices.[17] This use of unit value data presents three estimation problems not encountered with the use of price data. Specifically, there are problems with commodity heterogeneity, quality choice, and measurement error. Each problem will be discussed in turn.

Even though the 200 or so food items included in the SUSENAS surveys record consumption at a fairly disaggregate level, it is possible that a food good may be composed of two or more distinctive food items (e.g. the commodity 'sugar' may combine both refined and unrefined types). If this were true then the unit values should exhibit multimodal distributions. Hence we inspect the histograms and kernel density estimates of the unit values for each food good in order to detect the presence of multiple modes or gross outliers. Any gross outliers discovered were discarded, and none of the thirty-four food goods exhibited multimodal distributions in any survey year.

Following the example of Deaton and Tarozzi (1999), an automatic method for outlier detection was also employed where any unit value whose logarithm lies more than 3.5 standard deviations beyond the mean was discarded. In addition, if unit

---

[17] Two other studies that employ unit value data in poverty analysis are Chen and Ravallion (1996) and Wodon (1997), however, the methods adopted in these studies are different than those proposed here.

values are actually good proxies for true prices and prices vary regionally, there should be a high degree of unit value homogeneity within districts and a high degree of variation in unit values between districts.[18] Analysis of variance tests were conducted and determined that a significant and substantial portion of variance in unit values can be attributed to intercluster variation for all thirty-four food goods. We conclude that the unit values used in this study exhibit relatively few problems with commodity heterogeneity and behave similarly to true prices.

Quality choice is another problem that can confound the naive adoption of unit values. Previous work by Deaton (1988, 1997) has focused on how unit values can be utilized to estimate genuine price elasticities of various commodities. His estimation methods exploit the structure of household surveys such as SUSENAS that, in order to reduce survey costs, household information should be collected from clusters of households located close to each other. Deaton's approach makes the key identifying assumption that there is no within-cluster price variation for goods of identical quality. This assumption enables Deaton to exploit the intercluster variation in prices in order to estimate various price elasticities. Similarly, we make the assumption that food goods of identical quality have identical within-cluster prices. This structural assumption will then enable the imputation of a price for each food good while controlling for the level of quality typically purchased by a low-income household. Formally, UV_{gic}, the unit value of a particular food good g consumed by household i in cluster c, is a multiplicative function of the cluster price level λ_{gc} for good g and the intercluster price of quality chosen by household i, p_{gi}:

$$UV_{gic} = \lambda_{gc} p_{gi}.$$

We assume that the quality price p_g varies over a range $[p_{\text{upper}}, p_{\text{lower}}]$ and that this range of quality choice is available to all clusters. This structure forces the relative price, say, of high quality spinach to low quality spinach to be the same in every location. Since p_{gi} is a choice variable—households choose the quality of goods consumed—simple mean unit values may not accurately serve as a proxy for prices. We further assume that food quality can be treated as a one-dimensional measure and that the choice of a particular point in the quality continuum is determined both by a household's demographic composition and its level of living. That is, the choice of p_{gi} is a function of household expenditures X_i and household demographic variables Z_i:

$$p_{gi} = e^{f_g(X_i, Z_i)}.$$

Thus, the reported unit value is modelled as a function of cluster price levels and household characteristics. In log form the unit value is expressed as

$$\ln UV_{gic} = \ln \lambda_{gc} + \ln p_{gi} = \ln \lambda_{gc} + f_g(X_i, Z_i).$$

These structural assumptions enable estimations of the elasticity between the quality of a particular food good and total household expenditure. These elasticities are exactly the same as the 'expenditure elasticities of quality' first studied in the seminal work

---

[18] Note that the SUSENAS consumption surveys were executed in January or February of each survey year hence there should be little or no seasonal variation in the unit value data.

by Prais and Houthakker (1955) on household consumption patterns. This estimated elasticity of quality is used to 'quality correct' the unit values in order to proxy the price of a food good at a quality level typically bought by an arbitrarily defined group of poor households.

If indeed prices vary only across clusters, then a simple regression of unit values on household expenditures with cluster fixed effects and other controls will trace out the relation between the quality component of the unit value and the wealth level of the household. We estimate the following regression for each of the thirty-four food goods:[19]

$$\ln UV_{gic} = \alpha_g + \beta_g \ln X_i + \varphi_g Z_i + f_c + u_{gic}.$$

The vector of household demographic variables Z_i includes total household size, the proportion of household members in various age and gender categories, the number of adult workers in the household, and the age, gender, education, and marital status of the household head. The cluster fixed effect is denoted by f_c. In this specification the constant α_g is simply the intercluster log mean unit value for that good, that is, the mean $\ln \lambda_{gc}$. Once these coefficients are estimated, we then compute the estimated price for a good at a quality level consumed by a household at the twentieth percentile of household expenditure and with the mean demographic makeup of the bottom expenditure quintile. That is the price P_g^* is determined to be

$$\ln P_g^* = \ln \bar{\lambda}_g + \hat{\beta}_g \ln X_{20\text{th}} + \hat{\varphi}_g \bar{Z}_{\text{bottom quintile}}.$$

Appendix Table 8.A2 lists the mean unit values for each good from the 1993 SUSENAS along with the 'corrected' unit values (P_g^*) that will serve as the price proxy. As is readily apparent, the 'corrected' unit values for each good are less than the mean unit values, but quite close overall. If quality were a normal good, then we would expect the corrected price to be less than the mean unit value since at lower incomes, households purchase lower quality goods. However, the more homogeneous a food good in terms of quality, the smaller the range of quality choice a household has and hence the closer the corrected price is to the mean unit value. The fact that the corrected price of red onions is, for example, much closer to the red onion mean unit value than is the corrected price of chicken to its unit value, suggests that red onions may not vary in quality as much as chicken. Goods that have the largest quality expenditures of elasticity tend to be packaged goods like prepared noodles or tea. The quality corrected value for sugar is virtually identical to the mean unit value, perhaps reflecting strict price controls for sugar at that time. Although Appendix Table 8.A2 presents the mean unit values and corrected prices for the national sample in the 1993 SUSENAS, separate prices for each provincial rural/urban area can be and are estimated in the same manner.[20]

The third problem that prevents the naive adoption of unit values as a direct measure of price plagues all survey based analysis to varying degrees, measurement error. In the

---

[19] Various related functional forms were tried, with no noticeable improvement in fit.

[20] For certain goods and province pairs, it was not possible to estimate a local price due to lack of observations. In these few cases the price of the closest neighbouring province was adopted.

Table 8.A2. *The mean unit values and estimated prices (rupiahs) for the food bundle*

Item	Unit	Mean unit value (UV)	Corrected price (P^*)	P^*/UV
Local rice	kg	6.220	6.040	0.971
Hybrid rice	kg	5.822	5.749	0.988
Cassava	kg	1.474	1.321	0.896
Mackerel	kg	20.966	18.003	0.859
Preserved anchovies	ons	3.317	2.887	0.870
Beef	kg	67.340	64.119	0.952
Chicken	kg	34.126	31.319	0.918
Chicken eggs	kg	21.959	21.030	0.958
Spinach	kg	4.739	3.900	0.823
Water lilies	kg	4.051	3.357	0.829
String beans	kg	5.560	4.942	0.889
Tomatoes	ons	0.892	0.854	0.957
Eggplant	kg	3.608	3.133	0.868
Red onions	ons	1.937	1.843	0.952
Garlic	ons	5.150	4.770	0.926
Red pepper	ons	2.934	2.641	0.900
Cayenne pepper	ons	2.819	2.541	0.901
Peanuts	kg	18.419	17.339	0.941
Soft soybean cake	kg	9.195	8.512	0.926
Dried soybean cake	kg	10.226	9.710	0.950
Other bananas	kg	4.327	3.590	0.830
Coconut oil	l	12.639	12.333	0.976
Other cooking oil	l	12.752	12.373	0.970
Coconut	butir	2.397	2.225	0.928
Sugar	ons	1.329	1.324	0.997
Tea	ons	4.218	3.504	0.831
Ground coffee	ons	5.038	4.330	0.859
Salt	ons	0.497	0.433	0.871
Coriander seeds	ons	3.365	3.043	0.904
Red peppers	ons	5.445	4.775	0.877
Tamarind	ons	1.448	1.326	0.916
Fish paste	ons	2.697	2.328	0.863
Soy sauce	10 ml	0.550	0.521	0.948
Noodles (dried)	kg	20.922	15.777	0.754
Total cost of bundle (rupiahs)		15,349.930	14,556.770	0.948

Note: 1 ons = 100 g.

Source: SUSENAS 1993.

SUSENAS surveys, households must report the total quantity consumed in the past week of 200 or so food items as well as the total weekly expenditure of each item. Clearly, this is an exacting task for any household and may well lead to reporting errors. It is also likely that any misreporting of expenditures will be positively correlated with misreporting of quantity. For example, a household may inaccurately recall the quantity of a good consumed and then estimate expenditure based on some notion of price paid.

We adopt a simple model of consumption misreporting to investigate the potential consequences of measurement error in unit value data. Assume that the reported log quantity, $\ln q^*$, and log expenditure, $\ln x^*$, for a particular good (the subscript g is dropped for ease of exposition) are additive functions of the true quantity and expenditure, $\ln q$ and $\ln x$, as well as mean zero error terms u_q and u_x. Formally:

$$\ln q^* = \ln q + u_q,$$
$$\ln x^* = \ln x + u_x.$$

with $E(u_q) = E(u_x) = 0$. The assumption of mean zero error terms is obviously key. Differing approaches to modelling the error term can yield very different results. Assume that each right-hand side variable has variance σ_q, σ_x, σ_{uq}, and σ_{ux}. Also assume that the reporting error terms may have a non-zero covariance σ_{uqux}. All other potential covariance terms are assumed to be zero for ease of exposition with no loss in generality. As mentioned above, there are strong reasons to suspect that $\sigma_{uqux} > 0$ however this covariance is free to take any value. The statistic of interest in this study is the mean unit value for any particular good (or rather the mean value adjusted for quality effects) with the standard formulation:

$$\overline{\ln \text{UV}} = \frac{1}{n}\left(\sum_n \ln\left(\frac{x}{q}\right)\right).$$

However, instead of calculating the mean unit value with the true x and q we observe the error prone x^* and q^*. In order to explore the consequences of this measurement error for our poverty measurements, expressions for the expected mean and variance of the noisy unit values are solved in terms of the mean and variance of the true unit values.

$$E\overline{\ln \text{UV}^*} = E\left[\frac{1}{n}\sum_n \ln\left(\frac{x^*}{q^*}\right)\right] = \frac{1}{n}\left[\sum_n E(\ln x + \mu_x - \ln q - \mu_q)\right]$$

$$= \frac{1}{n}\sum_n (\ln x - \ln q) = \overline{\ln \text{UV}}$$

$$V\overline{\ln \text{UV}^*} = V\left[\frac{1}{n}\sum_n \ln\left(\frac{x^*}{q^*}\right)\right] = \frac{1}{n^2}\left[\sum_n V(\ln x + \mu_x - \ln q - \mu_q)\right]$$

$$= \frac{1}{n^2}\left[\sum_n (\sigma_x + \sigma_{\mu x} + \sigma_q + \sigma_{\mu q} - 2\sigma_{\mu x \mu q})\right]$$

$$= \frac{1}{n}(\sigma_x + \sigma_{\mu x} + \sigma_q + \sigma_{\mu q} - 2\sigma_{\mu x \mu q})$$

$$= V\overline{\ln \text{UV}} + \frac{1}{n}(\sigma_{\mu x} + \sigma_{\mu q} - 2\sigma_{\mu x \mu q}).$$

The above expressions make clear that, at least for large samples, the consequences of the measurement error are not especially severe. The mean of the noisy unit value measure is an unbiased estimate of the true mean and the variance of the noisy measure approaches the variance of the true measure as sample size increases. Hence we can conclude that

$$p \lim \overline{\ln UV}^* = \overline{\ln UV}.$$

Of course the mean estimate based on the observed finite sample unit values will have higher variance than a mean estimated without measurement error. Note, though, that if $\sigma_{uxuq} > 0$, as we suspect it is, then this mitigates the variance of the noisy measure. In fact, if σ_{uxuq} is relatively large in comparison with σ_{ux} and σ_{uq} then there are few negative consequences in the use of the noisy measure even for relatively small samples.

If indeed the error terms are mean zero, the mean unit values derived from the national sample yield unbiased estimates of the true mean unit value and, since the sample is large, the loss in efficiency is probably slight. Other conclusions can possibly be reached with different assumptions regarding the behaviour of the error term. Since the true nature of misreporting error is unknown, this study makes no attempt to correct for measurement error in the unit values. Regardless of the specific form of misreporting error, the calculated mean unit values for the provincial and urban/rural cells (the local price estimates) will be relatively less accurate due to the smaller sample sizes. These higher variances of local price estimates resulting from the smaller sample sizes must be kept in mind when reviewing the results.

It is these modified unit values, essentially mean unit values corrected to reflect quality choices made by low-income households, that are used to price the food bundle and yield the food poverty line z^f. However, even the poorest household must also consume some amount of non-food goods and the next subsection discusses two approaches to measure the cost of basic non-food goods.

Estimating Non-Food Expenditures

Household consumption data usually contains much less detailed information on non-food consumption, and the types of goods consumed are much more heterogeneous than the food goods listed in Appendix Table 8.A1. SUSENAS data is no exception to this rule. These differences make the construction of a non-food bundle very difficult. An alternative approach to estimating non-food expenditures, as put forth by Ravallion (1994), is to define a 'basic non-food good' as a good for which people are willing to forgo food in order to obtain. The goal, in other words, is to determine the non-food expenditure level that would displace some portion of basic food spending (z^f). This entails a look at the typical value of non-food expenditures by those households who can just afford basic nutritional requirements z^f but choose not to do so. This level of non-food expenditure plus z^f yields the lower poverty line, z^l. (An 'upper' poverty line will be defined below.) This level of non-food spending can be estimated with the simple food demand function:

$$s_i = \alpha + \beta_1 \log \left(\frac{X_i}{z^f} \right) + \beta_2 \left[\log \left(\frac{X_i}{z^f} \right) \right]^2 + \varphi Z_i + D_{\text{prov}} + u_i,$$

where s_i is the food share of total expenditures for household i, X measures household expenditures, Z conveys household demographic makeup as before, and D_{prov} is a vector of provincial dummy variables. The constant, α, estimates the average food share for those households where $X = z^f$, net of demographic and regional effects. The lower poverty line would then be constituted by z^f plus this estimated amount of non-food expenditure, $z^f - \alpha z^f$, or expressed more concisely as

$$z^l = z^f (2 - \alpha).$$

The parameter α is estimated separately for rural and urban households. In principle, this method can also be used to estimate non-food spending for each provincial and rural/urban cell. However, we encounter the same conceptual difficulties discussed earlier. That is, regional differences in income and living standards can be conflated with regional differences in taste for non-food goods or regional differences in availability of non-food goods. With respect to non-food goods the problem is exacerbated because little detailed information on non-food consumption is contained in the SUSENAS surveys. Because we cannot control for regional differences in the composition of non-food good consumption, separate food share equations for each local cell are not estimated. Instead only a national α is estimated and utilized, even if z^f is determined separately for each province with local price estimates.

Yet another more generous poverty line can be calculated by considering the level of non-food spending exhibited by those households where the food share actually reaches z^f. This amount of non-food expenditures can be considered as an upper bound on the allowance for basic non-food needs if those households that reach their food requirements also satisfy their non-food requirements. This amount of non-food expenditure added to z^f yields z^u, the upper poverty line.

To calculate z^u, we need to estimate s^*, the expected value of the food share when food spending equals the food poverty line. Once s^* is obtained, z^u is simply given as z^f / s^*. The value of s^* can be implicitly defined by

$$s^* = \alpha' + \beta_1 \ln \left(\frac{1}{s^*} \right),$$

where α' is the α of the previous regression net of provincial and demographic mean effects. If we approximate $\ln(s^*)$ by $s^* - 1$ (since s^* is close to zero) we can then generate a first guess of s^*: $s^* = (\alpha + \beta)/(1 + \beta)$. Using Newton's method we iterate until s^* converges with the following expression:

$$s^*_{t+1} = s^*_t - \frac{s^*_t + \beta \ln(s^*_t) - \alpha}{1 + \beta/s^*_t}.$$

This algorithm usually converges rapidly. Similar to the discussion of α above, s^* can be estimated separately for each province, however we refrain from doing so due to the inability to control for regional variation in the types of non-food goods consumed.[21]

Appendix Table 8.A3 gives the estimated national values for α and s^*, as well as z^f, z^l, and z^u, for both the rural and urban sectors in each of the five surveys. These poverty lines are very close to the actual poverty lines used in the study. The next step in this poverty estimation process is to generate household-specific poverty lines based on z^f, z^l, and z^u but adjusted by each household's specific caloric needs as determined by its demographic makeup.

Determining the Household-Specific Poverty Line

For the final step in the poverty line determination methodology we modify the three poverty lines so that they more accurately reflect the actual caloric needs of each household as determined by its demographic makeup. Previously, the food quantities consumed were scaled to ensure a caloric content of 2,100 daily calories. The 2,100-calorie figure is the usual benchmark caloric need for an active adult. However, caloric needs vary across individuals and these needs are in part determined by age, gender, and activity level.

A household with many young children or elderly would have a lower caloric need than an equivalent sized household of working adults. Hence, using the 2,100 caloric benchmark may inadvertently identify that first household as poor, even though the caloric needs of that household are actually being met. In an attempt to correct this type of bias, we recalibrate the estimated poverty lines to reflect the particular demographic makeup of each household and thus create a poverty line specific to each household. We do this by first obtaining the mean caloric needs for eight major demographic groups as calculated from WHO *et al.* (1985). The eight groups include: (i) male children aged 0–4, (ii) female children aged 0–4, (iii) male children aged 5–14, (iv) female children aged 5–14, (v) physically active adult men, aged 15–59, (vi) physically active adult women aged 15–59, (vii) partially sedentary elderly men, aged 60 and over, and (viii) partially sedentary elderly women, aged 60 and over. The household proportions of each of these eight demographic groups partially constitute the Z vector of demographic variables used in earlier regressions. The particular caloric requirements of each group are listed in Appendix Table 8.A3 alongside other summary information.

Once the caloric needs of each demographic good are determined, any poverty line z is simply scaled to reflect the demographic makeup of the specific household by the following expression:

$$z_i^* = \left(\sum_D \left(\frac{\tau_D}{2,100} \right) \left(\frac{D_i}{N} \right) \right) \cdot z,$$

---

[21] Similar problems plague the intertemporal comparison of basic non-food needs. Thus, the final values of α and s^* employed in the analysis are determined from the geometric means of the α and s^* parameters estimated separately in each survey year.

Table 8.A3. *Estimated values of various parameters and national poverty lines*

Measure		1984		1987		1990		1993		1996		1999	
		Urban	Rural	Urban	Rural	Urban	Rural	Urban	Rural	Urban	Rural	Urban	Rural
z^f	(rupiahs/person/month)	8,184	7,619	9,436	8,844	12,566	11,726	15,250	14,022	23,208	21,262	62,744	59,807
α		0.698	0.727	0.698	0.727	0.698	0.727	0.698	0.727	0.698	0.727	0.698	0.727
z^l	(rupiahs/person/month)	10,657	9,701	12,287	11,260	16,364	14,930	19,859	17,854	30,222	27,072	81,704	76,150
s^*		0.642	0.69	0.642	0.69	0.642	0.69	0.642	0.690	0.642	0.69	0.642	0.69
z^u	(rupiahs/person/month)	12,752	11,041	14,703	12,815	19,581	16,992	23,763	20,320	36,163	30,811	97,768	86,668

Daily calorific needs by age group and gender

Gender and age group (years)	Daily calories
Male, 0–4	1,456
Female, 0–4	1,289
Male, 5–14	2,545
Female, 5–14	2,253
Male, 15–59	2,432
Female, 15–59	1,982
Male, 60+	2,018
Female, 60+	1,609

Source: Author's calculations from SUSENAS various rounds; also WHO (1985).

where τ_D is the caloric requirement of demographic group D, D_i is the number of household members in that group, and N is the total family size. These modified poverty lines yield the particular expenditure levels employed to distinguish poor from non-poor households.

POVERTY MEASUREMENTS

After the determination of a particular poverty line, the next choice is an appropriate poverty measure. In fact three poverty measures are employed. All three poverty measures are additively decomposable with the proper population weights and are discussed at length in Foster *et al.* (1984). The general FGT poverty measure is given as

$$P_\alpha(x; z) = \frac{1}{n} \sum_{i=1}^{q} \left(\frac{z - x_i}{z} \right)^\alpha,$$

where q is the number of poor individuals (belonging to households where per capita income x is no greater than z) and n the total population. Differing values of the parameter α generate different poverty measures. The three particular poverty measures used in this chapter are as follows:

1. The poverty headcount index ($\alpha = 0$). This standard poverty measure gives the proportion of the population residing in households where the PCE is less than the poverty line. While easy to interpret, this measure is insensitive to the degree of poverty or the distribution of poverty among the poor. For example, if an already poor household suffers an even further decline in income then overall poverty increases yet the headcount measure remains unchanged.
2. The poverty gap index ($\alpha = 1$). This index relates the per capita consumption deficit of aggregate poverty as a proportion of the poverty line. The poverty gap index is simply the mean of the poverty deficit, $(z - x)/z$, averaged over the entire population. Similarly, the ratio P_1/P_0 yields the mean of the poverty deficit averaged over all poor households and thus represents the average transfer (expressed as a proportion of the poverty line) every poor individual would need to receive in order to bring all poor up to the poverty line. Unlike the headcount ratio, the poverty gap index conveys some measure of the depth of poverty.
3. The squared measure ($\alpha = 2$), here also known as the squared gap measure. Unlike the previous two measures, this measure is sensitive to income distributions among the poor and thus gives some indication of the severity of poverty. This measure is essentially a weighted average of the poverty gap index where the individual is weighted by the distance from the poverty line. Although this measure is the most difficult of the three measures to interpret, it will be an important measure in this study since it gives greater weight to the poorest of the poor.

REFERENCES

Atkinson, A. and A. Brandolini (1999). 'Promise and Pitfalls in the Use of "Secondary" Datasets: Income Inequality in OECD Countries', unpublished manuscript, Nuffield College: Oxford.

Ben-David, D. (1993). 'Equalizing Exchange: Trade Liberalization and Income Convergence', *Quarterly Journal of Economics*, 108(3): 653–79.

Bidani, B. and M. Ravallion (1993). 'A Regional Profile of Poverty in Indonesia', *Bulletin of Indonesian Economic Studies*, 29(3): 37–68.

Biro Pusat Statistik (1997). *Statistical Yearbook of Indonesia*, Biro Pusat Statistik: Jakarta.

Bruno, M., M. Ravallion, and L. Squire (1998). 'Equity and Growth in Developing Countries: Old and New Perspectives on Policy Issues', in V. Tanzi and K.-Y. Chu (eds) *Income Distribution and High Quality Growth*, MIT Press: Cambridge, MA.

Card, D. (1996). 'The Effect of Unions on the Structure of Wages: A Longitudinal Analysis', *Econometrica*, 64(4): 957–80.

Chen, S. and M. Ravallion (1996). 'Data in Transition: Assessing Rural Living Standards in Southern China', *China Economic Review*, 7(1): 23–56.

Deaton, A. (1988). 'Quality, Quantity, and Spatial Variation of Price', *American Economic Review*, 78(3): 418–31.

—— (1997). *The Analysis of Household Surveys*. Johns Hopkins University Press: Baltimore, MD.

—— and C. Paxson (1998). 'Economies of Scale, Household Size, and the Demand for Food', *Journal of Political Economy*, 106(5): 897–931.

—— and A. Tarozzi (1999). 'Prices and Poverty in India', unpublished manuscript, Research Programme in Development Studies, Princeton University: New Jersey.

Diewert, E. (1976). 'Exact and Superlative Index Numbers', *Journal of Econometrics*, 4(2): 114–45.

Dollar, D. and A. Kraay (2004). 'Growth Is Good for the Poor', in A. F. Shorrocks and R. van der Hoeven (eds) *Growth, Inequality and Poverty: Prospects for Pro-Poor Economic Development*, Oxford University Press: Oxford.

Easterly, W. and R. Levine (1997). 'Africa's Growth Tragedy: Policies and Ethnic Divisions', *Quarterly Journal of Economics*, 112(4): 1203–50.

Edwards, S. (1998). 'Openness, Productivity, and Growth: What Do We Really Know?', *Economic Journal*, 108(4): 383–98.

Foster, J. and A. Shorrocks (1988). 'Poverty Orderings', *Econometrica*, 56(1): 173–7.

——, J. Greer, and E. Thorbecke (1984). 'A Class of Decomposable Poverty Measures', *Econometrica*, 52(3): 761–6.

Frankenberg, E., D. Thomas, and K. Beegle (1999). 'The Real Costs of Indonesia's Economic Crisis: Preliminary Findings from the Indonesia Family Life Surveys', *RAND Working Papers* 99–04, RAND: Santa Monica, CA.

Friedman, J. and J. Levinsohn (2002). 'The Distributional Impacts of Indonesia's Financial Crisis on Household Welfare: A Rapid Response Methodology', *World Bank Economic Review*, 16(3): 397–423.

Huppi, M. and M. Ravallion (1991). 'The Sectoral Structure of Poverty During an Adjustment Period: Evidence for Indonesia in the Mid 1980s', *World Development*, 19(12): 1653–78.

Krugman, P. (1991). 'Increasing Returns and Economic Geography', *Journal of Political Economy*, 99(3): 483–99.

Levinsohn, J., S. Berry, and J. Friedman (2003). 'Impacts of the Indonesian Economic Crisis: Price Changes and the Poor', in M. P. Dooley and J. A. Frankel (eds) *Managing Currency Crisis in Emerging Markets*, University of Chicago Press: Chicago, IL.

McKenzie, D. (2001). 'Asymptotic Theory for Heterogeneous Dynamic Pseudo-Panels', manuscript, Stanford University: Stanford.

Prais, S. (1959). 'Whose Cost of Living?', *Review of Economic Studies*, 26(2): 126–34.

—— and H. Houthakker (1955). *The Analysis of Family Budgets*, Cambridge University Press: Cambridge.

Ravallion, M. (1994). 'Poverty Comparisons', *Fundamentals in Pure and Applied Economics* Vol. 56, Harwood Academic Press: Chur.

—— (1997). 'Can High Inequality Developing Countries Escape Absolute Poverty?', *Economics Letters*, 56(1): 51–7.

—— (2001). 'Growth, Inequality, and Poverty. Looking Beyond Averages', *World Development*, 29(11): 1803–15.

—— and B. Bidani (1994). 'How Robust is a Poverty Profile?', *World Bank Economic Review*, 8(1): 75–102.

—— and G. Datt (2002). 'Why Has Economic Growth Been More Pro-Poor in Some States of India than Others?', *Journal of Development Economics*, 68(2): 1453–73.

Rodriguez, F. and D. Rodrik (1999). 'Trade Policy and Economic Growth: A Skeptic's Guide to the Cross-National Evidence', *NBER Working Papers* 7081, National Bureau of Economic Research: Cambridge, MA.

Sachs, J. and A. Warner (1995). 'Economic Reform and the Process of Global Integration', *Brookings Papers on Economic Activity*, 1: 1–118.

Suryahadi, A., S. Sumarto, Y. Suharso, and L. Pritchett (2000). 'The Evolution of Poverty during the Crisis in Indonesia, 1996 to 1999', *Policy Research Working Papers* 2435, World Bank: Washington DC.

van de Walle, D. (1988). 'On the Use of the SUSENAS for Modeling Consumer Behaviour', *Bulletin of Indonesian Economic Studies*, 24(2): 107–22.

WHO/FAO/UNU Expert Panel (1985). 'Energy and Protein Requirements', *WHO Technical Reports* 724, WHO: Geneva.

Wiebe, F. (1994). 'Measuring Poverty in Indonesia: Identifying the Poor Under Heterogeneous Conditions', Ph.D. dissertation, Stanford University: Stanford.

Wodon, Q. (1997). 'Food Energy Intake and Cost of Basic Needs: Measuring Poverty in Bangladesh', *Journal of Development Studies*, 34(2): 66–101.

9

Reforms, Remoteness, and Risk in Africa: Understanding Inequality and Poverty during the 1990s

LUC CHRISTIAENSEN, LIONEL DEMERY,
AND STEFANO PATERNOSTRO

9.1. INTRODUCTION

Debates about the relationship between economic growth, income inequality, and poverty have a particular resonance in Africa. While the persistence of deep-seated poverty is undoubtedly a result of its slow economic progress over the past two decades, there remains a difference of opinion about whether growth benefits the poorest segments of African societies. The Dollar and Kraay (2000) view that growth *is* good for the poor has been disputed largely in the African context (see Forsyth 2000). Resolving these differences is made complex by the many changes that have affected people's lives and livelihoods during the 1990s. Reforms, shifts in external opportunities, and sharp movements in the terms of trade have all changed the economic environment. Some countries faced internal civil strife and political instability. Others had to endure severe drought. And there have been serious health shocks, such as AIDS and malaria, affecting rich and poor alike. This complexity makes for considerable debate about the impact of economic growth on the lives of poor Africans.

In their review of the cross-country growth literature, Collier and Gunning (1999) conclude that the slow economic progress in Africa is due to three sets of factors: geography (the land-locked, tropical character of many countries); macroeconomic

Some of this chapter previously appeared in the *World Bank Economic Review* 17(3), 2003: 317–47. It is reproduced here with the kind permission of Oxford University Press.

This chapter synthesizes and builds on the work of a large team of researchers who contributed to a series of poverty dynamics country studies in Africa, coordinated by the authors. It benefits enormously from their careful and competent analysis. The authors are grateful for helpful comments from Alan Gelb, John Hoddinott, and Jean Louis Arcand, and especially acknowledge the responsive and enthusiastic research assistance of Angelica Salvi. The chapter benefited from comments received from participants at the WIDER–Cornell–LSE Conference on Spatial Inequality and Development held at the London School of Economics, 28–30 June 2002. The work was generously supported by bilateral donors in Italy, the Netherlands, Switzerland, United Kingdom, and United States.

policies (notably economic policy volatility and a lack of openness to international trade); and microeconomic policies, which have disproportionately taxed rural producers, eroded social capital, undermined the provision of public services, and resulted in a retreat into subsistence by rural producers. Despite these important insights from cross-country analysis, the reasons for 'Africa's growth and poverty paradox' (Easterly and Levine 1997) remain open to debate. The limited number of countries, and the high correlation between the explanatory variables, means that the findings are often highly sensitive to the specification of the estimation model. The use of country-wide averages in this literature also limits what can be said about the distributional dimension of growth. It is unlikely, therefore, that cross-country analysis alone will resolve the growth–poverty issue (Bourguignon 2000; Brock and Durlauf 2000; Deininger and Okidi 2001). A more microeconomic approach is called for (Collier and Gunning 1999; Ravallion 2001). Only then can research establish 'why some poor people are able to take up the opportunities afforded by an expanding economy—and so add to its expansion—while others are not' (Ravallion 2001: 1,813). This study adopts this microperspective, and focuses on three key factors which govern how different groups in African society have been affected by recent economic growth (and also episodes of economic recession)—reforms, remoteness, and risk.

The main point of departure in the growth–poverty debate in the African context has been the assessment of how economic policy reforms have affected income distribution and poverty. This debate refuses to go away, in part because it was not well served by good data (both macro and micro). Expressing an 'African perspective', Mkandawire and Soludo (1999: 73) conclude that structural adjustment programmes did not place African economies on a 'poverty-reducing growth path'. And Stewart (1995: 155) draws a similar conclusion, albeit based on very flimsy data. On the other hand, the application of quantitative general equilibrium models suggested that policy reforms had mildly favourable effects (Sahn 1994, 1996; Sahn *et al.* 1997). Given the lags involved, the 1990s might be a more appropriate decade to examine the growth path induced by economic policy reforms in Africa (Collier and Gunning 1999). With more comprehensive and comparable household data (including emerging panel data), and with another decade of economic reform in many countries, it is now essential to revisit this issue.

Our second major theme is remoteness—the fact that many poor Africans live out their lives with little access to public services and markets. Only microdata can help unravel its effect on persistent poverty.[1] Regions, and households within these regions, may evolve differently due to spatial externalities related, for example, to knowledge diffusion and agglomeration effects (Ravallion 2002). The marginal cost of adopting new technologies or expanding into new activities (e.g. off-farm employment) typically declines as the necessary infrastructure becomes more widely available and more people

---

[1] While the importance of location has received somewhat less attention in the developing economics literature, the point is obviously not new. Quah (1996) even argues that in understanding regional convergence (or lack thereof) in Europe physical location and geographical spillovers matter more than national macro factors.

in the network become accustomed to the new technologies. A household's spatial position also affects its access to both input and output markets—coined 'cost' and 'demand linkages' by Davis and Weinstein (Chapter 6, this volume)—necessary for accumulating wealth and benefiting from the opportunities an overall economic upturn provides. Regional differences in living standards are obviously also linked to the agro-ecological characteristics of the environment (temperature, rainfall, altitude, slope, soil fertility, etc.) which affect the productive potential of the locality and its inhabitants. And the availability of public infrastructure and services (electricity, sanitation, health and schooling facilities, credit and extension services) often differs considerably across regions. There is a strong expectation, therefore, that growth in Africa is likely to have highly differentiated geographical effects.

The third factor which governs how poor people have been affected by economic growth in Africa is risk. Among the factors explaining poverty at the household level 'disease and climate feature most prominently, and these are largely omitted in the aggregate analysis' (Collier and Gunning 1999: 83). These growth-retarding risks might explain the 'Africa dummy' in growth regressions.[2] It is widely documented that households in Africa live and work in risky environments with insufficient access to credit or insurance to protect their consumption from shocks (Besley 1995; Morduch 1995). In the absence of such mechanisms they often engage in low-risk, low-return activities, which lock them into perpetual poverty. In the review that follows we focus on two main risk factors that have dominated Africa during the 1990s, disease and drought.

The study elaborates on the results of a series of poverty dynamics country studies[3] which exploit household survey data in Africa covering the 1990s. When available, household panel data have been used (Ethiopia and Uganda), though important insights were also obtained from repeated cross sections (Zimbabwe, Ghana, and Madagascar). It begins with a review in Section 9.2 of the trends in living standards during the 1990s, describing the evolution of income inequality and poverty and their relation with economic growth. Section 9.3 goes beyond the averages and identifies the main factors behind the observed trends—reforms, remoteness, and risk. Concluding observations are made in the final section.

9.2. LIVING STANDARDS DURING THE 1990s

Table 9.1 describes the evolution of private consumption, primary school enrolment, child malnutrition, and child mortality in our selection of countries during the 1990s. The first and obvious point is that living standards are still very low in these countries.

---

[2] In support of this hypothesis Guillaumont *et al.* (1999) find that economic, political, and natural volatility are important factors in explaining the poor growth performance of African economies.

[3] The selection of countries was based on the availability of comparable measures of consumption, and includes Ethiopia, Ghana, Madagascar, Mauritania, Nigeria, Uganda, Zambia, and Zimbabwe. These are reported in Bigsten *et al.* (2003), Dercon (2000, 2002), Coulombe and McKay (2001), Paternostro *et al.* (2001), McCulloch *et al.* (2000), Canagarajah *et al.* (2000), Appleton (2001), Appleton *et al.* (1999), Deininger and Okidi (2001), McCulloch *et al.* (2001), Alwang and Ersado (1999), and Alwang *et al.* (2002).

By the close of the decade, no country enjoyed an annual per capita consumption in excess of US$500, and in Ethiopia it was just US$86. All countries fell far short of universal primary enrolment, and in some (e.g. Ethiopia) primary enrolments were unacceptably low. Malnutrition was a very serious problem, especially in Madagascar and Ethiopia, where more than half the children exhibited signs of stunting or long-term malnutrition. Even in Ghana, Mauritania, and Zimbabwe, there is evidence of stunting in about a quarter of the population under five years of age. Perhaps the most poignant indicator of the very low welfare levels is the incidence of child deaths. Under-five mortality exceeded 100 (per 1,000) in all countries. In Zambia, almost one in five children failed to survive to their fifth birthday. Too many African children are dying needlessly.

Second, there are differences in the *changes* in these indicators over time. In four countries, economic living standards appear to have improved. But in Madagascar, average real consumption remained more or less unchanged, while it fell sharply in Nigeria, Zambia, and Zimbabwe. Similarly, improvements in primary school enrolment in Ethiopia, Ghana, Mauritania, and Uganda contrast with unsatisfactory outcomes in Zambia. Ethiopia and Mauritania experienced sharp reductions in long-term malnutrition, but there was little progress elsewhere. In all countries the long-term downward trend in child mortality appears to have continued through the decade, except in Zimbabwe, a result probably related to the AIDS epidemic (among other factors), and in Nigeria. Also the 2000/1 round of the Uganda Demographic and Health Survey suggests that child mortality in Uganda has been unchanged (and possibly even increased) since 1997 (UDHS 2001), despite economic gains.

Third, the trends in the indicators are generally consistent with each other, though there are some important exceptions. In the four countries experiencing economic growth (Ethiopia, Ghana, Mauritania, and Uganda) the trends in human development indicators match the improvement in economic well-being, albeit to different degrees. But in those experiencing stagnation and decline, the signals are noisier. In some cases the education indicator improved despite the stagnation or decline in economic living standards (Madagascar, Nigeria, and Zimbabwe). Child mortality improved in Zambia and child malnutrition improved in Zimbabwe during episodes of deteriorating economic circumstances. Such outcomes (and the experience of Uganda after 1995) serve as a reminder that focusing only on one dimension of well-being can be misleading when tracking poverty dynamics over time (World Bank 2000).

9.2.1. *Income Inequality*

We now turn to the distributional aspects of economic well-being, and to the issue of whether episodes of growth in the 1990s in Africa were associated with changes in income inequality.[4] Increasing reliance on markets and the withdrawal of the state

---

[4] As all our empirical measures of income are based on expenditures, we use the terms 'income' and 'consumption' interchangeably in the remainder of the text.

Table 9.1. *Evolving living standards in eight African countries during the 1990s*

	Real private consumption per capita (constant 1995 US$)[a]			Net primary school enrolment rates[b]			Child malnutrition[c]			Child mortality[d]		
	Year 1	Year 2	Annual growth rate (%)	Year 1 (%)	Year 2 (%)	Change (% points)	Year 1 (%)	Year 2 (%)	Change (% points)	Year 1 (per 1,000)	Year 2 (per 1,000)	Change (per 1,000)
Positive growth												
Ethiopia, 1994–7	80	86	2.6	19	25	+6	66	55	−11	190	175	−15
Ghana, 1992–8	275	304	2.0	70	82	+12	26	26	0	119	104	−15
Mauritania, 1987–95	297	361	3.6	28	41	+13	48	23	−25	—	149	—
Uganda, 1992–7	211	258	4.7	68	86	+18	43	39	−4	165	162	−3
Stagnation/decline												
Madagascar, 1993–9	223	222	0.0	48	64	+16	50	49	−1	170	149	−21
Nigeria, 1992–6	206	173	−3.4	94	98	+4	38	—	—	136	147	11
Zambia, 1991–8	362	266	−6.6	73	66	−7	40	42	+2	192	202	10
Zimbabwe, 1991–6	595	439	−5.2	83	86	+3	30	23	−7	80	90	10

[a] Growth rates calculated based on least squared method, which is less sensitive to the choice of base and terminal period.

[b] Net enrolment rates = percentage of children of school age enrolled in primary school as a fraction of the total number of children in that age group. Figures obtained from the surveys analysed in the Poverty Dynamics studies. First year figure for Ethiopia refers to 1996. Figures for Nigeria reflect gross enrolment rates in 1994 and 1996 and are obtained from World Development Indicators.

[c] Child malnutrition defined as the percentage of children stunted, that is, z-score of height for age which is less than −2; the reference periods for these figures approximate to those in column 1.

[d] Child mortality under 5 (per 1,000 live births); the reference periods approximate to those in column 1.

Source: World Bank data and country studies under the *Poverty Dynamics* study (see f.n. 3).

might be expected to increase income inequality (people with low levels of education, and limited access to public services and markets being less likely to take advantage of the opportunities growth presents). But on the other hand, given the previous tendency for the state to tax agriculture and the rural sector heavily, the removal of such interventions might result in improved national income distributions. We present Gini coefficients, a popular measure of inequality, to describe how income inequality evolved in our sample of countries (Table 9.2). All underlying 'welfare measures' are based on real total household expenditures.[5] The surveys were designed to enable comparisons over time within a country, though due to different survey designs caution is warranted in making comparisons across countries. Nonetheless, the differences in the degree of income inequality in our sample of countries are striking. At one extreme, Zimbabwe has a highly unequal distribution (a Gini ratio of over 0.6),[6] reflecting unequal land distribution, a result in part of its colonial history. Income distributions in Ghana and Uganda are far more egalitarian.

In terms of evolution, the picture is one of little change in *overall* income inequality in these countries,[7] except in Zambia. Reforms and growth have clearly not led to a significant deterioration in consumption inequality, as popular belief would hold (Forsyth 2000)—though Ethiopia forms an exception. Nevertheless, these aggregate measures of inequality can be misleading. They may in fact mask a great deal of distributional change, an issue we review further in Section 9.3.

9.2.2. *Trends in Income Poverty During the 1990s*

If growth episodes were not associated with significant changes in inequality, did they lead to poverty reduction? Table 9.3 reports poverty estimates for our countries. As with the inequality measures, real household consumption per adult equivalent (or in some cases, per capita) is taken as the central economic welfare measure. Poverty lines in all cases (except Mauritania) are derived from a food consumption basket, estimated to yield a minimum caloric intake, with adjustments made for essential non-food consumption. These poverty lines are typically much higher than the purchasing power parity US$1/day poverty line. The average poverty incidence in twenty-four spells of poverty change in African countries analysed by Ravallion (2001) was 31 per cent (based on the US$1/day line). This compares with (unweighted) average headcounts of 55 per cent in our sample of twelve spells, indicating higher poverty lines. Because of differences in survey design and in the specifics of how the

[5] For most countries, expenditure is normalized on the number of 'equivalent' adults in the household. In Ethiopia, Nigeria, and Madagascar, the welfare measure is real household expenditure per capita.

[6] Intuitively, the Gini index of a population represents the expected income difference between two randomly selected individuals or households. From Table 9.1 we know that in Zimbabwe real average per capita consumption in 1996 amounted to US$439. The corresponding Gini index is 0.64 (Table 9.2). Thus, in 1996 the per capita consumption of any two randomly selected Zimbabweans differed on average by US$281 (=0.64 × US$439)—a clear indication of high inequality given that average per capita consumption is only US$439.   [7] A similar picture emerges when using the Theil inequality measures.

Table 9.2. *Consumption inequality[a] during the 1990s in eight African countries*

Gini coefficient	Year 1	Year 2	Change
Ethiopia[b]			
1994–7 (Rural)	0.39	0.43	0.04
1994–7 (Urban)	0.40	0.45	0.05
All	0.39	0.44	0.05
Ghana 1992–8			
Rural	0.33	0.33	0.00
Urban	0.34	0.31	−0.03
All	0.37	0.37	−0.00
Madagascar 1993–9			
Rural	0.42	0.36	−0.06
Urban	0.41	0.38	−0.03
All	0.43	0.38	−0.05
Mauritania 1987–95			
Rural	0.43	0.37	−0.06
Urban	0.40	0.36	−0.04
All	0.43	0.39	−0.04
Nigeria 1992–6			
Rural	0.51	0.44	−0.07
Urban	0.51	0.51	0.00
All	0.51	0.47	−0.04
Uganda 1992–2000			
Rural	0.33	0.32	−0.01
Urban	0.39	0.40	0.01
All	0.36	0.38	0.02
Zambia 1991–8			
Rural	0.61	0.48	−0.13
Urban	0.47	0.43	−0.04
All	0.58	0.48	−0.10
Zimbabwe 1991–6			
Rural	0.58	0.57	−0.01
Urban	0.60	0.59	−0.01
All	0.68	0.64	−0.04

[a] Real expenditures per adult equivalent; real per capita expenditures for Ethiopia, Nigeria, and Madagascar.
[b] Purposively sampled villages and urban centres; not nationally representative.

Source: Country studies under *Dynamics of Poverty* study (see f.n. 3).

L. Christiaensen, L. Demery, & S. Paternostro

Table 9.3. *Consumption poverty in eight African countries during the 1990s*

	Poverty headcount (P_0)			Severity index (P_2)		
	Year 1	Year 2	% change	Year 1	Year 2	% change
Ethiopia						
1994–7	41	35	−14	8	6	−27
Ghana						
1992–8	51	39	−24	9	7	−22
Madagascar						
1993–7	70	73	5	17	19	12
1997–9	73	71	−3	19	19	0
Mauritania						
1987–95	58	35	−40	17	6	−65
Nigeria						
1985–92	46	43	−7	8	9	13
1992–6	43	66	53	9	17	89
Uganda						
1992–7	56	44	−21	10	6	−40
1997–2000	44	35	−20	6	5	−16
Zambia						
1991–6	70	80	14	30	31	1
1996–8	80	76	−5	31	26	−16
Zimbabwe						
1991–6	26	35	35	4	5	25

Source: World Bank data and country studies under *Dynamics of Poverty* study (see f.n. 3).

welfare measure and poverty lines are derived, the data in Table 9.3 are not comparable across countries. But the research has been designed to ensure comparable estimates over time.

The poverty measures we report here are derived from the familiar class of poverty indices after Foster *et al.* (1984). In addition to the poverty headcount (P_0), Table 9.3 also includes the severity poverty index (P_2) because it is sensitive to the distribution of income *among* the poor, and particularly to changes in the living standards of the poorest of the poor. The data suggest the following:

1. Most countries can be considered as having to deal with 'mass' poverty. Over 70 per cent were estimated to be poor in Madagascar and Zambia. And 66 per cent of Nigerians were estimated to be poor in 1996.
2. There is no uniform trend. While consumption poverty incidence declined substantially in several countries (Ethiopia, Ghana, Mauritania, and Uganda), it rose sharply in Nigeria and Zimbabwe. Poverty has fluctuated in Zambia and Madagascar, increasing marginally in the former and remaining more or less unchanged in the latter.

3. Where the incidence of poverty has declined, the data suggest that the poorest sections of the population have also benefited. This is suggested by the significant downward trend in P_2. In several cases the percentage fall in the P_2 measure was greater than that in P_0.

9.2.3. *Poverty, Inequality, and Economic Growth*

In some cases these changes in poverty occurred in a context of economic decline (Nigeria and Zimbabwe, and Madagascar and Zambia during the earlier periods). In others they accompanied overall economic progress (Ethiopia, Ghana, Mauritania, and Uganda). To shed more light on the relation between poverty, inequality, and growth, Table 9.4 presents a decomposition of poverty incidence into two components: changes explained by changes in mean consumption (keeping the *distribution* of consumption unchanged); and changes arising from changing consumption distribution (with mean consumption kept constant). The poverty measure decomposed in the table is the elasticity of headcount poverty with respect to changes in mean household expenditure.[8]

In most countries, changes in poverty incidence are due predominantly to changes in mean expenditure (Table 9.4). But the results of this exercise also serve as a caution against over-generalizing for Africa. Uganda's growth experience (in which reduction in inequality bolstered the effects of rising mean consumption) contrasts with that of Ethiopia, where inequality increased, and dampened the poverty reducing impact of growth. Where there has been recession, mean and redistribution effects typically have opposite signs, and the redistribution effect substantially mitigates the poverty increasing impact of lower mean incomes (in Madagascar, Nigeria, and Zimbabwe). Better-off groups clearly bear a heavier burden of income losses during periods of economic decline in Africa.[9] To assess further the extent to which these episodes of growth and recession are 'pro-poor' we follow Kakwani and Pernia (2000) in defining $\phi = \eta/\eta_g$ where η is the *observed* elasticity of headcount poverty with respect to changes in mean expenditure, and η_g is the elasticity of headcount poverty assuming that the distribution of income did not change during the period. ϕ can be defined as an index of 'pro-poor growth'. Growth can be considered pro-poor if $\phi > 1$.[10] Table 9.5 compares estimates of ϕ for these eight African countries with recent experience in Asia. On the basis of this sample of countries, growth and recession episodes in Africa have tended to be pro-poor,[11] and indeed more so than the Asian experience.

---

[8] This is defined as the proportionate change in headcount poverty divided by the proportionate change in mean per capita household expenditure. For details of the method used, see Kakwani and Pernia (2000).

[9] The tendency for income inequality to narrow as higher income groups bear the brunt of economic recession was also noted by Grootaert (1996) in analysing poverty changes in Côte d'Ivoire in the 1980s. Though this does not seem to have occurred in Zambia during 1991–6.

[10] When mean household expenditures are declining, $\phi = \eta_g/\eta$, so that a recession would also be considered pro-poor if $\phi > 1$.

[11] This should of course not be taken to mean that the poor did not suffer during recessions, but rather that the rich suffered relatively quite a bit more.

L. Christiaensen, L. Demery, & S. Paternostro

Table 9.4. *Relative importance of mean and distribution in the evolution of poverty incidence*

	Percentage change in:		Poverty elasticity w.r.t. mean expenditure	Explained by changes in:[b]	
	Mean per capita expenditure	Poverty headcount		Mean	Distribution
Ethiopia[a]					
1994–7	24.8	−13.8	−0.56	1.09	0.53
Ghana					
1992–8	24.9	−23.6	−0.95	−0.99	0.04
Madagascar					
1993–7	−17.5	4.7	−0.27	−0.77	0.50
1997–9	0.6	−2.7	−4.50	−0.78	−3.72
1993–9	−17	1.9	−0.11	−0.73	0.62
Mauritania					
1987–95	49.5	−40.4	−0.82	−0.75	−0.07
Nigeria					
1992–6	−41.1	53.6	−1.30	−1.32	0.02
Uganda					
1992–7	17.1	−20.7	−1.21	−1.06	−0.15
Zambia					
1991–6	−25.7	14.9	−0.58	−0.58	0.00
1996–8	13.2	−4.9	−0.37	−0.44	0.07
Zimbabwe					
1991–6	−28.8	35.3	−1.23	−2.22	0.99

[a] Purposively sampled villages and urban centres; not nationally representative.
[b] Decompositions based on Kakwani and Pernia (2000). Note that this method is an exact decomposition with no residual or interactive term.

Source: World Bank data and country studies under *Dynamics of Poverty* study (see f.n. 3).

Taking all eleven spells of poverty change in our sample of African countries reported in Table 9.4, we obtain a growth elasticity of poverty incidence of just −0.89 (Fig. 9.1).[12] While growth is 'pro-poor', its quantitative impact on the headcount is limited in this sample. This follows from the fact that inequality did not change significantly, and it reflects the depth of poverty—large numbers are subsisting well below the poverty line (and poverty lines are set well above modal consumption). The growth elasticity of the severity index (P_2), at −1.28 (with a standard error of 0.21) is higher, indicating that

[12] This is simply the slope coefficient in the regression of the proportionate change in headcount poverty on the proportionate change in the survey mean. The standard error on the slope coefficient is 0.11. When plotting the regression line, it runs almost through the origin, a reflection of the fact that income inequality has been stable over this period. The historical elasticities we observe for this sample of African countries are significantly lower than that estimated by Ravallion (2001) to be typical of low-income countries (−2.5). Given the different poverty lines used (he uses the much lower benchmark of PPP$1/day) and the different method of computation, his estimates are not comparable with ours.

Table 9.5. *Pro-poor growth indices (φ) in selected African and Asian countries*

Growth episodes			
Ethiopia, 1994–7	0.51	Thailand, 1992–6	0.61
Ghana, 1992–8	0.96	Lao PDR, 1993–8	0.21
Mauritania, 1987–95	1.10	Korea, 1990–6	1.03
Uganda, 1992–7	1.14		
Zambia, 1996–8	0.87		
Recession/stagnation episodes			
Madagascar, 1993–7	2.85	Thailand, 1996–8	0.73
Nigeria, 1992–6	1.02	Korea, 1997–8	0.84
Zambia, 1991–6	0.97		
Zimbabwe, 1991–6	1.81		

Note: For details of method see text. Asian country estimates are simple means across years within the subperiods shown.

Source: Kakwani and Pernia (2000: Table 4).

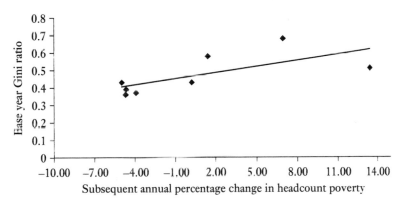

Figure 9.1. *Initial inequality and subsequent poverty trends*
Source: See text.

growth has improved the economic well-being of the poorest, though not enough to take many of them out of poverty.

As discussed above, countries with lower initial inequality typically grow more rapidly in subsequent years, and experience greater poverty impact from that growth. The experience of this (albeit small) sample of African countries seems consistent with this view (Fig. 9.1). The countries that had lower levels of initial inequality (as evidenced by the Gini ratios), were more likely to experience declines in poverty in subsequent years (Spearman correlation is 0.72 and statistically significant at 5 per cent level). Nonetheless, that said, there is also sufficient variation around this empirical regularity and the sample size is sufficiently small to counsel caution.

9.3. GROWTH AND SYSTEMATIC CHANGES IN INCOME DISTRIBUTION

The evidence from the African experience covered in this study indicates that growth and recession have been pro-poor. Yet, further decomposition of national inequality and poverty measures—by socioeconomic group and geographical location—indicates that the aggregate statistics often mask a wide variety of experiences. Some groups and regions gained disproportionately from the new opportunities following economic reforms and growth, while others lost out or even became impoverished. Similarly, overall Gini coefficients often appear stable over time despite substantial churning within and across geographical regions. These divergent experiences suggest that in addition to reforms in economic policy, other factors such as location and infrastructure, households' private endowments, and the occurrence of shocks further condition whether households can escape poverty in the wake of overall economic growth.

To disentangle the effects of these disparate events and factors on the different sections of African society, studies have often relied on economy-wide modelling techniques (Bourguignon and Morrison 1992; Sahn et al. 1997). These techniques can generate counterfactuals and provide important insights into the respective impacts of policies and other shocks. On the other hand, the models typically impose a strong structure which sometimes leads to questions about their realism. In addition, they are most often calibrated at one point in time. As a result, they cannot always confidently track changes over time—the economic history, which usually involves policy-induced structural changes in the economy. This study places emphasis instead on the microeconometric evidence emerging from the much improved and richer household survey data. We highlight in particular two poverty dynamics panel studies—Dercon (2002) on Ethiopia, and Deininger and Okidi (2001) on Uganda. Focusing on the factors they identify as key for economic growth and poverty reduction, we then assess the evidence from the other case studies which use either repeated cross-sectional regressions (Zimbabwe, Madagascar, Ghana) or simply an extensively documented narrative linking the macroevents to the observed evolutions in household welfare (Zambia and Mauritania).

The Ethiopia and Uganda studies are particularly informative. First, both involve the use of panel data, and their methodologies and results are similar. Second, both countries experienced far-reaching reforms in economic policy, inducing changes in market institutions, relative prices, and producer behaviour. The rural sector in Ethiopia had previously been largely ignored and heavily taxed. In the early 1990s agricultural reforms were initiated including the abolition of food delivery quota for farmers, and a relaxation (and later abolition) of restrictions on private grain trades. These measures substantially reduced the food marketing margins between surplus and deficit regions. The Birr was devalued by 142 per cent and the foreign exchange markets were liberalized. This positively affected the farmgate prices of tradables, such as coffee and chat, even though the effect was somewhat muted due to the existence of parallel markets. Producer prices for coffee also evolved favourably during the period because of increasing world prices.

In Uganda, government policy changed from the late 1980s on, dismantling the biases against rural producers. Coffee marketing and exports were liberalized, and direct export taxation was abandoned. Similar measures were taken in the cotton sector. The foreign exchange market was liberalized, leading to real exchange rate depreciation. The weighted mean real producer price of export crops in Uganda (77 per cent of which are coffee) increased by 78 per cent between 1989–91 and 1995–7. Decomposition of this increase underscores the importance of the liberalization of the export crop markets for the cash-crop producers. Changes in the nominal protection coefficient (producer price/border price), changes in the real exchange rate, and changes in the real world price contributed respectively 58, 9, and 11 per cent (Townsend 1999). Agricultural output recovered, averaging between 4 and 4.5 per cent per annum in real terms over the past decade, and this has played an important role in reducing poverty (Appleton *et al.* 1999).

Both Deininger and Okidi (2001) and Dercon (2002) use household panel data to assess how changes in economic policies and their effects on producer prices, influenced household welfare and rural poverty. Dercon (2002) uses panel data from six *rural* communities[13] in Ethiopia covering the period 1989–95. The change in household real consumption per adult is explained through a reduced form regression model with an Oaxaca-Blinder type decomposition. In this approach changes in consumption and poverty can be explained by changes in endowments over time and changes in returns to endowments. The main regressors were changes in real crop producer prices (which Dercon shows to be closely related to the macroeconomic and agricultural reforms implemented during this period), location (proxied by distance to an urban centre), access to roads, private endowments (land, labour, and education), and two shock variables, rainfall and ill-health. His results are summarized in Table 9.6.

Household consumption increased on average by 32 per cent between 1989 and 1995, and poverty—here defined as the poverty gap in logs—decreased by 29 percentage points. The growth in rural household incomes was largely fuelled by changes in relative food-crop prices,[14] and increased returns to location and access to road infrastructure. Dercon's simulations show that consumption would have *declined* by 13 per cent and poverty would have *increased* by 23 per cent had there been no peace and no economic and agricultural reforms.[15] Interestingly, all poor households (even those who fell into poverty) benefited from the relative price changes that occurred. These findings suggest that the reforms and increased political stability substantially improved well-being of the poor, directly through a favourable change in relative prices, and for those

---

[13] Because the study is not nationally representative, the results cannot be generalized to Ethiopia as a whole. Nonetheless, the methodology adopted as well as the empirical findings themselves provide important insights in the linkages between economic policy, growth, and poverty reduction.

[14] Coffee prices also improved, yet coffee was grown in only one of the six sample villages, and the coffee harvest had failed that year in that particular village due to pest attack and drought. The effect of changing export crop prices cannot be evaluated from this sample, but its importance has been assessed explicitly in the Uganda case study described later.

[15] Dercon (1995) shows that the cereal marketing margins mainly improved because of the liberalization of the grain markets and only on some routes did the end of the war have a significant effect.

Table 9.6. *Decomposition of consumption growth per adult and poverty gap ratio (percentage points) in Ethiopia*

| | Actual | | Counterfactual | | | |
| | | | No reform and peace | | No risk | |
	Growth	Poverty	Growth	Poverty	Growth	Poverty
Real crop price change	15	−18			15	−16
Change in returns to road access/location	19	−23			19	−21
Private endowments						
Increase in land	7	−10	1	−2	7	−8
Change in returns to land	3	0			3	−1
Increases in adult labour	3	−4	3	−4	3	−4
Changes in returns to educated adults	0	0			0	0
Change in adult equivalent units	−5	7	−5	7	−5	7
Shocks						
Relative rainfall shock	−8	13	−8	14		
Illness shocks	−4	5	−4	5		
Residual	0	0	0	3	0	0
Percentage growth and percentage point poverty change (sum of above)	30	−30	−13	23	42	−43

Source: Dercon (2002).

well connected to markets, indirectly through an increase in the returns to market connectedness as determined by road infrastructure and distance to urban centres.

In addition to public endowments, such as road infrastructure and location, private endowments are also found to be important for consumption growth and poverty reduction.[16] Increases in landholdings (through redistribution) or improvement in the quality of the land owned, and increases in adult labour reduced poverty by 14 percentage points. Returns to land also increased,[17] but because the poor typically possess little (and often less fertile) land, they profited much less than the average household from the increased returns to land. Finally, the occurrence of shocks (especially

[16] Adult education levels are extremely low, less than one year per adult, and they are assumed not to have changed. The effect of education as such, as opposed to changes in returns to education, has thus not been evaluated in this study.

[17] As the direct effect of changing producer prices has been controlled for, changes in returns to land result from other factors such as shifts in the underlying production technology potentially induced by the reforms.

rainfall, but also illness shocks) had a large negative effect, both on the growth process and poverty outcomes. If households had access to full insurance protection from rainfall and health shocks, poverty would have declined by 42 percentage points compared with 29 percentage points in its absence. Dercon shows that the reason why households fell into poverty during this period was mainly the combined effects of the rainfall and illness shocks. In sum, households that escaped poverty during the period not only benefited from better producer prices, they also enjoyed a more favourable location, and were endowed with good access to infrastructure and better land. Those who remained poor or who fell into poverty, despite their participation in the gains from the agricultural reforms, did so in part because they were badly placed in terms of location and land. They also suffered most from poor rainfall and from ill-health.

Deininger and Okidi (2001) analyse changes in consumption and income observed for a panel of about 1,200 Ugandan households during the period 1992–2000. They regress household level changes in consumption and income against variables representing the change in relative producer prices of coffee, access to infrastructure, initial endowments of physical and human capital, the initial health status of households, and their social capital. They found these variables to be significant in explaining growth in Ugandan household incomes during the 1990s. As in Ethiopia, the effect of changes in relative prices (in this case an increase in farmgate coffee prices largely brought about by market liberalization, but also by the devaluation and favourable world prices) on consumption growth was substantial.

Initial private endowments of education and other assets (mainly land) were also crucial for consumption growth. For example, if households had six years of completed schooling on average (instead of the observed three years)—equivalent to completing primary schooling—growth in consumption would have been 2 percentage points higher. A difference of one standard deviation in terms of initial asset value (about half of which is accounted for by land) put households on a 2 percentage point higher consumption growth path. Households which in 1992 were afflicted by health problems—reportedly related to malaria in over 80 per cent of cases—experienced consumption growth which was (other things constant) 1.8 percentage points lower than those not experiencing such problems. Households with access to electricity enjoyed consumption growth that was 6 percentage points higher than other households.

The above results offer insight into what determined the growth in income and consumption among Ugandan households. How did such growth affect poverty? To address this, Deininger and Okidi estimate a multinomial logit model of changes in poverty status (households are classified as either not changing their status, falling into poverty, or escaping from poverty). They find that the relative coffee price changes had a powerful poverty-reducing impact, indicating that their effect was broadbased and that price changes in tradable commodities directly benefited poor producers (and not only indirectly through the labour market). Moreover, households with higher education, more initial assets (land), better health, and better access to infrastructure (electricity) and location (distance to municipality) were far less likely than others to fall into poverty, and more likely to escape from it. The results from these microeconometric analyses of panel data suggest that the following factors are influential in determining the relationship between economic growth and poverty reduction:

- First, many poor rural households stand to benefit directly from reform—in this case liberalization measures, and the gains can be substantial. In so far as liberalization measures increase producer prices, rural producers gain, and to the extent that food marketing margins tend to decline, rural consumers will benefit as well. Nonetheless, some gain more than others, depending on the product- and consumption-mix of the household.
- Second, a household's remoteness appears key in conditioning the extent to which it will benefit from liberalization measures. Specifically, whether the household had access to infrastructure and urban markets was an immensely important factor in governing the growth in household income. It explains about half of household consumption growth and poverty reduction in Ethiopia during 1989–95, and it was also quantitatively important for growth in Ugandan household income. Connectedness to markets as captured by access to infrastructure (especially roads, and also electricity) and distance to urban centres is likely to be a major factor in determining how growth in any country transmits its benefits to the population.
- Third, the potential for economic growth and poverty reduction further depends on a household's private endowments. Households with larger private endowments— be it more and better qualified labour or land—not only tend to be less poor, they are also better placed to profit from new opportunities generated by liberalization and institutional change.
- Finally, it is vital to separate out the effect of shocks when assessing the role of policy changes. Dercon highlights rainfall and health shocks, both of which are certain to be relevant to poor households in most African countries. The importance of health shocks is also underscored by Deininger and Okidi for the Ugandan case. Export commodity price fluctuations, though not explicitly treated in these studies, form another important risk factor.

We now examine the evidence on distribution and poverty changes in other countries covered in this review, looking for echoes of the findings from the panel data of Ethiopia and Uganda, and focusing on three issues: reforms, remoteness, and risks.[18]

9.3.1. *Reform*

The changes in relative prices through exchange rate devaluations, the opening of domestic markets, and changes in the structure of production are certain to lead to shifts in income distribution, with producers of tradable goods (mostly exportables) benefiting directly from the economic policy reforms. The Ugandan and Ethiopian studies show that these effects were evident during the 1990s, and that they directly

---

[18] The importance of private endowments (human and physical capital assets and land) is also underscored by the two panel studies. Given the acceptance of these in the literature, we focus here on the three other themes.

Table 9.7. *Poverty incidence by rural activity, Ghana and Uganda in the 1990s*

	Uganda				Ghana			
	Population share (2000)	1992	2000	% reduction	Population share (1998)	1992	1998	% reduction
Food crop	45.9	63.3	45.7	−27.8	43.9	68.1	59.4	−12.8
Cash crop	21.3	62.7	29.7	−52.6	6.3	64.0	38.7	−39.5

Source: Appleton (2001); Coulombe and McKay (2001).

benefited poor households. The experience of Ghana in West Africa echoes these East African findings. Ghana experienced sharp poverty reductions among cash (export) crop producers during the 1990s, a result of more favourable world cocoa prices and an increase in cocoa production. Table 9.7 compares trends in poverty among crop producers in rural Uganda and Ghana.

In both countries about two-fifths of the population are food producing farmers, of whom about two-thirds were poor in the early 1990s. And in both countries, poverty fell among food producers, but the decline was not as great as that experienced by export crop producers. Most of the rural poor appear to have benefited from growth, but those producing export crops have benefited most. A much larger share of the population in Uganda grows cash crops (21 per cent) than in Ghana (6 per cent) which may explain the larger drop in poverty among food-crop producers in Uganda due to externality effects. Reviewing the existing evidence on the experience with agricultural reforms in sub-Saharan Africa, Kherallah *et al.* (2002) arrive at a similar conclusion — export-crop producers seem to have benefited more than food-crop producers. What needs to be better understood is the *transmission* mechanism that led to economic gains of households not producing for export.

Potential pathways include rural labour markets, with higher export-crop prices stimulating export-crop production leading to increased demand for agricultural wage labour and ultimately higher agricultural real wages. Abdulai and Delgado (2000) find that in Ghana a 1 per cent change in the domestic terms of trade between agriculture and non-agriculture leads to a 0.83 per cent change in the real agricultural wage rate in the long run, underscoring the importance of labour markets in transmitting the effects of economic reforms. Increased liquidity in rural economies from agricultural exports can also have important spin-off effects, through an expansion of both investment in export- and food-crop production, and increased consumption of goods and services produced with previously underutilized local labour, land, or capital. As a rule of thumb Delgado *et al.* (1998) posit that any policy-enhancing producer income from agricultural exports increases local rural income by twice the amount of the increased exports.

To understand the different evolution in poverty among food- and cash-crop producers, it is important to keep in mind that the former group tends to be much more heterogeneous than the latter. In export-crop growing regions, the effects of favourable export-crop prices were transmitted to the food-crop growing households—either through the labour market or the input and product markets, or both. Transmission of such benefits to areas unsuitable for export-crop production, especially when they are also remote, is much harder. For example, in Ghana food producers in more remote and less integrated regions (in the north) did not experience a similar reduction in their poverty as food growers in cash-crop (and better integrated) areas (Coulombe and McKay 2001). Similarly, food-crop producers in northern Uganda, which is also less accessible, appear not to have benefited from recent growth (Appleton 2001).

9.3.2. *Remoteness*

The panel analysis of Ethiopian and Ugandan households provides strong empirical evidence that location and geography are important in determining how growth influences income distribution. These findings are supported by the experiences in the other case study countries. In some, the decline in poverty is observed in both the rural and urban areas (Uganda, Mauritania, Ghana; see Table 9.8). In others, the change is confined mainly to urban areas (Zambia between 1991 and 1996). Striking differences in poverty changes are also observed across the administrative regions (Table 9.9). For example, while poverty incidence in Toliara (Madagascar) declined by just over 10 per cent during the 1990s, it increased by more than 40 per cent in Mahajanga (from 53 to 76 percentage points). In Uganda, the Central Province saw its poverty headcount halve between 1992 and 2000, though it declined by only 9 per cent in the Northern Province. Poverty dropped by 80 per cent in Greater Accra (Ghana), while it rose by one-third in the Upper East, and the regional discrepancies in the evolution of poverty observed in Zambia were of similar magnitude.[19]

Clearly, geography matters in conditioning growth and poverty reduction, and the reasons for this can be manifold (Ravallion 2002). The marginal cost of adopting new technologies, household access to input and output markets, agro-ecological characteristics of the environment, and the availability of public infrastructure can differ considerably across regions.

The evidence from the Ethiopian and Ugandan panel studies has especially pointed to the importance of market connectedness, as proxied by distance to urban centres and road infrastructure, and the role of public infrastructure (electricity). These themes also appear important in understanding the experiences from Ghana, Madagascar, and Zambia. Poverty in Accra fell sharply, but not in other urban areas (Fig. 9.2). In the Savannah zone poverty even *increased* in the urban areas, while it fell only marginally in the rural Savannah. Moreover, even after controlling for a host of household characteristics, community infrastructure variables and the agro-ecological environment (Coulombe and McKay 2001) living standards in the northern region appear much lower. Important clues as to why Ghanaians in the north did not benefit from growth are found in recent papers by Badiane and Shively (1998) and Abdulai (2000), which

---

[19] A similar pattern emerges when looking at average consumption growth across regions, as opposed to poverty change.

Table 9.8. *Headcount poverty trends in rural and urban areas of seven African countries during the 1990s (in %)*

	Rural				Urban		
	Population share in year 1	Year 1	Year 2	Change (points)	Year 1	Year 2	Change (points)
Ghana, 1992–8	67	64	49	−15	28	19	−9
Madagascar, 1993–9	81	74.5	76.7	2.2	50.1	52.1	2
Mauritania, 1987–95	56	68	48	−20	45	17	−28
Nigeria, 1992–6	62	46	69	23	37	58	21
Uganda, 1992–7	88	59	48	−11	28	16	−12
Zambia							
1991–6	62	88	90	2	47	62	15
1996–8	62	90	86	−4	62	59	−3
Zimbabwe, 1991–6	63	36	48	12	3	8	5

Source: Country studies under the *Poverty Dynamics* study (see f.n. 3).

Table 9.9. *Regional poverty change[a] in four African countries during the 1990s*

Country	Selected regions	Poverty headcount (P_0)		
		Year 1 (%)	Year 2 (%)	% change
Ghana (1992–8)	Greater Accra	26	5	−80
	Upper East	67	88	32
	Country total	51	39	−24
Madagascar (1993–9)	Toliara	81	72	−12
	Mahajanga	53	76	43
	Country total	70	71	2
Uganda (1992–2000)	Central	46	20	−55
	North	72	66	−9
	Country total	56	35	−37
Zambia (1991–8)	Northwestern	78	62	−21
	Lusaka	31	60	94
	Country total	69	76	10

[a] The regions with the largest positive and the largest negative change are reported for each country.

Source: Country studies under the *Poverty Dynamics* study (see f.n. 3).

conclude that markets (more specifically the maize market) in the remoter northern region are not very well integrated with the economy at large. This lack of integration most likely impeded the transmission of the benefits of growth to the region. The multivariate regression analysis by Coulombe and McKay (2001) further indicates that communities with access to electricity tend to be better off.

L. Christiaensen, L. Demery, & S. Paternostro

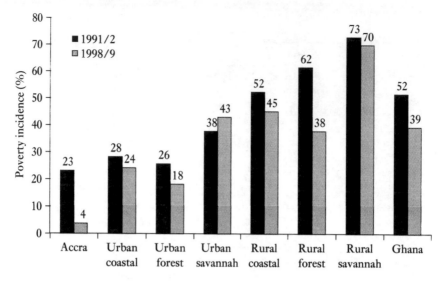

Figure 9.2. *Ghana, incidence of consumption poverty by zone, 1992–8*

Source: Coulombe and McKay (2001).

'Remoteness' is also important in understanding geographical differences in poverty outcomes in Madagascar. Paternostro *et al.* (2001) disaggregate poverty according to an index of remoteness, the latter being a weighted sum of indicators reflecting access to roads, bus stop, agricultural extension services, modern fertilizers, and distance to schools and health facilities (the weights were derived from factor analysis). Their findings (Table 9.10) indicate an association between the degree of remoteness and the likelihood of being in poverty. They also show that while overall rural poverty remained largely unchanged during 1997 and 1999, households assessed to be the most remote, experienced increased poverty—in contrast to the least remote quintile where poverty indicators actually improved. In a similar fashion a remoteness index was constructed for Zambia based on households' distance to the food market, the post office and a public phone, public transport (potential indicators of market connectedness), primary and secondary school and distance to the hospital (indicators of access to public services). Again households in the most remote areas appear substantially poorer than those in the least remote areas. These findings are replicated when households are only classified according to an index of market connectedness or an index of access to public services, suggesting that geography affects poverty both through market connectedness and the availability of public services.

While the evidence presented shows that location is crucial in conditioning growth and poverty reduction linkages, a better understanding of the transmission channels is called for. Does the Peruvian experience (Escobal and Torero, Chapter 5, this volume) that private and public assets are more important in explaining regional income variations than agro–ecological characteristics also hold in the African context? Do spatial

Table 9.10. *Rural poverty incidence by 'remoteness' quintile, Madagascar and Zambia (%)*

		Madagascar (P_0)		Zambia (P_0)	
		1997	1999	1991	1998
1	Most remote	79	84	86	75
2		82	78	81	76
3		76	76	83	73
4		72	72	82	74
5	Least remote	72	72	69	69

Source: Paternostro *et al.* (2001); and authors' computations.

externalities affect growth and poverty reduction as suggested by the findings from rural China (Ravallion 2002)? The policy ramifications of such insights are substantial, as they shed light on the longstanding debate about the economic desirability of public investment in resource poor areas vis-à-vis the promotion of outmigration or resettlement.

9.3.3. *Risk*

Poverty estimates provide a snapshot of the standard of living at a certain point in time and reflect both policy reforms as well as temporary external shocks such as droughts. When evaluating the evolution of poverty it is thus important to control for the effect of external shocks on comparative poverty figures. Controlling for all other factors, the Ethiopian panel analysis estimated that household income growth was reduced by about a fifth because of rainfall shortage (Dercon 2002). The role of rainfall variations in influencing household income growth was also an important feature of the Zimbabwean and Madagascar experience.

That poverty increased sharply in Zimbabwe during the 1990s is without question (Alwang *et al.* 2002). The decline in economic well-being (and increase in poverty) is evident from the leftward shift in the distribution of real household consumption (Fig. 9.3). The change occurred mainly in the vicinity of the poverty line (Z\$30 per month)—with a sharp increase in the numbers of people consuming just below, and a parallel decline in the numbers just above the poverty line. What is less clear is whether poverty increased because of the droughts that afflicted the country in 1991/2 and again in 1994/5, or because of the Economic Structural Adjustment Programme (launched in 1991) which was being implemented at the same time. Alwang *et al.* (2002) apply non-parametric methods to simulate what the 1995 distribution would have been if the 1990 rainfall patterns had applied that year. This exercise confirms that the drought led to an increase in poverty during the early 1990s, but it also indicates that the drought alone cannot explain the deterioration in economic well-being (Fig. 9.4(a)). As discussed before, actual changes in household location, assets,

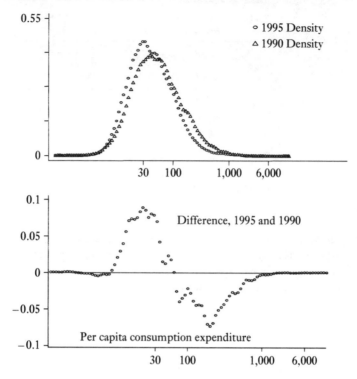

Figure 9.3. *Zimbabwe, shift in welfare distribution, 1990–5*

Source: Alwang *et al.* (2002).

and individual characteristics (notably the levels of educational attainment) would actually, other things constant, have *raised* consumption levels and reduced poverty (Fig. 9.4(b)). Without such changes, incomes would have deteriorated even more than they did. Evidence from Madagascar further underscores the importance of weather shocks in comparing poverty over time. Simulations indicate that 75 per cent of the predicted change in household economic well-being and poverty incidence can be traced back to the relative change in drought occurrence between 1993 and 1999. The insurance capacity of households against covariate shocks in many parts of Africa is clearly extremely limited.

9.4. CONCLUDING REMARKS

While it is true that *overall* income distributions (evidenced by the Gini ratio) have not changed during African episodes of growth, and that such growth (or recession) can be characterized as pro-poor in this aggregate sense, beneath these numbers exists a variety of experience. Neglect of this reality by policymakers—and sometimes also

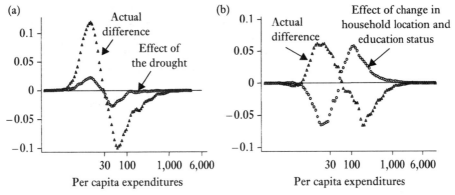

Figure 9.4. *Zimbabwe, simulated effects of (a) rainfall (rural distribution only) and (b) individual and household characteristics on changes in the welfare distribution, 1990–5*

Source: Alwang *et al.* (2002).

by academics—has often impeded a constructive and fruitful dialogue with 'civil society' about appropriate poverty reducing policies (Kanbur 2001). Our review of the microeconomic evidence shows that there have been systematic changes in income distributions and poverty in the countries covered. Of the main contours of these distribution changes, we have highlighted three key policy messages: the importance of economic reform for poverty reduction; the role of location and remoteness in conditioning how the benefits of growth are distributed; and the need to account for shocks in understanding distributional outcomes and poverty changes over time. The analysis of household panel data by Dercon (2002) for Ethiopia and Deininger and Okidi (2001) for Uganda provides the most systematic and empirically convincing cases that policy-induced changes in relative prices can have poverty-reducing effects. Microevidence from Ghana provides some corroboration from West Africa.

The second message is the need for a geographical perspective on poverty. The recent microeconomic evidence on poverty dynamics has shown that some regions, by virtue of their sheer remoteness, have been left behind somewhat as growth has picked up. Households with limited access to markets and public services have not benefited from growth during the 1990s. The provision of public goods (notably infrastructure services—from the Ethiopian case, especially roads and from the Ugandan case, electricity) is crucial to help poor households benefit from the opportunities generated by economic policy reforms and growth. Third, the microeconomic evidence underscores the importance of social protection in a poverty reduction strategy. The impact of rainfall variations and ill-health are the two risk factors featured. Dercon (2002) estimates that poverty reduction in the sample of Ethiopian rural communities would have been

18 percentage points greater had households been protected from the effects of ill-health and rainfall shortages. The importance of weather shocks for poverty changes was also underscored by the findings from Zimbabwe and Madagascar. Deininger and Okidi (2001) find that ill-health among Ugandans back in 1992 noticeably increased the probability of being in poverty eight years later. In light of households' greater exposure to disease, and to the vagaries of weather (and world commodity prices following liberalization), policies to help the poor manage their risks have become even more important nowadays.

REFERENCES

Abdulai, A. (2000). 'Spatial Price Transmission and Asymmetry in the Ghanaian Maize Market', *Journal of Development Economics*, 63: 327–49.

—— and C. Delgado (2000). 'An Empirical Investigation of Short- and Long-run Agricultural Wage Formation in Ghana', *Oxford Development Studies*, 28(2): 169–85.

Alwang, J. and L. Ersado (1999). 'Changes in Poverty in Zimbabwe: 1990–1996' (mimeo), Poverty Reduction and Social Development Africa Region, World Bank: Washington DC.

——, B. Mills, and N. Taruvinga (2002). *Why has Poverty Increased in Zimbabwe?*, Poverty Dynamics in Africa Series, World Bank: Washington DC.

Appleton, S. (2001). 'Poverty in Uganda, 1999/2000: Preliminary Estimates from the UNHS' (mimeo), University of Nottingham: Nottingham, January.

——, T. Emwanu, J. Kagugube, and J. Muwonge (1999). 'Changes in Poverty in Uganda, 1992–1997' (mimeo), Poverty Reduction and Social Development Africa Region, World Bank: Washington DC.

Badiane, O. and G. Shively (1998). 'Spatial Integration, Transport Costs, and the Response of Local Prices to Policy Changes in Ghana', *Journal of Development Economics*, 56: 411–31.

Besley, T. (1995). 'Savings, Credit and Insurance', in J. Behrman and T. N. Srinivasan (eds) *Handbook of Development Economics*, Elsevier Science: Amsterdam.

Bigsten, A., B. Kebede, A. Shimeles, and M. Taddesse (2003). 'Growth and Poverty Reduction in Ethiopia: Evidence from Household Panel Surveys', *World Development*, 31(1): 87–106.

Bourguignon, F. (2000). 'Can Redistribution Accelerate Growth and Development?', paper presented at the World Bank ABCDE-Europe Conference, 26–28 June, Paris.

—— and C. Morrisson (1992). *Adjustment and Equity in Developing Countries: A New Approach*, OECD Development Centre: Paris.

Brock, W. A. and S. N. Durlauf (2000). 'Growth Economics and Reality', *NBER Working Papers* 8041, National Bureau of Economic Research: Cambridge, MA.

Canagarajah, S., J. Ngwafon, and F. Okunmadewa (2000). 'Nigeria's Poverty: Past, Present, and Future' (mimeo), Nigeria Country Department, World Bank: Washington DC.

Coulombe, H. and A. McKay (2001). 'The Evolution of Poverty and Inequality in Ghana over the 1990s: A Study Based on the Ghana Living Standards Surveys' (mimeo), Office of the Chief Economist, Africa Region, World Bank: Washington DC.

Collier, P. and J. W. Gunning (1999). 'Explaining African Economic Performance', *Journal of Economic Literature*, 37(1): 64–111.

Deininger, K. and J. Okidi (2001). 'Growth and Poverty Reduction in Uganda, 1992–2000: Panel Data Evidence' (mimeo), World Bank: Washington DC, and Economic Research Council: Kampala, December.

Delgado, C. L. *et al.* (1998). 'Agricultural Growth Linkages in Sub-Saharan Africa', *IFPRI Research Reports* 107, International Food Policy Research Institute: Washington DC.

Dercon, S. (1995). 'On Market Integration and Liberalization: Method and Application to Ethiopia', *Journal of Development Studies*, 32(1): 112–43.

—— (2000). 'Changes in Poverty and Social Indicators in Ethiopia in the 1990s: (At Last) Some Good News From Ethiopia' (mimeo), Poverty Reduction and Social Development Africa Region, World Bank: Washington DC.

—— (2002). 'The Impact of Economic Reforms on Households in Rural Ethiopia: A Study from 1989 to 1995', *Poverty Dynamics in Africa Series*, World Bank: Washington DC.

Dollar, D. and A. Kraay (2000). 'Growth *is* Good for the Poor' (mimeo), Development Research Group, World Bank: Washington DC, March. Reprinted in A. Shorrocks and R. van der Hoeven (eds) (2004). *Growth, Inequality and Poverty: Prospects for Pro-Poor Economic Development*, Oxford University Press for UNU-WIDER: Oxford.

Easterly, W. and R. Levine (1997). 'Africa's Growth Tragedy: Policies and Ethnic Divisions', *Quarterly Journal of Economics*, 112(4): 1203–50.

Forsyth, J. (2000). Letter to *The Economist*, 20 June.

Foster, J., J. Greer, and E. Thorbecke (1984). 'A Class of Decomposable Poverty Measures', *Econometrica*, 52(3): 761–6.

Grootaert, C. (1996). *Analyzing Poverty and Policy Reform*, Avebury: Aldershot.

Guillaumont, P., S. Guillaumont, and J. F. Brun (1999). 'How Instability Lowers African Growth', *Journal of African Economies*, 8(1): 87–107.

Kakwani, N. and E. M. Pernia (2000). 'What is Pro-poor Growth?', *Asian Development Review*, 18(1): 1–16.

Kanbur, R. (2001). 'Economic Policy, Distribution and Poverty: The Nature of Disagreements', *World Development*, 29(6): 1083–94.

Kherallah, M., C. Delgado, E. Gabre-Madhin, N. Minot, and M. Johnson (2002). *Reforming Agricultural Markets in Africa*, Johns Hopkins University Press: Baltimore, MD.

McCulloch, N., B. Baulch, and M. Cherel-Robson (2000). 'Growth, Inequality and Poverty in Mauritania, 1987–1996' (mimeo), Poverty Reduction and Social Development Africa Region, World Bank: Washington DC.

——, ——, and —— (2001). 'Poverty, Inequality and Growth in Zambia during the 1990s', *WIDER Discussion Paper* 2001/123, UNU-WIDER: Helsinki.

Mkandawire, T. and C. C. Soludo (1999). *Our Continent Our Future, African Perspectives on Structural Adjustment*, Council for the Development of Social Science Research in Africa: Dakar and International Development Research Centre: Ottawa, and Africa World Press: Asmara.

Morduch, J. (1995). 'Income Smoothing and Consumption Smoothing', *Journal of Economic Perspectives*, 9(3): 103–14.

Paternostro, S., J. Razafindravonona, and D. Stifel (2001). 'Changes in Poverty in Madagascar, 1993–1999', *Africa Region Working Papers* 19, World Bank: Washington DC.

Quah, D. (1996). 'Regional Convergence Clusters Across Europe', *European Economic Review*, 40: 951–8.

Ravallion, M. (2001). 'Growth, Inequality and Poverty: Looking Beyond Averages', *World Development*, 29(11): 1803–15.

—— (2002). 'Externalities in Rural Development: Evidence for China', *World Bank Policy Research Working Papers* 2879, World Bank: Washington DC.

Sahn, D. (ed.) (1994). *Adjusting to Policy Failure in African Economies*, Cornell University Press: Ithaca, NY.

Sahn, D. (ed.) (1996). *Economic Reform and the Poor in Africa*, Clarendon Press: Oxford.

——, P. A. Dorosh, and S. D. Younger (1997). *Structural Adjustment Reconsidered: Economic Policy and Poverty in Africa*, Cambridge University Press: Cambridge.

Stewart, F. (1995). *Adjustment and Poverty: Options and Choices*, Routledge: London.

Townsend, R. (1999). 'Agricultural Incentives in Sub-Saharan Africa: Policy Changes', *World Bank Technical Papers* 444, World Bank: Washington DC.

UDHS (2001). *Uganda Demographic and Health Survey 2000–Preliminary Report*, Uganda Bureau of Statistics: Entebbe.

World Bank (2000). *World Development Report 2000/1: Attacking Poverty*, World Bank: Washington DC.

PART VI

TRADE, WAGES, AND REGIONAL INEQUALITY

10

Economic Polarization Through Trade: Trade Liberalization and Regional Growth in Mexico

ANDRÉS RODRÍGUEZ-POSE AND
JAVIER SÁNCHEZ-REAZA

10.1. INTRODUCTION

Trade and economic integration are generally considered to have a beneficial impact on economic growth. Two types of gains from trade have been identified by international trade theory. First, gains from exchange arise since differences in endowments or preferences make countries profit from trading with each other. Second, gains from specialization arise from trade, since specialization in a narrow range of activities brings about efficiency (Markusen *et al.* 1995). Gains from trade often result in countries with open economies outgrowing those with closed economies (Sachs and Warner 1995; Frankel and Romer 1999; OECD 1999). There is, however, greater controversy regarding the factors that impinge on trade. Models based on the Heckscher–Ohlin (H–O) approach focus fundamentally on factor structure; Ricardian models highlight technology; new economic geography models stress the importance of transportation costs, agglomeration, and backward and forward linkages; and dynamic trade models emphasize the importance of spillovers. There is also much discussion about the spatial distribution of the benefits of trade and economic integration. H–O models underline that engaging in trade leads to the equalization of factor prices (Mundell 1957; Markusen *et al.* 1995) and, although they tend to be more 'agnostic' regarding regional growth, some authors have hinted that factor mobility may also yield a reduction in territorial disparities (Wood 1994). Neoclassical growth theories with immobile factors do not consider trade, but predict that increases in investment and capital—which may or may not be related to trade—trigger economic convergence. New economic geography models do not make clear territorial predictions, although many indicate that increases in trade and in economic integration may result in the territorial concentration of economic activity (Fujita *et al.* 1999). And the territorial outcome of dynamic trade models depends on the specific framework.

This chapter explores what has been the territorial impact of trade reform and economic integration by analysing the evolution of regional disparities in Mexico since 1980. The choice of Mexico is not arbitrary. Mexico is arguably the country that has undergone the deepest process of economic liberalization and regional integration in the world since the mid-1980s. It first shifted its economic policy from a closed-economy approach to trade liberalization, and since 1994 to economic integration with the United States and Canada. The chapter focuses on how these processes have affected regional growth and its determinants during the three stages of Mexico's economic transformation since 1980: the import substitution industrialization (ISI) period until 1985; early trade liberalization and membership of (General Agreement on Tariffs and Trade) GATT, between 1985 and 1994; and increasing economic integration since the signing of NAFTA (North American Free Trade Agreement) in 1994.

The main question addressed in the chapter is whether trade and economic integration have had an impact on regional economic growth,[1] that is, whether progressive trade liberalization has led to changes in regional inequalities amongst Mexican states. The chapter also explores the factors behind such transformations. In order to achieve these goals the chapter is divided into four further sections. The first section of the chapter briefly describes the changes in economic policy in Mexico since the 1980s. Section 10.2 analyses the effects the opening of the Mexican economy has had on regional disparities. Section 10.3 tries to establish through the use of multiple regression analysis which factors have made the greatest contribution to regional growth in the three economic stages (ISI, GATT, and NAFTA) of the recent Mexican economic history. The conclusions are presented in Section 10.4.

10.1.1. *Economic Policy Changes in Mexico Since 1980*

The revival of growth theory since the late 1980s has brought the analysis of the genesis and evolution of regional disparities to the fore. Neoclassical and endogenous growth theories as well as the new economic geography approach have analysed the connection between factors such as capital accumulation, investment, technological change, economies of agglomeration, population growth, human capital and transport costs, among many others, and economic growth. Trade and economic integration have also played a relevant role in growth studies (Grossman and Helpman 1991). However, despite recent advances in growth theory, the effect of trade and economic integration on national and regional economic growth is still very much debated. Different theories and empirical analyses often reach contrasting results about the territorial impact of trade and economic liberalization. These range from those that highlight that trade leads to greater concentration of economic activity and greater polarization (Krugman 1991, 1993; Venables 1998; Venables and Limao 1999) to those that highlight that economic liberalization and increases in trade ultimately lead to a reduction of disparities (Sachs and Warner 1995).

---

[1] A series of recent studies, such as Esquivel and Messmacher (2002) or López-Córdoba and Moreira (2002), have focused on the link between shifts in policy and changes in productivity, rather than on GDP per capita, as is the aim of this chapter. The results of the analyses using productivity as the dependent variable largely corroborate our results.

The main aim of this chapter is to provide an empirical analysis of what has been the impact of the last three stages (final period of ISI, GATT, and NAFTA) of the passage from a closed economy to an increasingly open and regionally integrated economy on Mexican regional disparities. The choice of Mexico is determined by the profound economic reforms that the country has undertaken since the mid-1980s. The choice of periods is fundamentally based on economic policy decisions and the two breaking points coincide with the signature of the GATT by Mexico in 1986 and with the establishment of NAFTA in 1994, respectively. The main objective behind economic reforms was to achieve greater economic stability and sustainable growth through trade liberalization. Trade liberalization and economic integration have thus marked a radical change in the economic regime of a country that was until then notorious for its economic and political immobility. Since independence from Spain in the early nineteenth century until the 1980s, Mexico had only implemented two economic models: (i) the enclave-economy model, stemming from colonial times and which lasted until the 1930s and (ii) the ISI model, between the 1930s and 1985 (Villarreal 1988). The former model was characterized by relatively high levels of foreign investment, few links with domestic firms and the export of a high percentage of local production. The latter was characterized by the use of both tariff and non-tariff barriers to international trade in order to promote industrialization and protect national firms from foreign competition, although since the mid-1970s the ISI economy had basically ceased to exist and Mexico—as was the case under the enclave-economy model earlier—became increasingly dependent on exports of oil and other raw materials. This final state of the ISI model is thus also known as the period of the 'petrolization' of the Mexican economy.

Since the demise of the ISI model and of the petrolized economy in 1985 the rhythm of economic change has increased considerably. Import substitution has given way to economic liberalization, openness to trade, and to the establishment of an export promotion model. Two phases can be distinguished within this period: (i) the early trade liberalization phase, triggered by Mexico's signature of the GATT in 1985; and (ii) the economic integration phase, linked to the signing of NAFTA in 1994, and to the endorsement of a series of bilateral and multilateral agreements with other countries. The GATT years brought about a sustained increase in the export of intermediate goods and in the flow of foreign direct investment (FDI) to the country. A large percentage of this investment came under the maquiladora[2] scheme, which led to a substantial increase in the exchange of intermediate goods across the border (Weintraub 1988). Membership of NAFTA, together with the signature of other trade agreements with many Latin American countries, with the European Union and Israel in the 1990s, have also provoked significant changes in the Mexican economy. Mexico has undertaken reforms in the fields of intellectual property rights, equal treatment of foreign and domestic investors, and the participation of foreign individuals and firms in the financial sector. The benefits induced by economic integration include greater

---

[2] Assembly plants which import parts and components (mainly from the United States) in order to make finished goods for re-export. Most maquiladoras are located along the Mexican–American border.

stability and attraction of FDI, repatriation of capital, recognition by the international community, and the restoration of confidence in the Mexican economy.

In addition to the processes of economic liberalization and regional integration, the last two decades of the twentieth century in Mexico also featured a series of events that have caused significant macroeconomic turmoil. The steady decline in oil prices of the early 1980s provoked in 1982 the partial collapse of the economy which had grown increasingly dependent on oil revenues. The oil bust triggered a debt crisis that dominated Mexico's economy during the 1980s. The shift in presidency from Carlos Salinas de Gortari to Ernesto Zedillo in late 1994 was engulfed in another huge macroeconomic crisis ('the tequlia effect') which led to a serious dent in economic growth and to a considerable devaluation of the peso. Each of these two crises coincided closely with the shifts in trade regimes and, to a certain extent, are linked to them. The oil bust and the debt crisis of 1982 can be regarded as the trigger of the liberalization process as a result of the need to look for macroeconomic policy alternatives to the demise of oil dependency. The tequila effect is closely associated to costs of economic integration within the framework of NAFTA.

The implications for the Mexican economy of the changes in economic regimes are evident. Figure 10.1 depicts the evolution of trade as a percentage of GDP (left-hand axis) and GDP per capita (right-hand axis) between 1970 and 2000. The figure highlights that every change in trade regime has been accompanied by an almost immediate rapid rise in trade as a percentage of GDP. The signature of GATT led to an increase in trade as a percentage of GDP from a rate of 25 per cent in 1985 to 38 per cent in 1988. Membership of NAFTA—together with the 1994 devaluation of the Mexican peso—provoked a 20 point increase, from 38 to 58 per cent in 1995 alone (Fig. 10.1). Since then, trade expansion has continued, albeit at a slower rate. These changes have transformed Mexico within a period of little more than a decade, from a relatively closed country into one of the most open in the American continent with levels of trade as a percentage of GDP that are comparable to those of the more open European economies. Around 90 per cent of Mexican trade is with the United States. The connection between changes in trade regimes and growth in GDP per capita is less evident. Whereas the last stages of ISI were dominated by economic decline, the GATT years were associated to moderate economic growth, which has been replaced—despite a significant destruction of wealth in 1994—by high economic growth in the first years of NAFTA (Fig. 10.1). The processes of economic liberalization and integration have not been territorially neutral and had significant effects on regional inequalities in Mexico, which are explored in the following section.

10.2. THE TERRITORIAL IMPACT OF ECONOMIC LIBERALIZATION AND REGIONAL INTEGRATION

10.2.1. *The Territorial Effect of ISI*

Regional disparities have always existed in Mexico. The territorial legacy of the enclave-economy model is what can be defined as a dual economy. Economic activity

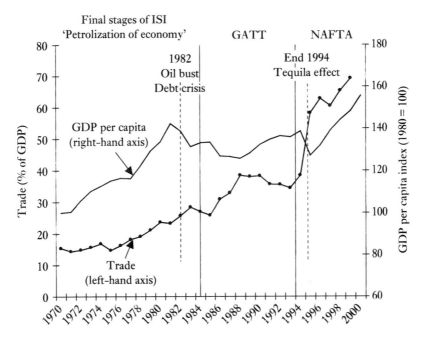

Figure 10.1. *The evolution of trade as a percentage of GDP and GDP per capita in Mexico, 1970–2000*

Note: GDP data calculated using 1993 Mexican pesos.

Source: World Bank (trade data) and INEGI (GDP data).

and industrial production had become concentrated in the centre of the country—in the states of the Federal District of Mexico (Mexico DF), Puebla, and Veracruz— and in the northern states. In contrast, most of the south had remained dependent, agricultural, and poor (López Malo 1960). The establishment of an ISI model in the 1930s further contributed to foster territorial inequalities in the country. Import substitution accentuated the economic decline of the states which relied on the export of natural resources—with the exception of oil and certain minerals—and agricultural produce, generally located along the Gulf of Mexico and in the south, and triggered a process of industrialization which favoured the concentration of economic activity in large metropolitan areas. Relatively large industrial poles emerged in and around Mexico City, in Jalisco, and along the Mexican–US border, especially in the state of Nuevo León. The industrial poles were associated with the large metropolitan areas of Mexico City, Monterrey, and Guadalajara, and with the establishment in 1966 of a maquiladora scheme restricted to the northern border (Smith 1990). High-income regions were also found in the oil-producing southern states of Campeche, Tabasco and, to a lesser extent, Veracruz, or in tourist states, such as Quintana Roo. In contrast, southwestern states and northern states not bordering the United States remained

242 A. Rodríguez-Pose and J. Sánchez-Reaza

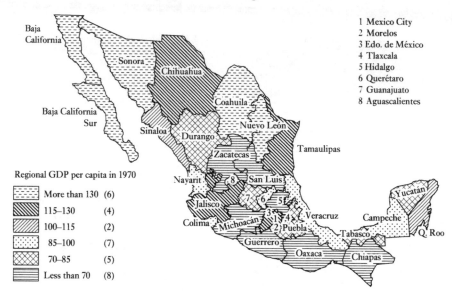

Map 10.1. *Regional GDP per capita in 1970 (national average = 100)*

relatively isolated from the whole process. Most of the northern states away from the border could only achieve very modest and precarious industrialization. Most states in the south, which did not rely on oil revenues, remained dependent on agriculture and backward.

In the final years of the ISI model, regional disparities in GDP per capita reflected the level of polarization in the country (Map 10.1). The highest GDP per capita was found in the northern border states, around Mexico City and Jalisco. The Pacific coastal state of Sinaloa, and Quintana Roo, in the Yucatán peninsula, also enjoyed relatively high levels of GDP per capita. The southern Pacific coastal states of Chiapas, Oaxaca, Guerrero, and Michoacán, as well as many of the central states surrounding Mexico DF had, in contrast, the lowest GDP per capita (Map 10.1). GDP per capita in the poorest state (Oaxaca) only represented one-quarter (26.7 per cent) of that of the richest state (Mexico DF). Similarly, the GDP per capita of the four poorest states (Oaxaca, Michoacán, Guerrero, and Zacatecas) was barely one-third (34.4 per cent) of that of the four richest states (Mexico DF, Nuevo León, Baja California, and Coahuila).

Most of the concentration of economic activities in the north of the country, Jalisco and in and around Mexico took place during the early stages of ISI. The final years of the ISI model witnessed, in contrast, a strong process of regional convergence, which contributed to a reduction in regional disparities (Sánchez-Reaza and Rodríguez-Pose 2002). Between 1970 and 1985 regional per capita growth rates in many lagging states such as Tlaxcala, Oaxaca, Chiapas, or Querétaro more than doubled those of Mexico DF, Nuevo León, or Baja California (Fig. 10.2). The β-convergence rate

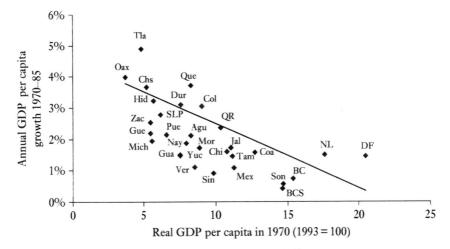

Figure 10.2. *Initial income and growth in the Mexican regions during the final stages of ISI*

across Mexican states during this period was 1.85 per cent per annum,[3] close to the rate of 2 per cent reported by many neoclassical empirical analyses.

The process of catchup in the 1970s and early 1980s came, however, to an abrupt end after the signature of GATT. The GATT and NAFTA years have been associated first with an overall decline in national growth (Juan-Ramón and Rivera-Batiz 1996), and second with a deepening of regional inequalities. National per capita GDP growth fell from 1.94 per cent per annum during the period 1970–85 to 1 per cent in the years between 1985 and 2000 (and only 0.58 per cent between 1985–98). At a regional level, the convergence of the 1970s and early 1980s became a β-divergence of 1.36 per cent per annum.[4] Many of the lagging regions in Mexico saw their growth rates decrease significantly. Chiapas, with an annual rate of per capita growth of −2 per cent, suffered the strongest fall in growth rates (Fig. 10.3). Tlaxcala, Nayarit, Veracruz, and Oaxaca were not far behind. Indeed, all the states south of the Mexico City agglomeration—with the exception of Campeche, Puebla, Quintana Roo, and Yucatán—had negative per capita growth rates throughout this period. The highest rates of growth took place in some of the richer states; the industrial states of Chihuahua and Aguascalientes and the tourist state of Quintana Roo had the highest growth, with annual rates close to or above 3 per cent, with Coahuila, Querétaro, and DF also faring relatively well (Fig. 10.3).

Trade liberalization and economic integration have thus led to a deepening of regional inequalities in Mexico. Mexico DF and the northern border states have

---

[3] The results of the regression are as follows: β–coefficient $= -0.0185$; t-statistic $= -4.417$; Adjusted $R^2 = 0.374$.

[4] The results of the regression are as follows: β–coefficient $= 0.0136$; t-statistic $= 2.281$; Adjusted $R^2 = 0.148$.

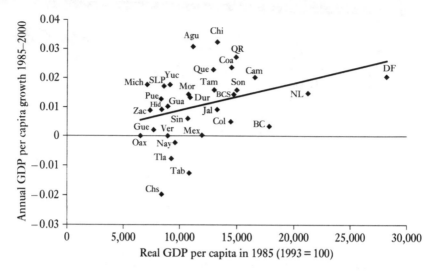

Figure 10.3. *Initial income and growth in the Mexican regions after trade liberalization*

reaped the lion's share from the opening of borders and North American economic integration, whereas the south—save the Yucatán peninsula—has become even more economically backward (Map 10.2). Overall, the shift in macroeconomic regimes has been associated with a radical change in the evolution of regional disparities. This change in trend is evident in Fig. 10.4, which depicts changes in Mexican σ convergence, that is, the evolution of the coefficient of variation of log-GDP per capita between 1970 and 2000, following Sánchez-Reaza and Rodríguez-Pose (2002). Whereas the final stages of ISI and the petrolization of the economy oversaw a 24 per cent reduction in regional disparities in the fifteen years between 1970 and 1985, the signature of GATT marked a clear reversal in the trend, with the coefficient of variation growing rapidly between 1986 and 1993 and returning by 1991 to the levels of disparities of the late 1960s. Since becoming a member of NAFTA, the evolution of the coefficient of variation has stabilized, but remains at levels above those of 1970 (Fig. 10.4).

As a whole, regional inequalities in Mexico are much greater than regional disparities in most developed countries, and roughly similar to those found in other countries of the so-called South, such as Brazil or India (Rodríguez-Pose and Gill 2003). In 2000, GDP per capita in Chiapas which had become the poorest state, was only 16.3 per cent that of Mexico DF, the richest state. The combined GDP per capita of the four poorest states—Chiapas, Oaxaca, Guerrero, and Tlaxcala—was just one-quarter of that of the four richest states (Mexico DF, Quintana Roo, Nuevo León, and Campeche) (Map 10.2).

What are the reasons behind the significant deepening of regional disparities in Mexico since the beginning of the process of economic liberalization? To what extent has membership of GATT and NAFTA contributed to turning regional convergence into regional divergence? What are the factors that have affected regional economic

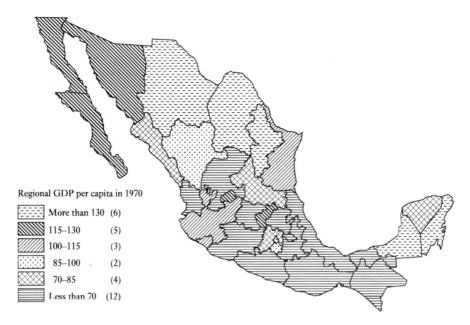

Regional GDP per capita in 1970

	More than 130	(6)
	115–130	(5)
	100–115	(3)
	85–100	(2)
	70–85	(4)
	Less than 70	(12)

Map 10.2. *Regional GDP per capita in 2000 (national average = 100)*

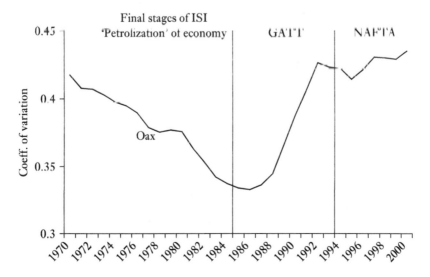

Figure 10.4. *Evolution of the coefficient of variation of regional disparities in Mexico*

growth in the different stages of economic liberalization? The following section tries to give an answer to these questions.

10.3. ECONOMIC LIBERALIZATION AND THE FACTORS BEHIND REGIONAL GROWTH

10.3.1. *The Model and the Variables*

In order to test whether trade liberalization and economic integration have had an impact on regional economic growth, we perform three ordinary least squares (OLS) regressions,[5] one for each of the three corresponding stages of economic liberalization: (i) the ISI period between 1980 and 1985, (ii) early trade liberalization and membership of GATT, between 1985 and 1994, and (iii) increasing economic integration since the signing of NAFTA, between 1994 and 2000. The model, used in the three stages, adopts the following form:

$$G_{i,t} = f\{y_0, m_0, \text{dismx}, \text{disus}, k_0, \text{ed}_0, \text{hsg}_0, \text{camtab}, \text{maq}_0, \text{pubinv}_0\},$$

where $G_{i,t}$ is regional real per capita GDP growth in each Mexican state for each period covered in the analysis (1980–5, 1985–94, and 1994–2000) and y_0 represents the natural logarithm of the initial regional GDP per capita. Net migration rates at the beginning of the period are represented by m_0. The natural logarithm of the distance in kilometres by road from the capital of each state to Mexico City is captured in dismx and that to the nearest border city with the United States in disus. k_0 and ed_0 refer to the per capita initial level of state commercial banking deposits and to initial level of education in each state, measured as the average years of schooling of the population, respectively. Higher levels of education in the labour market are depicted by hsg_0, which refers to the population weighted natural logarithm of the number of high school graduates at the beginning of each period. The final variables are used to control for biases in the structure of the economy, such as the effect of oil (camtab), maquiladora (maq_0), and public investment (pubinv_0). A more detailed description of each variable and its sources is included in the Appendix.

The choice of variables reflects a compromise between the factors that according to recent literature have shaped economic growth in Mexico and data availability. The oil (camtab) variable is introduced in the model in order to capture the expected distortionary effects of oil in what was a petrolized economy in the early 1980s.[6] The maquiladora (maq_0) represents a proxy for the location of foreign FDI at the

---

[5] Lack of adequate time-series regional data for Mexico has prevented us from using alternative techniques such as panel data analysis.

[6] Other studies of the evolution of regional disparities in Mexico have used different methods to control for the problems related to the concentration of the oil industry in the states of Campeche and Tabasco, and, to a much lesser extent, Veracruz and for the fluctuations in oil prices. Juan-Ramón and Rivera-Batiz (1996) conducted parallel analyses without the two most important oil-producing states, whereas Esquivel and Messmacher (2002) have used oil-corrected incomes as an alternative. The results of these analyses largely coincide with ours.

beginning of each period. This special export-oriented form of investment accounted for 47 per cent of recorded FDI in Mexico in 1998 (CNIE 1998) and has, despite its recent spread throughout the country, been heavily concentrated along the border with the United States (Hanson 1996; Sánchez-Reaza and Rodríguez-Pose 2002). The initial migration variable (m_0)—defined as the number of outmigrants minus immigrants— aims at encapsulating the constant flow over the last few decades of Mexicans from rural to urban areas, from the south and centre-north to Mexico City and the northern border states, and from the whole country to the United States (Durand *et al.* 2001). The level of education (ed_0) and the indicator of high school graduates (hsg_0) are proxies for the general improvement in human capital endowment and for the specific expansion of the qualified labour force at the beginning of the period; k_0 is used as a proxy for the availability of capital and $pubinv_0$ for the effects of public policies.

The reason for including the distance to Mexico City (dismx) and to the border of the United States (disus) in the regressions performed for each of the three economic stages is based on one of the new economic geography's determinants of concentration: proximity to markets. As Hanson underlines 'the importance of trade liberalization is that it changes the reference market for firms in a country. Given transport costs, we expect trade to shift resources to locations with relatively low-cost access to foreign markets, such as border regions and port cities' (1998*a*: 420). Trade liberalization and economic integration would have accordingly brought about a shift in the reference market from Mexico City during the ISI period to the United States during GATT, but especially under NAFTA (Krugman and Livas Elizondo 1996; Hanson 1998*a,b*). Therefore, the use of dismx and disus will help to compare the extent to which distance to Mexico City or distance to the US border plays a role in determining growth. The inclusion of distances to the main market will determine whether there has been in fact a shift in the relevant market, and if such shift is associated to particular trade policies.

10.3.2. *A Cautionary Note About Mexican Regional Data*

Researchers studying regional disparities in Mexico have to face numerous problems. Perhaps the most important one is that of lack of data. Despite having one of the most comprehensive subnational data compilations outside Europe and the United States and of recent improvements, many difficulties remain. With the exception of GDP indicators there is little regional information available prior to 1980, and whenever it can be found, questions arise about its reliability. This factor has limited our analysis to the post-1980 evolution of regional disparities. But even after 1980 Mexican regional data are often missing. There are, for example, no data on technological change, R&D investment, or capital accumulation. In some cases proxies can be used, as is the case of regional commercial banking deposits as a proxy for capital accumulation. In others, this is not possible. And even when regional data are available, they are often haphazard. Serious problems are encountered, for example, with migration indicators. Mexican migration rates at a regional level are not published on a regular basis.

For the 1990s, they are only available for 1990 (INEGI 1995) and 1995 (INEGI 1997). Therefore, the migration indicators used for the GATT and NAFTA periods in our analysis represent the year closest to the beginning of each period. For the ISI period we use regional inward migration statistics from INEGI (1986), as well as our own calculations of regional outward migration figures based on those provided by Partida Bush (1994). Given the above-mentioned difficulties with regional data availability and reliability, the results and interpretations of the analysis must be valued in light of the inherent limitations of the datasets.

10.4. THE RESULTS OF THE ANALYSIS

10.4.1. *Regional Growth in the Late Stages of ISI*

Which factors determined regional growth and the formation of regional disparities at the end of the ISI period, when the Mexican economy was already largely reliant on oil? Table 10.1 reports the results of regressing regional per capita growth rates for the period during 1980–5 on the independent variables. Five models are performed. The first four models include different subsets of independent variables: model 1 contains just the initial level of GDP per capita; model 2, the basic structural variables associated to economic growth in developing economies (dependence on raw materials and migration); model 3, the distances to the main market; and model 4, the structural variables associated with growth in more developed economies. Model 5 represents the most satisfactory simplification of the general model at a 90 per cent level of significance. VIF (variance inflation factor), Cook–Weisberg, and Moran's I tests have been carried out in order to check for multicollinearity, heteroskedasticity, and spatial autocorrelation, respectively. Any violation of the assumptions is reported at the bottom of the table.

Four factors emerge as the main determinants of growth during the final years of ISI. Almost half of the variance in growth across Mexican states during this period was explained by the initial levels of GDP per capita, the presence of oil, the initial general levels of human capital, and proximity to Mexico City (Table 10.1). As expected in a period characterized by regional convergence, high initial levels of GDP per capita (y_0) were inversely correlated with growth rates, meaning that the highest growth was concentrated in the poor southern states. The regional convergence rate during this period remains fairly stable even when other variables are introduced in the model.

Contrary to what could have been expected under an ISI regime—but not under an economy that had become increasingly dependent on oil revenues—the presence of oil had a positive and very significant correlation with growth rates (Table 10.1). The combination of raw materials (mainly oil, but also minerals) and agricultural produce contributed to the growth of those Mexican states with the highest endowment of natural resources and/or with the lowest labour costs. This factor fostered growth in the south and centre of Mexico, where large reserves of natural resources and the lowest labour costs could be found. The south of the country was also home to a large percentage of the outward migrants towards other parts of the country and the United States.

The general level of education (ed_0) is also significant and positively associated with growth, whereas the variable used as a proxy for the skilled workforce (hsg_0) has

Table 10.1. *OLS results for the end of the ISI period*

ISI indep. var.	Coeff.				
	(1)	(2)	(3)	(4)	(5)
y_0	−0.463*** *−2.864*	−0.267 *−1.119*	−0.375 *−1.366*	−1.253** *−2.179*	−0.942*** *−3.698*
camtab		0.391** *2.616*	0.432*** *2.768*	0.255 *1.100*	0.403*** *2.882*
m_0		−0.243 *−1.017*	−0.198 *−0.740*	0.025 *0.073*	
dismx			−0.093 *−0.519*	−0.218 *−0.897*	−0.285* *−1.721*
disus			−0.194 *−1.120*	−0.184 *−0.909*	
k_0				0.336 *0.729*	
ed_0				0.710* *2.047*	0.581** *2.278*
hsg_0				−0.626 *−1.443*	
maq_0				−0.051 *−0.225*	
$pubinv_0$				0.263 *0.817*	
F	8.202	5.714	3.596	2.372	7.868
Prob > F	0.008	0.004	0.013	0.046	0.001
df	*1.30*	*3.28*	*5.26*	*10.21*	*3.28*
R^2	0.215	0.380	0.409	0.530	0.457
Adj. R^2	0.189	0.313	0.295	0.307	0.399
Multicollinearity	No	No	No	Yes	No
Heteroskedasticity	No	No	No	No	No
Sp. autocorrelation	Borderline	Borderline	No	No	No

Notes: Standardized coefficients reported; *t*-statistics in italics under coefficients; ***, **, and * denote significance at the 99%, 95%, and 90%, respectively.

Source: See text.

a negative coefficient (Table 10.1). This result reinforces the view presented earlier for the Mexican economy in the final years of the ISI period as sharing some of the features of less-developed economies. During the late 1970s and early 1980s Mexico's national and regional economies had become extremely dependent on oil and other natural resources and agricultural goods. This reliance on natural resources and the relative absence of advanced manufacturing and services among the most dynamic export-oriented sectors of the economy, while positively associated by the general level of education of the population, rendered the presence of people with higher education levels somewhat redundant, as the highest skills were generally found in sectors orientated to the less lucrative national market. Finally, and in accordance with new economic geography postulates, the coefficient for the distance to Mexico City (dismx) is significant in model 5 and negatively associated with growth (Table 10.1). This underlines the importance of the Mexican capital as the reference market and the advantages of being geographically close to it.

Altogether, the regional growth panorama in Mexico in the final stages of ISI seems to reproduce many of the neoclassical postulates, highlighted by the fact that there is notable regional convergence. Some of the postulates defended by the new economic geography approach are also fulfilled, especially the importance of Mexico City, rather than the United States, as the main market during the final stages of economic protectionism. Centrifugal forces, however, prevailed over centripetal forces.

10.4.2. *Regional Growth During GATT*

Table 10.2 reports the results of regressing regional GDP per capita growth during the GATT years (1985–94) on the independent variables for that period. The procedure followed is the same as for the previous period. The results expose the existence of a radical shift in the factors connected to regional growth in Mexico after the demise of the ISI system. First and foremost the explanatory capacity of the model is severely reduced. If we take model 5—which represents the most satisfactory simplification of the general model—we find that the initial GDP per capita (y_0) and the initial number of high school graduates divided by population (hsg_0) are the only two significant variables, and that the model only explains less than a quarter of the variance in growth per capita in Mexico during the GATT period (Table 10.2). Factors such as exports or proximity to Mexico City as the main national market, that were among the main determinants of regional growth in the earlier period, are no longer relevant, as indeed are most of the other regional variables included in the model.

One of the important differences with the previous period is the shift from regional convergence to divergence. The sign of the coefficient of the initial GDP per capita becomes positive and significant in all models, bar model 4, which suffers from multicollinearity. As described earlier, economic growth in the wealthier regions of the north and centre of the country outstripped growth in the south. Apart from initial GDP per capita, only the proxy for the endowment in qualified human capital displays a negative association with regional growth (Table 10.2).

The coefficients of the two variables indicating distance to the two main markets show little sign of change in the reference market. The coefficient of dismx changes sign in model 3, but loses significance, and disus is not significant in any of the models (Table 10.2). This implies that whereas proximity to Mexico City has lost relevance as a determinant of regional economic growth during the GATT period,

Table 10.2. *OLS results for the GATT period*

GATT indep. var.	Coeff.				
	(1)	(2)	(3)	(4)	(5)
y_0	0.389**	0.307	0.459*	−0.140	0.391**
	2.314	*1.458*	*1.957*	*−0.299*	*2.411*
camtab		−0.015	−0.109	−0.148	
		−0.088	*−0.597*	*−0.631*	
m_0		0.150	0.127	0.267	
		0.718	*0.558*	*1.077*	
dismx			0.164	−0.194	
			0.822	*−0.674*	
disus			0.317	0.277	
			1.583	*1.264*	
k_0				0.886	
				1.513	
ed_0				0.079	
				0.204	
hsg_0				−1.299**	−0.295*
				−2.281	*−1.820*
maq_0				0.127	
				0.496	
$pubinv_0$				0.229	
				0.653	
F	5.353	1.873	1.674	1.407	4.539
Prob > F	0.028	0.157	0.176	0.244	0.019
df	*1.30*	*3.28*	*5.26*	*10.21*	*2.29*
R^2	0.151	0.167	0.244	0.401	0.238
Adj. R^2	0.123	0.078	0.098	0.116	0.186
Multicollinearity	No	No	No	Yes	No
Heteroskedasticity	No	No	No	No	No
Sp. autocorrelation	No	No	No	No	No

Notes: Standardized coefficients reported; *t*-statistics in italics under coefficients; ***, **, and * denote significance at the 99%, 95%, and 90%, respectively.

Source: See text.

there is still no sign of the new economic geography shift in the main market to the regions bordering the main Mexican export market, the United States.

Overall, the results of the analysis of the GATT years point more towards a country still under the shock of the collapse of its import-substitution strategy, rather than to a country starting to feel the effects of economic liberalization. The foundations of the later years of the ISI model, such as oil dependency and the reliance on natural resources, were being shaken, but no clear alternative was emerging. The Mexican economy could no longer rely on its traditional products for growth, but the incipient and still rather tentative process of economic liberalization had not yet generated an alternative economic system, in which other factors could have filled in the vacuum left by the steep decline in revenues caused by the collapse of the price of oil and other natural resources. The petrolization of the economy during the early 1980s resulted in a postponement of the structural change reform in the late stages of ISI (Smith 1990) and led to a doubling of public expenditure and to the expansion of external debt, which reached 61.9 per cent of GDP by the mid-1980s (Ramírez 1989). As a result, after the sharp decline of oil prices of the early 1980s the government was more concerned with cutting expenditure, reducing public deficit, and servicing the debt under a stabilization programme carried out under the auspices of the IMF (Auty 1994), than with preparing the Mexican economy for trade liberalization.

10.4.3. *Regional Growth During NAFTA*

Greater changes in the factors affecting regional growth can be observed after membership of NAFTA. After the transition of the GATT years, the results for the NAFTA period point in the direction of the emergence of what can be the seed of a new economic model of regional growth in Mexico. As evidenced by model 5—and considering the caveat that the model is marginally affected by a problem of spatial autocorrelation—three variables alone explain more than 40 per cent of the variance in regional growth in Mexico between 1994 and 2000. Initial GDP per capita (y_0) has the most robust and significant coefficient. As in the GATT years, the standardized coefficient is positive, pointing to the existence of regional divergence, which, in combination with other variables, tends to be stronger than in the previous period (Table 10.3).

The other two significant variables, initial migration (m_0) and the proxy for the endowment of qualified human capital (hsg$_0$), indicate that profound changes were happening in Mexican regional growth in the last few years of the twentieth century and corroborate claims by other authors of a significant structural change in the Mexican economy (Esquivel and Messmacher 2002; Esquivel *et al.* 2002). The standardized coefficient of hsg$_0$ takes on a positive sign (Table 10.3). This means that regional growth in Mexico, as in most developed areas of the world, is increasingly associated with the quality of the local human capital endowment. This variable, which was negatively associated with growth both during ISI and GATT, indicates that in the NAFTA period the skilled labour force not only starts to play a more important role (Esquivel 1999), but also that the returns to higher levels of education may be increasing, as shown by Esquivel and Messmacher (2002) when analysing the evolution of labour productivity in Mexico. In brief, education and skills are becoming more relevant and investment in this sector may be starting to yield greater returns. For the first time in the analysis, regions with higher levels of education and skills are growing faster than the rest of the country.

Table 10.3. *OLS results for the NAFTA period*

NAFTA indep. var.	Coeff.				
	(1)	(2)	(3)	(4)	(5)
y_0	0.448***	0.624***	0.692***	1.951***	0.629***
	2.745	3.563	3.694	4.475	3.888
camtab		0.081	0.038	0.066	
		0.521	0.234	0.363	
m_0		−0.400**	−0.469**	−0.969***	−0.474***
		−2.290	−2.415	−3.815	−2.868
dismx			0.204	−0.044	
			1.153	−0.170	
disus			0.084	−0.214	
			0.477	−1.210	
k_0				−1.327**	
				−2.494	
ed_0				−0.393	
				−1.480	
hsg_0				1.224**	0.329**
				2.147	2.229
maq_0				−0.125	
				−0.494	
$pubinv_0$				−0.703**	
				−2.737	
F	7.533	4.615	2.981	3.959	6.933
Prob > F	0.010	0.010	0.029	0.004	0.001
df	1.30	3.28	5.26	10.21	3.28
R^2	0.201	0.331	0.364	0.653	0.426
Adj. R^2	0.171	0.259	0.242	0.488	0.365
Multicollinearity	No	No	No	Yes	No
Heteroskedasticity	No	No	No	No	No
Sp. autocorrelation	Borderline	Borderline	Yes	No	Borderline

Notes: Standardized coefficients reported; *t*-statistics in italics under coefficients; ***, **, and * denote significance at the 99%, 95%, and 90%, respectively.

Source: See text.

The coefficient of the initial migration variable has a negative sign (Table 10.3). Migration within Mexico from the poorer areas to the more developed states and to the United States had been a common feature of the Mexican economic and social history of the last few decades. In many ways it represented a safety valve for poorer states since, first, it contributed to keep population growth in states with scarce economic potential at bay and, second, because the remittances from migrants represented an important source of income for the inhabitants of many states (Taylor 1999). The fact that the coefficient of migration is negative implies that losing human resources to other states can no longer be considered an asset for economic growth, which may be one of the factors behind the slowdown in the process of migration across states (Esquivel 1999). This evidence in combination with the positive sign of the endowment of qualified human capital point in the direction of the emergence of an economy which is less based on natural resources, basic agriculture, and undifferentiated manufacturing production and more reliant, albeit still in an initial stage, on knowledge. There is, however, no sign of a change in the relevant market from Mexico City to the United States. The fact that both dismx and disus are not significant may be an indication that the change in the relevant market (Hanson 1996, 1998*a*) may be happening at a lower rate than expected, if at all.

In sum, changes in the results of the analysis conducted during the NAFTA period herald an important structural transformation in the Mexican economy. The increasing regional divergence, the negative connection between outmigration and growth, the increasing returns of education may be signalling the possible emergence of a new, more knowledge-based economy linked to economic liberalization and regional integration.

10.5. CONCLUSION

The chapter has analysed whether changes in trade policies and economic integration in NAFTA have had an influence on regional growth and the evolution of regional disparities in Mexico. As mentioned earlier, problems linked to the availability and reliability of regional data imply that any conclusion should be considered with caution. Bearing this in mind, the results of the analysis have shown that the successive passage from a crumbling ISI system to incipient trade liberalization through membership of GATT, and then to economic integration in NAFTA, has provoked major changes in regional disparities and in the importance of the factors that generate growth.

First, trade liberalization and economic integration have brought about a shift in regional inequalities. Despite the fact that regional disparities and a north–south divide have existed in Mexico since industrialization took off in the 1930s (López Malo 1960), recent changes in economic regimes have been associated with a change in regional trends. Whereas the end of the ISI period was characterized by regional convergence, economic liberalization and integration have been connected to economic divergence and to a widening of the gap between a relatively rich north of the country and an increasingly poor south. Economic liberalization and integration have also spurred greater concentration of economic activity in the main economic poles of the country. The states bordering the United States have mainly benefited from this, but Mexico City has also fared well. Despite reducing its share of manufacturing jobs (Hanson 1998*b*), the capital is attracting high value-added services and becoming an important financial centre. In contrast, the agricultural and natural resource-dependent states of the south of the country have suffered severe relative declines. This is especially the case in some oil-producing states, such as Tabasco, whose GDP per capita has been seriously dented by the decrease in oil prices and the ebbing oil dependence of the Mexican economy. The rural and agricultural states of Chiapas, Oaxaca, Guerrero, and Tlaxcala also shared poor rates of growth.

Many of the explanations of the widening regional gap lay in the changes of the relative importance of the factors associated to regional growth. During the late stages of the ISI period, Mexican regional growth was mainly associated with the production of oil, raw materials, and agricultural produce. During this period the poorer southern states supplied the bulk of the exports. In this context, investing in improving human skills or in trying to generate endogenous growth opportunities in relatively poor states made little sense as a regional development strategy. Workers with the highest skills tended to find jobs in the less-productive, nationally orientated manufacturing and service sectors. The mobility of labour and exports of natural resources sufficed to reduce inequalities across states. Yet, this situation entailed serious risks which became evident once the ISI system collapsed. Mexico had become too dependent on oil and the exploitation of other natural resources, and their price decline contributed to the collapse of the ISI model and to the debt crisis that ravaged Mexico throughout most of the 1980s.

The demise of ISI led to economic liberalization and greater openness to trade. The signature of GATT was a capital step in this strategy. However, in terms of regional growth and the evolution of regional disparities, the GATT years were still dominated by the effects of the breakdown of the previous system. Increases in trade were associated with a reversal in the regional growth trends. Regional convergence, which had been the norm since the 1970s, gave way to regional divergence. Only during the NAFTA period have the full effects of trade liberalization and economic integration become more apparent. These forces seemed to have unleashed a process of greater economic concentration which has mainly benefited the relatively advanced regions of the north. Regional disparities have been reinforced, fundamentally in favour of those regions with the highest endowment in human capital and the lowest levels of outmigration. Centrifugal forces are currently less important than centripetal forces and there are initial signs of the emergence of an increasingly knowledge-based economy, which is likely to further widen regional disparities across Mexico.

In brief, trade liberalization and economic integration have not provoked a reduction in territorial disparities, but have led to greater polarization (Dussel Peters 1997). As predicted in some H–O models (Venables and Limão 1999), Mexican states close to the North American market have profited from integration, increasing their production and incomes, although there is no clear econometric indication yet of a change in the relevant market from Mexico City to the United States. States farther away from the United States have lost out in relative terms and have become more detached from the recent insertion of the Mexican economy in world markets. Although centrifugal forces may start playing a greater role in the future, once congestion and environmental degradation start to affect the efficiency of the main economic poles, greater policy intervention than hitherto may be needed in order to curb the spiralling of regional disparities. Industrial, educational, and regional development policies need to be developed fast in order to set up the bases for development in a series of Mexican states which, until recently, relied almost solely on migration and their natural resources to survive. In any case, further research is needed in order to determine what are the factors behind regional growth in Mexico in the last few years, since the traditional factors which influenced growth until very recently are giving way to new and less well-known factors which are likely to shape growth and regional disparities in Mexico in the years to come.

Appendix: Description of the Dependent and Independent Variables

The dependent variable included in the model ($G_{i,t}$) represents regional real per capita GDP growth in each Mexican state for each period covered in the analysis. The data sources are the economic censuses carried out in 1980, 1985, 1993, and the 2000 estimation made by INEGI (Instituto Nacional de Estadística Geografía e Informática (Mexico)—National Statistical and Geographical Institute) (INEGI 2000) for GDP, and the Presidencia de la República (1999) reports for the state population.

The independent variables reproduce—to the extent that available data allow—the factors highlighted by growth theories as the main determinants of growth. y_0 depicts the natural logarithm of the initial regional GDP per capita, extracted from the same data sources as the dependent variable, as a proxy for the agglomeration and initial concentration of economic activity.

Initial state net migration rates—calculated as the number of outmigrants minus the number of immigrants—are depicted by m_0. Apart from interregional migration, there are no data on factor mobility in Mexico. Net state migration rates at the beginning of each period are used in order to test to what extent the mobility of labour has played a role in the evolution of Mexican regional inequalities. Migration also represents a (somewhat imperfect) proxy for the remittances of immigrants, which have played a major role in the development of the Mexican economy (Conway and Cohen 1998; Taylor 1999).

Distance to the most important markets is a key variable for the new economic geography. This strand assumes that once trade is introduced a shift in the relevant market occurs. In the Mexican case the relevant market should be Mexico City during ISI, and the border with the United States during GATT and especially since the implementation of NAFTA (Hanson 1996, 1998a; Krugman and Livas Elizondo 1996). The natural logarithmic function of road distances, measured in kilometres, from the capital of each state to Mexico City (dismx) and to the nearest border with the United States (disus), are used to represent proximity to the two largest markets. Both variables are tested for all three periods, in order to assess whether the domestic or foreign market is the most relevant in each period.

Other factors considered by growth theorists as key determinants of growth are also included in the model. The natural logarithm of the initial state commercial banking deposits (k_0), measured in current pesos and weighted by the population of each state, is introduced as a proxy for capital accumulation. The average years of schooling (ed_0) of the adult population at the beginning of the period and the initial number of high school graduates divided by the population of each state (hgs_0) provide two measures of the educational attainment level of the population.

Other variables are used to control for other influences in the structure of the Mexican economy, such as the effect of oil on the economy (camtab), the initial location of maquiladora (maq_0) and public investment ($pubinv_0$). Oil, which has provoked significant distortions in regional disparities, has been included in the model as a dummy variable representing the two main oil-producing states, Campeche and Tabasco. These two states accounted for 94.65 per cent of the total Mexican oil production in 1998, and their GDP per capita have fluctuated enormously according to the price of oil and to the level of production (PEMEX 1999). The maquiladora scheme, which is becoming increasingly important and was until recently restricted to the border with the United States, has also been included as a variable in the form of maquiladora employment levels at the beginning of each period constructed using INEGI data (INEGI 1998). Finally, the natural logarithm of public investment, measured in current pesos in each Mexican state at the beginning of each period, is also included in the model.

REFERENCES

Auty, R. (1994). *Economic Development and Industrial Policy: Korea, Brazil, Mexico, India and China*, Mansell Publishing: London.

CNIE (1998). *Informe Estadístico sobre el Comportamiento de la Inversión Extranjera Directa en México*, Comisión Nacional de Inversiones Extranjeras: Mexico DF.

Conway, D. and J. H. Cohen (1998). 'Consequences of Migration and Remittances for Mexican Transnational Communities', *Economic Geography*, 74: 26–44.

Durand, J., D. S. Massey, and R. M. Zenteno (2001). 'Mexican Immigration to the United States: Continuities and Changes', *Latin American Research Review*, 36: 107–27.

Dussel Peters, E. (1997). *La Economía de la Polarización. Teoría y Evolución del Cambio Estructural de las Manufacturas Mexicanas (1988–1996)*, UNAM-Editorial Jus: Mexico DF.

Esquivel, G. (1999). 'Convergencia Regional en México, 1940–1995', *El Trimestre Económico*, 66(4): 725–61.

——— and M. Messmacher (2002). 'Sources of Regional (non) Convergence in Mexico', World Bank: Washington DC. Available at www.wbln0018.worldbank.org/lac/lacinfoclient.nsf.

——— D. Lederman, M. Messmacher, and R. Villoro (2002). 'Why NAFTA did not Reach the South', World Bank: Washington DC. Available at www.lnweb18.worldbank.org/external/lac/lac.nsf/Sectors/ChiefEconPres.

Frankel, J. and D. Romer (1999). 'Does Trade Cause Growth?', *American Economic Review*, 89(3): 379–99.

Fujita, M., P. Krugman, and A. Venables (1999). *The Spatial Economy*, MIT Press: Cambridge, MA.

Grossman, G. M. and E. Helpman (1991). 'Trade, Knowledge Spillovers and Growth', *European Economic Review*, 35: 517–26.

Hanson, G. (1996). 'Economic Integration, Intraindustry Trade, and Frontier Regions', *European Economic Review*, 40: 941–9.

Hanson, G. (1998a). 'Regional Adjustment to Trade Liberalization', *Regional Science and Urban Economics*, 28: 419–44.

—— (1998b). 'North American Economic Integration and Industry Location', *NBER Working Papers* 6587, National Bureau of Economic Research: Cambridge, MA.

INEGI (1986). *X Censo General de Población y Vivienda 1980, Resumen General*, Vol. II, Secretaría de Programación y Presupuesto: Mexico DF.

—— (1995). *Cuaderno de Información Oportuna Regional* No. 39, Geografía e Informática, Instituto Nacional de Estadística: Aguascalientes, Mexico.

—— (1997). *Conteo 1995, Resultados Definitivos, Tabulados Complementarios*, Geografía e Informática, Instituto Nacional de Estadística: Aguascalientes, Mexico.

—— (1998). *Industria Maquiladora de Exportación*, Geografía e Informática, Instituto Nacional de Estadística: Aguascalientes, Mexico.

—— (2000). *Banco de Información Económica*, Geografía e Informática, Instituto Nacional de Estadística: Aguascalientes, Mexico, 24 March 1999. Available at www.inegi.gob.mx.

Juan-Ramón, V. H. and L. A. Rivera-Batiz (1996). 'Regional Growth in Mexico: 1970–93', *International Monetary Fund Working Papers* 23, IMF: Washington DC.

Krugman, P. (1991). 'Increasing Returns and Economic Geography', *Journal of Political Economy*, 99(3): 483–99.

—— (1993). 'The Narrow and Broad Arguments for Free Trade', *American Economic Review*, 83: 362–6.

—— and R. Livas Elizondo (1996). 'Trade Policy and the Third World Metropolis', *Journal of Development Economics*, 49: 137–50.

López-Córdoba, E. and M. M. Moreira (2002). 'Regional Integration and Productivity: the Experiences of Brazil and Mexico', *Economic and Social Progress in Latin America Reports*, Inter-American Development Bank: Washington DC.

López Malo, E. (1960). *Ensayo sobre Localización de la Industria en Mexico*, UNAM: Mexico DF.

Markusen, J. *et al.* (1995). *International Trade: Theory and Evidence*, McGraw-Hill: Singapore.

Mundell, R. (1957). 'International Trade and Factor Mobility', *American Economic Review*, 47: 321–35.

OECD (1999). *Trade, Investment and Development: Policy Coherence Matters*, Organization for Economic Co-operation and Development: Paris.

Partida Bush, V. (1994). *Migración Interna*, Instituto Nacional de Estadística, Geografía e Informática: Aguascalientes, Mexico.

PEMEX (1999). *Informe de Labores 1998, Anexo Estadístico*, Petroleos Mexicanos: Mexico DF.

Presidencia de la República (1999). *Quinto Informe de Gobierno, Anexo Estadístico*, Presidencia de la República: Mexico DF.

Ramírez, M. D. (1989). *Mexico's Economic Crisis: Its Origins and Consequences*, Praeger: New York.

Rodríguez-Pose, A. and N. Gill (2003). 'Is There a Global Link Between Regional Disparities and Devolution?', *LSE Environmental and Spatial Research Papers* 78, LSE: London.

Sachs, J. and A. M. Warner (1995). 'Economic Convergence and Economic Policies', *NBER Working Papers* 5039, National Bureau of Economic Research: Cambridge, MA.

Sánchez-Reaza, J. and A. Rodríguez-Pose (2002). 'The Impact of Trade Liberalization on Regional Disparities in Mexico', *Growth and Change*, 33: 72–90.

Smith, P. (1990). 'Mexico Since 1946', in L. Bethel (ed.) *The Cambridge History of Latin America (Vol. 7), Latin America Since 1930: Mexico, Central America and the Caribbean*, Cambridge University Press: Cambridge.

Taylor, J. E. (1999). 'The New Economics of Labour Migration and the Role of Remittances in the Migration Process', *International Migration*, 37: 63–88.

Venables, A. J. (1998). 'The Assessment: Trade and Location', *Oxford Review of Economic Policy*, 14(2): 1–6.

——and N. Limão (1999). 'Geographical Disadvantage: A Heckscher–Ohlin-von Thünen Model of International Specialization', *Journal of International Economics*, 58(2): 239–63.

Villarreal, R. (1988). *Industrialización, Deuda y Desequilibrio Externo en México: Un Enfoque Neo-Estructuralista*, Fondo de Cultura Económica: Mexico DF.

Weintraub, S. (1988). *Mexican Trade Policy and the North American Community*, Centre for Strategic and International Studies: Washington DC.

Wood, A. (1994). *North–South Trade, Employment and Inequality*, Oxford University Press: Oxford.

J31 O15 R12
P33 P23 **11** O18 R23

International Trade, Location, and Wage Inequality in China

SONGHUA LIN

11.1. INTRODUCTION

Economists have long recognized the relationship between geographic location and income. Using international data, Moreno and Trehan (1997) provide evidence that being close to large markets contributes to income growth. Similarly, using a panel of US counties, Hanson (1998) finds that proximity to a large market has a positive effect on earnings. Recent literature on economic geography summarizes the channel through which location affects income (Overman *et al.* 2001). Location exerts its impact on both the demand and the supply side of an economy. On the demand side, when a location is far away from its target market, the potential demand for the goods and services in the location is less than in other locations closer to the market. On the production side, if a location is far away from the suppliers of intermediate inputs, the costs of production will be relatively high and value added is then reduced.

In this chapter, we examine the link between each province's geographic location and provincial wage rates in China. In particular, we investigate the extent to which the increasing wage gap between the coastal and the interior regions is associated with each province's access to international output markets and suppliers of intermediate inputs. This study uses Redding and Venables' (2000) methodology, which examines the role of geography in shaping the evolution of the cross-country distribution of income.

The Chinese case is interesting for several reasons. First, income inequality has always been an important and sensitive political issue since the foundation of the People's Republic of China in 1949. Kanbur and Zhang (2001) examine fifty years of regional inequality in China and find that there have been three phases of rising inequality during the past fifty years—one appeared in the late 1950s, one was in the

This chapter represents part of my Ph.D. dissertation. I would like to give special thanks to my adviser Robert Feenstra for his insightful guidance and comments. Discussions with Deborah Swenson and Lee Branstetter are gratefully acknowledged. I am grateful to Shuming Liang for providing useful materials and detailed information on China's geographic features. This chapter has benefited from the comments of the participants in the Macroeconomics Workshop and the Macroeconomics International Seminar at the University of California, Davis.

late 1960s, and one was in the 1990s. It is worth noting that the regional inequality in the 1990s is more serious than that experienced in the 1960s and is similar to that experienced in the 1950s. Many studies on China's income inequality suggest that foreign trade and investment might have caused China's income inequality in the 1990s.[1] To my knowledge, however, no research has been conducted to explicitly uncover the mechanism by which international trade affects regional wages. This chapter is the first attempt to explore the relationship between regional wage rates and international trade.

Second, the increasing income inequality in China after its trade liberalization in the late 1970s has coincided with the international trend towards an increasing wage gap between high- and low-skilled workers. During the last two decades, increasing wage inequality has been observed in many industrialized countries,[2] and in Mexico.[3] There are three explanations for the increasing wage gap—one is international competition from low-wage countries;[4] the second is skill-biased technological change due to the increased use of computers;[5] and the third is global outsourcing.[6] However, most of the literature has focused on industrialized economies, while wage inequality in developing countries has not drawn much attention.[7] China, the largest developing country in the world, underwent economic reform in the late 1970s and actively engaged in global outsourcing. Hsieh and Woo (1999) provide evidence that outsourcing from Hong Kong to China has been associated with an increase in the wage gap between skilled and unskilled labour in Hong Kong. It is natural, then, to expect that similar wage movements would take place in China.

Instead of examining the wage gap between skilled and unskilled workers, we explore wage inequality in a different dimension—the wage gap between the coastal and the interior provinces. As illustrated in recent studies, the wage inequality in China is manifesting itself more in the form of regional inequality rather than in wage inequality between skilled and unskilled workers, and regional wage inequality is strongly associated with the regional distribution of international trade.

Another reason for considering province-level data is that we are not able to apply the standard classification of skill in the Chinese labour market. The conventional approach distinguishes skill levels by classifying workers into non-production and production. Unfortunately, this distinction is not reported in the China statistical yearbook. Instead, an education index appears. The fact that college-educated workers account for a small percentage of the workforce in China makes the education index a poor way to classify workers.

[1] Jian *et al.* (1996), Kanbur and Zhang (1999), Tsui (1998), Hussain *et al.* (1994), Chen and Fleisher (1996), Khan *et al.* (1993).

[2] Freeman and Katz (1994), Katz and Autor (1999).

[3] Cragg and Epelbaum (1996), Feenstra and Hanson (1997), Hanson and Harrison (1999, 2001).

[4] Leamer (1993: 57–162, 1994), Borjas and Ramey (1993), Wood (1994).

[5] Davis and Haltiwanger (1991), Lawrence and Slaughter (1993), Berman *et al.* (1994).

[6] Katz and Murphy (1992), Feenstra and Hanson (1996: 89–127).

[7] Feenstra and Hanson (1997), Hanson and Harrison (1999) are two notable exceptions. Both examine the increase in relative wages or skilled workers in Mexico.

11.1.1. *Market Access*

My work follows recent literature on economic–geographic models which use market access as an important variable in determining income. Market access was first defined in Harris (1954), where he argues that the potential demand for goods and services in a location depends upon the distance-weighted GDP in all locations. Other related work includes papers by Hummels (1995), Leamer (1997), and Hanson (1996*a*,*b*). Krugman and Venables (1995) draw special attention to the implications of increasing returns to scale and include it in their framework. Redding and Venables (2000) extend the Krugman and Venables (1995) trade theory model to include transportation costs in trade and intermediate goods in production. They define 'market access' as the proximity of an exporting country to its output market, and 'supplier access' as the proximity of an importing country to its supply of intermediate inputs.

As a prelude to the analysis, using data on the Chinese provinces for the period 1988–98, we first estimate a gravity equation to construct market access and supplier access variables. Second, we estimate the wage equation using the constructed market access and supplier access. Having estimated the model, we compare the predicted wage gap obtained in the model to the one obtained from the observed data, and evaluate the extent to which the gap in wages can be explained by differences in regional market access and supplier access. The remainder of the chapter is organized as follows. In the next section, we briefly introduce China's spatial economy. Section 11.3 presents the theoretical model. Section 11.4 explains the estimation strategies. We describe the data sources and measurement in Section 11.5. Section 11.6 reports the estimation results and robustness tests. Finally, we offer concluding remarks and policy implications in Section 11.7.

11.2. CHINA'S SPATIAL ECONOMY

China is a very large country covering 6,000,000 square miles with thirty administrative divisions.[8,9] Geographic features in China differ greatly from one province to the next, though the variety of natural landscape is not the focus of this chapter. Here, we mainly introduce stylized facts about the spatial distribution of economic activity in China.

First, regional income varies dramatically across provinces. Table 11.1 presents the income inequality in China in 1995. There are three alternative measures of income: the average real wage rate, GDP per capita, and the average real wage rate in the manufacturing sector. The first row in the table shows the national average for each measure of income. We divide the Chinese provinces into two groups: coastal and interior regions.[10] Among the coastal group, the real wage rates in most provinces are

---

[8] Beijing, Tianjin, Hebei, Shanxi, Inner Mongolia, Liaoning, Jilin, Heilongjiang, Shanghai, Jiangsu, Zhejiang, Anhui, Fujian, Jiangxi, Shandong, Henan, Hubei, Hunan, Guangdong, Guangxi, Hainan, Sichuan, Guizhou, Yunnan, Tibet, Shaanxi, Gansu, Qinghai, Ningxia, and Xinjiang.

[9] Tibet is excluded from our sample due to the lack of data.

[10] Coastal regions include Beijing, Tianjin, Liaoning, Shanghai, Jiangsu, Zhejiang, Fujian, Shandong, Guangdong, and Hainan. Interior regions include Hebei, Shanxi, Inner Mongolia, Heilongjiang, Jilin,

Table 11.1. *Income inequality across provinces in 1995*

Province	Wage[a] (CNY)[c]	GDP per capita (CNY/person)	Wage in manufacturing sector[b] (CNY)
Average	1,514	1,480	1,437
Coastal			
Beijing	2,287	3,132	2,126
Tianjin	1,826	2,889	1,691
Liaoning	1,379	1,945	1,270
Shanghai	2,606	5,315	2,496
Jiangsu	1,669	2,049	1,593
Zhejiang	1,859	2,256	1,701
Fujian	1,645	1,918	1,666
Shandong	1,445	1,614	1,328
Guangdong	2,317	2,355	2,222
Hainan	1,500	1,413	1,443
Interior			
Hebei	1,359	1,243	1,268
Shanxi	1,326	997	1,148
Inner Mongolia	1,161	1,024	1,034
Jilin	1,244	1,243	1,160
Heilongjiang	1,164	1,529	1,019
Anhui	1,294	938	1,192
Jiangxi	1,183	861	1,106
Henan	1,220	927	1,133
Hubei	1,316	1,164	1,258
Hunan	1,347	971	1,274
Guangxi	1,434	993	1,491
Sichuan	1,304	889	1,298
Guizhou	1,257	502	1,321
Yunnan	1,446	850	1,594
Shaanxi	1,234	655	1,149
Gansu	1,543	795	1,541
Qinghai	1,616	638	1,337
Ningxia	1,426	965	1,333
Xinjiang	1,502	931	1,466

[a] Wage is the real wage rate of formal employees.
[b] Wage in the manufacturing sector is the real wage rate of formal employees in the manufacturing sector.
[c] Wage rates are in China Yuan Renminbi.

Source: CSPH (various).

higher than the national average except Liaoning, Shandong, and Hainan. Liaoning and Shandong are two provinces where there is much state-owned heavy industry, which used to play an important role in the local economy. Since China underwent economic reform, state-owned companies have faced competition from joint ventures and privately owned enterprises. State-owned enterprises are not as efficient as other enterprises, however they are still the majority in local Chinese economies. This may be the reason why real wage rates in Liaoning and Shandong are lower than the national average. Hainan Island is a new province (it split from Guangdong province in 1988), and its statistical reports, to some extent, are not consistent with its economic activity. Among the interior provinces, wage rates in most provinces are lower than the national average except in Gansu and Qinghai, two poor provinces in the far west which receive enormous subsidies from the central government every year.

The income gap between the coastal and the interior regions is not only large, it is also increasing. Figure 11.1 presents the wage difference between regional wage and national average wage level. Figure 11.1(a) shows the wage difference in the coastal provinces for 1988–98. Over the years, the wage rates have risen higher than the national average. In particular, the regional wages of Beijing, Shanghai, and Guangdong are much higher than the national average. Figure 11.1(b) presents the wage difference in the interior provinces for 1988–98; the wage rates are much lower than the national average. Comparing Figs 11.1(a) and (b), we observe the increasing wage gap between the coastal and the interior regions.

There is general consensus that China's income disparities in the late 1990s have been caused by trade liberalization. Kanbur and Zhang (2001) argue that openness and global integration from the late 1970s is the key variable in explaining regional inequality during the reform period. The important feature of global integration in this period in China is the concentration of international trade along China's east coast. Table 11.2 shows the average distribution of international trade broken down by customs regimes across the regions from 1988 to 1998. Guangdong has the highest share in all kinds of trade shares, and in the share of processing trade in particular.[11] Guangdong is also in the leading position for ordinary trade. Other coastal provinces account for 30 per cent of processing trade, 57 per cent of ordinary exports, and 73 per cent of ordinary imports.[12] It is obvious that the interior provinces did not play any notable role in either processing exports or processing imports. The share of processing trade in each interior province is less than 1 per cent. In terms of ordinary trade, a few interior provinces account for between 2 and 4 per cent of national ordinary exports. Compared to the performance of the coastal provinces, it is not impressive.

Anhui, Henan, Hubei, Hunan, Jiangxi, Guangxi Shaanxi, Sichuan, Xinjiang, Ningxia, Gansu, Qinghai, Yunnan, and Guizhou.

[11] In 1986, China established two foreign trade regimes: a processing trade regime, which is an export promoting regime; and an ordinary trade regime, which is an import substitution regime.

[12] Beijing outperformed all other provinces in the share of ordinary imports. This might be the result of the volume of trade generated by the national foreign trade companies assigned to Beijing for 1988–92.

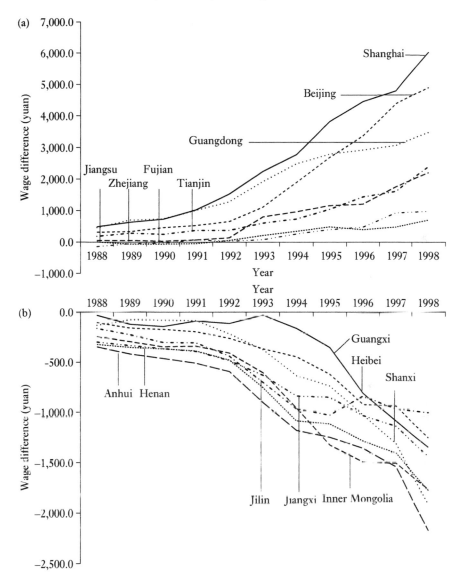

Figure 11.1. *Comparison of the provincial wage with the national average: (a) coastal provinces, (b) interior provinces*

The share of ordinary import by the majority of the interior provinces is less than 1 per cent, except Jilin, Hubei, and Sichuan.

Figure 11.2 depicts the association between the regional real wage rates and share of total export, which indicates a region's degree of openness. Most coastal provinces, except Hainan, are associated with high degrees of openness and high levels of real

Table 11.2. *Average distribution of international trade for 1988–98 (in %)*

Province	Share of			
	Processing export (1)	Ordinary export (2)	Processing import (3)	Ordinary import (4)
Coastal				
Beijing	2.72	9.57	4.28	52.45
Tianjin	2.70	2.83	2.63	1.80
Liaoning	3.54	8.77	3.49	2.45
Shanghai	8.87	8.26	7.13	7.92
Jiangsu	4.51	7.36	4.50	3.08
Zhejiang	2.34	7.04	2.18	1.81
Fujian	4.49	3.65	4.95	1.75
Shandong	3.74	6.95	3.53	1.84
Guangdong	62.31	19.22	62.75	14.95
Hainan	0.15	1.19	0.20	1.65
Interior				
Hebei	0.68	3.99	0.54	0.64
Shanxi	0.13	0.93	0.10	0.19
Inner Mongolia	0.13	0.61	0.12	0.28
Jilin	0.20	1.57	0.21	1.17
Heilongjiang	0.25	1.75	0.31	0.75
Anhui	0.37	1.40	0.31	0.48
Jiangxi	0.17	1.25	0.20	0.39
Henan	0.30	1.65	0.28	0.48
Hubei	0.64	2.12	0.51	1.03
Hunan	0.29	1.94	0.23	0.61
Guangxi	0.45	1.63	0.61	0.60
Sichuan	0.46	2.31	0.39	1.43
Guizhou	0.08	0.40	0.08	0.20
Yunnan	0.13	0.97	0.10	0.67
Shaanxi	0.22	1.20	0.17	0.65
Gansu	0.07	0.42	0.09	0.13
Qinghai	0.01	0.17	0.01	0.02
Ningxia	0.02	0.17	0.02	0.04
Xinjiang	0.02	0.62	0.03	0.29

Source: Calculated from Chinese trade data in MOFTEC (various years).

wage rates, whereas the interior provinces cluster around the low share of total exports and low real wage rates. Why does most trade take place in the coastal provinces? We argue that geographical location matters. The provinces located along China's east coast have advantages in trading with other countries as they are closer to China's major markets, such as Hong Kong and Japan, and have lower transportation costs.

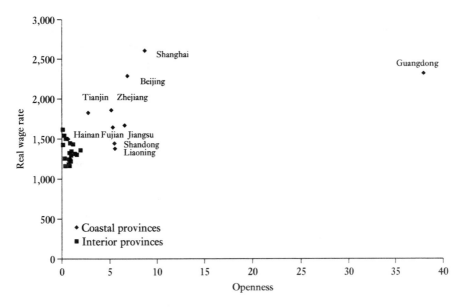

Figure 11.2. *Regional real wage and openness*

Table 11.3 lists average regional export share to Hong Kong and Japan, and distance from each province to Hong Kong and Japan.[13] Guangdong is the province closest to Hong Kong, and it is the province that accounts for 69.7 per cent of national export to Hong Kong for 1988–98. According to annual trade volumes, Hong Kong, Japan, and the United States are China's top three trading partners. Each province, however, has a different ordering of trading partners. Table 11.4 shows examples for a few provinces. For instance, Mongolia does not appear to be an important partner for most provinces except for Inner Mongolia, the province located at the far north of China and neighbouring on Mongolia. Another example is the Jilin province; it shares a border with North Korea and has a Korean–Chinese autonomous region within the province. Even though North Korea trades very little with the rest of the world, it is the fourth most important trading partner of the Jilin province. In this chapter, we find that distance strongly affects the volume of trade.

11.3. THEORETICAL MODEL

11.3.1. *Redding and Venables Model*

In the context of the Chinese provincial trade, we present the outline of the Redding and Venables (2000) model. It is based on a theoretical model in Fujita *et al.* (1999).

---

[13] Distance is the arc distance. In terms of arc distance, some of the coastal provinces are further away from Hong Kong and Japan than the interior provinces are. In reality, however, the coastal provinces either have their own ports or are near to ports, and transport goods through shipment, which leads to lower transport costs than in the interior provinces.

S. Lin

Table 11.3. *Average share of export and distance to major trading country*

Province	Export share to (in %)		Distance to (in miles)	
	Hong Kong (1)	Japan (2)	Hong Kong (3)	Japan (4)
Coastal				
Beijing	2.4	6.5	1,216	1,308
Tianjin	1.2	3.6	1,169	1,261
Liaoning	1.3	19.2	1,443	977
Shanghai	3.3	12.9	759	1,098
Jiangsu	2.5	10.6	724	1,229
Zhejiang	2.1	6.2	657	1,196
Fujian	4.0	4.8	289	1,507
Shandong	1.8	11.1	1,015	1,088
Guangdong	69.7	5.5	72	1,811
Hainan	0.8	0.5	294	2,087
Interior				
Hebei	1.1	5.9	733	1,405
Shanxi	0.2	0.5	1,069	1,510
Inner Mongolia	0.2	0.6	1,279	1,561
Jilin	0.5	1.9	1,642	900
Heilongjiang	0.5	1.5	1,759	978
Anhui	0.5	0.9	679	1,317
Jiangxi	0.7	0.5	445	1,475
Henan	0.8	0.9	851	1,471
Hubei	1.4	1.1	561	1,513
Hunan	1.1	0.7	404	1,649
Guangxi	1.3	0.5	370	2,083
Sichuan	1.1	1.5	680	1,970
Guizhou	0.1	0.3	546	2,045
Yunnan	0.4	0.6	778	2,315
Shaanxi	0.5	0.7	875	1,742
Gansu	0.2	0.3	1,125	2,006
Qinghai	0.0	0.3	1,227	2,110
Ningxia	0.1	0.1	1,200	1,848
Xinjiang	0.4	0.3	2,114	2,785

Source: First two columns are calculated using Chinese trade data in MOFTEC (various). Columns (3) and (4) are constructed using the information on the longitude and latitude.

In addition, it includes transportation costs in trade, and intermediate goods in production. Consider international trade between the administrative provinces in China and the rest of the world.[14] There are $i = 1, \ldots, 29$ provinces in China and the Chinese

[14] Here we assume that there is no interprovince trade in China, and the rest of world is trading only with the Chinese provinces. Since our concern here is wage rates in China, the second assumption will not affect our results.

Table 11.4. *Trade partners for some provinces*

Province	Partner	Province	Partner
Tianjin (12)	Japan Hong Kong USA South Korea Germany	Inner Mongolia (15)	Japan Hong Kong South Korea Mongolia Italy
Liaoning (21)	Japan USA South Korea Hong Kong Netherlands	Jilin (22)	Japan South Korea Hong Kong North Korea USA
Shanghai (31)	Japan Hong Kong USA South Korea Germany	Shandong (37)	Japan South Korea Hong Kong USA Germany

Note: The partner is ranked according the volume of trade.

Source: The volume of trade is calculated using Chinese trade data from MOFTEC (various).

provinces are trading with $j = 1, \ldots, J$ countries.[15] Let U_j denote the utility function in country j with CES form, c_{ijk} refers to the consumption of good k exported from province i to country j. Suppose province i produces N_i products. Then the representative consumer's utility function in country j is,

$$U_j = \sum_{i=1}^{29} \sum_{k=1}^{N_i} c_{ijk}^{(\sigma-1)/\sigma} = \sum_{i=1}^{29} N_i c_{ij}^{(\sigma-1)/\sigma}, \quad \sigma > 1. \tag{11.1}$$

The second equation arises at the assumption that consumption in country j is equal over all products $k = 1, \ldots, N_i$ sold by province i, that is, $c_{ijk} = c_{ij}$. Good k is used both in consumption and as an intermediate good, and in both uses there is a constant elasticity of substitution, σ. The problem facing a representative consumer in country j is to maximize (11.1), subject to budget constraints:

$$E_j = \sum_{i=1}^{29} N_i p_{ij} c_{ij}, \tag{11.2}$$

where E_j is country j's aggregate expenditure, p_{ij} is the price of goods produced in province i and sold in country j. Solving the maximization problem, we can derive

[15] The number of trading countries j has evolved over the years.

country j's demand for the product produced in province i,

$$c_{ij} = p_{ij}^{-\sigma} E_j P_j^{\sigma-1},\tag{11.3}$$

where P_j refers to country j's general price index, which is defined as:

$$P_j = \left[\sum_{i=1}^{29} N_i p_{ij}^{1-\sigma} \right]^{1/(1-\sigma)}.\tag{11.4}$$

Redding and Venables (2000) refer to the term $E_j P_j^{\sigma-1}$ in eqn (11.3) as country j's market capacity, which depends on total expenditure in country j and overall price.

Turning to the production side, consider a single representative firm in province i with increasing returns to scale production technology, and an imperfect competitive market. The firm uses labour and intermediate input with share θ and $1-\theta$ to produce output y_i, and then the firm's profit is,

$$\pi_i = p_i y_i - w_i^\theta P_i^{1-\theta}(\alpha + \beta y_i),\tag{11.5}$$

where p_i is a free on board (f.o.b.) price in province i, $y_i = \Sigma_j c_{ij} T_{ij}$, and T_{ij} is a transport costs factor, indicating that T_{ij} units of the product must be shipped to country j in order for one unit to arrive. The firm has fixed costs of α and marginal costs of β. Then the first term on the right-hand side is revenue and the second term is total costs.

With demand function (11.3), profit maximizing firms set a single f.o.b. price, p_i, such that prices for the sales in different countries are $p_{ij} = p_i T_{ij}$. The price p_i is a constant mark-up over marginal cost, and is given by,

$$p_i = \frac{\sigma}{\sigma - 1} \beta w_i^\theta P_i^{1-\theta}.\tag{11.6}$$

Substituting this pricing behaviour into the profit equation, profits of firm in province i are

$$\pi_i = \frac{w_i^\theta P_i^{1-\theta}}{\sigma - 1}[\beta y_i - (\sigma - 1)\alpha].\tag{11.7}$$

Therefore, the firm breaks even if the total volume of its sales equals,

$$\bar{y} = (\sigma - 1)\left(\frac{\alpha}{\beta}\right).\tag{11.8}$$

From the demand function, eqn (11.3), it will sell this many units if its price equals,

$$p_i^\sigma = \frac{1}{\bar{y}} \sum_{j=1}^{J} E_j P_j^{\sigma-1}(T_{ij})^{1-\sigma}.\tag{11.9}$$

At the equilibrium, combining eqns (11.6) and (11.9), profit-maximizing firms have

$$\left(\frac{\sigma}{\sigma-1} w_i^\theta P_i^{1-\theta}\right)^\sigma = \left(\frac{1}{\bar{y}}\right) \sum_{j=1}^{J} E_j P_j^{\sigma-1} T_{ij}^{1-\sigma}.\tag{11.10}$$

Redding and Venables (2000) call this the 'wage equation', which implies that the break-even level of costs, for provincial firm i, is a function of distance weighted market capacities.

Equation (11.10) can be further simplified using eqn (11.4). Given the prices for sale in different countries, eqn (11.4) can be rewritten as,

$$P_j = \left[\sum_i N_i (p_i T_{ij})^{1-\sigma} \right]^{1/(1-\sigma)} = \left[\sum_i N_i p_i^{1-\sigma} T_{ij}^{1-\sigma} \right]^{1/(1-\sigma)}. \qquad (11.11)$$

The term $N_i p_i^{1-\sigma}$ measures an exporting province's supply capacity, as defined in Redding and Venables (2000). Substituting eqn (11.11) into eqn (11.10) and rearranging, we have,

$$w_i = \left(\frac{1}{\bar{y}} \right)^{-\sigma/\theta} \left(\frac{\sigma-1}{\beta\sigma} \right)^{1/\theta} \left[\sum_{j=1}^{J} N_j (p_j T_{ij})^{1-\sigma} \right]^{(1-\theta)/\theta(\sigma-1)}$$

$$\times \left[\sum_{j=1}^{J} E_j P_j^{\sigma-1} T_{ij}^{1-\sigma} \right]^{1/\theta\sigma}$$

$$= A(\text{SA}_i)^{(1-\theta)/\theta(\sigma-1)} (\text{MA}_i)^{1/\theta\sigma}, \qquad (11.12)$$

where,

$$A = \left(\frac{1}{\bar{y}} \right)^{-\sigma/\theta} \left(\frac{\sigma-1}{\beta\sigma} \right)^{1/\theta}$$

$$\text{SA}_i = \left[\sum_{j=1}^{J} N_j p_j^{1-\sigma} T_{ij}^{1-\sigma} \right]^{(1-\theta)/\theta(\sigma-1)} \qquad (11.13)$$

$$\text{MA}_i = \left[\sum_{j=1}^{J} E_j P_j^{\sigma-1} T_{ij}^{1-\sigma} \right]^{1/\theta\sigma}.$$

The left-hand side of eqn (11.12) is the wage rate, w_i. The constant A on the right-hand side combines constants from eqn (11.10). SA and MA in eqn (11.13) are defined as 'supplier access' and 'market access'.

Supplier access is distance-weighted supplier capacity and measures the proximity of an importing province i to the supplier of manufactured goods. Market access is distance-weighted market capacity and measures the proximity of an exporting province i to its international markets. Then eqn (11.12) implies that provinces with high market access and high supplier access pay relatively high wages because provinces with high market access face high demand for their products, and provinces with high supplier access can obtain intermediate goods at lower cost. Neither market access nor supplier access is observable and will be estimated from a gravity equation in the next section.

11.3.2. Gravity Equation

The demand eqn (11.3) gives the volume of sales from province i to each country j. Multiplying varieties and prices on the both sides, we obtain a gravity type trade equation,

$$N_i p_{ij} c_{ij} = (T_{ij})^{1-\sigma} N_i p_i^{1-\sigma} E_j (P_j)^{\sigma-1}. \tag{11.14}$$

The left-hand side in eqn (11.14) is simply the value of trade between province i and country j. The right-hand side contains province information, trading country information, and transportation cost. The term $E_j(P_j)^{\sigma-1}$ is 'market capacity'. The term $N_i p_i^{1-\sigma}$ is 'supplier capacity', which depends on the number of firms and the prices they charge. Since we focus on the geographic features of trade, these two variables can simply take the form of regional fixed effects.[16] Using the export data from Chinese provinces to the rest of the world, we can estimate provincial market capacity, whereas the import data by Chinese provinces from the rest of world is used to obtain supplier capacity. Market capacity and supplier capacity will be weighted by the distance between province i and country j, which are market access and supplier access.

11.4. EMPIRICAL STRATEGY

11.4.1. Empirical Specification

A two-stage estimation procedure is used. First a gravity equation is estimated using values of trade and distances between the Chinese province and its trading partners. The estimates of market access and supplier access for each province are then constructed using the estimated coefficients in the gravity equation. The gravity equation can be estimated by taking logs of eqn (11.14),

$$\ln(N_i p_i c_{ij}) = (1 - \sigma) \ln(T_{ij}) + \ln(N_i p_i^{1-\sigma}) + \ln(E_j P_j^{\sigma-1}),$$
$$\ln(\text{VOT}_{ij}) = \alpha_0 + \beta_0 \ln(\text{dist}_{ij}) + \delta_i + \gamma_j + \omega_{ij}, \tag{11.15}$$

where,

$\text{VOT}_{ij} = N_i P_i c_{ij}$, values of trade between province i and country j,

$\text{dist}_{ij} = T_{ij}$, distance between province i and country j, \hfill (11.16)

$\delta_i = \ln(N_i P_i^{1-\sigma}), \quad \gamma_j = \ln(E_j P_j^{\sigma-1}).$

---

[16] Using the fixed effects still addresses the criticism of the conventional gravity equation made by Anderson and von Wincoop (2000).

δ_i is a provincial dummy and γ_j is a trading country dummy. We have two measures of distance: arc distance, which is the minimum-length arc between two locations, and internal–external distance, which measures the distance within China and outside of China. Internal distance is measured by the arc distance between the province and its closest ports, and external distance is measured by the external arc distance between China's large and other international ports. Then the specification of the gravity equation is,

$$\ln(\text{VOT}_{ij}) = \alpha_0 + \beta_1 \ln(\text{dist\_i}_{ij}) + \beta_2(\ln \text{dist\_e}_{ij}) + \delta_i + \gamma_j + \omega_{ij}, \qquad (11.17)$$

where dist_i and dist_e refer to internal and external distance, respectively.

In order to construct market access, we set the dependent variable as the value of exports from province i to province trading partner, country j. When we construct supplier access, the dependent variable is the value of imports by province i from country j. Market access and supplier access for eqn (11.15) are constructed using the formula,

$$\hat{\text{MA}}_i = \sum_{j=1}^{\mathcal{J}} e^{\hat{\gamma}_j} \times \text{dist}_{ij}^{\hat{\beta}_0}, \quad i = 1, \ldots, 29, \ j = 1, \ldots, \mathcal{J},$$

$$\hat{\text{SA}}_i = \sum_{j=1}^{\mathcal{J}} e^{\hat{\delta}_j} \times \text{dist}_{ij}^{\hat{\beta}_0}, \quad i = 1, \ldots, 29, \ j = 1, \ldots, \mathcal{J}. \qquad (11.18)$$

Market access and supplier access for eqn (11.17) are, thus,

$$\hat{\text{MA}}_i = \sum_{j=1}^{\mathcal{J}} e^{\hat{\delta}_j} \times \text{dist\_i}_{ij}^{\hat{\beta}_1} \times \text{dist\_e}_{ij}^{\hat{\beta}_2}, \quad i = 1, \ldots, 29, \ j = 1, \ldots, \mathcal{J},$$

$$\hat{\text{SA}}_i = \sum_{j=1}^{\mathcal{J}} e^{\hat{\gamma}_j} \times \text{dist\_i}_{ij}^{\hat{\beta}_1} \times \text{dist\_e}_{ij}^{\hat{\beta}_2}, \quad i = 1, \ldots, 29, \ j = 1, \ldots, \mathcal{J}. \qquad (11.19)$$

We run the gravity equation annually since the number of trade partners, $\mathcal{J}$, has increased over the years, as China has become more and more open to the outside world. The change in the number of trade partners directly affects the estimated coefficients on partner dummies. Therefore, provincial market access and supplier access evolve, given the fixed distance between each province and its trade partners. In the second step, given the provincial market access and supplier access, we specify the following log-linear wage equation in empirical estimation:

$$\ln w_i = \lambda_0 + \lambda_1 \ln \text{SA}_i + \lambda_2 \ln \text{MA}_i + u_i, \qquad (11.20)$$

where the dependent variable w_i is the real wage rate, or the real wage rate in the manufacturing sector in province i. λ_0, λ_1, and λ_2 are the parameters to be estimated.[17]

---

[17] Since market access and supplier access are generated from the gravity equation, the OLS standard errors are invalid. The standard errors are corrected by using the 'bootstrap technique'.

The error term includes technology differences and other forces that affect regional wage rates, such as spatial correlation. We will return to these forces in the following robustness section. The error term u_i also includes the residuals in the gravity equation since the regressors, supplier access and market access, are generated from the gravity equation.

We decompose the Chinese export and import data into two trade regimes. Thus, we have processing exports, processing imports, ordinary exports, and ordinary imports. Applying the various export and import data into the gravity eqns (11.15) and (11.17), and using definitions in eqns (11.18) and (11.19), we arrive at the processing market access, the ordinary market access, the processing supplier access, and the ordinary supplier access.[18] Then the basic wage equation is:

$$\ln w_i = \varphi_0 + \varphi_1 \ln \hat{PMA}_i + \varphi_2 \ln \hat{OMA}_i + \varphi_3 \ln \hat{PSA}_i + \varphi_4 \ln \hat{OSA}_i + \varepsilon_i, \quad (11.21)$$

where PMA and PSA refer to processing market access and processing supplier access, OMA and OSA are ordinary market access and ordinary supplier access.

We are also interested in the impact of the different trade regimes on the regional wage rates. Compared with the ordinary trade regime, processing trade is more concentrated along the coast. We expect the effects of processing trade on the wage rate to be higher than those obtained from ordinary trade, and processing trade can better explain the wage inequality than ordinary trade does. Thus, the alternative estimation is to separate processing market access and processing supplier access from ordinary market access and ordinary supplier access in the wage equation,

$$\ln w_i = \kappa_0 + \kappa_1 \ln \hat{PMA}_i + \kappa_2 \ln \hat{PSA}_i + \kappa_i, \quad (11.22)$$

$$\ln w_i = v_0 + v_1 \ln \hat{OMA}_i + v_2 \ln \hat{OSA}_i + v_i. \quad (11.23)$$

11.4.2. *Robustness Test*

The error term in eqn (11.21) includes technology differences across provinces and other factors that affect provincial wage rates. We need to examine the robustness of results with the inclusion of other factors.

The first experiment we conduct is adding provincial dummies into the wage equation to capture the differences across provinces. Then we explicitly consider the regional effects. We use educational level to indicate regional human capital development and capture the technology differences. Historically, educational level is higher on the coast than in the rest of China, though after 1978, the gap increased. Investment on the coast is more than double that of the interior and, in particular, there is more foreign direct investment flowing in because central government policies favour

---

[18] Processing market access measures the proximity of a province exporting processed goods to its international markets. Ordinary market access measures the proximity of a province exporting ordinary goods to its international markets. Processing supplier access measures the proximity of a province importing processing materials from supplier of manufactured goods. Ordinary supplier access measures the proximity of a province importing ordinary goods from supplier of manufactured good.

the coastal areas. We thus use a preferential policy index to represent the preferential policy and explicitly consider the policy effect.[19]

The construction of market access and supplier access involves international trade, which implies that we are measuring the provincial market access and supplier access to the international market, and the domestic supply and demand are ignored.[20] Instead of taking the domestic forces into account in the computation of market access and supplier access, we address the effect of domestic demand in the wage equation. The dataset we use is panel data, twenty-nine provinces over eleven years, but we will not consider time dummies. In the process of estimating the gravity equation, we observed the increasing volumes of exports and imports over the years. We think the coefficients associated with regional dummies pick up the dynamic changes, and they are carried into the estimated market access and supplier access. Therefore time dimensions are embodied in market access and supplier access and, hence, we omit time dummies in the robustness test.

11.5. DATA

We have three data sources. The first is disaggregate Chinese trade data obtained from the Customs General Administration, as part of the project described in Feenstra *et al.* (1998). This data source provides the value and quantity of exports and imports under the ordinary trade regime and the processing trade regime broken down by Chinese provinces for 1988–98. The trade data is five-digit SITC for 1988–91, six-digit HS for 1992–6, and eight-digit HS for 1997–8.

The second is the *China Statistical Yearbook* (CSPH various) which provides other economic variables for the provinces, such as average nominal wage rates, wage rates in the manufacturing sector, population, GDP, education level, and retail price deflators. The detailed definitions of these variables are presented in the Appendix. The arc distance data is obtained from the Internet.[21]

11.6. ESTIMATION RESULTS

11.6.1. *Gravity Equation*

The first stage of estimation is the gravity equation. We estimate the gravity eqns (11.15) and (11.17) annually. For some of the small countries we have not been able to obtain the longitude and latitude to calculate the distance and, therefore, these small countries and islands have been dropped from the sample. Given the detailed information on Chinese international trade, we aggregate export and import data up to

---

[19] The preferential policy index is constructed in Démurger *et al.* (2001).
[20] This is due to the lack of information on the interprovincial transactions.
[21] We obtain each location's latitude and longitude from www.mapblast.com/myblast/index.mb, and www.nau.edu/~cvm/latlongdist.html provides the distance calculation.

Table 11.5. *Gravity equation in 1995*

	Log value of:			
	Processing export (1)	Ordinary export (2)	Processing import (3)	Ordinary import (4)
Using arc distance				
Log(distance)	−1.139	−0.605	−1.508	−0.982
	[6.4]**	[4.5]**	[5.7]**	[3.3]**
Using internal–external distance				
Log(dist_i)	−0.618	−0.443	−0.423	−0.535
	[9.4]**	[16.5]**	[3.9]**	[4.95]**
Log(dist_e)	−0.696	−0.428	−0.599	−0.706
	[4.6]**	[3.77]**	[2.73]**	[2.72]**
Province dummy	Yes	Yes	Yes	Yes
Partner dummy	Yes	Yes	Yes	Yes
Observations	1,805	2,923	1,031	1,082
R^2	0.8	0.8	0.6	0.7

Notes: The table shows the estimation results in 1995. The estimated coefficients of external distance in other years are not all significant. *t*-statistics are in parentheses. *Significant at 5%; **significant at 1%.

the provincial level under two different trade regimes. The value of trade is converted into Chinese currency and deflated using the retail price index.

Table 11.5 reports the gravity equation estimation for 1995 using arc distance and internal–external distance. We are interested in the effect of different trade regimes; therefore, the dependent variables are the log values of processing exports, ordinary exports, processing imports, and ordinary imports, respectively. Independent variables include the distance between the Chinese province and its trading partner, Chinese province dummies, and each province's trading partner dummies. The estimated coefficients of distances, arc distance and internal–external distance, are correctly signed and statistically significant at the 1 per cent level. This is consistent with the hypothesis that location lends to more trading with nearby markets. The model explains 80 per cent of the cross-section variation in the export data, 60 per cent of the variation in processing import data, and 70 per cent of the variation in ordinary import data. We use the estimated coefficients of trade partner dummies to construct market access and supplier access variables, which are used as the explanatory variables in the second stage regressions.

The constructed market access and supplier access increase over the years, given the fact that China is gradually integrating into the world economy. Using the results in Guangdong as an example, Fig. 11.3 depicts the evolution of market access and supplier access under the processing trade regime for 1988–98. And other provinces, especially the provinces on the coast, have very similar patterns. The results from the ordinary trade regime follow the same increasing trend. Figure 11.4 presents the

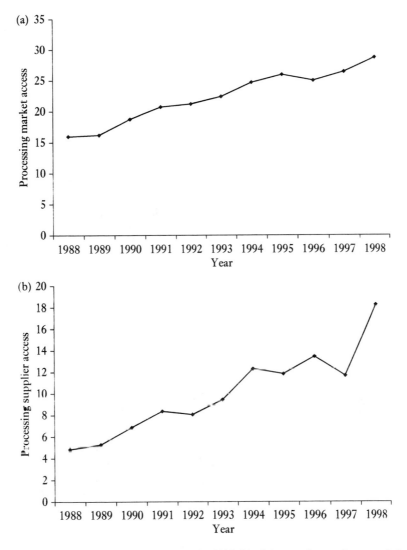

Figure 11.3. *Processing indices in Guangdong for 1988–98: (a) processing market access index and (b) processing supplier access index*

estimated market access across twenty-nine provinces in 1995. Light columns refer to market access in the coastal provinces, whereas the dark columns refer to market access in the interior provinces. Figure 11.4(a) presents the processing market access index. Almost all the coastal provinces have higher levels of processing market access than the interior provinces, except Hainan Island. Figure 11.4(b) shows a similar pattern as Fig. 11.4(a) but the variation in ordinary market access across provinces is smaller than those in processing market access.

(a)

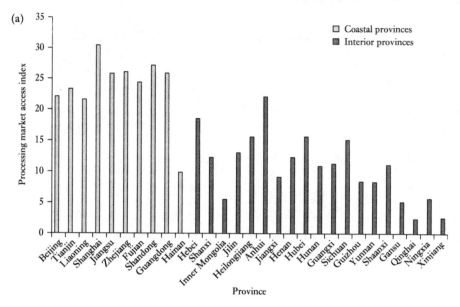

(b)

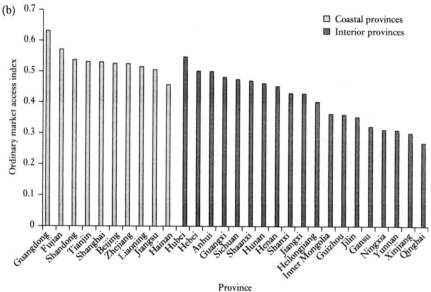

Figure 11.4. *Market access index in 1995: (a) processing market access index and (b) ordinary market access index*

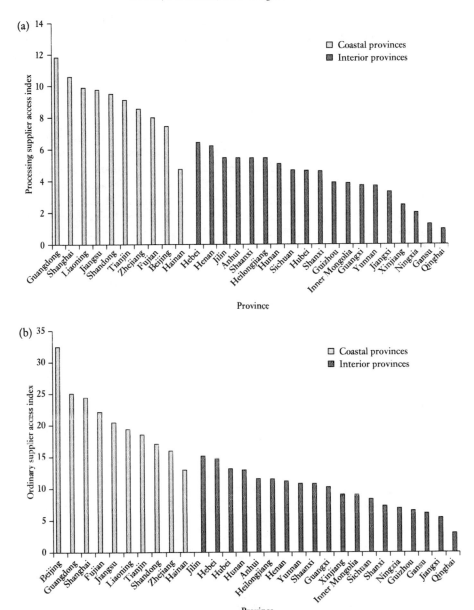

Figure 11.5. *Supplier access index in 1995: (a) processing supplier access index and (b) ordinary supplier access index*

Figure 11.5 presents the estimated supplier access across twenty-nine provinces in 1995. In both panels, the coastal provinces have a higher level of supplier access. The ordinary supplier access in Beijing reaches the highest level, which is consistent with our calculation in Table 11.3.

11.6.2. *Wage Equation: Basic Model*

The second stage of estimation is the wage equation. We use two different wage rate measures; the average provincial real wage rate and the average real wage rate in the manufacturing sector. The independent variables are processing market access, ordinary market access, processing supplier access, and ordinary supplier access. In the first stage, we estimate the gravity equation using different measures of distance, therefore we have two sets of estimated market access and supplier access. One is from the arc distance, and the other from the internal–external distance. We also estimate the basic wage equation using only processing trade data or ordinary trade data.

Table 11.6 presents the estimation results for the wage equation. The dependent variable is the log of average provincial real wage rate. The independent variables in the first three columns are market access and supplier access estimated using arc distance, and those in the other three columns are from the internal–external distance. Columns (1) and (4) show the results of regressing provincial real wage rate on estimated

Table 11.6. *Basic wage equation: real wage rate*

	Using arc distance			Using internal–external distance		
	(1)	(2)	(3)	(4)	(5)	(6)
Log(processing market access)	0.022 [5.24]**	0.027 [5.40]**		0.073 [8.94]**	0.023 [3.16]**	
Log(ordinary market access)	−0.01 [1.0]		0.005 [0.63]	−0.09 [0.31]**		−0.01 [1.15]
Log(processing supplier access)	0.021 [7.0]**	0.018 [6.0]**		0.023 [4.07]**	0.022 [4.78]**	
Log(ordinary supplier access)	0.022 [3.67]**		0.024 [4.86]**	0.042 [7.96]**		0.034 [7.80]**
Constant	7.309 [114.0]**	7.213 [323.80]**	7.139 [115.98]**	7.44 [101.93]**	7.06 [241.13]**	7.219 [103.35]**
Observations	317	317	319	317	317	319
R^2	0.20	0.12	0.08	0.35	0.19	0.1

Note: This table shows the estimation results for the basic wage equation. The dependent variable is the log of provincial real wage rate. Standard errors are corrected by using bootstrap techniques and *t*-statistics are in parentheses. * significant at 5%; ** significant at 1%.

processing market access, ordinary market access, processing supplier access, and ordinary supplier access using ordinary least square (OLS). Columns (2) and (5) consider the effects under processing trade regime, while columns (3) and (6) present the results only for ordinary trade regime. The coefficients on processing market access, processing supplier access, and ordinary supplier access are positive and statistically significant at the 1 per cent level in all specifications of wage equations.

We think the internal–external distance is a more precise measurement of the transportation costs than arc distance is. And we do find that the market access and supplier access constructed using the internal–external distance have larger effects on the real wage rate than those constructed using the arc distance. It holds for processing trade and ordinary trade. We also expect that processing market access and supplier access have stronger impact on the wage rate than ordinary market access and supplier access as the processing trade is involved in labour-intensive industries. This is true for processing market access, not for ordinary market access.

Table 11.7 presents the estimation results for the wage equation using the average real wage rate in the manufacturing sector. The structure of Table 11.7 is the same as Table 11.6. We find that, in any specification, the coefficients in Table 11.7 are smaller than those in Table 11.6. This is because the trade data includes both manufacturing and non-manufacturing sectors. The estimated market access and supplier access obtained from the gravity equation reflect the potential demand for all kinds of goods, not only

Table 11.7. *Basic wage equation: real wage rate in manufacturing sector*

	Using arc distance			Using internal–external distance		
	(1)	(2)	(3)	(4)	(5)	(6)
Log(processing market access)	0.014 [3.5]**	0.018 [3.91]**		0.057 [7.52]**	0.021 [3.24]**	
Log(ordinary market access)	−0.004 [0.57]		0.007 [0.92]	−0.056 [0.25]		0.007 [0.07]
Log(processing supplier access)	0.016 [5.33]**	0.014 [5.19]**		0.015 [2.84]**	0.019 [4.8]**	
Log(ordinary supplier access)	0.018 [3.91]**		0.019 [3.96]**	0.038 [7.83]**		0.03 [7.63]**
Constant	2.627 [43.76]**	2.578 [126.03]**	2.5 [44.56]**	2.67 [39.07]**	2.43 [92.35]**	2.51 [39.57]**
Observations	316	316	318	316	316	318
R^2	0.14	0.08	0.06	0.3	0.12	0.08

Note: This table shows the estimation results for the basic wage equation. The dependent variable is the log of provincial real wage rate in manufacturing sector. Standard errors are corrected by using bootstrap techniques and *t*-statistics are in parentheses. * significant at 5%; ** significant at 1%.

manufactured products. Thus, the effect of market access and supplier access on the provincial real wage rate, which reflects the general level of purchasing power during a certain period of time, is stronger than on the real wage rate in the manufacturing sector.

11.6.3. *Robustness Test*

First, we consider the robustness of results including regional effects. The regional effects capture all the differences across the provinces. The dependent variable is the average provincial real wage rate and the independent variables are processing market access, ordinary market access, processing supplier access, and ordinary supplier access. Columns (1) and (3) in Table 11.8 copy the results in columns (1) and (4) of Table 11.6, which are the results of the basic wage equation. Columns (2) and (4) report the estimation results including regional effects. The estimated coefficients on processing market access, processing supplier access, and ordinary supplier access are still highly statistically significant. In terms of the magnitude, the estimated coefficients are similar or slightly smaller than in their counterparts. This indicates the estimation results in Table 11.6 are robust. The estimated coefficients on most regional dummy variables are negative, and the dummies for the interior provinces are statistically significant at the 1 per cent level.

Second, we consider the provincial level of education. The provincial educational level is measured by the ratio of the number of students enrolled in the institutions of higher education to the regional population. Table 11.9 presents the robustness results. Columns (1) and (3) reproduce the results of Table 11.6. Columns (2) and (4) present

Table 11.8. *Wage equation: robustness test a*

	Using arc distance		Using internal–external distance	
	(1)	(2)	(3)	(4)
Log(processing market access)	0.022	0.021	0.073	0.047
	[5.24]**	[7.0]**	[8.94]**	[4.31]**
Log(ordinary market access)	−0.01	−0.008	−0.09	−0.107
	[1.0]	[1.38]	[0.31]**	[-7.78]
Log(processing supplier access)	0.021	0.021	0.023	0.021
	[7.0]**	[10.5]**	[4.07]**	[3.92]**
Log(ordinary supplier access)	0.022	0.021	0.042	0.027
	[3.67]**	[5.25]**	[7.96]**	[4.19]**
Constant	7.309	7.509	7.44	7.509
	[114.0]**	[84.8]**	[101.93]**	[84.8]**
Observations	317	317	317	317
R^2	0.20	0.50	0.35	0.50

Note: This table presents the estimation results on wage equation after taking regional dummies into account. The dependent variable is the log of provincial real wage rate. Columns (1) and (3) are copied from Table 11.6. Columns (2) and (4) have the fixed effects. * significant at 5%; ** significant at 1%.

Table 11.9. *Wage equation: robustness test b*

	Using arc distance		Using internal–external distance	
	(1)	(2)	(3)	(4)
Log(processing market access)	0.022	0.016	0.073	0.051
	[5.24]**	[4.0]**	[8.94]**	[5.89]**
Log(ordinary market access)	−0.01	−0.011	−0.09	−0.09
	[1.0]	[1.5]	[0.31]**	[−6.70]**
Log(processing supplier access)	0.021	0.018	0.023	0.019
	[7.0]**	[6.0]**	[4.07]**	[3.54]**
Log(ordinary supplier access)	0.022	0.018	0.042	0.03
	[3.67]**	[3.6]**	[7.96]**	[5.65]**
Log(education)		0.182		0.141
		[6.84]**		[5.58]**
Constant	7.309	7.579	7.44	7.73
	[114.0]**	[114.5]**	[101.93]**	[89.07]**
Observations	317	317	317	317
R^2	0.20	0.4	0.35	0.42

Note: This table presents the estimation results on wage equation after taking education level into account. The dependent variable is the log of provincial real wage rate. * significant at 5%; ** significant at 1%.

the estimated results after considering education levels. The coefficients on market access and supplier access are still statistically significant at 1 per cent, except ordinary market access. The magnitudes are smaller than their counterparts. As expected, the educational level positively and significantly affects the wage rate. The effect of educational level on the wage rate is larger than market access and supplier access, indicating that the level of education is the main factor determining the wage rate.

Third, we introduce policy dummies into the wage equation. We use the preferential policy index constructed in Démurger *et al.* (2001), and add dummy variables to the wage equation to capture the different degrees of deregulation, which are determined by the central government's preferential policy. Table 11.10 reports the results; the main results are still robust including policy dummies, and the effect on the wage rate is smaller than the counterparts in Table 11.6. Policy dummies are all statistically significant at 1 per cent, and positively affect the regional wage rates. Similar to educational level, the effect of preferential policy on the wage rate is larger than market access and supplier access, implying that preferential policy plays an import role in determining wage rate.[22]

[22] We also conduct the robustness test by adding the level of foreign direct investment (FDI) to the wage equation. The effect of FDI overpowers all other variables. And FDI is closely associated with international trade, in particular processing trade, which leads to the endogeneity. Hence the reason why we do not report the robustness test result using FDI.

Table 11.10. *Wage equation: robustness test c*

	Using arc distance		Using internal–external distance	
	(1)	(2)	(3)	(4)
Log(processing market access)	0.022	0.013	0.073	0.05
	[5.24]**	[3.25]*	[8.94]**	[6.15]**
Log(ordinary market access)	−0.01	−0.004	−0.09	−0.068
	[−1.0]	[−0.44]	[0.31]**	[−4.87]**
Log(processing supplier access)	0.021	0.008	0.023	0.013
	[7.0]**	[1.98]*	[4.07]**	[2.37]*
Log(ordinary supplier access)	0.022	0.013	0.042	0.031
	[3.67]**	[2.16]**	[7.96]**	[6.12]**
Policy dummy 1		0.223		0.186
		[4.4]**		[4.36]**
Policy dummy 2		0.242		0.194
		[5.5]**		[0.037]**
Policy dummy 3		0.348		0.374
		[6.3]**		[6.95]**
Constant	7.309	7.021	7.44	7.23
	[114.0]**	[88.8]**	[101.93]**	[88.6]**
Observations	317	317	317	317
R^2	0.20	0.3	0.35	0.45

Note: This table shows the estimation results after taking the preferential policy into account. The preferential policy index is constructed in Démurger *et al.* (2001), which indicates the various degrees of preferential policies. They are expected to be positive. * significant at 5%; ** significant at 1%.

Fourth, we consider the spatial correlations. Until now, we were mainly concerned with market access and supplier access to international markets, ignoring market access and supplier access to the domestic market. This is due to the lack of information on the interprovincial trade. In the second stage, to some extent, we are able to pick up the domestic factors by considering the wage rates of the nearby provinces. For illustration, we are interested in the real wage rate in province A. Then we choose another two provinces, B and C, which are close to province A. We take the wage rates of provinces B and C into account when we estimate the wage rate in province A besides market access and supplier access. Table 11.11 shows that the spatial correlation does play a role in explaining the real wage rate. At the same time, market access and supplier access still statistically affect the real wage rate.

11.6.4. *Model Prediction*

The values of R^2 in Table 11.6 indicate that 20 per cent of wage differences from the national average real wage rate can be explained by market access and supplier access.

Table 11.11. *Wage equation: robustness test d*

	Using arc distance		Using internal–external distance	
	(1)	(2)	(3)	(4)
Log(processing market access)	0.022	0.02	0.073	0.055
	[5.24]**	[2.22]*	[8.94]**	[7.22]**
Log(ordinary market access)	−0.01	−0.008	−0.09	−0.083
	[−1.0]	[−0.7]	[0.31]**	[−6.21]**
Log(processing supplier access)	0.021	0.018	0.023	0.017
	[7.0]**	[5.0]*	[4.07]**	[3.04]*
Log(ordinary supplier access)	0.022	0.017	0.042	0.042
	[3.67]**	[2.4]**	[7.96]**	[10.33]**
Log(Wage $n1$)		0.019		0.013
		[0.44]		[0.49]
Log(Wage $n2$)		0.01		0.048
		[0.86]		[0.74]
Constant	7.309	7.33	7.44	7.76
	[114.0]**	[40.8]**	[101.93]**	[31.55]**
Observations	317	317	317	317
R^2	0.20	0.3	0.35	0.43

Note: This table shows the estimation results after considering the spatial correlation. The independent variables Wage $n1$ and Wage $n2$ refer to the wage rates in provinces that are close to the province we are interested in. * significant at 5%; ** significant at 1%.

Processing market access and supplier access explains 12 per cent, and ordinary market access and supplier access explains 8 per cent. We are also interested in the model's prediction on wage inequality for each individual province. Using the estimated coefficient in column (1) in Table 11.6, we predict the wage difference between provincial wage rate and the national average, and compare it with the wage difference obtained from observations.

Table 11.12 presents the results: column (1) is the wage difference obtained by observation; column (2) is the predicted wage difference using our model; and column (3) takes the ratio of the first two columns. The results show that the model can explain about 23 per cent of the wage difference in the coastal provinces and 5 per cent in the interior provinces. The model overpredicts the wage difference for a few provinces. Overpredicted provinces either have ports within the province or are located near a coastal province. According to the model, these provinces should have relatively high wage rates while in actuality, the wage rates in the overpredicted provinces are lower than the national average. This implies that other factors counteract the impact of geographic location.

Column (4) in Table 11.12 reports the variance explained by the whole sample and subsample sets. Using the subsample that only contains the observations on the coast,

Table 11.12. *Wage differences explained by the model in 1995*

Province	Wage difference (CNY/year)		Ratio (%), (3) = (2)/(1)	Variance (R^2) (%) (4)
	From observation (1)	From model (2)		
Total coastal				20
Beijing	674	136	20	
Tianjin	239	118	49	
Liaoning	−181	99	−55	
Shaihang	1,045	159	15	
Jiangsu	142	110	77	
Zhejiang	250	117	47	
Fujian	214	165	77	
Shandong	−124	136	−110	
Guangdong	771	235	30	
Hainan	−8	−7	80	
Average			23	24
Interior				
Hebei	−184	62	−33	
Shanxi	−304	−45	15	
Inner Mongolia	−418	−128	31	
Jilin	−291	−93	32	
Heilongjiang	−433	−47	11	
Anhui	−259	67	−26	
Jiangxi	−346	−63	18	
Henan	−319	−14	4	
Hubei	−194	87	−45	
Hunan	−178	−9	5	
Guangxi	40	3	8	
Sichuan	−1,443	9	−1	
Guizhou	−1,576	−124	8	
Yunnan	−1,613	−161	10	
Shaanxi	−1,457	−5	0	
Gansu	−1,627	−175	11	
Qinghai	−1,693	−241	14	
Ningxia	−1,632	−180	11	
Xinjiang	−1,649	−197	12	
Average			5	15

Note: Column (1) is calculated using the real wage rate in *China Statistics Yearbook 1996*. Column (2) is calculated using the estimated coefficients in Table 11.6. Column (4) is the R^2 obtained from regression results using the whole sample and subsample. CNY = China Yuan Renminbi.

market access and supplier access can explain 24 per cent of the wage difference in 1995, whereas it is 13 per cent for the interior provinces. Compared with the average level in column (3), which is obtained from the model prediction, the coastal wage variance directly calculated from the sample is almost the same as the model prediction, and the interior wage variance is higher than the model prediction. This implies that the model captures the location advantage endowed by the coastal provinces and explains a significant portion of the wage differences for the coastal provinces.

11.7. CONCLUSION

Despite China's remarkable economic growth over the last two decades, a substantial increase in interregional wage inequality has occurred, which has depressed the economic growth and led to social tension. The empirical results of this chapter support the model's prediction that geographic location matters in determining returns to labour. In particular, about one-quarter of the wage differences in the coastal provinces and 15 per cent of the wage differences in the interior provinces can be explained by the province's market access and supplier access. The results are robust after taking into account other forces that are also important in determining regional wage rates.

The international experience shows that industrialization can improve a location's market access and supplier access. Hanson (1998) provides strong evidence that wage differentials in Mexico declined after establishing new industry centres along the United States–Mexico border with Mexico's trade liberalization. China's government is now moving in this direction. A Western Region Development Office has been established, targeted at promoting economic development in the western region.[23] This study indicates that more specific efforts should be devoted to the forces that affect market access and supplier access, such as increasing infrastructure investment and reducing transportation costs.

Appendix A: Data Description

This Appendix describes data sources and explains variables used.

Sources of Data

I have three data sources. First is the Chinese trade data (1988–98) obtained from the Customs General Administration as part of the project described in Feenstra *et al.* (1998). This data source provides detailed information on Chinese international trade. It contains the commodity codes, countries of origin/destination, countries of purchase/sale, value, quantity, unit of quantity, customs regime, firm type, and province of import or export. Second is the *China Statistical Yearbook* (CSPH various)

---

[23] The Western Region Development Office was established by the State Council in 2000 to launch a comprehensive development strategy and to coordinate its implementation.

which provides retail price index, average wage of formal employees, and average wage of formal employees in the manufacturing sector. All these economic indicators are at the provincial level. Third is the *Almanac of China's Foreign Economic Relations and Trade* (MOFTEC various) which provides average exchange rate of the renminbi against the US dollar.

Definition and Explanation of Relevant Data

Retail price index reflects the general change in prices of retail commodities. The change and adjustment in retail prices directly affect living expenditure of urban and rural residents, government revenue, purchasing power of residents, and equilibrium of market supply and demand, and the proportion of consumption and accumulation.

Average wage of workers and staff refers to the average wage in money terms per person during certain periods of time for workers and staff of enterprises, institutions, and government agencies, which reflects the general level of wage income during a certain period of time.

Exchange rate is the average exchange rate of renminbi against the US dollar in the China Exchange Market.

The total value of imports and exports at customs refers to the value of commodities imported into and exported from China.

Education Level

The education level is indicated by the ratio of the number of students enrolled in institutions of higher education to the population. Institutions of higher education refer to establishments set up according to government evaluation and approval procedures, enrolling graduates from high schools and providing higher education courses and training for senior professionals. They include full-time universities, colleges, and higher/further education institutes.

Appendix B: Distance Construction

We construct two measures of distance. The first is a measure of arc distance, in which we assume that goods are directly transported along the minimum arc distance that connects two locations. The second is internal–external distance, in which we assume that goods are first delivered from a province to Tianjin, Shanghai, or Guangdong, the three busiest harbours in China, and from there exported out of China.

Arc distance. Arc distance is the distance from the capital of a province to the capital of a country. To calculate arc distance, we first obtain the latitude and longitude points for each location at www.mpablast.com/myblast/index.mb. Then we input the latitude and longitude into the formula, which is provided at www.nau.edu/~cvm/latlongdist.html, and obtain the arc distance between any pair of locations.

Internal–external distance. It takes into account the fact that the interior provinces first transport the goods to the economic centre or harbours by rail, and from there the goods are exported out of China. This alternative distance measure corrects the arc distance measure (which ignores the geographic feature that the interior provinces are land-locked). The internal distance is the journey time[24] between the interior province and the economic centre (Beijing) or harbour cities (Tianjin, Shanghai, and Guangdong). The external distance is the shipping distance[25] from the harbour to the capitals of other countries.

REFERENCES

Anderson, J. and E. van Wincoop (2000). 'Gravity with Gravitas: A Solution to the Border Puzzle', *Boston College Working Papers in Economics* 485, Department of Economics, Boston College: Boston.

Berman, E., J. Bound, and Z. Griliches (1994). 'Changes in the Demand for Skilled Labour within US Manufacturing: Evidence from the Annual Survey of Manufactures', *Quarterly Journal of Economics*, 104: 367–98.

Borjas, G. J. and V. A. Ramey (1993). 'Foreign Competition, Market Power, and Wage Inequality: Theory and Evidence', *NBER Working Papers* 4556, National Bureau of Economic Research: Cambridge, MA.

Chen, J. and B. M. Fleisher (1996). 'Regional Income Inequality and Economic Growth in China', *Journal of Comparative Economics*, 22(2): 141–64.

Cragg, M. I. and M. Epelbaum (1996). 'Why Has Wage Dispersion Grown in Mexico? Is it the Incidence of Reforms or the Growing Demand for Skills?', *Journal of Development Economics*, 51: 99–116.

CSPH (China Statistical Publishing House) (various). *China Statistical Year Book*, China Statistical Publishing House: Beijing.

Davis, S and J. Haltiwanger (1991). 'Wage Dispersion Between and Within US Manufacturing Plants, 1963–1986', *Brookings Papers on Economic Activity, Microeconomics*, 3: 115–200.

Démurger, S., J. D. Sachs, W. T. Woo, S. Bao, G. Chang, and A. Mellinger (2001). 'Geography, Economic Policy and Regional Development in China', *Asian Economic Papers*, 1(1). 146–97.

Feenstra, R. C. and G. H. Hanson (1996). 'Foreign Investment, Outsourcing and Relative Wages', in R. C. Feenstra, G. M. Grossman, and D. A. Irwin (eds) *The Political Economy of Trade Policy: Papers in Honor of Jagdish Bhagwati*, MIT Press: Cambridge, MA.

—— and —— (1997). 'Foreign Direct Investment and Relative Wages: Evidence from Mexico's Maquiladoras', *Journal of International Economics*, 42: 371–94.

—— and —— (2001). 'Global Production Sharing and Rising Inequality: A Survey of Trade and Wages', *NBER Working Papers* 8372, National Bureau of Economic Research: Cambridge, MA.

——, H. Wen, W. T. Woo, and S. Yao (1998). 'The US–China Bilateral Trade Balance: Its Size and Determinants,' *NBER Working Papers* 6598, National Bureau of Economic Research: Cambridge, MA.

---

[24] Journey times are published in the official state railway time table.

[25] A world maritime transportation map was used for this purpose.

Freeman, R. and L. F. Katz (1994). 'Rising Wage Inequality: The United States vs. Other Advanced Countries', in R. Freeman (ed.) *Working Under Different Rules*, Russell Sage Foundation: New York.

Fujita, M., P. Krugman, and A. J. Venables (1999). *The Spatial Economy: Cities, Regions, and International Trade*, MIT Press: Cambridge, MA.

Hanson, G. H. (1996a). 'Localization Economies, Vertical Organization, and Trade', *American Economic Review*, 86(5): 1266–78.

—— (1996b). 'Economic Integration, Intra-industry Trade, and Frontier Regions', *European Economic Review*, 40(3–5): 941–9.

—— (1998).'Market Potential, Increasing Returns, and Geographic Concentration', *NBER Working Papers* 6429, National Bureau of Economic Research: Cambridge, MA.

—— and A. Harrison (1999). 'Trade, Technology, and Wage Inequality', *Industrial and Labour Relations Review*, 52(2): 271–88.

Harris, C. (1954). 'The Market as a Factor in the Localization of Industry in the United States', *Annals of the Association of American Geographers*, 44: 315–48.

Hsieh, C.-T. and K. T. Woo (1999). 'The Impact of Outsourcing to China on Hong Kong's Labour Market' (mimeo), Princeton University: New Jersey.

Hummels, D. (1995) 'Global Income Patterns: Does Geography Play a Role?', Ph.D. thesis, University of Michigan: Ann Arbor, chapter 2.

Hussain, A., P. Lanjouw, and N. Stern (1994) 'Income Inequalties in China: Evidence From Household Survey Data', *World Development*, 22(12): 1927–57.

Jian, T., J. D. Sachs, and A. M. Warner (1996). 'Trends in Regional Inequality in China', *NBER Working Paper* 5412, National Bureau of Economic Research: Cambridge, MA.

Kanbur, R. and X. Zhang (1999). 'Which Regional Inequality: Rural-Urban or Coast–Inland? An Application to China', *Journal of Comparative Economics*, 27: 686–701.

—— and —— (2001). 'Fifty Years of Regional Inequality in China: A Journey Through Evolution, Reform and Openness', *CEPR Working Papers* 2887, Centre for Economic Policy Research: London.

Katz, L. F. and D. Autor (1999). 'Changes in the Wage Structure and Earnings Inequality', in Orley Ashenfleter and David Card (eds), *Handbook of Labour Economics*, 3(A): 1463–55.

—— and K. M. Murphy (1992). 'Changes in Relative Wages, 1963–1987: Supply and Demand Factors', *Quarterly Journal of Economics* 107: 35–78.

Khan, A. R., K. Griffin, C. Riskin, and R. Zhao (1993). 'Sources of Income Inequality in Post-Reform China', *China Economic Review*, 4(1): 19–35.

Krugman, P. and A. J. Venables (1995). 'Globalization and the Inequality of Nations', *Quarterly Journal of Economics*, 101: 857–80.

Lawrence, R. Z. and M. J. Slaughter (1993). 'International Trade and American Wages in the 1980s: Giant Sucking Sound or Small Hiccup?', *Brooking Papers on Economic Activity: Microeconomics*, 2: 161–226.

Leamer, E. E. (1993). 'Wage Effects of a US–Mexico Free Trade Agreement', in P. M. Garber (ed.) *The US–Mexico Free Trade Agreement*, MIT Press: Cambridge, MA.

—— (1994). 'Trade, Wages and Revolving Door Ideas', *NBER Work Papers* 4716, National Bureau of Economic Research: Cambridge, MA.

—— (1997). 'Access to Western Markets and Eastern Effort', in S. Zecchini (ed.) *Lesson from the Economic Transition, Central and Eastern Europe in the 1990s*, Kluwer Academic Publisher: Dordrecht.

MOFTEC (Ministry of Foreign Trade and Economic Co-operation) (various). *Almanac of China's Foreign Economic Relations and Trade*, China Foreign Economic Relations and Trade Publishing House: Beijing.

Moreno, R. and B. Trehan (1997). 'Location and the Growth of Nations', *Federal Reserve Bank of San Francisco Working Papers in Applied Economic Theory* 97–02.

Overman, H., S. Redding, and A. J. Venables (2001). 'Trade and Geography: a Survey of Empirics', *CEPR Working Papers* 2978, Centre for Economic Policy Research: London.

Redding, S. and A. J. Venables (2000). 'Economic Geography and International Inequality', *CEPR Working Papers* 2568, Centre for Economic Policy Research: London.

Tsui, K.-Y. (1998). 'Factor Decomposition of Chinese Rural Income Inequality: New Methodology, Empirical Findings, and Policy Implications', *Journal of Comparative Economics*, 26(3): 502–28.

Wood, A. (1994). *North–South Trade, Employment and Inequality*, Oxford University Press: Oxford.

12

Spatial Inequality for Manufacturing Wages in Five African Countries

DIRK WILLEM TE VELDE AND OLIVER MORRISSEY

014
015 018 R23
J31 L60

12.1. INTRODUCTION

Within the broad context of spatial inequality, this chapter examines the issue of inequality in manufacturing wages. Specifically, we ask if workers with similar characteristics are paid higher wages (in purchasing power terms) if employed by firms located in the capital city than if employed by firms located elsewhere. Available evidence suggests that poverty is higher, and average incomes lower, in some regions of a country than in others, and typically incomes are highest in and around the capital city (or the major city if it is not the administrative capital) for the countries we consider. To a large extent, spatial inequalities reflect rural–urban divides in earning opportunities associated with the sector composition of employment—higher paid jobs in manufacturing and services are concentrated in urban areas, whereas low-paid agriculture sector jobs are in rural areas. However, it may be the case that even within the manufacturing sector there are spatial inequalities in wages, and this is the issue we investigate.

The availability of large-scale surveys has supported a noticeable increase in research on manufacturing enterprises in Africa. Much of this was initiated with the World Bank and the bilateral donor-sponsored Regional Programme on Enterprise Development (RPED), which funded surveys in a number of African countries during the 1990s. We use data from the first three waves of surveys (1990–3) for five countries: Cameroon, Ghana, Kenya, Zambia, and Zimbabwe. A particular advantage of the RPED data is that there are two datasets, one at the firm level with information on firm characteristics, and the other containing data on individuals (earnings and employee characteristics). Our primary concern is with the information on individual employees, and the firm-level data is used to identify the characteristics of the firms in which they are employed

This chapter constitutes the revision of a paper prepared for the WIDER-Cornell-LSE Conference on Spatial Inequality, held at the London School of Economics, 27–29 June 2002. We are grateful to the Department for International Development (DFID) for funding under grant R8003, to CSAE for making available the data used, and to an anonymous referee for helpful comments. Views and opinions expressed are those of the authors alone.

(in particular whether there is foreign ownership). We examine if firms located in the capital city pay higher earnings for equivalent workers when compared with firms located elsewhere, controlling for relevant firm characteristics.

A number of recent studies analyse these surveys (e.g. Bigsten *et al.* 1997, 1999, 2000; Söderbom and Teal 2001*a*, *b*; Strobl and Thornton 2002), but most are primarily concerned with firm-level data and none specifically address the questions raised in this chapter. Bigsten *et al.* (2000) examine rates of return on physical and human capital whereas Mazumdar (1995) and Strobl and Thornton (2002), using the same cross-country dataset that we use, are more concerned with the effect of firm size. te Velde and Morrissey (2001) use the same data to study the effect of foreign ownership on earnings. This chapter follows the same general approach and includes control variables identified as important in the previous studies, but with a focus on the effect of location on earnings and earnings differentials.

We do not present measures of spatial inequality, but rather present some evidence on location differences in manufacturing earnings. Although we do not know where firms not located in the capital city were actually based, the presumption is that most of the firms were located in other urban areas rather than in rural areas. Unfortunately, most of the information on spatial differences in inequality and poverty refers to rural–urban and/or regional differences. We review some evidence on Ghana and Zambia to give an indication of the magnitudes. As we in effect identify the wage premium of being employed in the capital city, to evaluate the significance of this we would like data on price or cost of living differences between the capital city and other urban areas. Such data were unavailable, requiring us to make a judgement on the likely magnitude of price differentials.

McCulloch *et al.* (2000) show that there were significant rural–urban and regional differences in poverty and inequality in Zambia in 1991. Mean per adult equivalent real consumption in urban areas was some three times the level of that in rural areas. They estimate, again for 1991, that some 70 per cent of the national population were below the upper poverty line; this figure was almost 90 per cent in rural areas but 47 per cent in urban areas (although there was a dramatic increase in urban poverty during the 1990s). Rural inequality was at the national level with a Gini of 0.56, compared to 0.45 in urban areas. The three most urbanized provinces (Copperbelt, Central, and Lusaka) had Ginis ranging from 0.47 to 0.52, whereas in rural provinces Ginis were mostly about 0.6. The general perception that poverty and inequality are higher in rural areas is confirmed for Zambia. However, as poverty and inequality are similar in the urbanized provinces, there is no reason to assume large price differentials between the capital city and other urban areas (where firms are likely to be located).

Coulombe and McKay (2001) compare poverty and inequality in Ghana between 1991–2 and 1998–9. Overall inequality increased, especially in rural areas, while inequality in Accra fell. Thus, urban–rural inequality rose. Almost 20 per cent of overall inequality was due to inequality between locations. They note that inequality fell for formal sector employees. Of greater relevance for our purposes, they report data on cost-of-living indices that suggest that the cost of living in Accra is about 12 per cent higher than in other urban areas. The corresponding differential may be even higher in Kenya. The average monthly basic minimum wage in Nairobi was 1,706 Kenyan Shillings in 1992, whereas that in other (small, rural) towns was 1,343, some 20 per cent lower (Republic of Kenya 1995) which does not give comparable price data.

We would expect to find that wages are higher in the capital city, if only because the cost of living is higher than in other urban areas. While there is no evidence that such a differential exists in Zambia, the differential is in the range of 10–20 per cent for Ghana and Kenya. Our aim is to see if the capital city premium is at least what would be explained by price differences, and to elicit some of the other factors that may explain higher capital city wages. We present estimates of a 'raw' and a 'pure' premium. The raw premium is the difference in the wage paid to similar workers, in terms of educational qualification or skill level. The pure premium adjusts this to control for the possibility that the types of firms that pay higher wages, such as larger or foreign-owned firms, are more likely to locate in the capital city.

The structure of the chapter is as follows. Section 12.2 presents some issues in the literature relating to wage inequality, identifying reasons why wages may be higher in the capital. This is brief as the literature has not specifically addressed the issue of spatial inequality. Section 12.3 then presents the wage determination model, essentially a Mincerian framework. Section 12.4 discusses the data and presents our results, assessing whether the location premium benefits specific types of workers. Conclusions are presented in Section 12.5 with a discussion of the significance of the location premium estimated.

12.2. FACTORS INFLUENCING SPATIAL INEQUALITY IN MANUFACTURING WAGES

There are at least three general reasons why workers employed by firms located in the capital city may earn higher wages than workers employed by firms located elsewhere. First, the distribution of *worker* characteristics may be skewed towards a particular location. While we can control for observed characteristics, such as educational attainment (level of schooling reached) or experience (measured as tenure), and therefore compare 'similar workers' (i.e. those with similar characteristics), there may be important unobserved factors. For example, workers in the capital city may be more motivated or better educated (e.g. urban schools may give better quality teaching, or the workers may have had higher exam marks) and are therefore paid more. Such unobserved characteristics will be part of any observed differences in earnings for apparently similar workers.

Second, the distribution of *firm* characteristics may be skewed towards a particular location and such features of firms can be associated with higher wages. Much of the literature on wage inequality is concerned with the effects of size and foreign ownership, especially foreign direct investment (FDI) by multinationals. Two issues arise. Do foreign or larger firms pay higher wages than local firms to similar workers? And do foreign or larger firms contribute to increasing wage inequality between skilled and unskilled workers? We will consider some of these issues indirectly, insofar as we account for size and ownership in the wage equations.

The literature on multinationals suggests that the presence of a firm-specific asset explains in part the observation of a wage differential between foreign-owned and local firms (Dunning 1993). Affiliates of multinationals use more up to date technologies, require more skilled workers, have access to better inputs, are more productive, face lower capital costs, and hence can pay more. But there are also other reasons for a wage differential (see te Velde and Morrissey 2001). Foreign firms may be more profitable than local firms and, as Blanchflower *et al.* (1996) argue, earnings can be positively correlated to profits, which is shown empirically in the case of Ghana (Söderbom and Teal 2001*a*). The firm characteristics that are known to be associated with higher earnings may be correlated with location in the capital city. In particular, workers in larger firms (measured by employment) have higher earnings—the 'size premium' identified by te Velde and Morrissey (2001) and Strobl and Thornton (2002), among others. Similarly, te Velde and Morrissey (2001) identify a 'foreign premium' as foreign-owned firms pay higher wages to equivalent workers. We will test for the possibility that firms with such characteristics, larger and/or foreign-owned, are more likely to locate in capital cities. This accounts for differences in the raw and pure premium in earnings for those employed in capital cities.

Third, workers in capital cities may earn higher wages than similar workers employed by similar firms located outside the capital city. This could simply be to compensate for a higher cost of living. Higher wages in the presence of a higher cost of living will help to maintain the balance between centrifugal and centripetal forces (see Krugman and Livas 1996; and Fujita *et al.* 1999). If wages are too high compared to consumer prices, firms may locate elsewhere. Similarly, if wages are too low compared to consumer prices, workers may choose to work elsewhere. Consumer prices may be higher in the capital city than elsewhere, therefore earnings have to be higher to maintain purchasing power. While we use a measure of real earnings, this is constructed from an aggregate country deflator and therefore does not capture regional price variations. We do not have information on regional price variability that is compatible with our wage data, and cannot account for this directly. We will consider if any estimated location premium (higher earnings in the capital city) is consistent with plausible magnitudes of regional price variations. Significant long-run variations in real earnings across space is only possible when labour markets are sufficiently segmented spatially, otherwise worker migration and/or firm location would erode the differential.

However, keeping a balance between centrifugal and centripetal forces does not explain the existence of a spatial wage differential in the first place. There are two different explanations for such wage differential and to distinguish between these explanations would require information on the effects of on earnings as well as productivity.[1] One possible reason is that unionization, or bargaining power more generally, is greater in the capital city. In other words, there are location reasons why wages (not productivity) in the capital city may be higher for similar workers. This may apply to a larger extent to skilled workers who would otherwise be poached by

---

[1] This study concentrates on the effects of location on earnings and, hence, may not be able to distinguish between both explanations appropriately.

other firms. Firms would not be able to afford paying higher wages over the long-run unless compensated for this in the form of lower costs for other inputs or in the form of higher production efficiency.

Another possible reason for higher wages in capital cities for otherwise similar workers is that capital cities may enhance the productivity of firms and workers within firms. Hence, firms in capital cities can afford to pay more to their workers than firms located elsewhere, in the short as well as the long-run. Urban economies may lead to greater production efficiency as they exhibit increasing returns to scale associated with three types of agglomeration economies (Wheaton and Lewis 2002). Urbanization economies could arise if larger cities provide more direct support services and industrial linkages. Localization economies may arise from knowledge transferred between firms in the same industry, through direct contact or spatial proximity, and could enhance skill accumulation and productivity. There may also be localization scale economies if agglomeration improves labour market search and matching, which in turn enhances specialization and productivity.[2] Agglomeration economies may lead to static or dynamic improvements in productivity, which can then lead to higher wages. It could be that skilled workers are able to capture more of such productivity gains through their ability to learn more from contacts than less-skilled workers, in which case skilled workers could benefit more from being employed by firms in the capital city.

12.3. LOCATION AND THE EARNINGS FUNCTION

We use and extend the framework of Mincer (1974) to examine the effects of location on earnings of individuals. This basic framework has been applied by Bigsten *et al.* (2000) and te Velde and Morrissey (2001) to the database we use. The starting point is to estimate the following equation:

$$\log(Y_{it}) = \alpha + \sum_j r_j S_{ij} + \beta_1 \text{age}_{it} + \beta_2 \text{age}_{it}^2 + \gamma_1 \text{ten}_{it} + \gamma_2 \text{ten}_{it}^2 + \varepsilon_{it}, \qquad (12.1)$$

where Y_{it} is a measure of the wage of individual $i = 1, \ldots, N$ at time $t = 1, \ldots, T$. S_{ij} is a binary dummy which is 1 for the highest level j of education completed (or number of years of schooling in the original Mincerian framework)—we include all levels of education except the first (no education), hence $j = 1, \ldots, \mathcal{J} - 1$, and r_j is the rate of return to the completion of education level j. Experience is captured by employee's age and ten, the number of years employed by the current firm (tenure), and the squared terms allow for non-linear effects. The substance of this chapter is to include location in (12.1) in a number of ways to assess the effect on earnings.

---

[2] Glaeser and Mare (1994) distinguish between two types of (dynamic) location economies. They find that faster urban wage growth can be explained by faster skill accumulation not by improved labour market outcomes in cities.

The first extension is to include a binary dummy $LOCC_i = 1$ if the firm in which individual i is employed in the capital city, and zero otherwise:

$$\log(Y_{it}) = \alpha + \sum_j r_j S_{ij} + \beta_1 age_{it} + \beta_2 age_{it}^2 + \gamma_1 ten_{it} + \gamma_2 ten_{it}^2 + \varphi LOCC_i + \varepsilon_{it}.$$

$$(12.2)$$

The coefficient φ is the percentage increase in earnings enjoyed by individual i because he or she is employed in a firm located in the capital—what we term the raw premium. The coefficient φ may overstate the true effects if location is correlated with control variables (Z_k, the firm characteristics such as size, foreign ownership, sector, etc.) that are positively correlated with the dependent variable. For example, it may be the case that larger firms locate in the capital city and it is established that there is a size premium in earnings. Thus, the coefficient on LOCC may be in part or wholly due to the fact that large firms locate in the capital city. A similar argument applies in the case of foreign-owned firms. Equation (12.3) therefore includes firm-level control variables ($k = 1, \ldots, K$).

$$\log(Y_{it}) = \alpha + \sum_J r_j S_{ij} + \beta_1 age_{it} + \beta_2 age_{it}^2 + \gamma_1 ten_{it} + \gamma_2 ten_{it}^2$$

$$+ \varphi_k LOCC_i + \sum_k \zeta_k Z_{ik} + \varepsilon_{it}. \qquad (12.3)$$

We then estimate (12.4) to assess whether the raw premium ($= \varphi_k$ in eqn (12.3)) occurs for workers in all sectors (control variables $Z_{SEC,l}$ equal 1 for sector $l = 1, \ldots, L$ and 0 otherwise), or workers in some sectors only.

$$\log(Y_{it}) = \alpha + \sum_J r_j S_{ij} + \beta_1 age_{it} + \beta_2 age_{it}^2 + \gamma_1 ten_{it} + \gamma_2 ten_{it}^2$$

$$+ \sum_l \varphi_l LOCC_i Z_{i,SEC,l} + \sum_k \zeta_k Z_{ik} + \varepsilon_{it}. \qquad (12.4)$$

Regression eqn (12.5) estimates (12.3), but interacts the variable LOCC with education level S (here for $j = 1, \ldots, J$) to assess whether location is beneficial for individuals regardless of the level of education completed.

$$\log(Y_{it}) = \alpha + \sum_{j=1,\ldots,J-1} r_j S_{ij} \beta_1 age_{it} + \beta_2 age_{it}^2 + \gamma_1 ten_{it} + \gamma_1 ten_{it}^2$$

$$+ \sum_{j=1,\ldots,J} \varphi_j LOCC_i S_{ij} + \sum_k \zeta_k Z_{ik} + \varepsilon_{it}. \qquad (12.5)$$

Finally, (12.6) repeats (12.5) but replaces levels of education with types of occupation (SKILLOCCUP = skilled occupations such as managers, supervisors, sales workers, and administrators, while other occupations are defined as less skilled) to assess whether foreign ownership affects individuals equally regardless of the type of occupation.

Given possible explanations discussed earlier, φ_j in eqn (12.6) could be higher with more complex and skilled occupations if skilled workers in capital cities are better at skill accumulation or better at wage bargaining than less-skilled workers in capital cities.

$$\log(Y_{it}) = \alpha + \sum_{j=1,\ldots,J-1} r_j S_{ij} + \beta_1 \text{age} + \beta_2 \text{age}^2 + \gamma_1 \text{ten} + \gamma_2 \text{ten}^2$$

$$+ \sum_{j=1,\ldots,J} \varphi_j \text{LOCC}_i \text{SKILLOCCUP}_{ij} + \sum_k \zeta_k Z_k + \varepsilon_{it}. \qquad (12.6)$$

When using the interaction terms between location and occupation/education we assume that observable worker and firm characteristics are the only determinants of worker earnings. If this is not so, for instance, if unobservable worker or firm characteristics affect earnings, the φ_j coefficients will be biased if location is correlated with the unobservables. One could allow for firm-specific effects by first differencing and availing of the panel nature of the firm-level data (e.g. Söderbom and Teal 2001a). However, it is not possible to allow for worker-specific effects as we have data on a repeated cross-section basis and not a panel for individual employees. The same firms are interviewed over time, but the workers interviewed within these firms are not necessarily the same.[3]

12.4. DATA DESCRIPTION AND RESULTS

The data in this chapter draw from firm-level surveys in Cameroon, Ghana, Kenya, Zambia, and Zimbabwe as part of the RPED conducted in repeated waves during the 1990s. In the dataset (which is available on the CSAE website) we used, there are three years (waves) of data for most of the five countries, covering firms in four manufacturing sectors: food, timber, textiles, and metal. The dataset includes formal and informal firms of various sizes, and is thought to be representative of the manufacturing sector in the respective countries.

We link two datasets, one containing data on firm characteristics (RPED), such as location, sector, ownership structure, and another containing data on individuals, such as education, occupation, tenure, age, and earnings. The two databases can be linked through a country-specific firm identifier in addition to data on waves. The data relate to two or three different years, and as there are insufficient time series, we pooled data across waves and focus on a static framework. Our core variable of interest is firms located in the capital city (LOCC = 1, otherwise 0). Other control variables are included. For example, the variable FOR is a 0/1 dummy to define if a firm is foreign-owned.

We use monthly earnings data (wages and benefits) in current domestic prices as the 'wage' variable, the measure commonly applied in studies using this data. The dependent variable in the regression analysis is in logs. An important part of the analysis

---

[3] Strobl and Thornton (2002) note that as some workers are interviewed more than once, there is a potential for correlated errors if multiple observations for the same worker are included. They try to test for this with the Ghanaian data and find no evidence for a bias in results.

in this chapter relates to the education and occupation variables. The data distinguish between five different levels of education: no education, some primary education, primary education completed, secondary education completed, and university. The data also distinguish occupation categories, which we allocate as skilled or unskilled (see te Velde and Morrissey 2001).

Appendix Table 12.A1 compares the mean of the log of earnings of workers in the capital city and elsewhere. It shows that average wages are higher in the capital city for all countries. As hypothesized previously, part of the explanation is in the *distribution of worker characteristics* across space: in all five countries the average number of years of formal schooling is higher for workers in the capital city than for workers elsewhere.

The distribution of firm characteristics across space is also likely to contribute to higher earnings in the capital city (the raw premium). Summary data on the sample classified according to location, ownership, and firm size is provided in Appendix Table 12.A2. This relates to a total of 2,824 firms (the regressions are based on employees linked to firms, hence the sample is much larger), 58 per cent are located in the capital city and 42 per cent are not. The sample is fairly evenly spread over the countries, largely reflecting their relative sizes: 25 per cent of firms are from Cameroon; 23 per cent from Kenya; 20 per cent from Zimbabwe; 18 per cent from Ghana; and 14 per cent from Zambia. Zambia is the only country for which fewer firms are located in the capital city (probably reflecting the importance of the copperbelt provinces), while the proportions are fairly even in Ghana. Considering all countries together, about 20 per cent of firms are owned by foreigners and such firms are more likely to be located in the capital city than are local firms (for all countries except Zambia).

There is a general tendency for larger firms to be located in the capital city, especially foreign-owned firms. This is not true for the largest size category (firms with more than 500 employees) overall, but is true if we define larger firms as those with more than fifty employees. Only in Zimbabwe are the largest firms more likely to be in the capital city; in Cameroon they are clearly less likely to be in the capital city, while for the other countries the number of firms in this category is very small. In all countries the smallest firms (ten or fewer employees) are almost all locally owned. In Cameroon and Kenya they are more likely to be in the capital city, in Ghana and Zimbabwe they are less likely, while numbers are evenly split in Zambia.

Table 12.1 presents the results of a simple logit estimation to see which characteristics are significantly correlated with location in the pooled sample (i.e. pooling all five countries). Allowing for country and sector effects, we find that in our sample larger firms tend to locate in the capital city but there is no significant tendency for foreign-owned firms to locate in the capital. As compared to Cameroon, firms are less likely to be located in the capital in Zambia and Zimbabwe and, to a lesser extent, Ghana. Firms in the metal sector appear most likely to locate in the capital.

Table 12.2 summarizes the results of estimating eqns (12.1)–(12.6) for manufacturing in five African countries.[4] The first row of Table 12.2 presents estimates of (12.2), the

---

[4] We began by estimating (12.1) for each country to check whether our results are consistent with those reported in Table 12.4 of the working paper version of Bigsten *et al.* (2000). The results were the same except

Table 12.1. *Influences on likelihood of location in capital*

Country	Logit regression
Ghana	−0.20 (−1.0)*
Kenya	0.14 (0.8)
Zambia	−0.71 (−3.6)*
Zimbabwe	−0.64 (−3.2)*
Foreign-owned firm	0.15 (1.2)
Wood and furniture sector	0.14 (1.1)
Textile sector	0.06 (0.4)
Metal sector	0.26 (2.3)*
Log(employment)	0.21 (6.3)*
Share of non-production workers	0.48 (1.6)
Constant	−0.4 (−1.8)
N	2,060
Maximum likelihood	−1,354.02

Notes: Cameroon is the omitted country, food the omitted sector. White heteroskedasticity-consistent, t-statistics in parenthesis; *indicates significance at least at the 5% level. Dependent variable = 1 if LOCC, 0 otherwise.

Source: Authors' computations.

raw premium. The effects of location are positive, substantial, and significant in all regressions. Earnings for individuals in firms located in the capital city are 34 per cent higher in Kenya, 32 per cent in Ghana, 19 per cent higher in Cameroon, 16 per cent in Zimbabwe, and 13 per cent in Zambia. The second row of Table 12.2 presents estimates of specification (12.3), confirming that the effects of LOCC on earnings are reduced when taking firm-specific control variables into account. Nevertheless, the pure location premium remains quite large at 12 per cent in Zimbabwe, 15 per cent in Cameroon and Zambia, 26 per cent in Ghana, and 28 per cent in Kenya. The location premium applies to all workers in Ghana and Kenya, but to skilled workers only in the other countries. There are no consistent patterns by sector of firm or education of workers.

12.4.1. *What Type of Worker Benefits from Spatial Inequality?*

To assess if the earnings 'premium' from location applies equally to different types of worker, we first estimate (12.4). The results, in row four of Table 12.2, suggest that the earnings premium does differ by sector for Ghana, Kenya, and Zimbabwe.

for minor differences, such as values of t-statistics, which may be due to the use of a different statistical package. Most coefficients are well determined and consistent with expectations. Details are available on request—we report here only the main results.

Table 12.2. *Summary of main results from wage equations*

	Cameroon	Ghana	Kenya	Zambia	Zimbabwe
LOCC premium					
No controls	0.19	0.32	0.34	0.13	0.16
Firm controls	0.15	0.26	0.28	0.15	0.12
Which workers?					
Sectors	ns	Wood	Wood	ns	Metal
		Food	Metal		Food
			Textiles		
			Food		
Education	ns	ns	No	ns	ns
			Education		
			Primary		
			Secondary		
Occupation	Skilled	Skilled	Skilled	Skilled	Skilled
		Less-skilled	Less-skilled		

Notes: Summary of results from Tables 12.2–12.6; ns implies non-significant differences in coefficients (based on *P*-values). LOCC premium is coefficient on LOCC in specifications (12.2), no controls, and (12.3), with firm-specific controls. Sectors are the significant interactive (LOCC*sector) terms in specification (12.4). Education are the significant interactive (LOCC*education) terms in specification (12.5). Occupation gives the significant interactive (LOCC*occupation) categories in specification (12.6): skilled or less-skilled occupations.

Source: Authors' computations.

The *P*-values (for *F*-tests) are smaller than 5 per cent, implying that the null hypothesis of equal coefficients (on sector*LOCC) can be rejected for these three countries. There are significant sector effects in Ghana (wood and food sectors), Kenya (all sectors), and Zimbabwe (metal and food), and hence workers in some sectors benefit more than workers in other sectors when they are located in the capital city.[5]

We then estimate specification (12.5) and present the results in Table 12.3. There are some patterns, but they are not very clear. The first three rows confirm that wages increase with education (as compared to no education); this is least for Ghana and most pronounced for Zambia. The size and foreign ownership premiums are also evident. A capital city premium applies for those with primary or secondary education in all countries, is considerable for those with no education in Kenya, Zambia, and Zimbabwe, but does not accrue to those with university education (except in Cameroon). In Zambia the location premium decreases with education whereas in Cameroon it increases (the other countries are more variable).

Table 12.4 presents results of estimating (12.6) using interaction terms between LOCC and occupation (skilled and less skilled) rather than LOCC and education.

---

[5] This compares well with evidence in Hanson (1997: Table 3) for Mexico. Wage differentials between Mexico City and other regions vary substantially by sector.

Table 12.3. *Earnings equations with education attainment, specification (12.5)*

	Cameroon	Ghana	Kenya	Zambia	Zimbabwe
PRIMC	0.09 (1.1)*	−0.03 (−0.3)	0.14 (3.4)*	0.36 (5.4)*	0.20 (3.6)*
SECC	0.49 (5.2)*	0.14 (1.3)*	0.35 (7.8)*	0.92 (11.6)*	0.60 (8.3)*
UNIVC	1.14 (9.1)*	1.18 (5.5)*	1.79 (10.9)*	1.99 (15.2)*	1.68 (5.7)*
Foreign ownership	0.08 (2.5)*	0.21 (6.5)*	0.17 (5.9)*	0.22 (4.55)*	0.12 (3.1)
Log(employment)	0.13 (8.8)*	0.15 (9.1)*	0.09 (10.4)*	0.10 (6.0)*	0.15 (12.3)*
LOCC*NONE	0.04 (0.5)	0.01 (0.1)	0.23 (5.6)*	0.26 (2.6)*	0.20 (3.2)*
LOCC*PRIMC	0.13 (2.5)*	0.27 (6.4)*	0.27 (9.3)*	0.23 (4.6)*	0.08 (2.2)*
LOCC*SECC	0.17 (2.6)*	0.36 (4.1)*	0.35 (9.6)*	0.05 (0.9)*	0.14 (2.5)*
LOCC*UNIVC	0.33 (2.8)*	0.13 (0.6)	−0.24 (−1.2)	−0.07 (−0.3)	−0.36 (−1.0)
Time dummies	Yes	Yes	Yes	Yes	Yes
Sector dummies	Yes	Yes	Yes	Yes	Yes
N	1,534	2,257	3,035	1,593	1,866
R^2	0.52	0.51	0.39	0.48	0.39
Test	$P = 0.24$	$P = 0.14$	$P = 0.01$	$P = 0.08$	$P = 0.20$

Notes: Dependent variable is log of monthly earnings in current domestic currency. White (1980) heteroskedasticity-consistent t-statistics in parentheses; *indicates significance at least at the 5% level. Equation as specified in the text. Standard worker controls (age, tenure, male, state ownership, foreign ownership, etc.) included in the regressions but not reported here (available upon request).

Source: Authors' computations.

The interpretation appears much clearer. For all countries, there is a clear difference in capital city premia between skilled and less-skilled occupations (indeed the premium for less skilled is negative in Zimbabwe). There are a number of general results:

- Workers in skilled occupations earn a premium (of 30–60 per cent) when they are employed by firms located in the capital city.
- Workers in less-skilled occupations earn a significant capital premium (of some 20 per cent) in Ghana and Kenya.
- Less-skilled workers do not earn a significant capital city premium in Cameroon and Zambia, while their premium is negative in Zimbabwe.

We now consider if the location wage premium varies by skill level after taking into account that LOCC tend to be larger firms, and the employer size premium varies by skill level (Strobl and Thornton 2002), and that the foreign ownership premium also varies by skill level (te Velde and Morrissey 2001). Are senior and more skilled workers paid more in firms located in the capital city simply because such firms tend to be larger or foreign-owned, or does a capital city wage premium remain after accounting for these factors? The results are in Table 12.5. Tests indicate that we cannot reject, for all countries, the hypothesis that the coefficients on LOCC*SKILLED and LOCC*UNSKILLED are equal. Thus, in general, the location premium applies

Table 12.4. *Earnings equations with occupations, specification (12.6)*

	Cameroon	Ghana	Kenya	Zambia	Zimbabwe
PRIMC	0.13 (2.9)*	0.06 (0.9)	0.09 (3.0)*	0.34 (5.8)*	0.11 (2.7)*
SECC	0.49 (10.3)*	0.24 (3.2)*	0.24 (6.8)*	0.79 (11.7)*	0.49 (9.0)*
UNIVC	1.26 (17.8)*	1.00 (7.7)*	1.22 (9.8)*	1.83 (15.6)*	1.04 (5.3)*
Foreign ownership	0.09 (2.8)*	0.21 (6.5)*	0.20 (5.7)*	0.23 (4.71)*	0.10 (2.6)*
Log(employment)	0.12 (8.4)*	0.15 (8.8)*	0.09 (8.6)*	0.10 (5.8)*	0.14 (12.2)*
LOCC*SKILLED	0.34 (8.0)*	0.51 (11.5)*	0.60 (13.6)*	0.29 (5.5)*	0.52 (12.1)*
LOCC*UNSKILLED	0.05 (1.1)*	0.19 (5.0)*	0.21 (8.1)*	0.04 (0.9)*	−0.03 (−1.2)*
Time dummies	Yes	Yes	Yes	Yes	Yes
Sector dummies	Yes	Yes	Yes	Yes	Yes
N	1,534	2,257	3,035	1,593	1,866
R^2	0.54	0.51	0.43	0.48	0.44
Test H_0: coefficients LOCC* SKILLED = LOCC* UNSKILLED	$P = 0.00$	$P = 0.00$	$P = 0.00$	$P = 0.00$	$P = 0.00$

Notes: Dependent variable is log of monthly earnings in current domestic currency. White (1980) heteroskedasticity-consistent t-statistics in parentheses; *indicates significance at least at the 5% level. Equation as specified in the text. Standard worker controls (age, tenure, male, state ownership, foreign ownership, etc.) included in the regressions but not reported here (available upon request).

Source: Authors' computations.

equally to all workers in each country—spatial inequality is not associated with skilled–unskilled wage differentials.[6] However, the size premium is significantly greater for skilled workers in all countries, as can be seen from the log(employment) interaction terms. This suggests that skilled workers were able to obtain a higher earnings premium in the capital city, compared to less-skilled workers, mainly because larger firms tend to locate in the capital city and such firms pay a premium to skilled workers. The foreign premium also favours skilled workers in Cameroon, Kenya, and Zambia, and this may contribute to a higher skill premium for workers located in the capital. In Ghana, the foreign premium favours unskilled workers.

12.5. CONCLUSIONS AND POLICY IMPLICATIONS

This chapter uses data on individual earnings in the manufacturing industry of five African countries (Cameroon, Ghana, Kenya, Zambia, and Zimbabwe) in the early 1990s to test whether location is associated with higher earnings for all education

---

[6] This compares well with similar evidence for Thailand (Matsuoka 2001). Controlling for other factors such as size and industry dummies, firms located in Bangkok and vicinity pay 39 per cent more to non-production workers and 36 per cent more to production workers than similar workers elsewhere.

Table 12.5. *Who benefits from location in the capital?*

	Cameroon	Ghana	Kenya	Zambia	Zimbabwe
Male	0.13 (3.6)*	0.09 (1.8)	0.16 (4.5)*	0.08 (1.8)	0.16 (4.7)*
Age	0.08 (4.8)*	0.18 (17.1)*	0.04 (3.6)*	0.05 (3.8)*	0.10 (9.2)*
Age^2	−0.0007 (−3.0)*	−0.002 (−14.6)*	−0.0004 (−2.9)*	−0.0004 (−2.5)*	−0.001 (−8.1)*
Tenure	0.011 (1.8)	0.01 (1.9)	0.007 (1.3)	0.03 (3.1)*	−0.007 (−1.2)
Tenure^2	−0.0001 (−0.4)	−0.0003 (−1.2)	−0.0000 (−0.0)	−0.0009 (−2.8)*	0.0002 (1.4)
PRIMC	0.13 (3.0)*	0.03 (0.4)	0.07 (2.4)*	0.28 (5.0)*	0.09 (2.4)*
SECC	0.49 (10.2)*	0.18 (2.4)*	0.20 (5.5)*	0.67 (9.9)*	0.43 (8.0)*
UNIVC	1.24 (17.5)*	0.88 (7.1)*	1.19 (9.7)*	1.61 (14.0)*	0.86 (4.3)*
Constant	8.1 (27.1)*	5.6 (29.3)*	6.6 (34.6)*	8.1 (38.4)*	3.3 (16.0)*
State ownership	−0.03 (−0.5)	0.01 (0.2)	−0.37 (−3.3)*	0.27 (4.2)*	0.01 (0.2)
LOCC*SKILLED	0.18 (3.2)*	0.24 (4.5)*	0.32 (5.8)*	0.12 (2.0)*	0.13 (2.3)*
LOCC*UNSKILLED	0.13 (3.0)*	0.28 (6.6)*	0.29 (11.1)*	0.17 (4.0)	0.12 (3.9)*
Log(employment)*SKILLED	0.15 (8.7)*	0.23 (11.9)*	0.15 (10.2)*	0.15 (8.0)*	0.22 (16.0)*
Log(employment)*UNSKILLED	0.10 (6.1)*	0.11 (6.5)*	0.07 (7.0)*	0.07 (4.4)*	0.11 (9.5)*
FOR*SKILLED	0.18 (3.7)*	0.03 (0.6)	0.34 (4.4)*	0.33 (4.8)*	0.07 (1.2)
FOR*UNSKILLED	0.03 (0.8)	0.28 (7.5)*	0.16 (4.2)*	0.11 (2.0)*	0.10 (2.4)*
Time dummies	Yes	Yes	Yes	Yes	Yes
Sector dummies	Yes	Yes	Yes	Yes	Yes
N	1,534	2,257	1,937	1,593	1,866
R^2	0.55	0.52	0.45	0.50	0.48
Test H_0: coefficients LOCC*SKILLED = LOCC*UNSKILLED	$P = 0.470$	$P = 0.55$	$P = 0.577$	$P = 0.451$	$P = 0.848$
Test H_0: coefficients FOR*SKILLED = FOR*UNSKILLED	$P = 0.014$	$P = 0.000$	$P = 0.029$	$P = 0.015$	$P = 0.712$
Test H_0: coefficients log(employment)*SKILLED = log(employment)*UNSKILLED	$P = 0.003$	$P = 0.000$	$P = 0.000$	$P = 0.000$	$P = 0.000$

Note: As for Table 12.3. Dependent variable is log of monthly earnings in current domestic currency.

Source: Authors' computations.

and occupation groups. Similar workers employed by firms located in the capital city do earn higher wages; the raw premium is in the range of 13–32 per cent. Controlling for firm characteristics, the pure capital city premium is significant: 12–15 per cent in Cameroon, Zambia, and Zimbabwe; 26–28 per cent in Ghana and Kenya. This location premium seems to apply to all types of workers, whether classified by education or skill level. While we found that skilled workers earn a higher wage premium in the capital city than less-skilled workers, this was not because of location effects per se, but rather because of firm characteristics associated with firms located in the capital city such as size and foreign ownership. This suggests that spatial inequality in itself does not directly contribute to skilled/less-skilled wage differentials.

We find some evidence for all three sources of spatial wage inequality identified in Section 12.2. First, the distribution of *worker characteristics* is skewed towards the capital city, for example, the number of years of formal education is higher for workers in the capital city. Note, however, that observed worker characteristics are accounted for and do not contribute to the premium. Second, *firm characteristics* are also important: larger and/or foreign-owned firms tend to pay a significant wage premium, generally favouring more skilled workers, and are more likely to locate in the capital city. The tendency of the types of firms that pay higher wages to locate in the capital accounts for about five percentage points of the raw premium in all countries except Zambia. Finally, workers in capital cities earn higher wages than similar workers employed by similar firms located outside the capital city, the pure premium estimated.

We do not have adequate data on spatial price variations to assess if the pure location premium corresponds to a premium on real earnings (purchasing power) differentials. In the case of Ghana and Kenya, where prices in the capital appear to have been 10–20 per cent higher than in other urban areas, the pure location premium could account for no more than a 10 per cent increase in real purchasing power. In Zambia, where evidence suggests little spatial variation in urban prices, the real premium also is no more than 10 per cent. In general, we do not find strong evidence that the earnings premium from being employed in the capital city contributes to spatial inequality to any appreciable degree. A potential real premium of 10 per cent could be accounted for by unobserved worker (and firm) characteristics and statistical confidence intervals. Migration and 'new economic geography' (agglomeration) theories would predict that, in equilibrium, real earnings are equalized across locations. In this sense our findings support such theories.

We can, however, be confident that a pure location premium exists, probably even in real purchasing power terms. The data available do not allow us to distinguish between the various explanations for a pure (real) location premium: unobserved characteristics, agglomeration economies (increasing productivity), or greater bargaining power of workers in cities. The new economic geography (NEG) approach of Fujita *et al.* (1999) cannot be directly tested, but we can make two observations. First, it is not evident that real earnings are equalized across urban locations, suggesting that there is a capital city agglomeration effect. In all likelihood, this is a combination of productivity and bargaining effects, both of which are unobservable characteristics in the data (hence, part of the pure premium). Second, and perhaps more conclusive, there is evidence for a firm location effect (the five percentage point difference between the raw and pure premiums in most countries). There is a tendency for larger and/or foreign-owned firms to agglomerate in the capital city. This is an effect that the NEG approach could explore further; market and supply-side explanations are equally likely.

The finding that wage inequality *within* manufacturing is unlikely to be a significant source of spatial inequality (i.e. relative to the significant rural–urban income differentials observed) does not imply that wage inequality is irrelevant. There are sources of wage inequality, and these tend to be interrelated (albeit with country variations). Larger firms tend to pay higher wages, as do foreign-owned firms (and these are not always one and the same firms), and such premia tend to favour more skilled and/or educated workers. Expanding manufacturing employment (spatially), which tends to be associated with larger firms and foreign investment, is a source of increased earnings. This may reduce spatial inequality, if workers are drawn out of low wage agriculture into higher wage (rural) manufacturing, but at the expense of increasing wage inequality (the skilled–unskilled differential). Wider opportunities for education and acquiring skills enhances the potential for all workers to benefit from manufacturing employment, and is more likely to attract investment in manufacturing. Manufacturing employment may be part of the solution to, rather than part of the problem of, spatial inequality.

APPENDIX

Table 12.A1. *Earnings and years of worker education by country and location (first wave)*

	Location (capital city = 1)	Log of monthly earnings in current domestic prices	Mean of formal years of worker education
Cameroon	0	11.06	9.83
	1	11.37	10.26
Ghana	0	9.40	9.79
	1	10.16	11.20
Kenya	0	7.69	8.62
	1	8.11	8.93
Zambia	0	10.51	10.10
	1	10.52	10.31
Zimbabwe	0	6.43	8.35
	1	6.61	8.79

Source: Authors' summary of the data.

Table 12.A2. *Cross tabulations by ownership, location, and firm size*

F/size	ALL		Cameroon		Ghana		Kenya		Zambia		Zimbabwe	
	0	**1**	**0**	**1**	**0**	**1**	**0**	**1**	**0**	**1**	**0**	**1**
Numbers												
F = 0												
1	380	411	62	113	99	64	108	136	60	64	51	34
2	313	403	55	103	92	102	53	90	64	57	49	51
3	183	345	7	38	16	51	35	105	51	30	74	121
4	117	65	89	13	1	0	4	12	5	6	18	34
All	993	1,224	213	267	208	217	200	343	180	157	192	240
F = 1												
1	23	28	11	10	3	9	3	5	0	1	6	3
2	48	91	15	46	6	26	14	12	7	7	6	0
3	76	234	15	86	6	34	7	51	18	13	30	50
4	51	56	28	20	3	0	5	3	3	2	12	31
All	198	409	69	162	18	69	29	71	28	23	54	84
Total	1,191	1,633	282	429	226	286	229	414	208	180	246	324
Percentage (100%)												
	42	58	40	60	44	56	36	64	54	46	43	57
F = 0												
1	13	15	9	16	19	13	17	21	15	16	9	6
2	11	14	8	14	18	20	8	14	16	15	9	9
3	6	12	1	5	3	10	5	16	13	8	13	21
4	4	2	13	2	0	0	1	2	1	2	3	6
All	35	43	30	38	41	42	31	53	46	40	34	42
F − 1												
1	1	1	2	1	1	2	0	1	0	0	1	1
2	2	3	2	6	1	5	2	2	2	2	1	0
3	3	8	2	12	1	7	1	8	5	3	5	9
4	2	2	4	3	1	0	1	0	1	1	2	5
All	7	14	10	23	4	13	5	11	7	6	9	15
Total	1,191	1,633	282	429	226	286	229	414	208	180	246	324

Notes: $F = 1$ indicates owned by a foreigner (individual or firm), otherwise locally owned. The size categories are 0–10 employees (1), 11–50 employees (2), 51–500 employees (3), and more than 500 employees (4).

Source: Authors' computations.

REFERENCES

Bigsten, A., P. Collier, and others (1997). 'Exports of African Manufactures: Macro Policy and Firm Behaviour' (mimeo), CSAE, University of Oxford: Oxford.

Bigsten, A., P. Collier, and others (1999). 'Investment of Africa's Manufacturing Sector: A Four Country Panel Data Analysis', *Oxford Bulletin of Economics and Statistics*, 61: 489–512.

—— *et al.* (2000). 'Rates of Return on Physical and Human Capital in Africa's Manufacturing Sector', *Economic Development and Cultural Change*, 48(4): 801–27.

Blanchflower, D. G., A. J. Oswald, and P. Sanfey (1996). 'Wages, Profits and Rent-Sharing', *Quarterly Journal of Economics*, 111(1): 227–51.

Coulombe, H. and A. McKay (2001). 'The Evolution of Poverty and Inequality in Ghana over the 1990s' (mimeo), World Bank: Washington DC.

Dunning, J. (1993). *Multinational Enterprises and the Global Economy*, Addison-Wesley: Boston, MA.

Fujita, M., P. Krugman, and A. J. Venables (1999). *The Spatial Economy*, MIT Press: Cambridge, MA.

Glaeser, E. and D. Mare (1994). 'Cities and Skills', *NBER Working Papers* 4728, National Bureau of Economic Research: Cambridge, MA.

Hanson, G. H. (1997). 'Increasing Returns, Trade and the Regional Structure of Wages', *Economic Journal*, 107(440): 113–33.

Krugman, P. and R. E. Livas (1996). 'Trade Policy and Third World Metropolis', *Journal of Development Economics*, 49(1): 137–50.

Matsuoka, A. (2001). 'Wage Differentials among Local Plants and Foreign Multinationals by Foreign Ownership Share and Nationality in Thai Manufacturing', *ICSEAD Working Papers* 15, International Centre for the Study of East Asian Development: Kitakyushu.

Mazumdar, D. (1995). 'Wage Differences by Size of Enterprise in African Manufacturing', *RPED Discussion Papers* 49, World Bank: Washington DC.

McCulloch, N., B. Baulch, and M. Cherel-Robson (2000). 'Poverty, Inequality and Growth in Zambia during the 1990s', *IDS Sussex Working Papers* 114.

Mincer, J. (1974). *Schooling, Experience and Earnings*, National Bureau of Economic Research: Cambridge, MA.

Republic of Kenya (1995). *Economic Survey* 1995, Central Bureau of Statistics, Ministry of Finance and Planning: Nairobi.

Söderbom, M. and F. Teal (2001a). 'Firm Size and Human Capital as Determinants of Productivity and Earnings', *CSAE Working Paper* 09, Centre for the Study of African Economies, Oxford University, Oxford.

—— and —— (2001b). 'Are African Manufacturing Firms Really Inefficient? Evidence from Firm-Level Panel Data', *CSAE Working Papers* 14, Centre for the Study of African Economies, Oxford University, Oxford.

Strobl, E. and B. Thornton (2002). 'Do Large Employers Pay More in Developing Countries? The Case of Five African Countries', *CREDIT Discussion Papers* 01, CREDIT, Nottingham University: Nottingham, downloadable from www.nottingham.ac.uk/economics/research/credit.

te Velde, D. W. and O. Morrissey (2001). 'Foreign Ownership and Wages: Evidence from five African Countries', *CREDIT Discussion Paper* 19, CREDIT, Nottingham University: Nottingham, downloadable from www.nottingham.ac.uk/economics/research/credit.

Wheaton, W. C. and M. J. Lewis (2002). 'Urban Wages and Labor Market Agglomeration', *Journal of Urban Economies*, 51: 542–62.

White, H. (1980). 'A Heteroskedasticity-Consistent Covariance Matrix Estimator and a Direct Test for Hetroskedasticity', *Econometrica*, 48: 817–38.

PART VII

SPATIAL INEQUALITY DURING TRANSITION

(Czech Republic, Hungary, Poland, Russia, Europe)

13

Regional Poverty and Income Inequality in Central and Eastern Europe: Evidence from the Luxembourg Income Study

MICHAEL FÖRSTER, DAVID JESUIT, AND
TIMOTHY SMEEDING

13.1. INTRODUCTION

Regional economic change is an important part of the economic development process in all countries—rich, poor, and middle income. The effects of regional economic change on poverty, inequality, social exclusion, population health, and other relevant social dimensions are just beginning to emerge. For instance, recent papers have shown that China's regional growth progress has varied considerably by region, leading to rising inequality within and between China's regions (Wei and Wu 2002). India shows a similar pattern. Studies of subnational (regional) poverty and inequality have also recently been completed for Europe and for other wealthy nations (Osberg 2000; Goerlich and Mas 2001; Rainwater et al. 2001; Jesuit et al. 2002; Stewart 2002).

One of the most rapidly changing regions of the world in the 1990s were the former centrally planned economies in Central and Eastern Europe (CEE), including the Czech Republic, Hungary, Poland, and Russia, which we study in this chapter. These CEE nations have undergone a very rapid change from planned economies to market-based societies. As a result, repressed inequalities in wages owing to the Soviet-style institutions of wage determination largely disappeared during the 1990s. These wage and earnings patterns were replaced by entrepreneurial and market-based returns to skills and risk-taking, producing overall national income and earnings inequality levels in the CEE by the end of the 1990s which resemble those in some West European and in other middle-income countries like Mexico (Förster and Tóth 1997; Smeeding 2002). Of course, these changes did not proceed on an even keel within each of these nations. Some areas prospered and others lagged behind.

The authors would like to thank the Ford Foundation for their support of the LIS Central and Eastern European research and data programme. They also would like to thank the Vienna Institute for International Economic Studies for providing expert assistance with regional macroeconomic performance indicators.

While comparative evidence on macroeconomic and labour market-related regional disparities in CEE is widespread and growing, most of these analyses are based on macroregional aggregate data. So far, and despite the significant contributions made by a recent World Bank report (2001), precious little is known on the microlevel of inequalities, that is, regional differences in household incomes and poverty (but see also Bailey 1997). This chapter seeks to fill some of these gaps and proposes an enhanced analysis of income inequality, poverty, and to a lesser extent economic growth, across the regions within four CEE countries. More specifically, is income inequality higher in some areas than in others within CEE countries? What are the contributions of inter versus intraregional inequalities in total income inequality within CEE countries? How does the adoption of a local rather than a national poverty line affect estimates of poverty within CEE regions? How do regions within CEE countries compare to regions within Western Europe? Finally, is there a relationship between economic growth, income inequality, and poverty across CEE regions, as some suggest?

13.2. SETTING THE SCENE: REGIONAL VARIATIONS IN MACROECONOMIC PERFORMANCES AND RECENT EVIDENCE AT THE MICROLEVEL

Pretransition governments pursued a centrally planned economic policy which, *inter alia*, led to specific industries (in particular heavy industries) being placed in specific regions according to political rather than economic criteria. It may therefore be expected, and has often been claimed, that at the start of transition regional disparities in terms of macroeconomic performance and employment structure were high in CEE. Furthermore, the transition to a market economy is believed to have accentuated those regional disequilibria.[1]

This seems, indeed, to have happened. Comparative cross-country studies generally point to an increase in regional disparities with regard to GDP and employment/unemployment in CEE countries. The *OECD Territorial Outlook 2001* (OECD 2001), for instance, reports that the coefficient of variation of per capita GDP across regions has risen between 1995 and 1997 in all three central eastern member countries of the Organisation for Economic Co-operation and Development (OECD): the Czech Republic (from 31 to 33), Hungary (from 31 to 36), and Poland (from 19 to 24). More precisely, for the Czech Republic the report defines the northwestern and southeastern regions as most deprived, while Prague and Plšen seem less affected (OECD 2001: 51). For Hungary, a 'significant widening of territorial disparities is reported' due to the fact that the capital region was the only one capable of withstanding a situation of declining real GDP and increasing unemployment (OECD 2001: 69). For Poland, a clear

---

[1] While we focus on the decompression of earnings as the key cause of rising income inequality during the transition, such factors such as privatization, land reform, the emergence of an entrepreneurial class, changes in public policies, and corruption, among others, have all been linked to its growth (e.g. see Atkinson and Micklewright 1992; Aghion and Blanchard 1994: 283–300; Commander and Coricelli 1995; Flemming and Micklewright 1999; World Bank 2001).

division between the richer western and poorer eastern part is described, disturbed by the richest region, the capital region around Warsaw.

As for regional labour market performances, an early study conducted in the first phase of transition (OECD 1995) suggests that 'spatial variations in unemployment rates materialized "at a stroke" after the introduction of market-oriented reforms in all transition countries ... (these variations) may last for a long time, because of the different capacities of regions to adapt to a market-based system' (OECD 1995: 11). Further, OECD (2001: 34) shows that the Czech Republic, Hungary, and Poland are part of those two-thirds of OECD countries in which regional disparities in unemployment have been widening in the second half of the 1990s; in the first two countries under a situation of increasing average (national) unemployment, and in Poland under a situation of decreasing average unemployment. The latter trend suggests a polarized pattern since positive employment growth is spatially differentiated.

How do the absolute levels of regional disparities compare with 'traditional' OECD countries? Hungary stands out. As far as the regional concentration of total GDP is concerned, as much as 42 per cent of national GDP is concentrated in its richest region,[2] the capital region around Budapest. On OECD average, 25 per cent of GDP is concentrated in the respective richest regions of countries, and this percentage is slightly lower in the Czech Republic and Poland (22 and 20 per cent, respectively). The coefficient of variation of per capita GDP is above OECD average in Hungary,[3] around average in the Czech Republic, and below average in Poland (OECD 2001: 33).

As for regional variations in unemployment rates, levels in the Czech Republic and Hungary (no information for Poland is available) actually do not diverge much from those experienced in other OECD countries (coefficient of variation of 31 for Hungary and 41 for the Czech Republic) and they are lower than in the two countries with highest regional variation in unemployment: Germany[4] (44) and Italy (61) (OECD 2000: 39). In addition, a decomposition analysis of the variance in unemployment rates shows that most of the explained variation in unemployment across regions is accounted for by education in the Czech Republic and Hungary (OECD 2000: 42). In sum, regional disparities in CEE countries are high but, with the exception of GDP concentration in Hungary, they do not seem to be extraordinarily high when compared to OECD countries.

In the most recent in-depth analysis of regional macroeconomic and unemployment variations, Römisch (2001) shows for nine CEE countries that, at the beginning of this decade, there exist large disparities between the capital city regions and the rest of CEE regions as well as an East–West pattern in terms of GDP and GDP per capita. Similar patterns are also found in terms of unemployment variations, with a few exceptions. In Hungary and Poland, for instance, unemployment rates in the eastern regions are not significantly higher despite GDP levels well below the national average. Römisch relates this to the high share of agriculture in those regions which do not

---

[2] This is the highest value across OECD.

[3] In fact, the fourth highest value is for Mexico, the United Kingdom and France show still higher coefficients.   [4] This only holds for reunified Germany but not West Germany taken apart.

generate high GDP but (unlike in Western Europe) are able to absorb or hide open unemployment.

As for the trend between 1993 and 1998, in accordance with the OECD figures quoted above, Römisch (2001: 5–7) reports regional variations of both total GDP and GDP per capita[5] on the rise throughout CEE countries. To situate the three countries included in the present chapter in the frame of other CEE countries, it should be noted that their levels of variation of per capita GDP are around average, with lower variation occurring in Lithuania and, in particular, Bulgaria and higher variation in Estonia and the Slovak Republic.

A kernel density analysis of the data suggests that 'without the capital cities, the distribution (of per capita GDP) has been stable and neither convergence nor divergence has occurred across the majority of the (poorer) regions in the countries' (Römisch 2001: 9). It also reveals that regions with above-average unemployment at the start are likely to have even higher unemployment in the following. In explaining the existence of regional disparities, Römisch's results point to the importance of the services sector on relative GDP and unemployment levels.[6] Other factors explaining a region's economic performance are their distances to the West and capital city regions, which both seem to generate positive spillovers. Finally, agglomeration effects were found to exert a significant and positive influence on regional GDP and unemployment levels (Römisch 2001: 15–18).

While comparative evidence on macroeconomic and labour-market-related regional disparities in CEE is widespread and growing, relatively little is known on the micro-level of inequalities, that is, regional differences in household incomes and poverty in a comparative perspective. In his major study on income, inequality, and poverty in transition countries, Milanovic (1998), for instance, attributes one paragraph to the regional aspect of poverty. Comparing microdata for the Czech Republic, Hungary, Poland, and Slovakia from the early to mid-1990s, he concludes that 'poverty rates decline with increase in the size of locality' (Milanovic 1998: 106). This finding relates to the larger share of highly skilled people in capital cities and the low level of income of farmers. The analysis, however, is based on large versus smaller cities and villages rather than on geographical regions.

A recent report published by the World Bank (2001) addresses many of the shortcomings of previous research on the market transition in CEE that we have thus far identified. Indeed, the report offers an exhaustive set of indicators on income inequality and poverty based on microdata from most of the countries in CEE. Furthermore, these microdata are also aggregated at the subnational levels of analysis so that intra-country disparities may be analysed. One of the key findings of this report is that the transition has resulted in divergent economic outcomes in the CIS (Commonwealth of Independent States) countries, such as Russia, and in Central and Southeast European

---

[5] The (unweighted) nine-country average of the Gini coefficient for the regional GDP distribution increased from 0.275 to 0.300, and the coefficient of variation of per capita GDP increased from 0.237 to 0.284 between 1993 and 1998.

[6] Regression results were significant also in the specification without the capital city regions.

and Baltic countries such as Poland (2001: 163–4). Another important conclusion from this report is that the capital cities in CEE countries have lower rates of poverty than in their nations as a whole and that there are some regions within countries where the risk of poverty is more than three times greater than the national rate (2001: 74–80). Despite the significant contribution that this report makes, there are a few remaining gaps that this chapter seeks to fill.

Unlike the World Bank report, we adopt a harmonized definition of household income and offer a more detailed aggregation of households at the regional level of analysis. We also make use of more recent data and examine at least two cross-sections for each country in order to investigate changes over time. Furthermore, we estimate income inequality within regions and use both a local and national standard when measuring poverty, neither of which has been previously accomplished. In addition, we compare regions within CEE countries to those in West European nations in order to assess the magnitude of interregional disparities among current EU members, three candidate countries and Russia. Finally, we offer some very preliminary evidence concerning the relationship between poverty, income inequality, and economic growth in CEE regions.

13.3. DATA AND METHODS

This chapter examines income inequality and income poverty using the harmonized microdata made available through the efforts of the Luxembourg Income Study (LIS) for the following countries and years: the Czech Republic (1992, 1996), Hungary (1991, 1994), Poland (1992, 1995, 1999), and Russia (1992, 1995).[7] The core concept used in this chapter is that of *disposable* income. More precisely, gross wages and salaries, self-employment income, cash property income, pension income, and social transfers of all household members are added and income taxes and mandatory employee contributions are subtracted to yield household disposable income.[8] In order to account for differences in household size, this chapter adopts the standard approach of taking the square root of the number of household members to calculate equivalent disposable income (Atkinson *et al.* 1995: 21).[9]

Another important measurement decision made in this chapter concerns top and bottom coding. We bottom code the LIS datasets at 1 per cent of equivalized mean

---

[7] Detailed information on the characteristics of the underlying surveys can be obtained from the LIS technical documentation site www.lisproject.org/techdoc.htm. In general, sample sizes of surveys vary between approx. 3,000 (Hungary) and 27,000 (Czech Republic). It bears mentioning that the quality of the surveys included in the LIS varies somewhat. For example, the LIS datasets for the Czech Republic and Poland are based upon official sources and are of higher quality than the 'unofficial' sources of data for Russia and Hungary (see Smeeding 2001).

[8] Unfortunately, income from home food production is not available in the Wave III datasets and, thus, it is not included in our income concept.

[9] There is an important debate focusing on the various equivalence scales one should adopt when examining CEE countries (e.g. see Lanjouw *et al.* 1998). However, research has shown that the choice of equivalency scale is most important when examining a subgroup of the population, such as children or the elderly. Since we are examining the entire population, our results are not as sensitive to this choice.

income and top code at ten times the median of non-equivalized income for the nation sample (Gottschalk and Smeeding 1997: 661). This procedure limits the effect of extreme values at either end of the distribution. Finally, we exclude all records with zero disposable incomes in the measures of income poverty that we report. This decision is consistent with Atkinson *et al.* (1995) and with the method used and recommended by the LIS key figures reported on the LIS website.[10] A final methodological decision is whether to consider inequality and poverty among households or persons (say, to count a couple with two children four times rather than once). As our concern is with the position of citizens and to treat each citizen as equal in the distribution, our results refer to 'person weights' which equal the household weight times the number of household members.[11]

Finally, many argue that household consumption (expenditure) is preferable to income when estimating economic well-being (e.g. see Ravallion 1994). Indeed, we concede that irregular pay and income under-reporting make reliance on income as the estimate of well-being somewhat problematic, especially in Russia (World Bank 2001: 367–8). For these reasons, the recent World Bank report on CEE countries (2001) favours household consumption when measuring poverty,[12] but reports both income and consumption inequality. In fact, previous research has demonstrated that within the affluent countries findings are very similar whichever approach is adopted. This is also true within the CEE countries when calculating income inequality, with the exception of CIS countries such as Russia (see also World Bank 2001: 143–4). However, when comparing our poverty results to those published by the World Bank (2001: Appendix D), our rates are consistently higher although our ranking of countries remains the same. Furthermore, contributing to these discrepancies is the fact that we use different years (and a different survey in the case of Hungary) as well as different equivalency scales. Nonetheless, in future research we hope to obtain harmonized estimates of household expenditures for sake of comparison.

13.3.1. *Defining Regions*

Unfortunately, not all of the national-level surveys from Central or Eastern European countries included in the LIS report the respondent's region/state/province of residence. In the countries we include in this regional analysis, the units tend to be well defined politically, territorially, and culturally. The exception to this is found in the case of Hungary, where we were only able to identify Budapest as a geographical unit while the other categories are based on an urban versus rural definition. In addition, in some cases we decided to aggregate regions even when a more detailed breakdown

---

[10] www.lisproject.org.

[11] This is in line with the current practice in European and international research. Atkinson *et al.* (2002: 29), for instance, argue 'We are not suggesting that individuals should be considered in isolation; but each person should count for one'.

[12] Except for Hungary and the Slovak Republic (World Bank 2001: 376).

was available so that we could maintain comparability across the LIS data waves[13] (e.g. in Poland and in Russia). Finally, due to the reform of Poland's provinces in 1999, the regional aggregations for Poland 1999 are not exactly comparable to the groupings in 1992 and 1995.[14] However, we believe that this has had little effect on our results since, in order to maintain comparability between Poland's Wave III and IV regions, we aggregate households into nine regions rather than provinces. Specifically, we aggregate households at the level of Czech regions (8); Hungary's capital city (Budapest), major cities, towns, villages, and farmsteads; and Polish (9) and Russian regions (9).[15] The list of regions, including the number of observations from which the measures of inequality and poverty are derived and 95 per cent confidence intervals for the estimates we report, is included in the Appendix.

13.3.2. *Measures of Income Inequality and Decomposition*

We use three general measures to estimate income inequality in our study: the Theil Index, the Gini coefficient, and the ratio of regional and national median incomes. The Theil Index is an additively decomposable index of income inequality, allowing one to estimate each subgroup's contribution to total income inequality within a population (Cowell 2000: 109). In this case, we compute the Theil Index using regions as our subgroup. We also report Gini coefficients at the regional and national levels of analysis. Gini scores are based on the Lorenz curve, which plots cumulative percentages of the population against their cumulative aggregate incomes. A value of zero indicates 'perfect equality', in which every individual has the same income. A value of one indicates 'perfect inequality' and results if one person has all the income. The advantage of this measure is that its computation includes the entire income distribution. Furthermore, it is the best-known measure of inequality in the social sciences. Also significant for our study, the Gini coefficient is an appropriate estimator of intra-regional income inequality. Finally, as a complementary way of capturing interregional inequality within a country, we report the regional/national median income ratio. This is simply computed as the ratio of a region's median household equivalent income to the national median household equivalent income. However, all of these measures are most sensitive to changes around the median and, thus, may not be as useful in quantifying changes at the bottom (or at the top) of the income distribution, a major concern of this study (see Atkinson *et al.* 1995: 23). Accordingly, we also compute relative poverty rates using both national and local poverty lines.

---

[13] In the following, the term 'LIS Data Wave III' refers to the early 1990s, 'Wave IV' to the mid-1990s, and 'Wave V' to the late 1990s.

[14] This administrative reform took effect on 1 January 1999 having become legislation in 1998, with Poland's forty-nine provinces reorganized into sixteen new provinces. In any case, we use nine geographic groups rather than the provinces thus limiting the effect this has on our results.

[15] Ideally we would be able to aggregate households into smaller and/or more relevant subnational units such as primary sampling units or those having administratively significant boundaries. However, we are limited to these definitions for practical reasons of data availability, confidentiality, and comparability. Nonetheless, our regional aggregations offer an improvement over previous research.

13.3.3. *Local and National Standards in the Measure of Poverty*

The most basic decision poverty researchers confront is whether to adopt an absolute or relative approach to measuring poverty. The former entails estimating a 'market basket' of goods and determining an absolute poverty line that is the cost of purchasing these goods for households of various sizes. The latter bases the poverty line on the distribution of income and establishes a point, such as 50 per cent of the median, below which households are considered 'poor'. Most cross-national research on poverty within affluent countries uses the second method and this is the official approach to measuring poverty adopted by Eurostat (1998, 2000). In addition to this, however, researchers conducting regional investigations are confronted with another choice—the definition of the reference society—whichever approach (absolute or relative) they adopt since 'there is also the possibility of variations in standards for defining poverty across the regions of a nation' (Rainwater *et al.* 1999: 4). For example, if one is using the absolute approach to defining poverty, the market basket is adjusted to reflect local prices rather than a national average. Thus, the poverty line varies regionally according to the costs of the goods in the basket (see also Citro and Michael 1995).[16]

In most comparative research on poverty, the poverty line is defined as a fraction of the *national* median equivalent income (commonly 50 per cent, though 40 and 60 per cent are also often used). Applying this 50 per cent approach to regional analyses, we are confronted with the choice between using this national standard or substituting a regional one as a reference group. Rainwater *et al.* argue that the regional standard

... approximates much better, although not perfectly, the community standards for social activities and participation that define persons as of 'average' social standing or 'below average' or 'poor'. . .

Using a local relative standard takes into account whatever variations in the cost of living are relevant and relevant differences in consumption, and relevant differences in social understanding of what consumption possibilities mean for social participation and related social activities. (Rainwater *et al.* 1999: 5, see also Rainwater 1991, 1992)

On the other hand, adopting a national-relative standard is sensitive to the wealth of a region relative to the national standard. This interregional approach more clearly captures disparities in wealth between regions and does not reflect intraregional income inequality per se. This will be more clearly demonstrated in Section 13.4. Rather than deciding which approach more accurately measures economic well-being, we use both in this chapter.[17]

---

[16] Note that, under certain policy-related considerations such as the allocation of structural funds in an enlarged European Union, there are also arguments to look at supranational poverty thresholds, taking the whole of Europe as a reference society. Förster *et al.* (2002), for instance, estimate indicators for income and consistent poverty for selected EU candidate countries under European-wide thresholds. See also Beblo and Knaus (2000).

[17] See Jäntti and Danziger (2000: 326–33) for an overview of alternative measures of poverty, including the often used Foster *et al.* (1984) class of indicators. In future research we hope to exploit some of these measures.

The alternative is to use an absolute approach at either the subnational or national level. The World Bank, for instance, uses different absolute poverty lines for each of the world's regions: $1 per person per day in Africa; $2 per person per day in Latin America; $3 per person per day in Central Asia; and $4.3 for CEE. The United States, on the other hand, has its own 'absolute' poverty line of $10–15 per person per day, depending on family size (Smeeding *et al.* 2001). However, absolute poverty standards can be captured nationally only when we can define comparable baskets of goods in 'real' terms across a set of countries. This process can be achieved using purchasing power parities (PPPs) such as those developed by the OECD. However, these PPPs are not well suited for microdata and do not account for wide differences across nations in the way that public goods such as healthcare, education, and the like are financed (Smeeding and Rainwater 2002). Also, differential quality of microdata may affect the results since PPPs are calculated relative to aggregate national account statistics, not microdata (see Smeeding *et al.* 2001). And even if the national absolute approach could be tolerated, one would not be able to actualize the absolute local approach unless regional (local) price indices were also calculated. For all of these reasons, we use the relative approach in this article.

13.4. RESULTS

In the following tables and figures, we report levels of income inequality and poverty for the four countries we examine and their thirty-one regions over three points in time in the 1990s. Confidence intervals based on the bootstrap standard errors of the estimates are also reported, allowing us to make conclusions with greater statistical certainty.[18] We begin at the national level, where we find that there are considerable differences in levels of income inequality and poverty between countries and that these levels increased in all of the countries during the 1990s. Next, we examine intra and interregional inequality and report regional figures and conclude that there is substantial variation with respect to levels of economic well-being within each of the countries. In this section we also explore the effects of using different poverty lines and find that there are often significant consequences associated with using a regional or national poverty line threshold. Finally, we look at trends in micro and macroeconomic disparities for two regions with different growth patterns in the Czech Republic in the 1990s.

13.4.1. *National Rates and Trends*

Before moving to our regional results, it is useful to examine national levels and trends in income inequality and relative poverty. Table 13.1 reports overall Theil Indices, Gini coefficients, and relative poverty rates (at 50 and 60 per cent of the median) for each of the datasets we examine. As shown in this table, levels of income inequality and

---

[18] We use 300 iterations of the bootstrap in order to calculate our standard errors and confidence intervals (see Osberg and Xu 1999; Osberg 2000).

Table 13.1. *National income inequality and poverty*

Country	Income inequality		Relative poverty	
	Theil	Gini	50% median	60% median
Czech Republic				
1992	0.082	0.207	2.3	6.5
1996	0.120	0.259	4.9	10.5
Hungary				
1991	0.145	0.283	8.2	14.3
1994	0.185	0.323	10.1	15
Poland				
1992	0.123	0.274	7.7	13.7
1995	0.190	0.318	11.6	17.7
1999	0.170	0.293	8.6	15.2
Russia				
1992	0.273	0.395	19.3	25.9
1995	0.351	0.447	20.1	25.7

Source: Authors' calculations from LIS.

relative poverty varied considerably between the four CEE countries and there is a clear ranking. Namely, the Czech Republic consistently reported the lowest levels of income inequality and poverty, followed by Hungary and Poland, which have similar levels, and then by Russia, which reported the largest levels of income inequality and poverty among the four countries. Although one should be cautious when interpreting trends from just two points in time, the results indicate that income inequality and poverty increased in all of the countries between the early and mid-1990s. However, the figures for Poland 1999, the only result from the late 1990s we include in our analysis, suggests that this trend reversed towards the end of the decade.[19] Nonetheless, there was still a net increase in income inequality and poverty within Poland over the course of the decade of the 1990s. In future work, we will determine if this same trend is evident in the other countries that we examine.

13.4.2. *Intra and Interregional Income Inequality*

As a first step in our regional analysis, Fig. 13.1 displays Theil Indices for each of the countries we examine, plus Italy. We include Italy as a reference since it is a country widely known to have large regional disparities.[20] As discussed, the Theil

[19] Trend estimates for Hungary point to a similar pattern; increasing inequality in the early and again mid-1990s, followed by a stabilization in the late 1990s (Förster and Pellizzari 2000; Szivosz and Tóth 2001).

[20] See Jesuit *et al.* (2002) for results on regional poverty within West European countries. In some of the following figures, we also compare our results to seventy-five regions from five West European countries since three of our four countries are EU candidate countries.

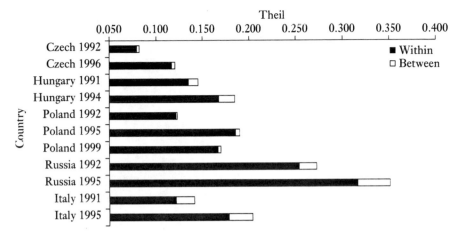

Figure 13.1. *Theil coefficients, within versus between regions*

Source: Authors' calculations using LIS.

is a decomposable index of income inequality that makes it particularly suited for our regional analysis (see Cowell 2000). In this case, we can determine the proportion of income inequality attributable to intraregional inequalities versus interregional inequalities. As shown in the figure (and Table 13.1), inequality increased in all of the countries between the early and mid-1990s. Furthermore, the decomposition shows that both intra and interregional inequality increased between the early and mid 1990s. However, the results from Poland—the only country for which we have LIS data available for Wave V, at the moment—suggest that inequality may have receded in the late 1990s. In terms of ranking the countries, interregional disparities were greatest in Russia in 1995 (even larger than in Italy) and lowest in Poland in 1992. Finally, by converting the Theil Indices to proportions, it is evident that the vast majority of inequality in each of the countries is due to intraregional, rather than interregional disparities, ranging from 90.1 per cent in Russia in 1995 to as much as 98.7 per cent in Poland in 1992—this is also clearly shown in the figure by the relative sizes of the bars. Contrary to conventional wisdom, the interregional part of income inequality in EU candidate countries is thus lower than in some of EU member countries.

Although Fig. 13.1 provides a general portrait of regional inequalities in CEE countries, Figs 13.2–13.5 offer a more detailed description of intra and interregional inequality, respectively. In Fig. 13.2, we plot the distribution of regional Gini coefficients using modified 'box and whiskers' plots (see Tukey 1977). In these summary plots, the line across the box represents the median regional Gini coefficient while the box indicates the interquartile range (difference between the regional Gini at the twenty-fifth and seventy-fifth percentiles). The whiskers, or lines extending above and below the box, report the maximum and minimum reported Gini coefficient within each country. Each box represents a country and the number of regions within each

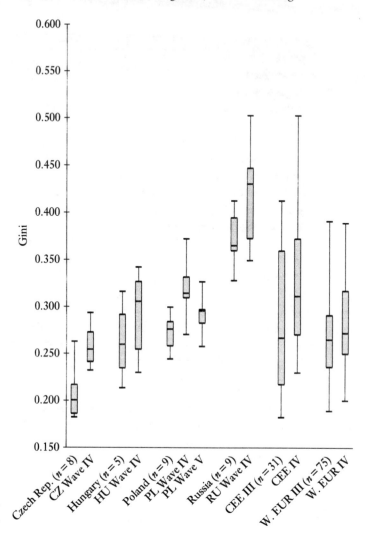

Figure 13.2. *Regional Gini coefficient box plots*

Source: Authors' calculations using LIS.

is reported along the *x*-axis. We also include an aggregation of the thirty-one CEE regions we examine in Waves III and IV and an aggregation of regional figures from five West European countries reported in Jesuit *et al.* 2002.[21] This latter figure allows us to make more direct comparisons to regional disparities within West and CEE regions.

---

[21] The five countries comprising the seventy-five West European regions are: Finland (1991, 1995), France (1989, 1994), Italy (1991, 1995), the United Kingdom (1991, 1995), and West Germany (1989, 1994).

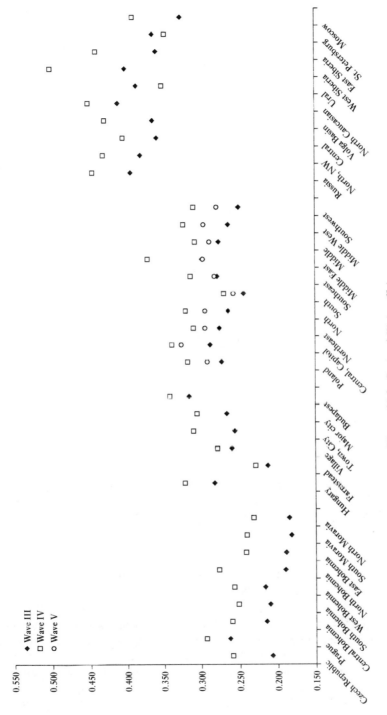

Figure 13.3. *Regional Gini coefficients*

Source: Authors' calculations using LIS.

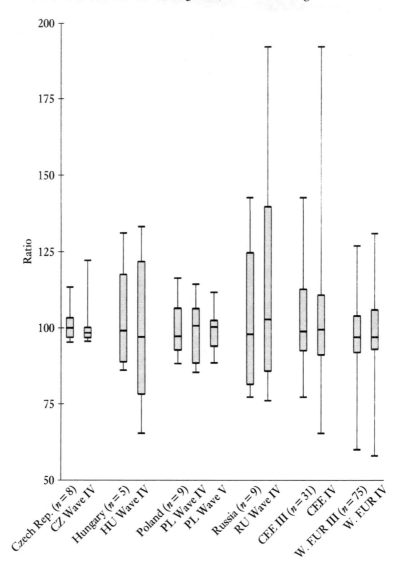

Figure 13.4. *Ratio of regional to national median household income box plots*

Source: Authors' calculations using LIS.

By examining both the lengths of the boxes (interquartile range) and the range between the minimum and maximum values (the whiskers), Fig. 13.2 illustrates that intraregional inequalities varied widely in the countries under examination. In fact, studies limited to the national level of analysis miss a great deal of intracountry variance in levels of income inequality. For example, the Gini coefficient for the whole of the Czech Republic in 1992 equalled 0.207. In Prague, however, the gap between

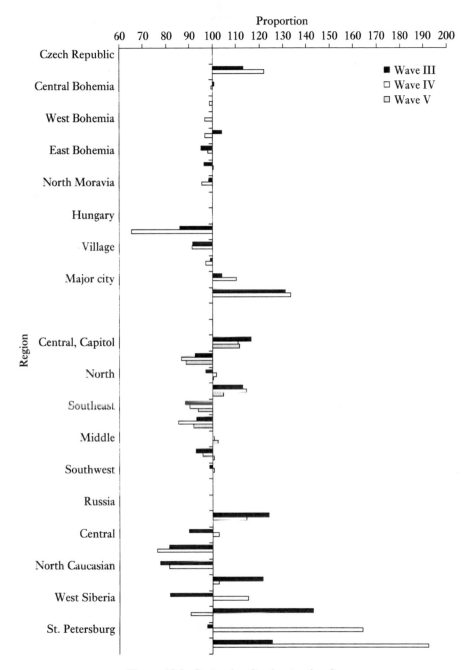

Figure 13.5. *Regional median / national median*

Source: Authors' calculations using LIS.

the rich and the poor was considerably wider and the Gini equalled 0.263 in the same year (also represented by the top of the whisker extending from the box in Fig. 13.2; the maximum value in the Czech Republic is in 1992). In Poland and Hungary, there are similar findings in that income inequality was higher in the urban capital cities than within the nations as a whole, though we are unable to conclude that this was the case in Poland for 1992 or for either year in Hungary with 95 per cent certainty. In Russia, on the other hand, income inequality in the urban capital Moscow was significantly lower than the national figures—Moscow (1992) Gini = 0.328; Russia (1992) Gini = 0.395. It follows that the levels of income inequality in the capitals Budapest, Warsaw, and Moscow were more similar than in their respective countries. Furthermore, it is evident that the regional levels of income inequality, as well as the range of regional inequality indicated by the length of the boxes in Fig. 13.2 (the interquartile ranges), increased in all of the countries between the early and mid-1990s. This trend was witnessed most dramatically in the Czech Republic and Russia where the median regional Gini coefficient increased to 0.254 from 0.200 and to 0.430 from 0.365, respectively. On the other hand, the evidence shows once again that income inequality declined between 1996 and 1999 in Poland. In many cases the confidence intervals we report do not overlap and thus indicate that we can be at least 95 per cent sure of these changes in regional inequality over time. Finally, when compared to the seventy-five EU regions in Western Europe, Fig. 13.2 suggests that the range of intraregional income inequality within CEE is considerably wider than in Western Europe. However, much of this is due to the inclusion of Russia, which is not currently a candidate for entry into the European Union. If we were to exclude these regions from the box plot, we would find that the levels of intraregional inequality with CEE are, in fact, similar to levels in the West.

In contrast to the preceding figures detailing intraregional income inequality, Figs 13.4 and 13.5 offer a more precise picture of interregional disparities within each of the countries. In this case, we plot the ratio of each region's median household income to the national median household income. Examining the countries, we find that interregional disparities were significantly greater in Russia and Hungary[22] than in the Czech Republic and Poland. For example, in Fig. 13.4 we can see that in Poland in 1992 the interquartile range equalled 92.8 per cent at the twenty-fifth percentile and 106.4 per cent at the seventy-fifth percentile while these figures equalled 81.5 and 124.7 per cent, respectively, in Russia in the same year. Finally, in the two countries with wider regional disparities, Hungary and Russia, the gap between the regions widened in the 1990s. The interregional gap in the Czech Republic and Poland, on the other hand, essentially remained stable and perhaps narrowed between the waves. Finally, we once again find that the range of regional inequality is greater in the CEE countries than within western EU regions but it is also clear that these distributions are again influenced by the considerably wider distribution within Russia.

[22] Caution has to be applied when interpreting the results for Hungary. As noted earlier, regions in Hungary do not refer to administrative entities such as in the other countries but rather to socioeconomic rural–urban categories, a fact which may overstate income disparities.

When examining Fig. 13.5 more closely, it is evident that some regions were 'winners' relative to the national median income while others were 'losers'. For example, Prague, Budapest, and Moscow were all winners in that the gap between these regions and the nation as a whole widened in the early 1990s. Whereas North Bohemia in the Czech Republic, farmsteads in Hungary, and East Siberia in Russia are all examples of losers. In fact, one general pattern that emerges from Fig. 13.5 is that the urban–rural gap grew within CEE countries during the first half of the 1990s. In sum, there is a good deal of regional variation in levels of income inequality within the countries we examine. In fact, it is evident that national income inequality figures mask a great deal of within-country variance in the level of inequality. Furthermore, regional disparities are greater in Russia and Hungary than they are in the Czech Republic and Poland. We also found strong evidence indicating that both intra and interregional inequalities grew in the countries under examination during the first half of the 1990s. With regard to the latter point, this is especially true in the countries that had the largest initial levels of income inequality, Hungary and Russia. However, the evidence from Poland in Wave V suggests that this trend may have been reversed in the second half of the 1990s.

Finally, when compared to regions within Western Europe, we found that both intra and interregional inequality was greater in CEE in the 1990s, a conclusion which has perhaps become part of the 'conventional wisdom' when discussing regional disparities in CEE versus the West. However, if we were to exclude Russia from the CEE regional aggregation, we would find that the rates of inequality are more similar than is often claimed, although regional disparities still tend to be somewhat greater within CEE countries than in the West.

13.4.3. *Regional Poverty*

Although the preceding description of regional income inequality provided some important insights, it told us little about the economic well-being of individuals within CEE regions. Accordingly, we chose to focus more attention on the bottom of the income distribution and estimated relative poverty in the thirty-one regions. Thus, Figs 13.6 and 13.7 report regional poverty rates for the countries we examine using the national poverty line for Waves III, IV, and V (Poland only). The box and whiskers plot shown in Fig. 13.6 and the plot of values and confidence intervals displayed in Fig. 13.7 clearly demonstrate that there is a great deal of regional variation in the rate of poverty across the CEE regions. For example, the interquartile range across the thirty-one regions we examined in Wave III, as shown in Fig. 13.6, extended from 3.2 to 13.7 per cent poverty, with a median poverty rate equal to 7.7 per cent. For comparison, the same figures for the West European regions are 5.7 and 12.8 per cent for the interquartile range with a median equal to 7.9 per cent. Furthermore, there is also a good deal of variation in the rate of poverty within countries. In Russia, the country that showed the largest regional variation in poverty in both waves, the interquartile range extended from 12.9 to 25.2 per cent in 1992 and the median regional poverty rate equalled 19.0 per cent in this same year. Furthermore, in 1992 poverty ranged from

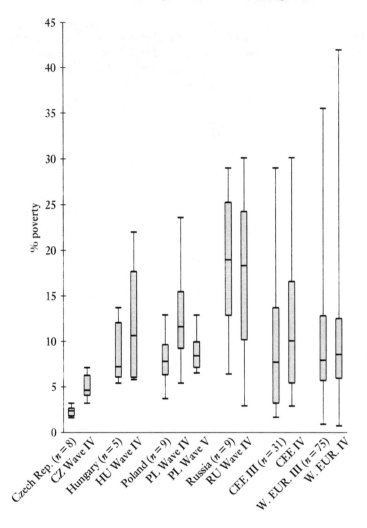

Figure 13.6. *Poverty rates using the national line*

Source: Authors' calculations using LIS.

a low of 6.4 per cent in Moscow to a high of 29 per cent in West Siberia. This latter point is also shown clearly in Fig. 13.7 and we can conclude with 95 per cent statistical certainty that poverty was lower in Moscow than in nearly every other region in Russia (with the exception of East Siberia where the confidence intervals overlap slightly).[23]

---

[23] In fact, we are being rather restrictive in our use of the confidence intervals since we only want to be 95 per cent certain that the poverty rate in one region is higher than in another. When confidence intervals do not overlap it indicates a 'stricter condition' that a region's poverty rate is higher than a value x and, independently, that another region's rate is lower than x (see Stewart 2002: 14).

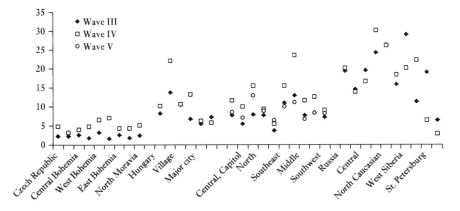

Figure 13.7. *Regional poverty rates, national lines*

Source: Authors' calculations using LIS.

In the Czech Republic, on the other hand, we found considerably less variance in the rate of poverty across the regions. As shown in Fig. 13.6, the interquartile range in the poverty rate in 1992 extended from 1.8 to 2.6 per cent and ranged from a low of 1.6 per cent in North Bohemia to a high of 3.2 per cent in West Bohemia. Nonetheless, the national poverty rate for the Czech Republic of 2.3 per cent (shown in Fig. 13.7) would still hide some regional variation.

Figures 13.6 and 13.7 also clearly show that the interregional poverty gap within all countries widened between Waves III and IV, as evidenced by the lengthening of the boxes and the whiskers in Fig. 13.6. This is most clearly seen in Hungary and Poland. Interestingly, the gap between regions narrowed considerably in Poland between Waves IV and V. In fact, the interquartile range in Poland in Wave V is slightly smaller than the range reported in Wave III (down to 0.7 per cent from 2.2 per cent). Despite this narrowing, the regional median poverty rate was higher in Poland in Wave V than in Wave III and thus poverty did shift upwards during the decade of the 1990s. Finally, it is important to note that the poverty estimates increased in every region between LIS Waves III and IV. In fact, this increase was statistically significant in about half of the regions examined.

As discussed previously, measuring poverty at the regional level of analysis involves the question of: what is the more appropriate reference society, the local community (region) or the nation as a whole? In Figs 13.8 and 13.9, we report regional poverty rates using a *local* poverty line to compare the results using the national line just discussed. As shown in Fig. 13.8, there continues to be a wide variance in regional poverty even when a local poverty line is adopted. For example, the interquartile range for the thirty-one regions we examined in Wave III extended from 4.3 to 15.6 per cent. Within most countries, however, the reported regional disparities in the rate of poverty are lower when the local line is adopted. This is most clearly shown in the results for Russia. Comparing these box plots to the distributions reported in Fig. 13.4 we

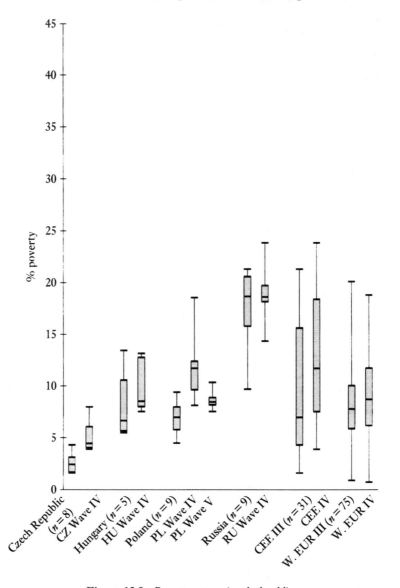

Figure 13.8. *Poverty rates using the local line*

Source: Authors' calculations using LIS.

find that the interquartile range in regional poverty extends from 15.8 to 20.6 per cent in Wave III using the local line, while the national line yielded a range from 12.9 to 25.2 per cent. This is true in the other countries with the exception of the Czech Republic, where the range in values is actually slightly wider using a local line. Finally, the most striking difference between Figs 13.6 and 13.8, which plotted the box and

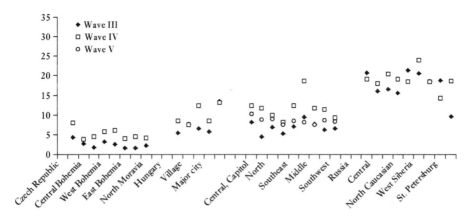

Figure 13.9. *Regional poverty rates, local lines*

Source: Authors' calculations using LIS.

whiskers using the national poverty line, is the comparison with the seventy-five West European regions. Specifically, when a local line is adopted it appears that regional disparities in the rate of poverty are wider in CEE than in West Europe. This is not due to higher variations in poverty in CEE countries when using local poverty lines (they are, in fact, slightly lower than when using national poverty lines) but to a much lower variation in western EU countries.

More significantly, there are some considerable differences that arise from using different poverty lines. This can be seen when comparing the results shown in Fig. 13.9 with the results displayed in Fig. 13.7. For example, the poverty rate in West Siberia, Russia was reported at 29 per cent using the national line and was equal to 20.5 per cent when the local line was adopted. Similarly, in Wave IV in the Volga Basin in Russia the poverty rate using the national line equals 30.1 per cent while it equals 20.4 per cent using the local line. Based upon the confidence intervals, which do not overlap on these estimates, we can conclude that the rates of poverty using these various lines differ. In Hungary, the rate of poverty among farmers is more than halved when a 'local' line is adopted, although we cannot say that these estimates differ with any statistical certainty. In these regions, and many others, using a national line could result in overestimating the extent of poverty in a region. On the other hand, in other regions the adoption of a local line results in regional poverty rates that are higher than reported when using a national line, indicating that the use of the former could result in significantly understating the level of poverty in a region. In Moscow in Wave IV, for example, the poverty rate using the national line equals about 3 per cent while the same figure increases to almost 19 per cent when a local line is used. The same is true in Budapest, where the use of a local line indicates that poverty in the capital city is equal to about 13 per cent while the poverty rate using a national line equals roughly 6 per cent. These results raise questions about the finding that poverty tends to be lower in the capital cities of CEE countries than in the rest of the countries, which was a

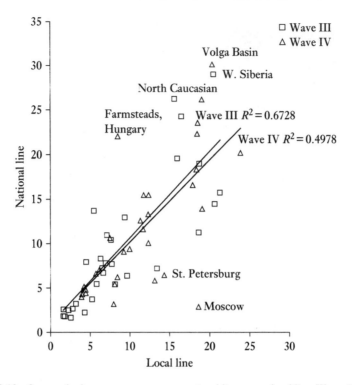

Figure 13.10. *Scatterplot between poverty rates, national line versus local line, Waves III and IV*

Source: Authors' calculations using LIS.

major conclusion of the World Bank report (2001: 74–6) and which we also found some evidence of using national lines. In short, national standard poverty lines fail to account for local standards *and* costs of living, which vary considerably across the regions within CEE countries. Once again, the confidence intervals for these differing rates indicate that we can be at least 95 per cent certain that the reported poverty rates differ.

   Despite these important discrepancies, there is a fairly strong relationship between both measures of poverty, as we would expect. This is more clearly demonstrated in Fig. 13.10, which plots the two estimates of poverty. As shown in this figure, between one-half and about two-thirds of the variance between the poverty rate using the local line and the rate using the national line is shared in Waves III and IV. Furthermore, this figure also emphasizes the important discrepancies between the two rates of poverty we just discussed. Namely, the use of a national or local poverty line only has significant consequences in countries where there is considerable regional diversity, such as in Russia or Hungary. The explanation for this is straightforward since the regional poverty thresholds are determined by the median incomes of the nation and the region. Where there is a larger divergence between these two figures, we can expect a larger

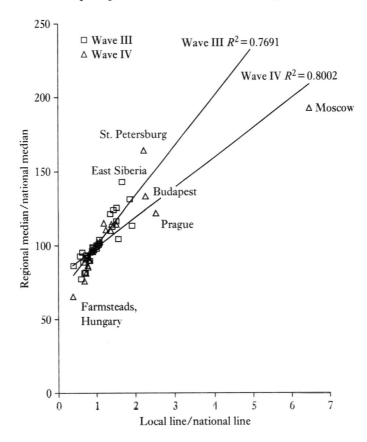

Figure 13.11. *Scatterplot between the ratio of median incomes and the ratio of poverty lines, Waves III and IV*

Source: Authors' calculations using LIS.

discrepancy between the two poverty rates. This is clearly shown in Fig. 13.11, which plots the ratio of poverty rates to the ratio of median incomes. Using a national line we are able to rank regions by their relative wealth and determine which regions are further away from their country's national standard. In effect, the national line allows us to gauge a nation's *interregional* inequality in economic well-being. For example, the fact that more than one-quarter of Russians living in the Volga Basin fell below the Russian poverty line in both waves reflects the fact that the Volga Basin is poor compared to Russia as a whole, as demonstrated in Fig. 13.7. Such an approach also more clearly approximates the European Union's current criteria for the allocation of Objective 1 funds, which may be an issue due to prospects of pending enlargement in three of the four countries examined (European Commission 1999).

The local poverty line, on the other hand, captures intraregional poverty or inequality. Furthermore, the local line takes into account differing standards of living across regions and, to a certain extent, varying prices.[24] Using the Volga Basin as an example once again, it is evident that there are still many poor people in this region even after adopting a local line. However, the point is that they are poor compared to others in their region, not only compared to Russians as a whole. In addition, there are regions that are relatively wealthy and where local standards as well as the cost of living are higher compared to the nation as a whole. We identified Moscow, Prague, and Budapest as such instances. In these cases, we may actually understate the level of poverty within a region and hence fail to identify persons who are in danger of being marginalized and quite possibly in economic need. Nonetheless, despite the proposed theoretical advantages associated with a local approach, both methods complement each other in presenting us with a clearer portrait of regional poverty within countries.

13.4.4. *Regional Growth and Inequality in the Czech Republic and Poland: Tentative Evidence*

Our final analysis focuses on the relationship between income inequality and economic growth. Due to data limitations, we are only able to examine seventeen regions in two countries: the Czech Republic and Poland. Furthermore, we cannot examine the same periods of time for both countries and thus results must be considered very tentative. Table 13.2 reports annual per capita GDP growth within these regions and the countries as a whole, adjusted using PPPs. The regions we consider in this section include the most 'dynamic', as well as those that lagged behind. We also report annual per cent changes in the income inequality and poverty measures we use in this chapter as well as two additional indicators: the share of total income received at the top and bottom quintiles of the population. These summary indicators enable us to tentatively examine whether there is a systematic relationship between economic growth and poverty/inequality, and whether inequality trends are driven by movements at the top and bottom of the income distribution (i.e. 'rich getting richer' and/or 'poor getting poorer').

It is important to note that the national trends in income inequality and poverty diverged. This could be due to the time periods under examination and differences in the economic cycles. Nonetheless, at first sight, Prague and the Warsaw regions stand out as having the highest rates of annual growth. In fact, annual economic growth in the Warsaw region was nearly double the rate in the country as a whole. This confirms our earlier findings that capital cities tended to be the largest beneficiaries of the transition. The annual increase in both poverty and inequality in Prague was only half that recorded in the whole country, while the least dynamic region in the Czech Republic (South Moravia) witnessed an above-average increase in inequality and the highest rise in poverty throughout the country. This suggests that higher economic growth is associated with a slower growth of poverty and inequality in the Czech Republic. However, the more recent results for Poland point in the inverse

---

[24] In future research, we hope to develop a spatial price index to directly capture varying costs of living across regions.

Table 13.2. *Regional annual per cent changes in growth and inequality*

Region	GDPpc		Poverty		Percentile ratios		Income shares	
	(PPP)	Gini	National	Local	P90P50	P10P50	Top 20%	Bottom 20%
Czech Republic[a]	7.1	5.7	20.8	—	3.6	−2.4	2.5	−4.0
Prague	8.7	2.7	8.5	14.3	1.9	−2.9	0.9	−3.6
Central Bohemia	6.2	4.6	9.6	7.9	3.8	−1.8	2.4	−3.0
South Bohemia	6.1	4.3	21.9	20.2	2.6	−2.7	1.7	−3.6
West Bohemia	6.9	4.2	16.5	13.4	2.5	−2.2	1.7	−3.6
North Bohemia	7.1	9.0	30.6	19.7	4.6	−3.4	4.6	−6.3
East Bohemia	5.8	6.0	11.9	20.0	3.2	−2.4	2.7	−3.6
South Moravia	5.3	6.8	19.9	22.4	3.9	−3.0	2.8	−4.7
North Moravia	8.3	5.5	16.6	14.3	2.9	−2.0	2.5	−3.4
Poland[b]	6.5	−2.1	−7.8	—	−0.2	2.6	−0.7	4.1
Central, Capitol	11.1	−1.0	−9.0	−4.6	1.3	2.3	−0.1	3.8
Middle	4.7	−1.6	−14.2	−11.6	0.1	3.8	−0.1	4.9
Middle East	3.5	−5.7	−20.7	−22.8	−1.0	12.2	−2.2	12.6
Middle West	6.6	−2.2	−10.6	−6.9	−0.6	1.9	−0.7	3.9
North	6.2	−2.1	−1.5	−2.4	−0.9	0.6	−1.0	2.3
Northeast	6.2	−1.2	−4.6	−7.4	0.6	3.4	0.1	5.0
South	4.5	−1.2	4.5	−1.9	−0.5	0.0	−0.5	1.3
Southeast	6.4	−2.7	−11.7	−10.1	−0.5	4.2	−1.0	4.9
Southwest	6.0	−2.7	−2.4	−2.9	−0.9	0.3	−1.6	2.3

[a] GDPpc between 1993 and 1996. Inequality measures between 1992 and 1996.
[b] All figures between 1995 and 1999.

Note: All figures computed using annual growth trends (exponential curve algorithm ($y = b \times m^x$)).
Source: Computations from LIS microdata; WIIW (2002).

direction: inequality and poverty decreased nationwide between 1995 and 1999, but they increased most in the least dynamic region (Central East) and least in the Warsaw region. Examples from other regions, such as North Bohemia in the Czech Republic and the North East in Poland, qualify these findings further. In both regions, the economy grew per capita by as much as in the whole nation but the performance of indicators of inequality and poverty was well below the national average. Some of the explanation is given in the sixth to ninth columns of Table 13.2, which show trends in the upper and lower part of the distribution. In the economically less dynamic regions of Central East and Central in Poland, and South Moravia and East Bohemia in the Czech Republic, the higher incomes lost relatively more in the Polish regions and gained relatively less in the Czech regions than in other regions in their countries. The lower incomes tended to lose less in these same regions in the Czech Republic and gain more in Poland relative to the other regions. In fact, the less well-off did best in the region with the lowest reported rate of economic growth, the Central East in Poland. To the contrary, the top income segment in the dynamic region of Prague gained much less than the top in the rest of their country, while the poorer segments lost less or as much as elsewhere in the Czech Republic. These few figures seem to challenge the conventional assumption according to which inequality in dynamic regions of CEE countries increases mainly because the 'rich get richer' and it increases in regions lagging behind mainly because the 'poor get poorer'.

Simple bivariate correlations between regional economic growth and the measures of income inequality and poverty did not show any significant correlation (tables not reported). However, for a number of reasons including varying starting conditions across regions and the impossibility to identify trends below the surface of averages and other measurement issues, finding no correlation between growth, inequality, and poverty across regions is not the same as saying that there is no impact of economic growth, as Ravallion (2001: 11–14) rightly points out. However, for a sound and thorough evaluation we would need to include more regions and counties in our analysis.

13.5. CONCLUSIONS

This chapter has shed some light on the effects of regional economic change on poverty and inequality within four CEE nations. But this is only a start. Much remains to be accomplished in our research. For instance regional growth should be linked to regional change in inequality in a consistent and exhaustive way. And economic change needs be linked to demographic change (emigration, immigration, and fertility) within declining and growing regions. Finally, it is our long-term goal to link regional economic and social change to health outcomes and schooling patterns (e.g. see Stewart 2002). Still, our initial results are promising and sensible. The following preliminary findings emerge from our analyses:

1. We find that capital cities and major urban areas are mainly winners, while regions which are longer distances from central cities and which are further from their richer western neighbours characterize losers. This has led to rising differences between rich and poor regions as well as greater inequality within regions.
2. We show that the contribution of intraregional inequalities to overall inequality largely outweighs the interregional contribution and, contrary to conventional wisdom, the latter is less important in CEE countries than in some of the western EU countries.
3. In the three EU candidate countries included in our analysis, inequality was higher in capital cities than within the nations as a whole, but the inverse was true for the Russian Federation.
4. The urban–rural gap seems to have increased in all countries.
5. Variations in poverty and inequality across and within regions are considerably higher in the Russian Federation than in the three EU candidate countries. In these three countries, variations are somewhat but not considerably higher than in western EU countries.

6. With the notable exception of the Czech Republic, regional disparities in the rate of poverty are lower when a local poverty threshold is adopted.

While these results are somewhat tentative at this time, they point to both winners and losers in the changeover from planned to market economies in the four countries. They also suggest that the transition may have exacerbated regional differences and that national and international authorities need to pay greater attention to regional disparities within and across nations as they design economic and social policies.

APPENDIX

See Tables 13.A1, 13.A2, 13.A3, 13.A4, and 13.A5 in the following pages.

Table 13.A1. *List of regions, poverty rates, and Gini coefficients with 95% confidence intervals*

Region	Poverty						Inequality				n
	Estimate National	95% c.i.		Estimate Local	95% c.i.		Estimate Gini	95% c.i.		Ratio	
		Lower	Upper		Lower	Upper		Lower	Upper		
Wave III											
Czech Republic	2.3	2.0	2.5	—	—	—	0.207	0.203	0.212	—	16,234
Prague	2.2	1.7	3.0	4.3	3.5	5.5	0.263	0.245	0.282	113.4	1,988
Central Bohemia	2.7	1.9	3.4	2.8	2.1	3.6	0.215	0.202	0.229	100.6	3,225
South Bohemia	1.8	1.2	2.6	1.8	1.1	2.5	0.210	0.194	0.230	100.0	3,085
West Bohemia	3.2	2.3	4.2	3.2	2.1	4.2	0.217	0.200	0.231	100.0	1,374
North Bohemia	1.6	1.2	2.2	2.6	2.1	3.4	0.190	0.183	0.199	104.2	1,113
East Bohemia	2.6	2.0	3.3	1.6	1.2	2.2	0.189	0.180	0.199	95.3	1,818
South Moravia	1.8	1.5	2.2	1.6	1.3	2.1	0.182	0.174	0.192	96.4	1,953
North Moravia	2.5	2.0	3.0	2.3	1.8	2.8	0.185	0.177	0.193	98.4	1,678
Hungary	8.2	6.9	9.7	—	—	—	0.283	0.269	0.297	—	1,979
Farmstead	13.7	0.0	29.3	5.5	0.0	18.5	0.213	0.147	0.302	86.1	22
Village	10.4	7.7	12.7	7.7	5.5	9.5	0.260	0.237	0.284	91.6	703
Town, City	6.7	4.9	9.5	6.7	4.7	9.7	0.256	0.235	0.287	99.1	566
Major city	5.4	3.6	8.2	5.8	3.9	8.7	0.267	0.238	0.304	103.9	291
Budapest	7.2	4.3	10.8	13.4	10.1	16.8	0.316	0.287	0.345	131.1	397
Poland	7.7	6.8	8.6	—	—	—	0.274	0.267	0.281	—	6,597
Central, Capitol	5.4	3.9	7.1	8.2	6.2	10.3	0.289	0.268	0.318	116.4	910
Northeast	7.9	4.4	12.4	4.5	1.9	7.2	0.276	0.244	0.321	92.6	385
North	7.8	4.6	12.2	7.0	3.8	10.5	0.265	0.244	0.287	97.3	878
South	3.7	2.5	5.3	5.2	3.6	6.8	0.244	0.233	0.258	112.8	368
Southeast	10.9	8.3	13.9	7.1	5.1	9.7	0.279	0.261	0.302	88.3	665
Middle East	12.9	9.3	17.1	9.4	5.3	13.2	0.300	0.263	0.338	93.2	705

Middle	7.7	5.2	10.5	7.8	5.1	10.5	0.277	0.253	0.304	100.1	574
Middle West	8.3	6.1	11.3	6.3	4.4	8.9	0.265	0.249	0.285	92.9	1,287
Southwest	7.2	4.5	9.9	6.5	3.6	9.4	0.252	0.234	0.268	98.9	825
Russia	19.3	18.2	20.3	—	—	—	0.395	0.384	0.405	—	6,294
North, NW	14.5	11.3	17.9	20.6	17.5	23.8	0.382	0.355	0.408	124.0	884
Central	19.6	17.3	22.2	16.0	14.0	18.2	0.359	0.340	0.382	89.7	578
Volga Basin	24.3	20.6	27.6	16.5	13.2	20.2	0.365	0.346	0.390	81.2	773
North Caucasian	26.2	23.3	29.4	15.6	13.1	18.7	0.412	0.383	0.449	77.3	981
Ural	15.7	13.6	18.1	21.3	19.3	23.9	0.387	0.368	0.408	121.3	351
West Siberia	29.0	25.3	33.7	20.5	17.1	24.0	0.402	0.373	0.442	81.7	1,209
East Siberia	11.3	8.7	14.3	18.7	15.9	22.5	0.360	0.340	0.387	142.7	624
St Petersburg	19.0	15.6	23.1	18.8	15.8	23.0	0.365	0.330	0.410	97.9	340
Moscow	6.4	4.3	9.8	9.7	6.6	12.8	0.328	0.290	0.382	125.4	554
Wave IV											
Czech Republic	4.9	4.6	5.2	—	—	—	0.259	0.255	0.263	—	28,131
Prague	3.2	2.4	4.0	8.0	6.8	9.3	0.293	0.280	0.310	122.2	5,463
Central Bohemia	4.0	3.2	4.8	3.9	3.2	4.7	0.260	0.250	0.277	99.5	3,646
South Bohemia	4.8	3.5	6.0	4.4	3.4	5.6	0.251	0.236	0.265	98.7	2,428
West Bohemia	6.6	5.6	8.1	5.7	4.5	6.9	0.257	0.245	0.277	96.9	3,444
North Bohemia	7.1	5.9	8.2	6.2	5.0	7.4	0.277	0.263	0.293	96.7	2,077
East Bohemia	4.3	3.5	5.1	4.0	3.1	4.8	0.242	0.232	0.253	98.1	3,143
South Moravia	4.4	3.8	5.0	4.4	3.8	5.3	0.241	0.234	0.248	100.3	5,888
North Moravia	5.2	4.5	5.9	4.2	3.7	5.0	0.232	0.224	0.239	95.6	2,042
Hungary	10.1	8.8	11.6	—	—	—	0.323	0.311	0.338	—	1,929
Farmstead	22.0	0.0	49.1	8.5	0.0	28.9	0.230	0.162	0.322	65.3	18
Village	10.6	8.5	14.2	7.5	5.2	9.9	0.279	0.260	0.310	91.2	589
Town, City	13.3	10.3	17.3	12.3	9.9	15.9	0.311	0.287	0.336	97.0	476

Table 13.A1. (Continued)

Region	Poverty Estimate National	95% c.i. Lower	Upper	Estimate Local	95% c.i. Lower	Upper	Inequality Estimate Gini	95% c.i. Lower	Upper	Ratio	n
Major city	6.2	3.5	10.5	8.5	4.7	13.9	0.306	0.258	0.362	110.3	215
Budapest	5.8	3.4	7.7	13.2	10.7	16.7	0.342	0.322	0.366	133.2	631
Poland	11.6	11.1	11.9	—	—	—	0.318	0.314	0.322	—	31,985
Central, Capitol	10.1	8.8	11.1	12.4	11.2	13.5	0.339	0.327	0.353	110.8	1,674
Northeast	15.5	13.5	17.7	11.8	10.3	13.5	0.310	0.296	0.326	86.6	1,864
North	9.4	8.2	10.8	10.0	9.0	11.4	0.321	0.305	0.334	101.9	4,635
South	5.4	4.7	6.1	8.1	7.3	8.9	0.270	0.263	0.278	114.4	4,478
Southeast	15.5	14.1	16.8	12.4	11.5	13.5	0.314	0.303	0.324	90.2	3,463
Middle East	23.6	21.1	25.9	18.6	16.7	20.6	0.372	0.355	0.393	85.4	2,878
Middle	11.6	10.2	13.1	11.7	10.1	13.0	0.309	0.294	0.321	100.8	3,196
Middle West	12.6	11.4	13.8	11.3	10.2	12.5	0.324	0.312	0.334	95.8	3,936
Southwest	9.1	8.1	10.1	9.3	8.2	10.4	0.311	0.297	0.326	100.8	5,861
Russia	20.1	18.9	21.5	—	—	—	0.447	0.436	0.462	—	3,373
North, NW	13.9	8.0	19.0	19.1	12.2	24.5	0.432	0.385	0.477	114.6	611
Central	16.6	13.6	20.0	17.9	15.4	20.8	0.406	0.378	0.432	102.8	393
Volga Basin	30.1	26.2	34.4	20.4	17.5	23.1	0.430	0.404	0.467	76.1	248
North Caucasian	26.2	22.4	32.3	19.0	15.3	22.9	0.452	0.415	0.500	81.2	508

Ural	18.3	15.0	22.1	18.4	15.0	21.7	0.353	0.327	0.376	102.6	656
West Siberia	20.2	16.1	24.4	23.9	19.8	27.2	0.503	0.476	0.531	115.1	236
East Siberia	22.3	17.5	28.7	18.5	13.4	23.9	0.442	0.400	0.484	90.4	415
St Petersburg	6.5	1.9	13.5	14.3	4.8	22.8	0.349	0.308	0.396	164.3	101
Moscow	2.9	1.0	6.5	18.6	13.2	26.3	0.392	0.355	0.427	192.3	205
Wave V— 1999											
Poland	8.6	8.2	8.5	—	—	—	0.293	0.289	0.297	—	30,558
Central, Capitol	7.1	6.2	8.0	10.3	9.3	11.6	0.327	0.317	0.338	111.7	3,933
Northeast	12.9	11.3	14.7	8.9	7.4	10.2	0.296	0.282	0.312	88.5	2,144
North	8.9	7.5	10.0	9.1	7.7	10.1	0.296	0.285	0.311	100.3	2,912
South	6.5	5.7	7.3	7.5	6.7	8.3	0.258	0.250	0.267	104.6	4,965
Southeast	9.9	9.0	11.1	8.4	7.8	9.5	0.283	0.274	0.291	94.0	4,765
Middle East	11.1	9.6	13.2	8.2	6.9	9.5	0.298	0.283	0.314	91.9	1,704
Middle	6.8	5.8	8.1	7.5	6.5	8.7	0.290	0.278	0.306	102.5	2,579
Middle West	8.4	7.5	9.3	8.7	7.8	9.6	0.297	0.286	0.308	100.8	4,248
Southwest	8.3	7.3	9.5	8.3	7.3	9.3	0.280	0.271	0.290	100.0	3,308

Table 13.A2. *LIS Czech Republic regions*

	Nuts, Level 3	Code
Prague	Praha	010
Central Bohemia	Støední Èechy	020
South Bohemia	Budìjovický	031
West Bohemia	Plzeòský	032
	Karlovarský	041
North Bohemia	Ústecký	042
	Liberecký	051
East Bohemia	Královéhradecký	052
	Pardubický	053
South Moravia	Jihlavský	061
	Brnínský	062
	Zlínský	072
North Moravia	Olomoucký	071
	Ostravsko	80

Table 13.A3. *LIS Polish regions*

	Provinces, 1991 and 1995	Provinces, 1999
Central, Capitol	Warszawskie	Mazowieckie
	Ciechanowskie	
	Ostroleckie	
	Radomskie	
	Siedleckie	
Northeast	Bialostockie	Podlaskie
	Lomzynskie	Warminsko–mazurskie
	Olsztynskie	
	Suwalskie	
North	Elblaskie	Zachodnio-pomorskie
	Gdanskie	Pomorskie
	Koszalinskie	
	Slupskie	
	Szczecinskie	
South	Bielskie	Opolskie
	Czestochowskie	Slaskie
	Katowickie	
	Opolskie	
Southeast	Kieleckie	Malopolskie
	Krakowskie	Podkarpackie
	Krosnienskie	Swietokrzyskie

Table 13.A3. (*Continued*)

	Provinces, 1991 and 1995	Provinces, 1999
	Nowosadeckie Przemyskie Rzeszowskie Tarnobrzeskie Tarnowskie	
Middle East	Bialskopodlaskie Chelmskie Lubelskie Zamojskie	Lubelskie
Middle	Lodzkie Piotrkowskie Plockie Sieradzkie Skierniewickie	Lodzkie
Middle West	Bydgoskie Kaliskie Koninskie Leszczynskie Pilskie Poznanskie Torunskie Wloclawskie	Kujawsko-pomorskie Wielkopolskie
Southwest	Gorzowskie Jeleniogorskie Legnickie Walbrzyskie Wroclawskie Zielonogorskie	Dolnoslaskie Lubuskie

Table 13.A4. *LIS Russian regions*

	Districts/Provinces
North, NW	Komi ASSR Komi Assr, Usinsk, and Usinsk raion Leningrad oblast, Volosovskii district
Central	Moscow oblast Smolensk oblast, city and district Kalinin oblast, Rzhev and Rzhev district Tulskaia oblast and city Kaluzhskaia oblast and Kuibyshev district

Table 13.A4. (*Continued*)

Districts/Provinces

	Lipetskaia oblast, city, and district
	Tambov oblast, Uvarovo city, and district
Volga Basin	Gorkovskaia oblast, Gorkii
	Chubashshaia ASSR, Alatyr city, and district
	Pezinskaia oblast, Zemetchinskii district
	Tatarskaia ASSR, Kazan
	Saratov oblast, city, and district
	Saratov oblast, Volskii gorsvet, and district
	Volgagrad oblast, Rudian district
North Caucasian	Dagestan ASSR, Tsumadinskii
	Rostov oblast, Bataisk
	Krasnodar city and krai
	Stavropolskii, Georgievskii
	Krasnodarskii, kushchvskii
Ural	Cheliabinskii oblast and city
	Kurgan oblast and city
	Udmurtskia ASSR, Glasov
	Orenburg oblast and Orsk
	Permskaia oblast, Solikamsk
	Cheliabinskaia, Oktiabrskaia
West Siberia	Tomsk, KhantyMansiiskii, Surgut
	Altaiskii krai, Biisk city, and district
	Altaiskii krai, Kurinskii district
	Krasnoiarskii krai, Krasnoiarsk
	Krasnoiarskii krai, Nazarovo
East Siberia	Primorskii krai, Vladivostok
	Amurskaia, Arkharinskii
St Petersburg	St Petersburg Metro
Moscow	Moscow Metro

Table 13.A5. *GDP per capita (PPP method)*

	Year	
	1995	**1999**
Poland		
Total	6,299	8,249
Central, Capitol	7,684	12,303
Middle	6,214	7,527
Middle East	5,005	5,766

Table 13.A5. (*Continued*)

	Year	
	1995	1999
Middle West	6,202	8,152
North	6,415	8,302
Northeast	4,810	6,215
South	7,244	8,717
Southeast	5,201	6,766
Southwest	6,394	8,196
	1993	**1996**
Czech Republic		
Total	9,613	11,992
Prague	16,375	21,492
Central Bohemia	7,696	9,315
South Bohemia	9,018	10,878
West Bohemia	9,412	11,660
North Bohemia	8,677	10,805
East Bohemia	8,656	10,362
South Moravia	9,001	10,601
North Moravia	8,587	11,149

REFERENCES

Aghion, P. and O. Blanchard (1994). 'On the Speed of Transition in Central Europe', *NBER Macroeconomic Annual*, National Bureau of Economic Research: Cambridge, MA.

Atkinson, A. B. and J. Micklewright (1992). *Economic Transformation in Eastern Europe and the Distribution of Income*, Cambridge University Press: Cambridge.

——, L. Rainwater, and T. Smeeding (1995). *Income Distribution in OECD Countries: Evidence from the Luxembourg Income Study*, OECD: Paris.

——, B. Cantillon, E. Marlier, and B. Nolan (2002). *Social Indicators: The EU and Social Inclusion*, Oxford University Press: Oxford.

Bailey, D. (1997). 'Separate but Equal? Comparing and Decomposing Inequality in Central and Eastern Europe', paper presented at the EBRD Conference on Inequality and Poverty in Transition Economies, 23–24 May, London.

Beblo, M. and T. Knaus (2000). 'Measuring Income Inequality in Euroland', *Luxembourg Income Study Working Papers* 232, Center for Policy Research, Syracuse University: Syracuse.

Citro, C. and R. Michael (1995). *Measuring Poverty: A New Approach*, Academy of Sciences Press: Washington DC.

Commander, S. and F. Coricelli (eds) (1995). *Unemployment, Restructuring, and the Labour Market in Eastern Europe and Russia*, Economic Development Institute Development Studies, World Bank: Washington DC.

Cowell, F. (2000). 'Measurement of Inequality', in A. Atkinson and F. Bourguignon (eds) *Handbook of Income Distribution*, Elsevier Science: Amsterdam.

European Commission (1999). *6th Periodic Report on the Social and Economic Situation and Development of the Regions of the European Union*, Office for Official Publications of the European Communities: Luxembourg.

Eurostat (1998). 'Analysis of Income Distribution in 13 EU Member States', *Statistics in Focus* 11, European Statistical Office: Luxembourg.

—— (2000). *European Social Statistics: Income, Poverty and Social Exclusion*, European Statistical Office: Luxembourg.

Flemming, J. and J. Micklewright (1999). 'Income Distribution, Economic Systems and Transition', *Innocenti Occasional Papers, Economic and Social Policy Series* 70, UNICEF International Child Development Centre: Florence.

Förster, M. and M. Pellizzari (2000). 'Trends and Driving Factors in Income Inequality and Poverty in the OECD Area', *OECD Labour Market and Social Policy Occasional Papers* 42, OECD: Paris.

—— and I. Tóth (1997). 'Poverty, Inequalities and Social Policies in the Visegrad Countries', *Economics of Transition*, 5(2): 505–10.

Förster, M., G. Tarcali, and M. Till (2002). 'Income and Non-Income Poverty in Europe: What is the Minimum Acceptable Standard in an Enlarged European Union?', paper presented at the 27th Biennial Conference of the International Association for Research in Income and Wealth (IARIW), 18–24 August, Stockholm.

Goerlich, F. J. and M. Mas (2001). 'Inequality in Spain: 1973–91: Contribution to a Regional Database', *Review of Income and Wealth*, 47: 361–78.

Gottschalk, P. and T. Smeeding (1997). 'Cross-National Comparisons of Earnings and Income Inequality', *Journal of Economic Literature*, 35: 633–86.

Jesuit, D., L. Rainwater, and T. Smeeding (2002). 'Regional Poverty within the Rich Countries', in J. A. Bishop and Y. Amiel (eds) *Inequality, Poverty and the Redistribution of Income (Research on Economic Inequality* Vol. 9). Elsevier Science: New York.

Lanjouw, P., B. Milanovic, and S. Paternostro (1998). 'Poverty and Economic Transition: How Do Changes in Economies of Scale Affect Poverty Rates for Different Households?', *Policy Research Working Papers* 2009, World Bank: Washington DC.

Milanovic, B. (1998). *Income, Inequality and Poverty During the Transition From Planned to Market Economy*, Regional and Sectoral Studies, World Bank: Washington DC.

OECD (1995). *The Regional Dimension of Unemployment in Transition Countries*, OECD: Paris.

—— (2000). 'Disparities in Regional Labour Markets', *Employment Outlook 2000*, OECD: Paris.

—— (2001). *Territorial Outlook 2001*, OECD: Paris.

Osberg, L. (2000). 'Poverty in Canada and the USA: Measurement, Trends and Implications', *Luxembourg Income Study Working Papers* 236, Center for Policy Research, Syracuse University: Syracuse.

—— and K. Xu (1999). 'Poverty Intensity: How Well do Canadian Provinces Compare?', *Luxembourg Income Study Working Papers* 203, Center for Policy Research, Syracuse University: Syracuse.

Rainwater, L. (1991). 'The Problem of Social Exclusion', *Human Resources in Europe at the Dawn of the 21st Century*, European Statistical Office (Eurostat): Luxembourg.

—— (1992). 'Social Inequality in Europe and the Challenge to Social Science', in M. Dierkes and B. Bievert (eds) *European Social Science in Transition: Assessment and Outlook*, Westview Press: Boulder, CO.

Rainwater, L., T. M. Smeeding, and J. Coder (1999). 'Child Poverty Across States, Nations and Continents', paper presented at the International Conference on Child Well-being, Child

Poverty and Child Policy in Modern Nations: What Do We Know?, 30 September–2 October, Luxembourg.

——, ——, and —— (2001). 'Child Poverty Across States, Nations and Continents', in K. Vleminckx and T. M. Smeeding (eds) *Child Well-being, Child Poverty and Child Policy in Modern Nations: What Do We Know?*, The Policy Press: Bristol.

Ravallion, M. (1994). *Poverty Comparisons*, Harwood Academic Publishers: Chur.

—— (2001). 'Growth, Inequality and Poverty: Looking Beyond Averages', *World Bank Working Papers* 2558, Poverty and Human Resources Development Research Group, World Bank: Washington DC.

Römisch, R. (2001). 'Regional Disparities Within Accession Countries', paper presented at the East–West Conference of the Austrian National Bank, 5–6 November, Vienna.

Smeeding, T. M. (2001). 'Procuring Microdata Files for the LIS Project Databank: Progress and Promise', *Luxembourg Income Study Working Papers* 250, Center for Policy Research, Syracuse University: Syracuse.

—— (2002). 'Globalization, Inequality and the Rich Countries of the G-20: Updated Results from the Luxembourg Income Study (LIS) and Other Places', paper presented to the G-20 Workshop on Globalization, Living Standards and Inequality, 26–27 May, Sydney.

—— and L. Rainwater (2002). 'Comparing Living Standards across Nations: Real Incomes at the Top, the Bottom and the Middle', *Luxembourg Income Study Working Papers* 266, Center for Policy Research, Syracuse University: Syracuse.

——, ——, and G. Burtless (2001). 'United States Poverty in a Crossnational Context', *Luxembourg Income Study Working Papers* 244, Center for Policy Research, Syracuse University: Syracuse.

Stewart, K. (2002). 'Measuring Well-being and Exclusion in Europe's Regions', *CASE Working Papers* 53, Centre for Analysis of Social Exclusion, London School of Economics: London.

Szivós, P. and I. G. Tóth (eds) (2001). *Tíz év. Tárki Monitor jelentések* (Ten years. Tárki Monitor Reports), TÁRKI: Budapest.

Tukey, J. W. (1977). *Exploratory Data Analysis*, Addison-Wesley: Reading, MA.

Wei, S.-J. and Y. Wu (2002). 'Globalization and Inequality: Evidence from within China', paper presented to the G-20 Workshop on Globalization, Living Standards and Inequality, 26–27 May, Sydney.

WIIW (2002). Vienna Institute for International Economic Studies, database on regional economic indicators in Central and Eastern Europe.

World Bank (2001). *Making Transition Work for Everyone: Poverty and Inequality in Europe and Central Asia*, World Bank: Washington DC.

348-97

D31 P23 I32

14 P25 R23

Quo Vadis? Inequality and Poverty Dynamics Across Russian Regions

RUSLAN YEMTSOV

14.1. INTRODUCTION

The increase of inequality during the transition appears particularly large in Russia compared to countries in Central and Eastern Europe[1] (CEE). The economic recovery, on the other hand, has been retarded. As a result of high inequality and depressed real incomes, poverty has become widespread. These two facts—high and rising inequality and protracted transitional recession—appear to be linked in the perception of the Russian transition by many scholars.[2] Many of these perceptions are based on a stark contrast between the high inequality in Russia and moderate levels of inequality observed in more successful transition economies. The magnitude of the inequality increase in Russia remains perplexing and demands explanation. Very often the comparison of inequality across countries in transition overlooks differences in their size, geography, and heterogeneity within the units that are being compared. Russia with its climatic, ethnic, and economic variety stands to have a higher underlying level of inequality than more homogeneous countries, and the direct comparison of its inequality to other countries is therefore not very informative.

This version of the study reflects considerable revisions after its first presentation at the WIDER-Cornell-LSE Conference on Spatial Inequality and Development, at the London School of Economics on 28–30 June 2002, and at the WIDER Workshop on Microsimulation of Tax Benefit Reform in Russia, in Helsinki 2–3 August 2002. The author is indebted to Tony Shorrocks for detailed comments and many helpful suggestions. I am also grateful to Jim Davies and to David Weinstein for reviewing the first draft. The study was prompted by the author's involvement in the poverty work on Russia at the World Bank led by Radwan Shaban. The study, however, does not represent any form of an official statement on the part of the World Bank. Ravi Kanbur motivated the author to pursue the study of regional inequality in Russia, and Martin Ravallion encouraged the work. The invaluable assistance provided by the staff of the Household Budget Survey Department of the Russian Goskomstat, in particular Elena Frolova and Tatyana Velikanova is acknowledged. Ksenia Krivenko, Vladimir Medvedev, and Oleksyi Ivashenko helped to process the data. Finally, huge thanks go to Lorraine Telfer-Taivainen for her careful editorial work on the text, along with extremely useful suggestions on the readability of the study.

[1] As reported in Milanovic (1999a), the Gini coefficient in Russia increased from 0.22 to 0.48 between 1989 and 1995, in contrast to 0.26 to 0.36 increase in Poland over the same time period. World Bank (2000) and Förster *et al.* (Chapter 13, this volume) confirm this conclusion.

[2] See, for example, the review in Campos and Coricelli (2000).

This chapter looks closely at the contribution of regional variations to the overall inequality in Russia. In contrast to previous studies on the subject, which relied on small-scale survey data,[3] this chapter uses data from the regionally representative Russian Household Budget Survey (HBS) over 1994–2000, and therefore provides a full regional extended time coverage.[4] The share of inequality due to differences in mean real incomes across regions is found to represent one-third of the total inequality in Russia—significantly more than in any country in Europe. The chapter also finds that the increase in national inequality between 1994 and 2000 can be mostly accounted for by increasing interregional inequality. But, still at least two-thirds of the total inequality in Russia at any point in time is accounted for by inequality of within-region distributions. Having established that inequality in real incomes across Russian regions is indeed a key driving force behind the increase of the inequality at the national level, the chapter focuses on two particular questions. How and why have Russian regions become increasingly diverse in their mean real incomes? And what determines the evolution of inequality *within* regions?

The first question boils down to a known problem of convergence. A convergence framework can be applied to countries, or regions, to see whether over time there is a tendency for them to converge at income levels. The simple convergence model overlooks, however, complex dynamics across the entire distribution, and several studies have looked at the issue of convergence through a mobility analysis which takes into account the full spectrum of distribution. Researchers have applied either the first[5] or second[6] approach to study interregional inequality in Russia. However, the existing studies rely on a rather poor welfare indicator,[7] and a systematic study combining both approaches is not yet available. Despite data limitations, this chapter concludes that there is *no* apparent tendency towards convergence, especially for the latter period under study (1997–2000). The transition matrix approach suggests emerging divergence across regions, with the poor regions staying poor or getting even poorer, and the rich regions getting richer.

The second question—whether regions increasingly look alike in their internal distribution of incomes—receives an affirmative answer. The study applies a test for inequality convergence[8] to Russian regional data and finds statistically significant, albeit slow, convergence in regional levels of inequality towards a common (and high) level. Based on this finding, the chapter argues that the future of the poverty dynamics in Russia is determined by the interregional inequality. As the inequality is found

---

[3] Such as Commander *et al.* (1999) and Förster *et al.* (Chapter 13, this volume) for Russia.

[4] Kolenikov and Shorrocks (2003) used HBS data for only one year, 1995, to study the underlying factors of poverty and inequality at the level of regions; Fedorov (2002) used only data on money incomes.

[5] Mikheeva (1999); Carluer and Sharipova (2001).   [6] Dolinskaya (2002).

[7] They use CPI to deflate the nominal money incomes to constant prices to a base year. This approach overlooks the poor quality of regional CPI data in Russia, especially for the earlier years, and/or assumes the equality of price levels across regions at a base point. We apply a robust measure which is based on the regional cost of the minimum subsistence (or poverty) basket as deflator.

[8] As developed by Ravallion (2001), based on an initial attempt by Benabou (1996).

to be a very significant factor of poverty dynamics in Russia,[9] the issue of economic divergence across Russian regions has far-reaching social and political consequences. Observed differences between regions in their *current* levels of inequality can be interpreted as deviations from a common level of inequality, determined by the fundamental market forces. But it is important to establish what explains these deviations, and this is what the last part of this chapter attempts to do.

This chapter is organized into four sections. Section 14.2 briefly presents data and reviews basic trends for poverty and inequality for the country as a whole and its regions. Section 14.3 applies decomposition techniques to inequality at the national level and establishes trends in regional levels of inequality and regional real incomes, and their implications for poverty. Section 14.4 attempts to disentangle key factors behind variables and uneven changes in inequality across Russian regions. Section 14.5 concludes. To sum up, the first part of this chapter distills the data on regional inequality from published series, the second attempts to understand the resulting data structure, and the third brings in additional information to interpret this structure.

14.2. DATA, METHODOLOGIES, AND TRENDS

The HBS, conducted by the Russian statistical agency (Goskomstat), has until now remained relatively unexplored as a source of welfare data in Russia. Given its unparalleled geographical coverage, it is surprising that published poverty data based on this source are little used in the economic literature on Russia—in contrast to a widespread use of similar data sources in other countries (European Union, India, Brazil, etc.). This section briefly presents the context important to the interpretation of such data, by showing trends in incomes, inflation, poverty, inequality, and regional differences in Russia over 1990–2000.

14.2.1. *Data on Regional Incomes, Poverty, and Inequality*

Researchers focusing on poverty and inequality during Russia's transition have, to a large extent, relied on the only publicly available microdataset on household welfare in Russia, the Russian Longitudinal Monitoring Survey (RLMS).[10] However, this dataset, known to provide nationally representative data, is too small to give regionally representative results and can, thus, be of only limited use to study the regional determinants of poverty and inequality. The HBS conducted on a regionally representative sample of close to 50,000 households[11] provides an alternative dataset. These data constitute the basis for the published official series on poverty and inequality in Russia starting in the late 1980s. However, the primary records of HBS remain unavailable

---

[9] Shorrocks and Kolenikov (2001).

[10] More details are provided at the website www.cpc.unc.edu/rlms. A modified RLMS dataset represents Russia in the Luxembourg Income Study Database www.lisproject.org.

[11] The Russian microcensus of 1994 was used to completely revamp the sample in 1996 with a specific aim to achieve regional representativeness.

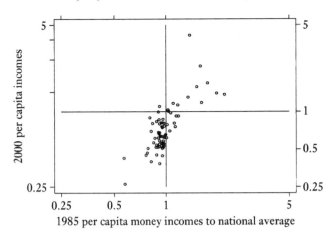

Figure 14.1. *Per capita incomes in Russian regions, 1985 and 2000*

Note: Average weighted by population size, log scale.

Source: Data from Goskomstat (2001).

to researchers. Published data, more exactly, regionally disaggregated poverty data, is the main data source for this chapter.

There are significant inconsistencies in the official methodology of compiling national-level data on inequality and poverty from regional distributions.[12] This chapter is not aimed at assessing the peculiarities of such methods applied by Goskomstat, but it is important to mention its major drawback here; since national-level estimates are produced with their own methods, they cannot be disaggregated into regional components. The chapter uses results of a consistent method to estimate the national inequality and poverty based on regional data. This method uses the properties of distribution (log-normal) used by Goskomstat to adjust the household-level data, and obtains a full set of distribution parameters from only a limited set of published figures—the method is discussed in detail in Yemtsov (2003).[13] This method also allows the calculation of inequality indices by region, so far not published by Goskomstat.

14.2.2. *Context: Regional Trends in Nominal Incomes in 1985–2000*

Even before the economic reform of 1992, Russian regions were characterized by quite noticeable differences in incomes. These widened by 2000, as shown in Fig. 14.1. To avoid problems with comparability of price levels over time, all regional average

---

[12] As demonstrated, for example, in Sheviakov and Kiruta (2001).

[13] The idea behind the estimate is to use the officially published data on poverty by region. Jointly with the data on regional poverty lines and mean incomes, it gives a parameter of inequality consistent with Goskomstat derivation of distribution statistics using log-normal function for each region. The regional distributions are then aggregated back to obtain consistent inequality measures at the national level.

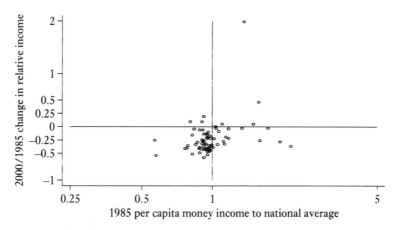

Figure 14.2. *Change in relative regional incomes over 1985–2000 versus initial (1985) values*
Note: Weighted by population. Log scale on horizontal axis.

Source: Computed based on Goskomstat (2000).

incomes are expressed in the figure as a ratio to the national mean per capita money income in the current year. All dots (each representing one region of Russia) at the beginning of the period (1985) were in the interval ranging from 0.5 to 2 of national mean incomes (horizontal axis). The spread has noticeably increased by 2000, and the range between maximum and minimum incomes per capita extended to 0.25–5 of national mean incomes. Thus, the regions were drifting clearly apart. Crossing lines represent the national means (=1) for 1985 (vertical) and 2000 (horizontal). If the interregional inequality is to be measured by the spread, it has increased noticeably over the transition.

Next, Fig. 14.2 demonstrates very peculiar dynamics of this widening. The figure plots the change over the period in the relative incomes—with regions with incomes increasing faster than national means plotted as positive values, and regions with falling incomes compared to national mean as negative values—against initial position of each region in 1985 (on the horizontal axis). All but three regions with initial incomes *below* the national average (i.e. to the left of the vertical line on Figs 14.1 and 14.2) have seen their position vis-à-vis national mean deteriorate by 2000 (falling below the vertical line on Fig. 14.2).

Many regions have seen their standing deteriorate very significantly; from 25 to 50 per cent. One region above the national mean in 1985, Moscow, has improved its incomes from just over 35 per cent above the national mean in 1985 to four times the national average. Its move is represented by an outlier position on the top of the graph. Most of the regions slightly above the national average in 1985, however, slipped down, or have maintained their relative position. Interestingly enough, bar Moscow, the number of regions improving their standing is equal (to three) for regions originally below and above the mean. Figure 14.2 reveals complex dynamics, suggesting intense reranking. Initial position seems to matter relatively little in determining the performance over the transition. The conclusion from Figs 14.1 and 14.2, however, has to be cautioned for at least two reasons. First, it does not take into account the differences in price levels across regions of Russia. Second, it assumes that incomes of the regions' populations are measured with the same precision in 1985 as in 2000.[14] We will now examine in detail the implications of the first to address the second problem, and will from now on limit the period of analysis to 1992–2000.

14.2.3. *Regional Differences in the Cost of Living*

Noticeable differences in price levels were observed in Russia already in 1985, and they widened considerably during the inflation which followed price liberalization in early 1992, amounting to some 2,500 per cent in 1992. Inflation declined to 22 per cent in 1996, to rise again during the crisis of 1998–9, with prices more than doubling between the third quarter of 1998 and the second quarter of 1999. The national price level, as measured by the consumer price index (CPI) between 1992 and 2001, increased 700 times. Within this national inflation there were substantial differences across regions. Researchers working with regional statistics tend to take these differences into account by applying some form of price index (most often CPI) to the base (1985 or 1991).[15] Such an adjustment, however, overlooks the fact that already in 1992 regions had very different price levels. The only way to correct for these is to take into account differences in the cost of a fixed basket of goods. In Russia this widely accepted fixed basket of goods has existed since 1992 as an official national poverty line based on a subsistence minimum (referred to as the minimum subsistence income or MSI).[16] Over the period under study, the cost of the minimum subsistence basket per capita rose from RR635 in January 1992 to RR379,000 in December 1996, and then increased further to 908 new rubles[17] by the end of 1999 (RR908,000 in old rubles)—more than a thousand-fold increase. Most importantly, the costs of this basket were monitored and reported regionally during 1992–2000.[18]

[14] Pretransition series are known to contain significant measurement errors, as documented in Atkinson and Micklewright (1995).   [15] Example of such an approach is Mikheeva (1999).

[16] The basis for establishing a poverty basket, or MSI, was a presidential decree on 2 March 1992. This decree allowed preparation of the official guidelines for region-specific baskets by the labour ministry published on 10 November 1992. These guidelines remained unchanged until the first quarter of 2000, when new methodology was introduced. This methodology itself takes its origin in a federal law of 24 October 1997 (No. 134) and the corresponding guidelines issued by the labour ministry and Goskomstat on 28 April 2000 (No. 36/34).

[17] The redenomination in January 1998 lopped off three zeros from the Russian currency. The government took elaborate precautions to ensure the population's confidence in the new currency with the old ruble notes circulating alongside the new ones for the whole of 1997. The old notes were exchangeable for the new currency until 1 January 2002.

[18] Note that the composition of the basket varies across six climatic zones, and cannot be judged as a fully fixed bundle. The analysis in this chapter assumes that these regional differences in the composition of the

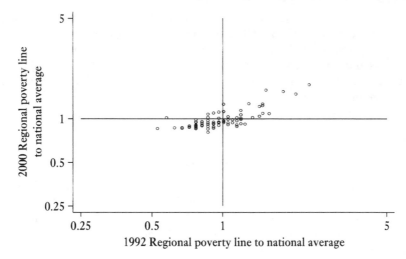

Figure 14.3. *Regional poverty lines in 1992 and 2000 to the national average poverty line*
Note: Average weighted by population size, log scale.
Source: Goskomstat (various).

Figure 14.3 plots regional poverty lines in 1992 against 2000. To maintain consistency with previous figures, the values used are regional poverty lines divided by the national average poverty line for the corresponding year, and the figure uses the same scaling options. Figure 14.3 shows that there has been already a very high differentiation of regional living costs in 1992, and these differences, though narrowing somewhat over time, have not dwindled much by 2000. Therefore an obvious solution to achieve comparability of welfare measure across regions is to take a ratio of nominal regional incomes to the current cost of MSI. Methodological and measurement issues related to the adaptation of such a measure are fully discussed in Yemtsov (2003).

This study uses regional money incomes divided by the regional poverty lines as a welfare indicator.[19] The alternative welfare indicator used in the literature—based on regional CPI indices with a base of 100 in 1992—gives quite different results, as the cost of the CPI basket differs significantly from the cost of a basket of food items consumed by the poor. This difference has to be kept in mind while comparing results presented in this chapter with other studies.

basket do not represent differences in the utility levels, and take into account only differences in local tastes and climatic conditions.

[19] Money incomes may seem somewhat an inferior indicator of living standards especially in the presence of significant in-kind components of consumption. However, money income is the only welfare index defined consistently over 1992–2000. Moreover, this is the only indicator used to officially assess the extent of poverty by regions in Russia. Due to upward adjustments to the household income data to match macroeconomic estimates of incomes, practised by Goskomstat, money incomes are consistently higher than household survey-based measures of total consumption (Yemtsov 2003).

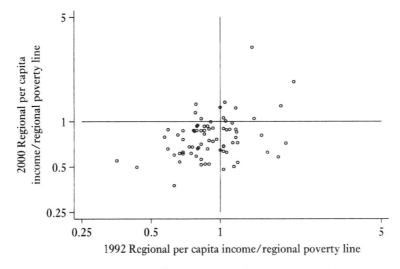

Figure 14.4. *Regional per capita income to regional poverty lines in 1992 and 2000, expressed as ratio to national averages*

Note: Average weighted by population size, log scales.

Source: Calculated based on Goskomstat (various) and annually reported poverty lines.

14.2.4. *Regional Real Per Capita Incomes Between 1992 and 2000*

Adjusting incomes by the regional differences in the cost of living substantially enriches the story on the regional dynamics of living standards. Figure 14.4 shows the regional variation of incomes per capita divided by the corresponding poverty lines, expressed as a ratio to all-Russia means for 1992 and 2000. All scaling conventions of previous figures are retained. Unlike the graph on relative *nominal* incomes, this one shows more dispersion across regions and significant reranking in region position vis-à-vis national average. The regions form a cloud rather than a line, but there is no sign of convergence or divergence prima facie, in that poorer regions are not necessarily catching up or increasingly lagging behind. The figure suggests seemingly chaotic movement in all directions. These actions mostly happened in the middle of the distribution. It is also clear that the position of the region at the start of transition does not seem to have predetermined its performance by the year 2000. Figure 14.4 captures regions at the start of transition and eight years later. Such a comparison does not fully capture movements between the extreme points in time. The period of 1992–2000 was remarkably turbulent and produced very rich dynamics.

14.2.5. *Poverty and Inequality Between 1992 and 2000*

Figure 14.5 shows on a national level the evolution of per capita incomes relative to the cost of the poverty basket (dashed line). The second line captures the evolution

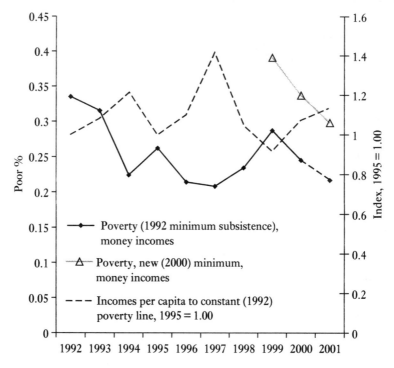

Figure 14.5. *Real incomes and poverty in Russia, 1992–2001*

Note: Officially published poverty headcount and calculated changes in per capita money incomes using published poverty lines, 1992–2001. The 2001 poverty rate with the old basket is the author's extrapolation based on published distribution (grouped data).

Source: Goskomstat (various) and author's calculations.

of poverty incidence as measured by the share of the population with money incomes below the poverty line. The graph also illustrates the impact on the measured welfare index from an introduction of the new (higher) poverty line adopted as the new official minimum subsistence level in 2000 (the line marked with triangles for 1999–2001). The figure shows that starting with the shock of 1992, the evolution of real incomes in Russia follows a clear two-hump trajectory: rising before 1995, with a subsequent fall in the (now forgotten) crisis of 1995, and rising again to a historic high of 1997, to fall in the 1998–9 crisis. Although the costs associated with the 1998 meltdown were considerable—real GDP fell by 5 per cent—the recession proved to be short-lived. By the end of 2000, poverty returned to its precrisis level and by 2001 real incomes were at 10–15 per cent above the level of 1992, if one uses the poverty line deflators. The corresponding story of poverty looks like a mere reflection of the trend depicted by the evolution of money incomes. Extrapolating the poverty rate based on the old line to 2001 data (dotted line), the figure reveals that by 2001 poverty had gone down to the lowest levels of the 1992–2000 period, if measured with a constant standard.

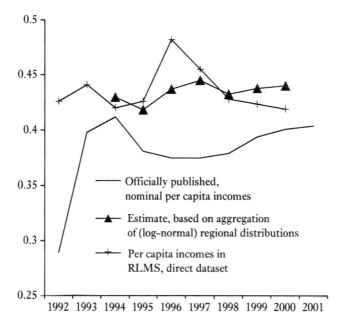

Figure 14.6. *Gini index for incomes per capita, Goskomstat*

Source: Darker line; Goskomstat (various) for official data on inequality in nominal incomes. Crossed line; RLMS and estimates (money incomes to regional poverty lines) Commander *et al.* (1999) for 1992–3, and Lokshin (2001) for subsequent years. Triangles: author's estimates based on regional data published by Goskomstat.

The fact that there is such stability in the relationship between average real money incomes (expressed as a ratio to poverty line) and the poverty rate, as depicted by the figure, would suggest that inequality has remained roughly stable.[20] The officially published data on inequality do not support this conclusion. These data, however, have been a subject of controversy in the research literature, and are known to contradict the evidence from publicly available surveys (RLMS).[21]

The series for official data on inequality and RLMS-based measures are plotted in Fig. 14.6. It also plots regionally consistent series on inequality computed by Yemtsov (2003). Unfortunately, regionally disaggregated data are available only from 1994. This cuts two starting years from our analysis and leaves 1994–2000 as the time frame for analysis in this study. The figure shows notable difference not only in the levels, but also in the trends for inequality for data from different sources. According to

---

[20] Any change in poverty can be decomposed to the change in the mean and the distribution, as shown by Datt and Ravallion (1998). Shorrocks and Kolenikov (2001) propose an approach that explicitly includes changes in the poverty line in this decomposition framework. However, as our measure of real incomes are money incomes divided by (a constant in real terms) poverty line, this factor can be omitted from future analysis. [21] As documented in Commander *et al.* (1999).

official data, highest inequality was observed in Russia in 1994. In the estimated series
inequality highs are recorded in 1996–7, the time when the inequality was decreasing
according to Goskomstat data. In the 1998–9 crisis inequality did increase according to
officially published data, but consistent estimates based on the same sources show that
it actually went down. This chapter is based on own estimates of the inequality (series
marked by triangles), which is the index consistently decomposable by all regions.

14.2.6. *Regional Inequality in Russia*

Figure 14.4 presented the scale of regional disparities in Russia in 1992 and in 2000.
Averaging over the years 1992–2001, the richest region in Russia was Moscow with
incomes on average exceeding three times the national mean. At the opposite extreme,
the Ingush Republic in North Caucasus was the least prosperous, with real money
per capita equal to around 30 per cent of the average. Tuva Republic and Chita
Oblast in Siberia, and Dagestan Republic in North Caucasus, were second to last
with 50–70 per cent. Among the locations with the highest welfare are the predominantly resource-rich and/or export-oriented regions of Siberia (the oblasts of Irkutsk,
Kemerov, Tomsk, and Tyumen, and Krasnoyarsk Krai) and the northwest republics of
Komi and Murmansk. In the richest group there are also several industrially developed
regions of the Volga Basin (Tatarstan Republic, and the oblasts of Rostov, Perm, and
Samara). The poorest Russian regions comprise, in addition to those already men-
tioned, South Siberia and several agrarian regions of the Volga Basin (the republics of
Marii El, Chuvash, and Mordova, and Penza and Kirov oblasts).

The distribution of regions by their real incomes was not constant over time. The
extent of such changes is revealed from the distribution of regions by the ratio of
the regional average money income per capita to official subsistence levels or regional
poverty lines (see Fig. 14.7). For example, this ratio in 2000 was below 1.25 in thirteen
regions, but above 2.5 in seven regions. Figure 14.7 shows that the histogram of distribution by real incomes was characterized by twin peaks in 1997, 1998, and 2000. Such a
distribution form suggests a tendency towards polarization. The figure records notable
instability in the distribution of regions by their levels of welfare over 1994–2000. It
also shows a significant shift in the distribution by groups in 1999 following the crisis,
and a subsequent recovery mirroring the precrisis distribution.

Data also suggests that, when measured by an alternative measure of living standards,[22] the regional disparities in the living standards are almost as high as in the case of
monetary incomes. A simple Spearman correlation of the ranks between them is 0.75
and 0.79 for 1997–2000, and the Kendall's tau is between 0.50 and 0.60. Most of the
regions are ranked as the poorest according to both monetary incomes and disposable
resources. Therefore whichever measure is applied the size of regional disparities in
Russia is large. When measured by the ratio of incomes in the top to bottom decile
of regions, regional economic inequalities in Russia over this period (1 : 2.8) are at par
with differences between regions of *countries* constituting the European Union, and

---

[22] See Yemtsov (2003) for a detailed discussion.

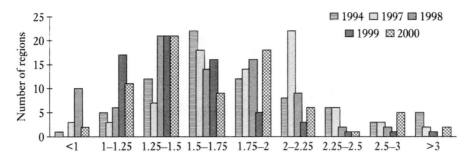

Figure 14.7. *Distribution of Russian regions by the average money income/poverty line ratio, 1994–2000*

Source: Ovcharova *et al.* (2001). For 2000, author's calculations using Goskomstat data.

much bigger than those between *states* in the United States.[23] The size and persistence of European regional inequalities has attracted much attention in the economic literature and is one of the key policy concerns of the European Union, whereas in Russia it has only recently become a widely discussed policy topic. The spread of regions by their levels of inequality is substantial. Russia embraces both very egalitarian and very unequal places. The Gini coefficient in 1999 varied from a low of 0.212 (Republic of Karachaevo–Cherkessk) to a high of 0.626 (Moscow). Noteworthy, the rates of poverty in these locations in the same year were 64.6 and 23.3 per cent, respectively. This suggests that while in some regions of Russia people can be equally poor, in others they are unequally well-off.

Figure 14.8 presents a histogram depicting changes over 1994–2000 in the distribution of regions by the level of their Gini indices for per capita incomes (expressed as ratios to the median level of inequality in the country). Regions with values below one have levels of Gini index below the inequality in the median Russian region for the corresponding year, and those above one, record higher inequality. The distribution of Russian regions by their own inequality levels has not experienced radical changes as their distribution by income levels. The figure shows that while most regions remained grouped quite closely to the median level of inequality, some important changes have nevertheless occurred. Specifically, the group of regions with inequality just above the median level (from 1 to 1.1) has increased dramatically between 1994 and 2000, while the group of regions with extreme values of inequality either vanished (group of less than 75 per cent of the median level), or was reduced.

This section shows that the performance of the Russian regions in transition is very diverse. Some regions have experienced dramatic changes in the level and the distribution of real incomes, and none of the regions were unaffected by changes. Overall, the set of dynamics produced in the Russian transition is very complex and

---

[23] See Boldrin and Canova (2001) for a review.

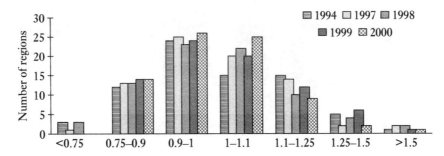

Figure 14.8. *Regional Gini indices for per capita incomes at ratio to the corresponding median value of Gini for 1994–2000*

Source: Yemtsov (2003) based on published regional data.

these represent an unrivalled subject to study determinants of the variation in regional poverty and inequality.

14.3. TRENDS IN REGIONAL INEQUALITY AND POVERTY IN RUSSIA

Section 14.2 of this chapter demonstrated a very complex set of dynamics across Russian regions over 1994–2000 in terms of real income and their distribution. This section will establish whether one can discern any orderly trends in these movements. Section 14.3.1 presents an integral view of the distribution as an aggregate of its regional components. Sections 14.3.2 and 14.3.3 analyse convergence or divergence across regions in their mean incomes. Section 14.3.4 reveals trends in within-region inequality. Section 14.3.5 examines the implications for poverty. Each topic starts with a short review of the literature, followed by the theoretical framework and analysis of Russian data.

14.3.1. *Russian Regions in 1994–2000: More Inequality Between the Unequal*

To what extent is the growing inequality in Russia due to increased regional variation? As the transition started, several regions, such as Moscow, St Petersburg, and Tyumen, benefiting from their natural resources, unique geographical position and accumulated human capital, significantly improved their standing vis-à-vis other regions. None of the popular representations of Russian realities is more dramatic than a huge contrast between the prosperity of Moscow and desperately grim images from Russian provinces. Is it possible to explain Russian inequality by this gap between a limited group of successful regions and a lagging majority?

These questions have prompted several researchers to analyse the regional dimension of inequality in Russia. Decomposition of inequality provides a useful accounting framework to assess the relative importance of between regional inequality and within regional distribution. Earlier attempts to decompose inequality (see Commander *et al.* 1999) suggested that regional differences play a very important role in explaining inequality changes at the national level. But this attempt relied on RLMS with its limited regional dimension. The findings of Commander *et al.*, however, are quoted in the literature[24] and provide motivation for further analysis. Now, when the basic picture of inequality inside each region based on HBS is established, one may attempt to provide a more accurate representation of the regional inequality and its sources.

Disentangling components of inequality is a useful step in the analysis of regional polarization,[25] another hotly discussed topic in the transition literature. In the Russian context, Fedorov (2002) introduced an explicit distinction between regional inequality and regional polarization in Russia. Relying on monetary income and expenditures per capita he finds that although regional inequality and polarization increased rapidly during 1991–6, the increases levelled off in the late 1990s. It shows that the main dimensions of increasing polarization are not so much that west–east, capitals–provinces, or ethnic Russian–national republics divides, but that factors such as export shares of regions or the relative sizes of their capitals do have effects. Fedorov posed questions on how the inequality between regions is related to inequality within regions, and how important was the increase in the interregional inequality in the Russian transition as an engine of overall inequality. Because of the data limitations these questions remained without answer. This section addresses the gap.

Commonly used inequality indices, such as Gini index or decile ratios are not strictly decomposable by population groups. But following Bourguignon (1979) and Shorrocks (1980) one can decompose the total level of inequality as measured by the Theil generalized entropy inequality indices exactly into the sum of W_g, inequality from within each of the groups in the partition of the population n into G disjoint groups (where a subgroup g consists of n_g individuals), plus the term representing the inequality between groups, B. Here groups are regions. A similar approach to the Gini index would leave a residual component due to the overlap of distributions, which is difficult to interpret.

Let y_i be an income of the ith household (out of population n). The Theil entropy index T is defined by:

$$T = \frac{1}{n}\sum_i^n \frac{y_i}{\mu} \log \frac{y_i}{\mu},\qquad(14.1)$$

where μ is the mean income, while the Theil mean log deviation index T_0 is given by:

$$T_0 = \frac{1}{n}\sum_i^n \log \frac{\mu}{y_i}.\qquad(14.2)$$

---

[24] Dolinskaya (2002).

[25] As one of the indices of polarization uses the relationship between, the between and within components of inequality (Kanbur and Zhang 1999).

If total inequality is divided in the components B (between groups inequality) and W_g (within groups), then T and T_0 are:

$$T = W + B = \sum_{g=1}^{G} \left[\frac{n_g}{n} \frac{\mu_g}{\mu} \left(\frac{1}{n_g} \sum_{i \in g}^{n_g} \frac{y_i}{\mu_g} \log \frac{y_i}{\mu_g} \right) \right] + \sum_{g=1}^{G} \frac{n_g}{n} \frac{\mu_g}{\mu} \log \frac{\mu_g}{\mu}$$

(14.3)

$$T_0 = W_0 + B_0 = \sum_{g=1}^{G} \left[\frac{n_g}{n} \left(\frac{1}{n_g} \sum_{i \in g}^{n_g} \log \frac{\mu_g}{y_i} \right) \right] + \sum_{g=1}^{G} \frac{n_g}{n} \log \frac{\mu}{\mu_g},$$

where W and W_0 represent the sum of the contribution to the overall inequality (as measured by T and T_0, respectively) due to the inequality *within* each of the subgroups of the population, and B and B_0 in the contribution to the national inequality due to the inequality *between* mean incomes μ_g for subgroups $g = 1, \ldots, G$. If the weight of gth group in the population is given by w_g, the income share by v_g, and T_{0g} and T_g are correspondingly Theil mean log deviation and Theil entropy indices for the region g, the following basic formula for decomposing both Theil Indices into the within groups (first term) and between groups (second term) components holds:

$$T = W_g + B = \sum_{g=1}^{G} v_g T_g + \sum_{g=1}^{G} v_g \log \frac{v_g}{w_g},$$

(14.4)

$$T_0 = W_{0g} + B_0 = \sum_{g=1}^{G} w_g T_{0g} + \sum_{g=1}^{G} w_g \log \frac{w_g}{v_g}.$$

A question such as 'how much inequality can be attributed to the inequality between households in different regions?' might have two interpretations: (i) 'how much less inequality would be observed if regional differences are the only source of income differences?'; and (ii) 'by how much would inequality fall if region-related differences were eliminated?' Only by using T_0 measure do we get numerically equivalent answers to these two questions, and we will rely mostly on this measure. However, we will also report results from the decomposition of T.

The log-normal distribution has a useful property,[26] according to which two Theil indices for each region g are:

$$T_{0g} = T_g = \frac{\sigma_g^2}{2},$$

(14.5)

parameters σ_g for each region g are estimated based on published data. Note, however, that the national distribution is a sum of regional log-normal distributions (and thus generally not a log-normal distribution itself), and the two national level Theil indices do not have to be the same. As Theil indices are seldom used to assess the level and trends of inequality we also compute the Gini coefficient for each aggregate distribution,

---

[26] One of the two parameters defining log-normal distribution (variance) is σ. This property can be used to test for log-normality of the empirical distribution.

using a simple numerical approach (with partition of the whole distribution into a sufficiently large number of intervals of real income and summing regional distributions by these intervals with population weights).

Table 14.1 presents results of Theil T_0 decomposition for per capita real money incomes. The table is organized as follows: each column represents one year from 1994 to 2000; the two last columns report the total change in index over the entire period (in absolute value) and the change expressed as percentage to the initial value. The table has two panels, I and II. Panel I reports results for a full set of regions, while Panel II presents the simulated national distribution, from which Moscow, St Petersburg, and Tyumen are removed. This hypothetical example helps to understand to what extent changes in the overall distribution were driven by these three regions known as outliers. The first row in Panel I is the Theil mean log deviation index for Russia. Over the period it rose from 0.297 to 0.339, a 14 per cent increase.[27] Note that the Gini coefficient (reported at the bottom of the first panel) for the same period has changed only slightly by 2 per cent. This discrepancy is not very surprising, as Theil mean log deviation and Gini indices are sensitive to changes in different parts of the distribution. The middle rows of the first panel report the W_0 and B_0 contributions to inequality. As usually revealed by such decompositions, the bulk of inequality can be attributed to the within-group components (75 per cent in 1994). Nonetheless, a sizeable and, more importantly, growing share of inequality is the result of the between-group differences, which accounted for 25 per cent of overall inequality in 1994 and for 32 per cent in 2000. This shift alone accounts for 84 per cent of the total increase in inequality in Russia between 1994 and 2000. The share of interregional inequality even at the beginning of the period was several times higher than similar shares in other European countries (see Förster *et al.*, Chapter 13, this volume). The first conclusion from this analysis is that regional differences are playing an increasingly important role in determining overall inequality. Up to 85 per cent of the total inequality increase during 1994–2000 can be attributed to the widening of interregional inequities.[28]

Repeating this decomposition while removing Moscow, St Petersburg, and Tyumen from the distribution offers valuable insights. The last row in the second panel shows that Gini index of this hypothetical distribution would be significantly lower than the actual one (by about 16 per cent), but the inequality would increase faster compared to what was actually observed (the Gini would increase by 5 per cent as opposed to just two).[29] The second conclusion therefore is that, contrary to popular opinion,

---

[27] This level of inequality is substantially higher than in other countries. Using World Bank data (2000) for comparable per capita income, we find that inequality was in 1998, 0.17 in Poland, 0.11 in Slovenia, Hungary, and the Czech Republic, and 0.22 in Croatia.

[28] Use of the Theil entropy index T yields qualitatively similar results. The share of inequality explained by the between component has increased from 25 per cent in 1994 to 29 per cent in 2000. Overall 54 per cent of the total inequality change as measured by T can be explained by the increase in the interregional differences in means.

[29] For the Theil entropy index T the level of inequality would be reduced by as much as a half in 2000 if the three regions will be removed from the distribution, but the overall size of inequality increase will remain unaffected by this experiment.

Table 14.1. *Inequality decomposition by regions of Russia for per capita real money incomes using Theil mean log deviation index*

	1994	1995	1996	1997	1998	1999	2000	Change over the period 1994–2000	
								Absolute value	% to initial value
I. Total inequality in per capita real incomes at the national level									
Theil mean log deviation of which:	0.297	0.282	0.316	0.337	0.314	0.319	0.339	0.041	+14
Between regions	0.073	0.076	0.083	0.079	0.088	0.103	0.108	0.035	+47
As a share of total, %	25	27	26	23	28	32	32	84	
Within regions	0.224	0.206	0.234	0.258	0.226	0.216	0.231	0.007	+3
As a share of total, %	75	73	74	77	72	68	68	16	
Gini index	0.430	0.418	0.437	0.445	0.432	0.438	0.440	0.010	+2
II. Hypothetical distribution without Moscow, St Petersburg, and Tyumen									
Theil mean log deviation:	0.192	0.171	0.198	0.230	0.212	0.209	0.225	0.033	+17
Between regions	0.049	0.051	0.054	0.044	0.045	0.051	0.051	0.003	+5
Within regions	0.143	0.12	0.144	0.186	0.167	0.158	0.174	0.030	22
Gini index	0.350	0.325	0.344	0.378	0.362	0.345	0.368		+5

Source: Author's estimations based on published data.

inequality in Russia is *not* the inequality within these three regions and between these three regions and the rest of the country.

The inspection of the middle rows of Panel II in Table 14.1—representing changes in inequality by components with the three above-mentioned regions removed—shows indeed that the inequality as measured by T_0 would increase by a sizeable 0.033 compared to 0.044 actually observed. But the decomposition shares would change considerably. In contrast to the actually observed changes, most of the change in inequality would come from interregional distribution, while the share of intraregional differences would remain stable. This exercise highlights the empirical importance for Russia in 1994–2000 of both stylized facts; the increased gap between high-income regions (such as Moscow, Tyumen, and St Petersburg) and the rest of the country, and increasingly unequal distributions within other regions. We will now examine the first, that is increased variation between regions, before investigating the trend in the second factor.

14.3.2. *Regional Convergence in Russia*

Reading the press reports one gets an impression that the outcome of transition by regions so far has been largely predetermined by the initial conditions, ultimately by the place of a region in the Soviet hierarchy, and that the market has moved the initially somewhat unequal regions further apart. Those who were doing better under communist rule are prospering under the market by reforming, privatizing, and changing. But those who were poor are set to remain so in a self-perpetuating circle of impoverishment and poor policies. This image sadly contradicts the view of market reforms with opportunities for most to advance. How accurate is this representation and how persistent are regional inequities? The answer to this question requires an application of a set of models that were developed to study convergence across countries. Empirical studies on economic convergence are also extended to convergence across regions of countries.[30] This framework was recently enriched with the analysis of mobility of regions across the entire distribution, which we will review in detail in the next section.[31]

It is interesting that among researchers studying the Russian transition a consensus over the lack of convergence was achieved, even before any data became available.[32]

---

[30] The regional studies by Barro and Sala-i-Martin (1991, 1992) for states within the United States and Europe, de La Fuente (1996) for Spain, Shioji (1996) for Japan, Coulombe and Lee (1995) for Canada, and Persson (1994) for Sweden, all conclude that there is indeed convergence across regions of the countries under investigation. What is important, is that the nature of convergence is absolute, which is often taken as evidence that regions within national boundaries are more likely to share similar economic and social characteristics. Regional convergence studies were long restricted to regions within developed nations because of the lack of data, but recently the literature on regional convergence expanded to developing nations. See the study by Cashin and Sahay (1996) and Bandyopadhyay (2004) on Indian states, Filiztekin (1999) on Turkish provinces, and Andalon and Lopez-Calva (2002) on Mexican states.

[31] See, for example, Bandyopadhyay (2004) on the convergence across Indian states.

[32] See Mikheeva (1999) for a thorough review.

Until very recently there were only a very few papers on regional convergence in Russia. Hanson and Bradshaw (2000), in their literature review on the regional dimension of systemic transformations in Russia, noted 'It is generally accepted that economic transition has widened the gap between the rich and the poor, both in terms of individuals in society and regions in the federation. Yet there has been a relative lack of academic research examining the relationship between transition and regional inequality'.[33]

Authors of early contributions, with the exception of Mikheeva (1999) used the coefficient of variation as an inequality measure and applied it to several economic and social indicators including industrial output, housing availability, and consumption of several food items. Russian convergence in a standard theoretical framework was thoroughly studied by Mikheeva (1999) using data for 1980–97. She found no convergence in real per capita incomes and some signs of divergence for the part of the data representing transition (1990–7). Similar results were obtained for Russia by Carluer and Sharipova (2001), who found no absolute convergence for nominal per capita income between 1985 and 1999, and only weak conditional convergence in regional gross products and industrial output per capita. Importantly, both studies have shown that the standard growth model framework constituting a base for convergence analysis cannot be usefully applied to transition dynamics. These studies, however, are plagued by two problems: data and weak conceptual frameworks. This study uses regional money incomes divided by regional poverty lines as welfare indices, and shows that this measure gives a more accurate representation of the regional variation compared to commonly used CPI deflated indices.

The problems with theoretical framework are more serious. Often 1990, 1991, or even 1985, are selected as starting points in the convergence analysis, overlooking crucial assumptions underlying convergence analysis. Neoclassical growth theory with standard assumption about decreasing returns to reproducible factors yields the following transitional dynamics of the output per capita around the steady state:

$$\ln(y_t) = e^{-\beta T} \ln(y_0) + (1 - e^{-\beta T}) \ln(y^*), \qquad (14.6)$$

where y_t is the output per capita y_0 and y^* are the initial level and the steady-state level of output, respectively. This equation implies that the average growth rate of output per capita over an interval from time 0 to time T is

$$\left(\frac{1}{T}\right) [\ln(y_T) - \ln(y_0)] = x + \left[\frac{1 - e^{-\beta T}}{T}\right] [\ln(y^*) - \ln(y_0)], \qquad (14.7)$$

where x is the growth rate of steady-state level of output. Holding steady-state growth rate and convergence rate constant across time and economic units, the equation shows that the growth rate of output is negatively related to initial level of output,

---

[33] Recently, the results of two major studies of regional economies in Russia have been published, one by Hanson and Bradshaw (2000), and another by Westlund *et al.* (2000). The Russian language periodical *Regions: Economics and Sociology* has published a series of papers on regional inequality (Kournishev 1999; Lavrovsky 1999; Mikheeva 1999; Treivish 1999).

and convergence rate, β, which can be estimated from regression of the value of y at point in time T to its value at previous period t:

$$\ln \frac{y_T/y_t}{T-t} = c - b\ln(y_t) + u_t \tag{14.8}$$

with usual assumptions about the error term and using that:

$$b = \left[\frac{1-e^{-\beta(T-t)}}{T-t}\right]. \tag{14.9}$$

Extending to i regions and assuming equal rate of convergence yields absolute convergence result if $b > 0$. This framework critically depends on the assumption of the same steady-state values and trends across time. This assumption is hard to defend in the context of transition, and therefore the starting point t has to be moved forward. But this movement shrinks already short data series available to even shorter period. This dilemma is a blight on all convergence tests for Russia. Generally, with the liberalization of economic activity and reduced fiscal resources characterizing early transition years, one should expect a considerable widening of the distribution. As demonstrated by Adelman and Vujovic (1998), central planning by trying to redistribute in favour of lagging regions within socialist economies artificially held back the regions with highest potential for growth. These pressures, however, never fully impacted and at the start of transition the distribution of regions can be represented as a compressed distribution compared to the one implied by economic forces. Thus at first it is expected that regions will diverge, moving to their equilibrium income levels. But once the market forces are unleashed, other mechanisms, including political economy, start to work that could eventually lead to a reduction of the spread. This observation underlines the need for utmost care in selecting time periods for studying convergence.

The point is illustrated by the comparison of Figs 14.9 and 14.10. Both figures plot the average annual growth rates of real money incomes per capita in Russian regions against their initial values (in logs), but they take different starting points: Fig. 14.9 plots average growth rates over 1992–2000 to 1992 values, while Fig. 14.10 takes 1994 as a starting point. Casual inspection of Fig. 14.9 may suggest the existence of convergence, as higher level values of real incomes in 1992 are associated with lower subsequent growth rates (one can fit the downward sloping line through dots that would yield a certain rate of convergence). Indeed the cross-sectional regression produces a statistically significant estimate of β (eqns (14.9) and (14.10)) of 0.06. This apparently strong correlation completely vanishes in Fig. 14.10. There are no more clear signs of convergence, as regions seem to form a cloud rather than a line, and the estimate of β gives only weakly significant values (at 15 per cent confidence) of convergence around 2 per cent per year. Both these finding are in contrast with earlier studies cited earlier, which relied on 1991 or 1985 as starting points and CPI deflated incomes, suggesting that these choices influenced the results. The assumption of equality of steady states across regions is removed in the definition of σ-convergence, which is a simple tendency of regions to move closer to each other; specifically, the values of

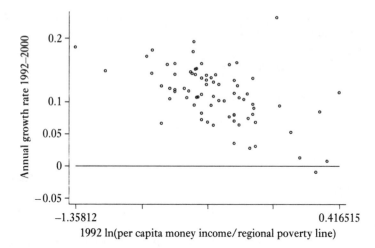

Figure 14.9. *Real per capita income by region in 1992 (log) and average annual growth rate in real per capita income over 1992–2000*

Source: Author's estimates (growth rates) based on published data.

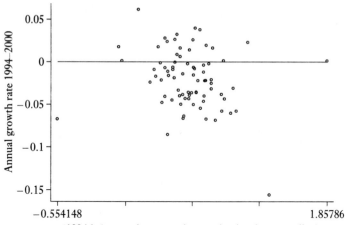

Figure 14.10. *Real per capita income by region in 1994 (log) and average annual growth rate in real per capita income over 1994–2000*

Source: Author's estimates (growth rates) based on published data.

standard deviation of the mean of the log of a variable of interest have to decrease, that is, for a period $\tau > t, \sigma_\tau < \sigma_t$, where σ_t is:

$$\sigma_t = \left[\frac{1}{n} \sum_i (\log y_{it} - \mu_t)^2 \right]^{1/2} \tag{14.10}$$

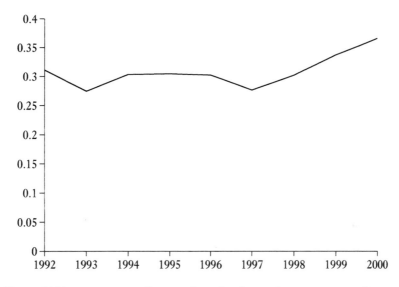

Figure 14.11. σ-*convergence for per capita regional money incomes to poverty lines over 1992–2000*

Source: Calculation based on published data on average per capita incomes and poverty lines by years and regions.

and in the case studied in this chapter, y_{it} is per capita real incomes to poverty lines in region i in year t, μ_t is the average value of $\log y_{it}$

Figure 14.11 plots the value of σ_t for real incomes per capita in Russian regions. It suggests rather stable values of variation across regions over 1992–7, and a robust increase in 1997–2000. Mikheeva (1999) reports falling levels between 1990 and 1994, one year jump in 1995, followed by no change over 1996–7. Both the level and the tendency are in striking contrast with results reported in Mikheeva (1999) for money incomes per capita deflated by CPI. The analysis of absolute and conditional convergence shows that it is difficult to discern any definite trend of convergence across Russian regions, data problems are key. The period 1992–2000 seems to include two subperiods with different trends: 1994–7 and 1997–2000.

14.3.3. *Mobility of Russian Regions Across the Distribution*

Studies of convergence using the standard regression framework briefly reviewed in the pervious part of this section consider average or representative behaviour and say little about prospects of interregional mobility. An alternative approach uses mobility across the distribution in time to uncover long-term tendencies in the evolution of the distribution across the full spectrum of income levels.[34] The formulation of the

---

[34] See the application of a full version of stochastic kernels to Indian states by Bandyopadhyay (2004).

approach relies on a key assumption (first-order Markov chain) that given the current realization of a process determining mobility, its future realizations are independent of the past. Although the assumption of first-order Markov process was criticized by Shorrocks (1976) in its applications to individual-level data on income mobility, it gained a wider use in the analysis of aggregated, such as country- or region-level, data. For Russia, this method was applied by Dolinskaya (2002) to study the regional mobility in real incomes per capita in the period 1970–97, and in particular 1991–7. Her analysis reveals a very rich and complex set of dynamics, suggesting polarization into rich and poor convergence clubs and provides insights into the determinants of regional mobility. It suffers, however, from the same problems as the previously mentioned studies—the choice of both the base period (1991) and the final point (1997), and the use of a 'noisy' deflator based on CPI. The welfare index used in this study may help to address some of these limitations, and it is useful to briefly review the theoretical framework for such analysis before applying it to the data on hand.

The transition matrix approach to studying dynamics of income distribution, pioneered by Quah (1993), focuses on capturing how the whole distribution evolves over time. At any point in time t regions occupy a certain position in the distribution F in the country. The movement to the next period $t+1$ can be described by a (stochastic) operator T, so that

$$F_{t+1} = TF_t. \tag{14.11}$$

The task is to infer T from the observed data. In practice, this task is simplified by partitioning F into n finite states, or intervals of income, in which case T becomes a matrix $M(n \times n)$. Each element m_{ij} in this matrix can be estimated from a sequence of observed transitions and represent a probability of moving from an initial state i to a state j. The sequence of M_t describing all transitions in the future converges to a limiting matrix (such that it will remain unchanged from t to $t + 1$) if F_t is described by the distribution $\bar{\lambda}$, called ergodic. It is shown that this distribution is unique, and

$$\bar{\lambda} = \bar{\lambda}M. \tag{14.12}$$

The approach requires meaningful partition of F into intervals. Following the approach developed by Dolisnkaya (2002), this study partitions the distribution of regions by their level of real incomes into five intervals, as reported in Table 14.2: the poorest with incomes below 0.7 of the national mean; next is between 0.7 and 0.9 of the mean; followed by the 'middle' between 0.9 and 1.1; by the upper middle (1.1 to 1.3); and finally the rich (above 1.3). The table consists of four different panels. Panel A takes a snapshot of the mobility by comparing the position of each region in 1994 to its position in 2000. This period is then broken on Panels B and C into two subperiods (1994–7 and 1997–2000). Finally, the last Panel D represents the last period 1997–2000 as an aggregation of all transitions that occurred in 1997–8, 1998–9, and 1999–2000.

Matrices presented in Table 14.2 are self-explanatory. For example, the first element in the matrix presented in Panel A shows that with probability of 0.67 the poorest regions in 1994 will remain poor in 2000; they will move one class up with the probability of 0.17. Probabilities sum to one across columns in each row. The diagonal of each

Table 14.2. *Dynamics of the regional distribution in Russia by the level of real per capita income 1994–2000*

A. Whole period: actual transitions between 1994 and 2000 positions (classes of income) (one six-year transition)

2000 / 1994	<0.7	0.7–0.9	0.9–1.1	1.1–1.3	>1.3
<0.7	**0.67**	0.17	0.00	0.17	0.00
0.7–0.9	0.19	**0.41**	0.26	0.15	0.00
0.9–1.1	0.08	0.40	**0.28**	0.12	0.12
1.1–1.3	0.00	0.18	0.45	**0.18**	0.18
>1.3	0.13	0.00	0.38	0.13	**0.38**
Starting frequency (regions in each class in 1994)	0.08	0.35	0.32	0.14	0.10
Ending frequency (regions in each class in 2000)	0.16	0.31	0.29	0.14	0.10
Ergodic distribution	**0.24**	**0.28**	**0.24**	**0.15**	**0.09**

B. First subperiod: transition between 1994 (starting position) and 1997 positions (classes of income) (one three-year transition)

1997 / 1994	<0.7	0.7–0.9	0.9–1.1	1.1–1.3	>1.3
<0.7	**0.50**	0.50	0.00	0.00	0.00
0.7–0.9	0.07	**0.52**	0.33	0.07	0.00
0.9–1.1	0.08	0.20	**0.48**	0.16	0.08
1.1–1.3	0.00	0.09	0.55	**0.27**	0.09
>1.3	0.00	0.13	0.13	0.50	**0.25**
Starting frequency (regions in each class in 1994)	0.08	0.35	0.32	0.14	0.10
Ending frequency (regions in each class in 1997)	0.09	0.31	0.36	0.17	0.06
Ergodic distribution	**0.11**	**0.31**	**0.37**	**0.15**	**0.06**

C. Second subperiod: transition between 1997 (starting position) and 2000 positions (classes of income) (one three-year transition)

2000 / 1997	<0.7	0.7–0.9	0.9–1.1	1.1–1.3	>1.3
<0.7	**0.86**	0.14	0.00	0.00	0.00
0.7–0.9	0.21	**0.54**	0.17	0.08	0.00
0.9–1.1	0.04	0.32	**0.50**	0.14	0.00
1.1–1.3	0.00	0.08	0.31	**0.38**	0.23
>1.3	0.00	0.00	0.00	0.00	**1.00**
Starting frequency (regions in each class in 1997)	0.09	0.31	0.36	0.17	0.06
Ending frequency (regions in each class in 2000)	0.16	0.31	0.29	0.14	0.10
Ergodic distribution	**0.12**	**0.06**	**0.03**	**0.01**	**0.78**

Table 14.2. (*Continued*)

D. Second subperiod: year to year transition between 1997 (starting position) and 2000 (final position) positions (classes of income) (average of three one-year transitions)

2000 1997	*<0.7*	*0.7–0.9*	*0.9–1.1*	*1.1–1.3*	*>1.3*
<0.7	**0.89**	0.11	0.00	0.00	0.00
0.7–0.9	0.11	**0.79**	0.10	0.00	0.00
0.9–1.1	0.00	0.17	**0.61**	0.23	0.00
1.1–1.3	0.00	0.00	0.36	**0.57**	0.07
>1.3	0.00	0.00	0.00	0.00	**1.00**
Starting frequency (regions in each class in 1997)	0.09	0.31	0.36	0.17	0.06
Ending frequency (regions in each class in 2000)	0.16	0.31	0.29	0.14	0.10
Ergodic distribution	**0.19**	**0.18**	**0.10**	**0.06**	**0.47**

Note: The entries in italic denote the real income intervals (regional per capita money incomes to regional poverty lines, with values normalized by the country's mean).

Source: Author's estimates.

matrix is in bold print as it shows the persistence of the distribution. In addition to the matrix of transitions, each panel also contains three rows that provide useful insights into the dynamics of the distribution by income classes. The first row below the matrix presents the initial distribution by income classes, the second row the final distribution, and the third row the ergodic distribution which would prevail in the long-run provided that transition dynamics remain unchanged. For example, by glancing over these three rows in Panel A for the first income interval (regions with incomes below 70 per cent of the national mean), one observes a very worrying expansion of this class from only 8 per cent of all regions in 1994 to 16 per cent in 2000, and poised to increase further in the long-run to 24 per cent of all regions.

Each element in the transition matrix is essentially a stochastic parameter which is estimated based on data from actual transitions. The precision of an estimate will depend on how many transitions are assessed. By taking only starting and ending points, as in Panels A–C, the analysis uses only limited information. On the other hand, the use of all transitions by years between starting and ending points, as Panel D in Table 14.2 does, may blur the long-term tendencies with short-term fluctuations. Table 14.A1 in Appendix II shows different aggregations across years to estimate transition matrices, and assess the accuracy of predictions. Over the entire period under study, 1994–2000, the transition matrix and the ergodic distribution of Russian regions by their income levels display somewhat less persistence than suggested by the analysis in Dolinskaya (2002). For example, the probability of remaining rich, estimated using data from two three-year transitions between 1991 and 1997, is shown to be 0.75, while Table 14.A1 shows it, using data from 1994–2000, at 0.54 with the same methodology. The probability for remaining in the lowest income class though is exactly the same, 0.69. Properties of ergodic distribution are also similar; there is a sizeable group of poor regions (24 per cent in the Panel A) forecast to remain poor, and a small but persistent group of rich regions (9 per cent in Table 14.2, and 17 per cent according to Dolinskaya 2002).

Disaggregation into subperiods produces new findings. Transitions over 1994–7 presented on Panel B display weak persistence and smaller tails in the ergodic distribution, suggesting greater convergence to the middle class, than the whole 1994–2000 period. These dynamics were reversed in 1997–2000. Panels C and D show significant persistence at the tails of the distribution (the poor staying poor with almost 90 per cent probability, and the rich stuck with 100 per cent probability of remaining rich). As a result, the ergodic distribution displays classical features of polarization into two convergence clubs; richer regions, and a smaller but sizeable group of very poor regions, with a vanishing middle section. This conclusion is robust to the aggregation method as the comparison of Panels C and D would suggest. The finding of emerging tendency towards polarization for 1997–2000 should be taken with several caveats. Table 14.A1 in Appendix II compares predicted probabilities based on the Markov first-order process assumptions with the actual ones, and reveals significant imprecision in the model's prediction. But even with these limitations one can claim that there is no apparent sign of convergence across regions of Russia.

14.3.4. *Convergence in Inequality: Are Russian Regions Becoming Equally Unequal?*

Despite the increasing role of interregional differences, the bulk of inequality is still coming from within the regions. Table 14.1 demonstrates that on aggregate there has been stability in the contribution of this component over time. What is behind it? Is it possible to identify trends and regularities in within-region changes in inequality? In other words, is inequality trended in any particular sense in each Russian region? Is there an identifiable convergence between regions in terms of inequality? How are the short-term dynamics influenced by longer-term trends?

The motivation behind attempting to study convergence in the levels of inequality is clear as, ultimately, it is a test of market operations. Neoclassical growth models imply not only convergence in average incomes, but also in the distribution. Countries or regions with the same fundamentals should trend towards the same invariant distribution of wealth and pretax income. Application of the optimal taxation models to transition economies settings[35] revealed also factors mapping the pretax (or market) income into the distribution of disposable income. Key parameters defining this mapping are features in the fiscal system, and the extent of public goods provision by the state. Once the regions are characterized by similar parameters in these dimensions, one may expect the fiscal systems to operate in a way (given all of its general equilibrium effects) that would produce similar post-redistribution inequality levels across regions.

---

[35] Kanbur and Tuomala (2002).

Regions of Russia prima facie have very different inequality aversion parameters, as may be revealed by a spread of regions across the political spectrum and significant regional differences in voting patterns. The observed behaviour, however, might be endogenous.[36] As shown in Ravallion and Lokshin (1999) proper treatment of revealed preferences gives significant differences in the attitudes to redistribution across some groups, such as urban and rural populations, but does not produce significant regional effects. Given the common history and commonality of some cultural institutions it should not be surprising that inequality aversion will not differ much across regions of Russia. Normally such preferences are known to differ across countries (as shown in Alesina et al. 2002), but not within the countries.

Key parameters of reductions of the public sector were common across regions of Russia (World Bank 1996), and produced similar outcomes. Regions did differ in the fiscal capacity considerably, but the system of fiscal federalism in Russia was known to produce a common set of rules and a common fiscal space (Zhuravskaya 2000). Only some regions (so called 'donor' regions with positive fiscal balances, rich regions in our classification) clearly stand out amidst these trends. Within these common patterns, regions of Russia display substantial differences in particular forms of adjustment and/or in the speed at which it occurred. Thus, one may expect to see a very gradual and uneven convergence in the levels of inequality as determined by the fundamentals.

A simple intuition is presented in Fig. 14.12. The figure plots original (1994) values of regional Gini indices for per capita incomes on the horizontal axis, against subsequent change in the region's Gini index over the period 1994–2000 on the vertical axis. The horizontal line through the scatter plot represents no change of Gini over time, and the vertical line depicts median level of Gini observed across regions in 1994. Two outliers are labelled on the graph: Moscow with the level of inequality already close to 0.6 in 1994; and North Ossetia on the top left with very low original inequality which more than doubled over the entire period. The graph reveals evidence of convergence. The higher the initial level of inequality, the more likely was a region to see a fall in its inequality by the year 2000. In contrast to the growth literature, there has been only a handful of studies looking at this inequality convergence, concentrating exclusively on cross–country datasets.[37] Clearly, no such attempt has ever been undertaken using data for Russia.

Borrowing from the literature on convergence in mean income, the simplest test for inequality convergence across regions is to regress observed changes over time in inequality (measured, say, by the Gini index) to its initial values. Keeping the same notations as in Ravallion (2001), let G_{it} denote the observed measure of inequality in a region i for $t = 0, 1, \ldots, T$ period; the test equation for convergence is then

$$G_{iT} - G_{i0} = a + bG_{i0} + e_i, \tag{14.13}$$

---

[36] And lead to more redistribution in more unequal places, as shown in cross-country studies such as Milanovic (1999b). This might be a mechanism that eventually equalizes regions in terms of their levels of inequality.   [37] See Ravallion (2001) for a review.

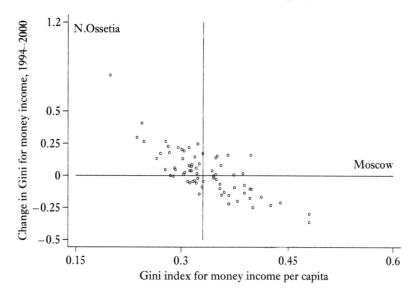

Figure 14.12. *Initial level of inequality (Gini index) in 1994 against the change in inequality over 1994–2000*

Source: Data from Yemtsov (2003) based on published data from HBS.

e_i is an error term. If the convergence parameter b (analogous to β in means convergence literature) is negative, then there is inequality convergence, and for non-zero b, steady-state inequality converges to an expected value similar across regions of $-a/b$. Application of this simple test to the actual data, as shown by Ravallion (2001), requires serious examination of concerns about the measurement error in the inequality indices, because these problems may have considerable effects on the results of convergence tests. If the initial level of inequality is underestimated (and there are reasons to believe it is in the context of Russia), the application of the simple framework will lead to overestimation of the subsequent trend. Thus, the dynamic structure of regional inequality has to be taken into account to determine its trend. Measurement error in the inequality data will bias a convergence test in the direction of suggesting convergence. We therefore employ a version of the test proposed by Ravallion (2001) that is robust to measurement error in the inequality data; it also uses panel structure of the data. Test equation to be estimated on Russian regional data can be written, as in Ravallion (2001)

$$G_{iT} - G_{i1} = (\alpha + \beta G_{i1})(t - 1) + e_{it}, \qquad (14.14)$$

where, as shown by Ravallion, composite error term e_{it} is such that it cannot be assumed that $\text{cov}(G_{it}, e_{it}) = 0$. But one can use G_{i0} (level of inequality in 1994) as an instrument for 'error free' G_{i1}^* in 1995; this estimation can be also performed together with other data to control for initial conditions that are supposedly not correlated with

Table 14.3. *Inequality convergence: test results*

Dependent variable is $G_{iT} - G_{i1}^*$	Intercept (α)	Slope (β)	R^2	N	Long-run Gini
Panel OLS[a]	0.0617073 (0.0105084)	−0.1812326 (0.0278383)	0.5376	383	0.340
Panel OLS on restricted sample[b]	0.0700591 (0.0114166)	−0.2088037 (0.0308504)	0.623	373	0.335
IVE with Gini only[c]	0.0563303 (0.109525)	−0.1609836 (0.296237)	0.3794	383	0.350
IVE, large instrument set[d]	0.0621956 (0.0157239)	−0.1778161 (0.042447)	0.4221	383	0.350
IVE large set, restricted sample[e]	0.0775095 (0.0187333)	−0.2297803 (0.0526736)	0.5052	373	0.337

Notes: Data on regional Gini indices for real money per capita incomes; dependent variable is expressed in points. Stata command xtpcse is used which produces panel corrected standard error (PCSE) estimates for linear cross-sectional time-series models; when computing the standard errors and the variance–covariance estimates, the disturbances are assumed to be heteroskedastic. IVE: instrumental variables estimation.
[a] Panel regression using actual data for 1994, no instruments.
[b] Same as note 'a' but with Moscow and Tyumen removed.
[c] Uses the value of Gini in 1994 as an instrument for Gini in 1995.
[d] Uses Gini in 1994 initial conditions and time-invariant characteristics of the region to instrument for Gini in 1995, which is then used as initial value 0.
[e] As note 'd', but with Moscow and Tyumen removed.
Bold marks preferred estimate, standard errors in parenthesis.

the measurement error to obtain as accurate an estimate as possible of error free G_{i1}^*.[38] The equation to be estimated then becomes

$$G_{iT} - G_{i1}^* = (\alpha + \beta G_{i1}^*)(t - 1) + e_{it}. \qquad (14.15)$$

This equation can be generalized to a linear panel data model of a measure of inequality on the region-specific initial level of inequality in 1995 (instrumented with 1994 level), and a time trend. Results of the test are reported in Table 14.3. These are regressions of the change in Gini index between each year and 1995 (although the OLS estimate could have used 1994 data also, but these are removed to maintain comparability). As in Ravallion (2001), there are only small differences between robust specification allowing for the measurement error and straightforward OLS formulation. The table reports strong indication of convergence. The long-run Gini implied by this estimate are all around 0.35; rather close to actually observed mean level of inequality. The slope coefficients are significant and imply much faster convergence than obtained in cross-country estimate by Ravallion (2001). This estimate allows the identification of

[38] Results from the instrumental variable regression are reported in Appendix IV.

Table 14.4. *Estimates for short-run dynamics of regional Gini indices based on their long-term trends*

Dependent variable: observed Gini for money incomes in the current year		Coeff.	s.e.	z
Gini for money incomes in the previous year	φ	0.682991	0.030216	22.604
Trend value for Gini index based on IV initial value	$1 - \varphi$	0.331475	0.03201	10.355

Notes: Panel data, gtee with ar(1) option in Stata. Number of observations $= 460$, $\chi^2 = 43636.91$ Pearson's $\chi^2(454) = 0.86$, Pearson's dispersion 0.00189. Test on equality of $(1 - \varphi + \varphi) = 1$, $\chi^2 = 7.66$, P-value $= 0.0056$.

short-term dynamics as well. These dynamics imply that each region is converging to its 'true' level of inequality which is given by the long-term trend.

Assuming that each region has a true underlying trend of inequality R_i, which can be revealed using the original instrumented value of G_{i1}^*

$$G_{it}^* - G_{i1}^* = R_i(t - 1) + v_{it}, \qquad (14.16)$$

v is a zero-mean innovation term. Disentangling trends in short-term dynamics requires a simple assumption that the observed inequality index is only partially adjusted at any given point in time to its underlying true value. Now imposing the restriction of the equality of autoregression coefficients across regions, the observed measure of inequality in a given region in a given period of time can be estimated using the following model:

$$G_{it} = \varphi G_{it-1} + (1 - \varphi)G_{it}^* + \varepsilon_{it}, \qquad (14.17)$$

where G^* is the true (error free) measure of inequality, and ε is an error term showing the difference between the true underlying inequality and measured inequality, which is assumed to be first-order autocorrelated. Table 14.4 reports estimates of the short-run parameter ψ for 1995–2000 (1994 data had to be used to create an instrument). This estimate φ implies that the short-run movements of inequality are rather slow. Assume that the region has a current level of Gini index value of 0.45, while its underlying level for this year is 0.4. Then the estimate implies that next year the inequality will change to 0.4399, or by 2.3 per cent. This estimate implies that whatever is the long-run level of inequality, Russian regions will reach it very slowly, pointing to the persistence of differences in the inequality over time and complex dynamics. The empirical dynamics of inequality changes and implied long-term trends are illustrated in Fig. 14.13 for two Russian regions.

Figure 14.13 is composed of two parts. Figure 14.13(a) represents Ivanovskaya oblast with originally low inequality level; Fig. 14.13(b), Chitinskaya oblast, gives the dynamics of inequality within the region with high initial values of Gini index. The figure shows a (common) long-term level of inequality based on regression results presented in Table 14.3. This level is shown as a horizontal line on Figs 14.13(a) and (b).

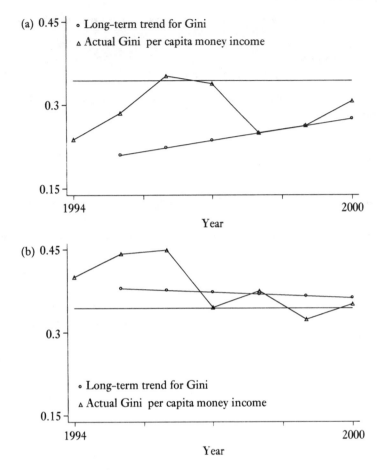

Figure 14.13. *Actual Gini, long-term Gini, and the implied trend for Gini in two representative Russian regions: (a) Ivanovskaya oblast and (b) Chitinskaya oblast*

Source: Predictions based on Table 14.3.

The estimated short-term trend from parameters reported in Table 14.4 is plotted as an upward slopping line on Fig. 14.13(a) (in this region the initial level of inequality is below its long-term value, thus it has to increase), and downward sloping line on the right panel (the opposite is true; initially the region had a higher Gini than long term 0.35). The actual movement of Gini from year to year is shown by bumpy lines. This figure illustrates well both the long-term dynamics and the extent of short-term fluctuations around it, explaining the slow convergence estimated from results reported in Table 14.4. This part of the chapter establishes robust results on inequality convergence across Russian regions in 1994–2000. Evidence of convergence towards some common level of inequality fits the general expectations well based on conceptual framework linking the forces determining the shape of distribution in transition.

14.3.5. *Poverty Projections and Preliminary Conclusions*

Both trends in regional mean real incomes and trends in within-region distributions matter for poverty changes at the national level. Trends in regional means determine the share of the population living in poor regions. Intraregional distributions matter, because given a regional mean it can be determined how many people will be poor in that region. Poverty at the national level can change if the number of poor in regions changes, or if inequality within-regions shifts.

The analysis in this section highlights the lack of convergence in the regional means and convergence to similar levels of inequality across the regions. How would national inequality look if these trends were to persist? A simple simulation using the decomposition framework presented in Section 14.3.1 is informative. Instead of taking the actual values of the Theil mean log deviation index, we can now derive the long-term Theil index which will be equal across all regions using the long-term value of Gini index derived in Section 14.3.4.[39] Based on this calculation it is easy to reckon that the within-region component of the Theil mean log deviation index will be reduced by about 15 per cent compared to its 2000 value. If the inequality between regions remains at its 2000 level, this will mean the reduction in the national level inequality by 10 per cent as measured by Theil T_0 index. A more intuitive measure, the Gini index, will record only a slight improvement falling from 0.44 to 0.425. This simulation is, of course, very hypothetical. It is unrealistic, based on the results presented in Sections 14.3.2 and 14.3.3, to assume that interregional inequality will stay at its 2000 levels. Thus, inequality in Russia is poised to increase. But such an increase could occur only gradually, as receding within-region inequality may compensate to a certain extent the unequalizing effect of regional divergence. The level of inequality implied by the Gini index between 0.425 and 0.45 that are projected in this simulation are informative, as they suggest that Russia will belong to the high inequality club, despite the fact that within each region the distributions are likely to converge to a middle level of inequality of 0.35.

One can go a step further and combine projected levels of inequality with the likely growth paths of the regional real income levels derived from the transition matrices depicted in Table 14.2. To reflect the most recent dynamics, simulation takes the values from Panel D which represent an aggregate of 1997–2000. Such aggregations are normally considered as robust estimates of transitions. For each region its future real income level is projected based on its 2000 value, and the cumulative probabilities derived from ten times repetition of the process depicted by the matrix in Panel D. Subsequently, the table projects future level of poverty if regions are to converge in ten years to a common level of inequality as established in Section 14.3.3. To derive poverty rates, simulation assumes that the shape of the real income distribution within each region will remain approximated by the log-normal form. Finally, it is assumed that the national mean will grow at a rate of 3 per cent per annum over ten years. Results

[39] Which, conveniently for log-normal distribution assumed to prevail within each region is Gini $= 2\Phi(\sigma/2) - 1$, where σ is the parameter defining Theil index, and Φ denotes the standard normal distribution function.

Table 14.5. *Poverty incidence by income class, actual and simulated for 2010*

2000 income intervals, to national mean	Actual 2000	Projected				
		Inequality convergence	Income mobility	Convergence and mobility combined	Only equi-proportional growth	All combined
<0.7	0.49	0.50	0.39	0.40	0.34	0.26
0.7–0.9	0.34	0.36	0.29	0.31	0.19	0.18
0.9–1.1	0.23	0.24	0.19	0.20	0.11	0.10
1.1–1.3	0.17	0.17	0.15	0.15	0.08	0.07
>1.3	0.14	0.06	0.14	0.06	0.08	0.02
Poverty incidence, all-Russia	0.25	0.24	0.21	0.20	0.14	0.11

Note: Intervals are based on the regional per capita money incomes in 2000 to regional poverty line, expressed as ratios to the national average. All poverty incidence figures are weighted by the population of regions in 2000. Poverty incidence is the share of regional population with incomes below the poverty line.

Source: Author's estimates.

with projected poverty incidence are presented in Table 14.5. Each row represents the initial (2000) income class where regions are grouped by the level of regional real income (expressed as ratio to regional poverty lines) compared to the national average real income (exactly as in Table 14.2). The columns report values for poverty incidence under various scenarios.

The first column of Table 14.5 reports actual values for 2000. The poverty incidence varied in 2000 from 49 per cent on average in the group of poorest regions to 14 per cent in a group of rich regions. The second column gives estimates of poverty if the trend towards inequality convergence is to bring all regions to the same inequality levels. Interestingly, this trend will affect poverty only minimally in all groups, except the richest regions where it will go down to 6 per cent of the population. The third column simulates the results of divergence based on the transition matrix approach. No assumptions are introduced about the growth of the overall all-Russia mean incomes so far, and all observed effects are only results of the mobility across income classes. Reductions of poverty for the low-income regions are quite substantial: in the group of poorest regions poverty is projected to decrease from 49 per cent in 2000, to 39 per cent in ten years. But relatively well-off regions are almost unaffected. Thus, despite the divergence, the overall vector of changes as suggested by the mobility over 1997–2000 is uplifting. The fourth column further enriches this scenario, combining the results of mobility projections with the trend determined by the inequality convergence. Since most of the 'action' in poverty rates are driven by the mobility across income classes these results are not that substantially different from what is reported in the third column. The fifth column introduces explicit assumptions about growth of national mean real incomes of equal 3 per cent per annum growth over ten years for all regions and all parts of the distribution (i.e. inequality within regions is assumed to remain constant). In other words, the whole distribution simply shifts to higher real incomes. The effect on poverty is significantly more pronounced than the impact of mobility per se. Thus, better overall economic performance is likely to have a very significant impact on poverty. Finally, the last and most informative column combines mobility, inequality convergence, and national mean growth. The projection shows that a combined effect of these factors will reduce the poverty rate in Russia to 11 per cent; less than half of its level in 2000. It is striking that the effect on the richest regions is particularly large; poverty is almost completely eliminated (falling to just 2 per cent of the population from 14 per cent in 2000) in the group with real incomes per capita more than 30 per cent over the national mean in 2000.

While the overall outcome seems very positive at first glance, it is informative that the last column suggests that 56 per cent of Russia's poor will be concentrated in a group of regions with income levels below 90 per cent of the national average, and only 3 per cent will be found in the upper income group. This is a dramatic change compared to 2000 when the corresponding shares were 47 and 11 per cent. That the regions seem to converge to some predetermined levels of poverty should not misguide anyone. It does not mean that policies are of no effect. First we have seen that this conclusion is based on historically short period and needs to be revisited if and when more data comes on stream. Second, as we have seen, this process, if left to operate on its own, will polarize the country. The economic distance between the rich and the poor regions presents an important indicator of differences in values and aspirations. If the rich and the poor share no common economic and social reality, there will be little or no agreement on common social goals or vehicles to achieve these goals.

14.4. CHANCE, CHOICE, OR FORTUNE? FACTORS DETERMINING REGIONAL INEQUALITY

So far we have assumed that underlying forces at work reveal within-region distributions determined by economic fundamentals. To what extent do regions differ in their paths of inequality changes and to what extent is it determined by their policies? Viewed from its end-point (convergence) inequality at a given point in time in a region is a product of its initial level and the region-specific trend. This section starts with the analysis of factors determining the initial level (1994) of inequality in a given region. Since we know that regions are converging to some (common) inequality level, the current level can be presented as 'excess' inequality in each region; that is, inequality compared to its long-term trend value. Using this idea, the section seeks to explain the differences between regions in their short-run deviations from the long-run inequality trends.

14.4.1. *Inequality in the Early Transition Years*

As demonstrated in Section 14.3.4, the process of regional convergence towards a common level of inequality operated rather slowly during the period 1994–2000 in Russia, and because of this low speed of convergence, a region's observed level of inequality at any given period of time was primarily determined by the 'initial' (1994) values of the Gini index. What can explain why certain regions had a higher level of inequality than others?

Milanovic (1998) proposed a simple two-sector model to analyse drivers of inequality in the early transition. Its values were calibrated to fit the generally observed patterns of inequality dynamics in the pretransition period and immediately after the transition. The parameters of the distribution were defined by the share of state sector employment, the number of private sector workers (tagged as self-employed), the share of pensioners (transfer recipients), their relative incomes and distribution within each 'sector'. The transition is modelled as a shrinking of the state sector accompanied by the emergence of the private sector and an increase in the variation of incomes both across and within sectors (part of which is determined through a state budget constraint). The latter factor, however, is secondary and the key predictions of numerical experiments point to the direction of intersectoral dynamics as key determinant of inequality change following transition. Inequality may display considerable inertia, therefore one needs to control the initial pretransition inequality to allow pretransition parameters of the distribution to survive the transition (such as the schedule of wage distribution in the state sector).

Unfortunately, almost none of the key parameters of this simple model can be directly traced to Russian regional data. But some indirect measures can be helpful. What is important is to catch in the model the factors determining, (i) the size of the state sector and the level of remuneration for the state sector workers (resources available to maintain employment and income levels in the state sector), assuming that the distribution of incomes within the sector does not change considerably; (ii) the size of the private sector, its relative income level and changes in inequality within this sector (including its level of productivity, entry conditions, etc.); and (iii) the number of transfer recipients. Since the parameters of the distribution and the income level for the latter group are primarily defined at the national level, it is enough simply to have a good measure of the size of this sector. Clearly, there are complex interaction and simultaneity between all of these factors. For this reason, it is important to include lagged values in the analysis of the current inequality levels.

The transition model offers a useful taxonomy of factors driving inequality. The initial level inequality is a product of initial geographic and economic conditions of a region, its employment structure, productive endowments, and policies aimed at redistributing incomes. The model to be estimated to assess the factors which determine the initial values of inequality can be represented as:

$$\text{Gini 1994} = F \text{ (initial conditions, employment structure, demography,}$$

$$\text{infrastructure, geography).} \qquad (14.18)$$

A detailed discussion of regionally disaggregated data on various indicators and their links to factors of inequality changes can be found in Appendix III. It also explains the basic logic behind including or excluding certain variables in regressions that follow.

Kolenikov and Shorrocks (2003) also use a rather ad hoc regression framework to establish determinants of inequality in Russian regions in 1995. Specifications adopted in this study are quite close to their approach. However, our aims are different. We seek to establish the relative importance of various factors, whereas Kolenikov and Shorrocks strive to increase the share of the explained interregional variance to conduct full Shapley–Owen–Shorrocks decompositions of poverty at the regional level.

For the first block of inherited parameters, this study assumes that the 'usual' level of inequality in the region can be proxied by the ratio of money incomes in 1985 to the national mean, and by car ownership (the most unequally distributed asset under socialism). Human capital available in the region (measured as percentage of the population with higher education in 1990) has an influence on both the size of the private sector (more skilled labour force presumably facilitates private sector development), its relative income level, and the inequality of earnings distribution. But because the latter factor can be inequality-reducing, the overall impact of this factor on inequality is hard to predict. The share of workers in private firms and the number employed in small- and medium-sized enterprises (SMEs) per 1,000 population in 1992, directly measure entrepreneurial climate and predict the size of this sector by 1994. These two variables are likely to have a positive inequality-increasing effect. However if the hypothesis about smaller private sectors (in 1992) reflecting more hostile business environments[40] is true, then smaller private sectors with more risky (and thus significantly more unequal) incomes may push up inequality compared to regions with larger private sectors and lower business risks and, thus, less unequal incomes. Variables showing the number of persons employed in industry in 1992 and the level of regional budget dependency on transfers from the central budget are both linked to the exposure to transitional recession and reveal the downward trend in the state sector. The higher these values, the more likely the region is to display some retardation in the decompression of the distribution.

The variable measuring the level of demographic dependency rate aims at establishing the size of the transfer recipients sector—one of the factors countervailing increases in inequality. The higher the dependency rate, the lower inequality would be, other things being equal. Another set of variables aims at capturing the levels of productivity, wages or rents in the new private sector— road quality, telephone lines/population, index of natural resources, and the prevalence of price controls (human capital also has a role here). The higher the indicators, the higher inequality one may expect as the relative income level in the private sector will be higher. Finally, the share of urban population, population density, distance to Moscow, control for large regional (>800,000) capital, and the region's share of population residing in the five largest cities all act as controls for geographical conditions.

Kolenikov and Shorrocks (2003) also classify the variables of the model into large classes such as natural resources, reform process, demographic, macroeconomic, politics, human capital, and geography. Each class includes three and more variables. The dependent variable is the level of inequality 1995 by regions. Table 14.A2 in Appendix IV reports results of four alternative specifications for the framework adopted in this study: for population weighted and unweighted regressions, and for the full

---

[40] See Basareva (2002), and Earle and Sakova (1999).

set of regions as opposed to the sample without Moscow, St Petersburg, and Tyumen. The results show that all factors, where the unambiguous assessment of expected influence on inequality can be made, have predicted signs. A large industrial sector, higher reliance on central transfers, higher demographic dependency rates in 1992, all reduce initial (1994) levels of inequality. The share of workers employed by SMEs in 1992 is linked to higher inequality by 1994; however, this effect is not robust to removal of the three regions from the distribution. The extent of price controls in 1992 definitely contributed to higher inequality two years later.

It is informative to find out that proxies for 'inherited' inequality (level of income in 1985 and car ownership) have insignificant impact as determinants of inequality in transition. On the other hand, a higher level of education seems to be one of the strongest and most significant factors reducing inequality. Unexpectedly, the share of private sector in employment by 1992 has an opposite sign compared to the share of SMEs; it tends to reduce the level of inequality. It is likely that we see here an effect of rents discussed above.

Most of the geography variables are either weak or insignificant. The natural resources, however, acted quite strongly to reduce inequality, contrary to expectations. What is observed here is, possibly, an indirect effect from more abundant natural resources through local fiscal revenue leading to the greater affordability of redistribution. The regression produces overall good fit and there is a consistency in the signs and size of estimated coefficients across its modification. But it gives only a static view on the distribution.

14.4.2. *Changes in Inequality*

To describe the factors behind the transitional dynamics, one needs a formal representation, accounting for the role of each factor and the interplay between them. Following Aghion and Blanchard (1994), the key channels of redistribution in transition can be formalized in a two-sector model in which the reallocation of labour and capital across *state* and *private* sectors (and unemployment as a transient step between the two) is seen as the determining feature of transition. The model is primarily concerned with the labour allocation, labour incomes, and transfers and, hence, can provide the paths (short- and medium-term dynamics) of inequality and poverty over the transition. In a number of modifications of the model some simulations were presented which provide a set of simple benchmarks for understanding the size of likely effects from within-sector inequalities, restructuring, and closure probabilities for state firms and the relative productivity of both state and private sectors.

The model produces a rich set of trajectories and paths depending on the key parameters; unfortunately it does not have a formal solution that would allow the development of a functional form for estimation. Simulations using versions of the model and their applications to study cross-country variation are described in detail in Commander and Tolstopiatenko (1996).[41] The simulations show that short- and

---

[41] The economy consists of two sectors, state and private, and three basic labour market states, state employment, private employment, and unemployment. The model assumes standard production functions

medium-term dynamics of inequality are influenced by the dynamics of sectoral employment, differences in sectoral productivity, and by the levels of inequality within each sector, all of which are predetermined in the model. What is interesting is that within a general trend towards rising inequality to its long-term steady-state level, there are substantial variations in the speed of such a movement across even a slight modification of parameter values. The path depends on the specific parameters of production and investment functions in each sector, but also on exogenously set probabilities of closure, and on taxation and benefit regime. The path is also sensitive to the initial level of inequality.

Simulations using this model and a set of parameters show that raising unemployment benefits results in a decrease in inequality. An increase in the probability of restructuring or closure leads to an increase in inequality. The taxation level does not have a clear impact on inequality under certain configuration of parameters, but does affect inequality, in other settings.

14.4.3. *Empirical Results*

Based on the insights provided by the restructuring model, this study adopts a very parsimonious specification for the empirical test. To empirically estimate the role of various factors affecting regional inequality, the test will relate the current level (t) of the Gini index to its initial 'error free' level, as well as to a number of factors which reveal the speed of convergence to a (common) steady state. A large instrument matrix and panel data are used, but no assumptions are made on the autocorrelation of residuals. The equation to be estimated is now modified to include initial level of inequality G^* (instrumented with a set of variables described above), and time-variant policy parameters.

$$\text{Gini}_t = F\ (G^*, \text{ initial conditions, employment structure, demography,}$$

$$\text{infrastructure, policies, geography}). \tag{14.19}$$

The results are presented in Table 14.6. Three estimators were used: the simple pooled OLS regression with instruments, and two panel regression set-ups (the between estimator and the random effect panel regressions). Most of the results are stable across methods. These results suggest that regional current levels of inequality depend critically on the initial conditions—the Gini index is strongly related to its initial level (instrumented to address the measurement error issue),[42] but this is not the only factor

and a given distribution of workers by skills and productivities, as well as utility functions. It endogenizes the decision of closure and restructuring by assuming that they depend on the difference between values of staying in different sectors compared to the value of being unemployed and to the value of being in the unrestructured firm. In addition a key parameter, probability of closure, is determined by exogenous institutional and financial factors. There are also exogenously chosen policy parameters, such as taxation and unemployment benefits, which make this model somewhat less 'closed' than in the optimal taxation models as analysed in Kanbur and Tuomala (2002) referred to in the previous section.

[42] Inequality convergence suggests that the coefficient for the initial level of inequality should be less than one and greater than zero, which is the case in Table 14.6.

Table 14.6. *Factors determining current levels of inequality*

Dependent variable: current level of Gini	OLS IV			Random effect panel			Between panel		
	Coeff.	s.e.	P-values	Coeff.	s.e.	P-values	Coeff.	s.e.	P-values
R^2									
Between				0.1896			0.0006		
Within				0.6866			0.6877		
Overall		0.5621		0.5763			0.5081		
Wald test				162.28		0.000	122.58		0.000
Level of Gini in 1994 (instrumented)	*0.560*	*0.114*	*0.000*	*0.596*	*0.183*	*0.001*	*0.767*	*0.206*	*0.000*
Experience of current governor in office	0.002	0.002	0.145	0.002	0.002	0.369	0.001	0.003	0.686
Legislature controlled by communists	−0.025	0.013	0.058	−0.030	0.021	0.159	−0.035	0.022	0.112
Price controls	0.000	0.000	0.093	0.000	0.000	0.178	0.000	0.000	0.246
Unemployment rate	0.397	0.125	0.002	0.352	0.120	0.003	0.560	0.288	0.052
Share of people employed in industry	−0.004	0.001	0.000	−0.005	0.001	0.000	−0.003	0.001	0.059
Share of people employed at SMEs	0.047	0.099	0.636	0.065	0.117	0.578	−0.088	0.194	0.652
Index of ownership restructuring	−0.025	0.078	0.751	−0.021	0.129	0.871	0.010	0.131	0.940
Index of sectoral shifts in employment	−0.472	0.148	0.002	−0.493	0.242	0.041	−0.512	0.250	0.041
Openness to trade	0.010	0.011	0.010	0.001	0.010	0.271	0.012	0.014	0.090
Wage arrears to civil servants	−0.143	0.044	0.001	−0.192	0.037	0.000	0.109	0.153	0.474
State transfers as share of population income	−0.176	0.102	0.086	−0.180	0.122	0.142	−0.194	0.195	0.321
Constant	0.317	0.061	0.000	0.351	0.090	0.000	0.193	0.117	0.100
σ_u				0.042507					
σ_e				0.041481					
ρ				0.512211					

Note: Instruments: urban, density, resource rich, distance to Moscow, large (>800,000) capital, dependency rate, road quality, telephone lines, early privatizer, number of SMEs in 1992.

which determines the observed level of regional inequality. The current economic conditions, expressed by the unemployment rate, are the second key factor. It is related to inequality in a predictable manner—the higher the unemployment rate, the stronger the level of inequality deviates upwards from its initially set values, other factors being controlled for.

Policy-related variables have predictable signs, but most of them are insignificant except for communists being in charge of the legislature which does reduce the current level of inequality, other things being equal. Price controls, which are normally associated with attempts to reduce inequality, do not have an independently measurable impact on slowing down the inequality changes. Regions which inherited larger industrial sectors have persistently lower levels of inequality, again *ceteris paribus*. All variables characterizing the business environment and the degree of restructuring have the right signs; they accelerate the move to a higher inequality.

Governance of the public sector also matters for inequality. It may be surprising that higher wage arrears act to reduce the level of inequality, but if one accepts the interpretation of arrears to civil servants as a politically manipulated phenomenon used by regional authorities to bargain more resources and transfers from the centre (see Treisman and Gimpelson 2000; Zhuravskaya 2000), then its role in hampering market forces is consistent with negative effects on inequality. In a more narrow sense, transfers reduce inequality, as one may expect.

Estimations presented in this section are aimed to measure the impact of various economic fundamentals on the path of inequality convergence. The result looks consistent with the models of restructuring and suggests that inequality dynamics is determined by a complex combination of many factors, which all determine how fast the regions move to a distribution determined by market forces and fundamentals. But the fact that it occurs in all parts of Russia, and that even the least advanced reformers also move in the same direction, albeit slowly, shows the broadbased nature of on-going reforms.

14.5. CONCLUSIONS

A recent debate around poverty and inequality demonstrated the crucial importance of good quality comprehensive data covering sufficiently long periods of time to underpin the analysis. This is exactly where the information on Russian regions remains scarce and largely not up to the task. Despite these limitations, the analysis of data from HBS sheds light on many issues of regional dynamics pertaining to the socioeconomic impact of the Russian transition. It is especially relevant to discern tendencies suggested by this particular dataset, as it is effectively a mirror in which Russian politics is reflected—that of official statistics.

This study finds that the share of inequality in Russia coming from within its regions is dominant, but unlike in other countries in Europe where it accounts for 90–95 per cent of the total inequality, in Russia its share is 70 per cent. Inequality between regions is growing over time, and accounts for 85 per cent of the increase in the national inequality over 1994–2000. The analysis suggests that, on the one hand, the regions seem to exhibit divergence in per capita incomes (especially over 1997–2000), but, on the other hand, they converge in their inequality levels (to a common value of Gini index around 0.35). Projections show that if observed trends are to continue into the future, by 2010 the absolute majority (56 per cent) of Russia's poor will be concentrated in a few permanently impoverished regions (with incomes below 90 per cent of the national average), while relatively more affluent regions will become virtually free of poverty. The study shows that rather large observed differences between regions in their current levels of inequality can be traced to a set of economic, political, and geographic factors that determine the evolution of income distribution. Over time the 'inherited' factors play lesser roles, and the labour market situation emerges as a particularly important factor of the inequality dynamics.

This chapter is by far not the final word in economic studies of Russian regional dynamics. Economic fundamentals, especially those related to the rate of technological progress, need to be properly revealed before one attempts further to understand the regional convergence or divergence in Russia. The relevance of conclusions from the analysis of data presented in this chapter, however, depends on the validity of assumptions underlying data processing techniques used by Goskomstat, some of which, as shown in the literature, are controversial. A recent study by Mistiaen and Ravallion (2002) argues that measures of inequality depend crucially on the assumptions about the behaviour regarding participation in the survey. A thorough reassessment of results has to rely on the raw data. The recently initiated joint Russian government–DFID–World Bank project aims at putting the data in the public domain, thus one can hope that significant advances in understanding the nature and dynamics of inequality in transition will be made in the near future.

Appendix I: Definition of Regions

By 1992 there were seventy-three statistically distinct units in the Russian Federation (seventy-two without Chechnya, which stopped cooperation on statistical matters rather early). According to the hierarchy accepted after the break up, and prior to the adoption of the new constitutions, Russian statistics and politics comprised seventy-seven oblasts, krais, and republics (without Chechnya). The difference between seventy-two and seventy-seven is due to the fact that several republics of North Caucasus, Adygeya, and Karachaevo-Cherkessiya were not earlier covered by regular statistical monitoring, and by very late (1992) granting of the status of 'subject' of the Russian Federation to three Siberian regions (Altai, Evreiskaya, and Chukotskij). The definition of regions has again changed in the new constitution to represent subjects of the federation, numbering eighty-nine territorial units.

The federative structure of the Russian federation as it emerged in the new constitution is somewhat peculiar. It consists of eighty-nine politically equal federation members, including twenty-one republics (national–territorial entities), fifty-five krais and oblasts (administrative–territorial entities), two cities of federal significance, Moscow and St Petersburg, and eleven smaller okrugs and oblasts (autonomous national–territorial entities). Previously autonomous okrugs and oblasts, for statistical purposes, were considered as part of the respective krais or oblasts, but after adoption of the new constitution they are on par with other members. Goskomstat did not respond to these changes immediately, but starting in 1999[43] all information published referred to eighty-nine federation subjects (eighty-eight in practice, as there were no data on Chechnya). No data, however, exist for autonomous okrugs and oblasts prior to 1999. The introduction of federal okrugs in 2000 changed the groupings of regions again, but confirmed and reinforced the equal treatment of all eighty-nine regions for statistical purposes.[44] However, the total number of economically distinct regions for the entire period is narrower as earlier data were available only for a classification of seventy-seven regions (and seventy-two regions prior to 1992).

A region represents a meaningful aggregation level for the purposes of inequality analysis. In addition to similar geographic, historic, and social conditions, regions are the agents of fiscal, structural, and social policy. They have the right to levy local taxes, invest in local infrastructure, provide subsidies to enterprises, legislate on local social transfers, supplement federally mandated transfers, and provide housing and utility subsidies to the households. At the same time authorities in some regions employ several quasi-legal methods of impeding free movement of capital, goods, services, and labour. There is a wealth of data published for each of the regions. Understanding the true meaning of some of the published data, presented in this table, does require a special description of methodological issues, provided in Appendix III.

Appendix II

Table 14.A1. *Transition matrices for regions between income states*

A. Year-to-year distribution dynamics: average of one-year transitions between 1994 and 2000 positions (classes of income) (six one-year transitions)

2000 / 1994	<0.7	0.7–0.9	0.9–1.1	1.1–1.3	>1.3
<0.7	**0.78**	0.20	0.02	0.00	0.00
0.7–0.9	0.12	**0.69**	0.18	0.01	0.00
0.9–1.1	0.00	0.19	**0.60**	0.20	0.01
1.1–1.3	0.00	0.00	0.40	**0.51**	0.10
>1.3	0.00	0.00	0.03	0.21	**0.76**
Starting frequency (regions in each class in 1994)	0.11	0.30	0.33	0.18	0.08
Ending frequency (regions in each class in 2000)	0.12	0.29	0.33	0.18	0.08
Ergodic Distribution	**0.17**	**0.30**	**0.30**	**0.16**	**0.07**

[43] Goskomstat (1999).

[44] Data published from the 1997 HBS was in line with the new member-level groupings (again, in practice eighty-eight regions).

Table 14.A1. (*Continued*)

B. Three-year average: distribution dynamics between 1994 (starting position) and 2000 (position at completion) (two three-year transitions)

2000 \ 1994	<0.7	0.7–0.9	0.9–1.1	1.1–1.3	>1.3
<0.7	**0.69**	0.31	0.00	0.00	0.00
0.7–0.9	0.14	**0.53**	0.25	0.08	0.00
0.9–1.1	0.06	0.26	**0.49**	0.15	0.04
1.1–1.3	0.00	0.08	0.42	**0.33**	0.17
>1.3	0.00	0.08	0.08	0.31	**0.54**

	<0.7	0.7–0.9	0.9–1.1	1.1–1.3	>1.3
Starting frequency (regions in each class in 1994)	0.08	0.33	0.34	0.16	0.08
Ending frequency (regions in each class in 2000)	0.12	0.31	0.32	0.16	0.08
Ergodic distribution	**0.19**	**0.32**	**0.28**	**0.13**	**0.07**

C. Actual distribution dynamics between 1994 and 2000 (actual initial and final positions, classes of income)

2000 \ 1994	<0.7	0.7–0.9	0.9–1.1	1.1–1.3	>1.3
<0.7	**0.67**	0.17	0.00	0.17	0.00
0.7–0.9	0.19	**0.41**	0.26	0.15	0.00
0.9–1.1	0.08	0.40	**0.28**	0.12	0.12
1.1–1.3	0.00	0.18	0.45	**0.18**	0.18
>1.3	0.13	0.00	0.38	0.13	**0.38**

D. Predicted distribution dynamics from six one-year transitions between 1994 and 2000 positions (classes of income)

2000 \ 1994	<0.7	0.7–0.9	0.9–1.1	1.1–1.3	>1.3
<0.7	**0.45**	0.36	0.14	0.03	0.00
0.7–0.9	0.21	**0.40**	0.27	0.10	0.02
0.9–1.1	0.07	0.27	**0.39**	0.21	0.07
1.1–1.3	0.02	0.18	0.41	**0.27**	0.14
>1.3	0.00	0.06	0.26	0.29	**0.40**

E. Predicted distribution dynamics from two three-year transitions between 1994 and 2000 positions (classes of income)

2000 \ 1994	<0.7	0.7–0.9	0.9–1.1	1.1–1.3	>1.3
<0.7	**0.52**	0.38	0.08	0.02	0.00
0.7–0.9	0.19	**0.40**	0.29	0.11	0.02
0.9–1.1	0.11	0.30	**0.37**	0.16	0.07
1.1–1.3	0.04	0.19	0.38	**0.23**	0.16
>1.3	0.02	0.13	0.23	0.29	**0.35**

Note: The entries in italic denote real income intervals (regional per capita incomes to regional poverty lines, with values normalized by the country's mean). Panels C–E are the predictions of dynamics based on transition matrix models.

Appendix III: Variables for Regional Analysis of the Inequality Convergence

Variables used to characterize factors of inequality levels are as follows.

Endowments and Initial Conditions of the Regions

To characterize natural resource endowments we use a complex assessment score developed by Lavrovsky, which in addition to mineral resources includes also data on climatic conditions, soils, etc. Alternatively, a simple dummy for the eight richest regions in terms of minerals is used.

To characterize population age profile (and labour resources available) we use demographic dependency rate (the sum of those below and above working age to total population). We also look at changes during 1985–95. Regions differ quite a lot, from 0.47 dependant for one person of working age up to 0.90. Changes in the demographic burden differ from 0 to 12 per cent increase. None of the regions witnessed a decrease in this rate.

Capital size is reported to be an important factor identified in the literature (see Fedorov 2002) as a good proxy for the opportunity for agglomeration, scale economies, concentration of wealth, and therefore inequality.

Measures of education at the regional level are very poorly reported by statistical agencies. The latest available published information refers to microcensus.

Physical assets are difficult to measure. The existing accounting method does not adequately capture the market value, etc. We approximate this endowment by the share of employment in industry.

To characterize the state of the infrastructure we use two proxies. 'Road quality' is the percentage of all roads that are paved; the latest available figures for 1995 give regional variations between 59.2 and 100 per cent. The second is an infrastructure proxy: the density of telephone lines (urban only); regionally density varies tremendously from nine to 193 telephone lines per 100 urban families.

Restructuring Policies: Advanced Reformers Versus Lagged Regions

The study identifies two groups of factors: proxies for 'quality of policies' that determine the investment climate, and the measures of the business climate.

A number of policy-related indicators are available for Russian regions, such as the dominant party in the parliament, the political orientation of governors, the number of governors since the start of transition, the experience of ruling governors, etc. One of the key indicators of governance at the regional level is an early start in the privatization process. By 1995, the total share of productive assets in mixed, private, or foreign ownership varied between regions from a low of 7 per cent to a high of 94 per cent (with an average of around 50 per cent). The list of lagging regions corresponds well with the known group of regions lead by conservative (communist) governments opposed to market reforms. A completely different though plausible proxy for governance quality can be fiscal data. Many scholars agree that wage arrears were a major sign of the breakdown of state authority in Russia. One can argue that wage arrears to civil servants can have especially detrimental consequences and reflect quite closely the degree of disorganization in the provision of basic state services. As measured by this indicator, regions ranged in 1997 between 0 (no arrears) and 25 per cent of the annual wage bill owed to civil servants as unpaid wages (with a national average of 3 per cent). In 1998 the situation deteriorated dramatically with 17 per cent of the total wage bill owed, with a peak of 45 per cent (implying that in some regions wages have been almost half a year late). The year 1999 saw a dramatic improvement with the national average standing at 1.3 per cent (with a high of 35 per cent).

Development of SMEs is a clear outcome indicator for governance quality reflecting the investment climate. Russian statistics of SMEs, which rely on surveys or census-type registration, is quite problematic especially where the dynamic story and comparisons over time are concerned—but as a measure of regional ranking it is quite acceptable. We use the share of SME employment to total employment measured by Goskomstat as a more reliable indicator of the real importance of SMEs (compared to sales or the number of firms, which seems to be particularly biased). The most business-friendly Russian regions in 1996 had a high of 40 per cent of all workforce employed by SMEs (average of 12), but in the worst regions this index was below 3 per cent. We also use the per capita number of SMEs in 1992 to control for the initial entrepreneurial abilities of the population. Basareva (2002) in her study of regional aspects of SME development revealed two significant facts: links of entry to self-employment and SMEs to the entrepreneurial climate in the region (broadly defined); and links of entry to the level and dispersion of entrepreneurial incomes. She demonstrates that the level of SME development in 1992 reflected some general local preferences and largely predetermined the evolution of the sector in transition.

The dispersion of foreign direct investment (FDI) share across regions in the gross regional product is, as one expects, exceptionally high but only a handful of regions have received substantial investments. Openness to trade is a better proxy for the overall effort of the regional government to integrate into the market economy. The ranking of regions according to this indicator has remained very stable over time. There are also all sorts of measurement problems (place of registration of import and export firms is different from the origin/final destination, etc.). Thus, the Republic of Ingushetia (with a special tax regime) serves clearly as a tax haven for many such firms, having a sum of export and import exceeding six times its regional gross product. The lowest share of around 2 per cent is registered in the Siberian Tuva Republic. However, as a general tendency this share is an informative indicator of both firms' and regional authorities' efforts to facilitate international trade and can therefore be used alongside other policy proxies.

An index of structural change (the sum of changes in the sectoral shares of employment) was originally proposed by Layard et al. (1991) in the analysis of unemployment. This index seems to perform well in assessing the depth of industrial restructuring by a certain date.

Economic Shocks

Regions were exposed to different shocks depending on their output composition. These shocks clearly influenced the transitional dynamics of inequality. Unemployment and employment rates as measured by the labour force survey (LFS) can be used to identify the magnitude of shocks to regional employment. Regions differ quite substantially in these indices; the unemployment rate in 1998 ranged from 5 to 50 per cent.

Transfers: Main Types, Role, Variation Across Regions; Transfer Dependent Versus Transfer Independent

We distinguish two types of transfers: budgetary transfers to regions; and transfers from regional budgets to populations. On average, a Russian region receives around 20 per cent of its spending budget from the federal budget as an interbudgetary transfer, with a low of only 3 per cent and a high of 90 per cent. The share of social public transfers in total population income varies in response to regional social policies and the demographic structure of the population, to produce a rather wide range between 5 and 31 per cent during 1997–9.

Appendix IV

Table 14.A2. *Instrumental variables regressions for the initial level of inequality (Gini index in 1994), regression results*

Dependent variable is: Gini for real money incomes in 1994	Full sample unweighted[a]			Weighted by population[b]			−Moscow + Tyumen[c]			−Moscow + Tyumen, weighted by population[d]		
	Coeff.	s.e.	t	Coeff.	s.e.	t	Coeff.	s.e.	t	Coeff.	s.e.	t
Money income in 1985 to national average	−0.0180	0.0125	−1.4420	−0.0189	0.0126	−1.5020	−0.0189	0.0126	−1.5020	−0.0126	0.0113	−1.1140
Car ownership in 1990 (per 1,000 population)	−0.0002	0.0005	−0.5120	−0.0005	0.0004	−1.2880	−0.0003	0.0005	−0.5930	−0.0005	0.0004	−1.1030
% of population with higher education, 1990	−0.5552	0.1815	−3.0580	−0.3047	0.1687	−1.8070	−0.5464	0.1887	−2.8960	−0.2351	0.1753	−1.3410
Share of workers in private firms, 1992	−0.3982	0.1807	−2.2040	−0.3223	0.1818	−1.7730	−0.4044	0.1813	−2.2310	−0.3145	0.1829	−1.7200
SME per 1,000 population, 1992	0.0115	0.0032	3.6510	0.0110	0.0025	4.4640	0.0083	0.0042	1.9980	0.0068	0.0052	1.3090
Employed in industry, population, 1992	−0.8191	0.2467	−3.3200	−0.7859	0.2080	−3.7790	−0.7255	0.2590	−2.8010	−0.7037	0.2152	−3.2690
High dependency on budget transfers	−0.0243	0.0179	−1.3580	−0.0142	0.0148	−0.9590	−0.0215	0.0182	−1.1780	−0.0104	0.0150	−0.6940
Middle dependency on budget transfers	−0.0542	0.0217	−2.5020	−0.0413	0.0193	−2.1460	−0.0589	0.0220	−2.6780	−0.0465	0.0197	−2.3620
Score for price controls, max. = 1	0.1108	0.0326	3.4030	0.0898	0.0308	2.9120	0.0951	0.0368	2.5850	0.0707	0.0349	2.0260
Relative price level, to average Russia	−0.0582	0.0269	−2.1640	−0.0645	0.0249	−2.5860	−0.0632	0.0274	−2.3090	−0.0676	0.0254	−2.6640
Middle level of demographic dependency rate	−0.0456	0.0216	−2.1120	−0.0358	0.0181	−1.9730	−0.0500	0.0221	−2.2630	−0.0389	0.0185	−2.1030
High level of demographic dependency rate	−0.0515	0.0271	−1.8990	−0.0400	0.0243	−1.6480	−0.0553	0.0278	−1.9880	−0.0426	0.0249	−1.7130
Middle level of road quality	0.0250	0.0151	1.6500	0.0227	0.0131	1.7240	0.0223	0.0155	1.4440	0.0185	0.0134	1.3760
High level of road quality	0.0264	0.0159	1.6640	0.0267	0.0137	1.9500	0.0263	0.0160	1.6470	0.0249	0.0137	1.8200
Middle level of telephone lines/ population	−0.0084	0.0142	−0.5910	−0.0147	0.0128	−1.1510	−0.0069	0.0144	−0.4830	−0.0111	0.0130	−0.8590
High level of telephone lines/population	−0.0212	0.0150	−1.4090	−0.0109	0.0132	−0.8300	−0.0174	0.0154	−1.1300	−0.0055	0.0136	−0.4010
Share of urban population	0.1259	0.0914	1.3780	0.1259	0.0820	1.5350	0.0905	0.0958	0.9450	0.1019	0.0835	1.2200
Population density	0.0000	0.0002	0.0830	0.0000	0.0001	−0.4140	0.0000	0.0002	−0.1560	−0.0001	0.0001	−0.4950
Index of natural resources	−0.0373	0.0195	−1.9110	−0.0199	0.0172	−1.1530	−0.0400	0.0197	−2.0290	−0.0240	0.0178	−1.3500
Distance to Moscow	0.0000	0.0017	0.0250	−0.0011	0.0016	−0.6900	0.0007	0.0018	0.4190	−0.0005	0.0016	−0.2920
Dummy for large (>800,000) capital	0.0073	0.0159	0.4580	0.0046	0.0122	0.3780	0.0119	0.0163	0.7300	0.0082	0.0124	0.6620
Share of regional population in 5 largest cities	−0.1128	0.0911	−1.2390	−0.0895	0.0833	−1.0750	−0.1319	0.0931	−1.4170	−0.1146	0.0849	−1.3500
Constant	0.7010	0.1026	6.8300	0.6223	0.1010	6.1630	0.7437	0.1090	6.8200	0.6447	0.1036	6.2250

[a] Number of observations = 75; $F_{(22, 52)} = 4.07$; Probability > $F = 0$; $R^2 = 0.6328$; Adjusted $R^2 = 0.4775$; Root MSE = 0.04419.

[b] Number of observations = 75; $F_{(22, 52)} = 11.23$; Probability > $F = 0$; $R^2 = 0.8261$; Adjusted $R^2 = 0.7525$; Root MSE = 0.0349.

[c] Number of observations = 73; $F_{(22, 50)} = 2.71$; Probability > $F = 0.0018$; $R^2 = 0.5437$; Adjusted $R^2 = 0.3429$; Root MSE = 0.04428.

[d] Number of observations = 73; $F_{(22, 50)} = 3.22$; Probability > $F = 0.0003$; $R^2 = 0.5861$; Adjusted $R^2 = 0.404$; Root MSE = 0.03559.

REFERENCES

Adelman, I. and D. Vujovic (1998). 'Institutional and Policy Aspects of Transition: An Empirical Analysis', in A. Levy-Livermore (ed.) *Handbook on the Globalization of the World Economy*, Edward Elgar: Cheltenham.

Aghion, P. and O. Blanchard (1994). 'On the Speed of Restructuring' (mimeo), MIT: Cambridge, MA and EBRD: London.

Alesina, A., R. Di Tella, and R. MacCulloch (2002). 'Inequality and Happiness: Are Europeans and Americans Different?' (mimeo), National Bureau of Economic Research: Cambridge, MA.

Andalon, M. L. and L. F. Lopez-Calva (2002). 'The Many Mexicos: Income Inequality and Polarization in Urban Mexico During the 90s', paper presented at the WIDER-Cornell-LSE Conference on Spatial Inequality and Development, 28–30 June, London.

Atkinson, A. and J. Micklewright (1995). *Economic Transformation in Eastern Europe and the Distribution of Income*, Cambridge University Press: Cambridge.

Bandyopadhyay, S. (2004). 'Twin Peaks: Distribution Dynamics of Economic Growth across Indian States', in A. Shorrocks and R. van der Hoeven (eds) *Growth, Inequality and Poverty*, Oxford University Press for UNU-WIDER: Oxford.

Barro, R. and X. Sala-i-Martin (1991). 'Convergence Across States and Regions', *Brookings Papers of Economic Activity*, 1: 107–58.

—— and —— (1992). 'Convergence', *Journal of Political Economy*, 100: 223–51.

Basareva V. (2002). 'Institutional Features of New Enterprise Formation in Regions of Russia', *EERC Working Papers* 02/02, Economics Education and Research Consortium: Moscow.

Benabou, R. (1996). 'Inequality and Growth', in B. Bernanke and J. Rotemberg (eds) *NBER Annual*, MIT Press: Cambridge, MA.

Boldrin, M. and F. Canova (2001). 'Inequality and Convergence: Reconsidering European Regional Policies', *Economic Policy*, 32: 207–53.

Bourguignon, F. (1979). 'Decomposable Income Inequality Measures', *Econometrica*, 47(4): 901–20.

Campos, N. F. and F. Coricelli (2000). 'Growth in Transition: What We Know, What We Don't, and What We Should' (mimeo), World Bank: Washington DC and CEPR: London.

Carluer, F. and E. Sharipova (2001). 'Regional Convergence in Russia? Or When Economic Geography Confirms Macroeconomic Analysis', *Russian-European Centre for Economic Policy Working Papers*, June.

Cashin, P. and R. Sahay (1996). 'Internal Migration, Centre-State Grants, and Economic Growth in the States of India', *IMF Staff Papers*, 43: 123–71.

Coulombe, S. and F. Lee (1995). 'Convergence Across Canadian Provinces, 1961 to 1991', *Canadian Journal of Economics*, 28: 886–98.

Commander, S. and A. Tolstopiatenko (1996). 'Restructuring and Taxation in Transition Economies' (mimeo), EBRD: London.

——, ——, and R. Yemtsov (1999). 'Channels of Redistribution: Inequality and Poverty in the Russian Transition', *Economics of Transition*, 7(2): 411–47.

Datt, G. and M. Ravallion (1998). 'Why Have Some Indian States Done Better Than Others?', *Economica*, 65(257): 17–38.

de La Fuente, A. (1996). 'On the Sources of Convergence: A Close Look at the Spanish Regions', *CEPR Discussion Papers* 1543, Centre for Economic Policy Research: London.

Dolinskaya, I. (2002). 'Transition and Regional Inequality in Russia: Reorganization or Procrastination?', *IMF Working Papers* 169, International Monetary Fund: Washington DC.

Earle J. S. and Z. Sakova (1999). 'Entrepreneurship from Scratch: Lessons on the Entry Decision into Self-Employment from Transition Economies', *IZA Discussion Papers* 79, Forschungsinstitut zur Zukunft der Arbeit: Bonn.

Fedorov, L. (2002). 'Regional Inequality and Regional Polarization in Russia, 1990–1999', *World Development*, 30(3): 443–56.

Filiztekin, A. (1999). 'Convergence Across Turkish Provinces and Sectoral Dynamics' (mimeo), World Bank: Washington DC.

Goskomstat (1999). 'Results of the Household Budget Survey', *Statistical Bulletins* 11(61), Goskomstat: Moscow.

—— (2000). *Regions of Russia*, Goskomstat: Moscow.

—— (2001). *Regions of Russia*, Goskomstat: Moscow.

—— (various). *Russian Statistical Yearbook*, Goskomstat: Moscow.

Hanson, P. and M. Bradshaw (2000). *Regional Economic Change in Russia*, Edward Elgar: Cheltenham.

Kanbur, R. and M. Tuomala (2002). 'Understanding the Evolution of Inequality during the Transition: The Optimal Income Taxation Approach' (mimeo), Cornell University: Ithaca.

—— and X. Zhang (1999). 'Which Regional Inequality? The Evolution of Rural–Urban and Inland–Coastal Inequality in China from 1983 to 1995', *Journal of Comparative Economics*, 27(4): 686–701.

Kolenikov, S. and A. F. Shorrocks (2003). 'Regional Dimensions of Poverty in Russia', paper presented at the UNU-WIDER Conference on Spatial Inequality in Asia, 28–29 March, Tokyo.

Kournishev, B. B. (1999). 'Kontseptualnie Podkhodi k Snizheniyu Ekonomicheskoi, Sotsialnoi i Pravovoi Asymmetrii v Razvitii Regionov Rossiskoi Federatsii (Conceptual Approaches to Addressing Economic, Social, and Legal Asymmetry in Regional Development of the Russian Federation)', *Regions: Economics and Sociology* 2 (Russian-language periodical).

Lavrovsky, B. (1999). 'Regionalnaya Asymmetria i Razvitie' (Regional Asymmetry and Development), *Regions: Economics and Sociology*, Special Issue (Russian-language periodical).

Layard R., S. Nickell, and R. Jackman (1991). *Unemployment*, Oxford University Press: Oxford.

Lokshin, M. (2002). 'Results of RLMS. Poverty and Inequality Changes' (mimeo), World Bank: Washington DC.

Mikheeva, N. (1999). 'Analysis of Interregional Inequality in Russia', *EERC Studies on Russian Economic Development* (10)5, Economics Education and Research Consortium: Moscow.

Milanovic, B. (1998). *Income, Inequality, and Poverty during the Transition from Planned to Market Economy*, World Bank: Washington DC.

—— (1999a). 'Explaining the Increase in Inequality during the Transition', *World Bank Policy Research Working Papers* 1935, World Bank: Washington DC.

—— (1999b). 'Do More Unequal Countries Redistribute More? Does the Median Voter Hypothesis Hold?' *World Bank Policy Research Working Papers* 2264, World Bank: Washington DC.

Mistiaen J. A. and M. Ravallion (2002). 'Survey Compliance and the Distribution of Income', *World Bank Policy Research Working Paper* 2956, World Bank: Washington DC.

Ovcharova L. *et al.* (2001). 'Working Towards a Poverty Eradication Strategy in Russia: Analysis and Recommendations' (mimeo), United Nations Theme Group on Poverty, ILO Moscow Office.

Persson, J. (1994). 'Convergence in Per Capita Income and Migration Across the Swedish Counties 1906–1990' (mimeo), IIES Stockholm University: Stockholm.

Ravallion, M. (2001). 'Inequality Convergence', *World Bank Policy Research Working Papers* 2645, World Bank: Washington DC.

—— and M. Lokshin (1999). 'Who Wants to Redistribute? The Tunnel Effect of 1990s Russia', *World Bank Policy Research Working Papers* 2150, World Bank: Washington DC.

Sheviakov, A. and A. Kiruta (2001). *Economic Inequality, Standards of Living and Poverty of Population in Russia (Measurement Methods and Analysis of Causal Dependencies)*, Centre for Socioeconomic Measurement, Russian Academy of Sciences: Moscow, and Economics Education and Research Consortium: Moscow.

Shorrocks, A. F. (1976). 'Income Mobility and the Markov Assumption', *Economic Journal*, 86: 566–78.

—— (1980). 'The Class of Additively Decomposable Inequality Measures', *Econometrica*, 48(3): 613–25.

—— and S. Kolenikov (2001). 'Poverty Trends in Russia during the Transition' (mimeo), UNU–WIDER: Helsinki.

Shioji, E. (1996). 'Regional Growth in Japan', *CEPR Discussion Papers* 1425, Centre for Economic Policy Research: London.

Treivish, A. I. (1999). 'Novie Tendentsii v Razvitii Regionov Rossii i ih Asymmetria (New Tendencies in the Development of Regions in Russia and Their Asymmetry)', *Regions: Economics and Sociology*, Special Issue (Russian-language periodical).

Treisman, D. and V. Gimpelson (2000). 'Political Business Cycles and Russian Elections, or the Manipulations of Chudar', *CIRJE Working Papers* 39, CIRJE, Faculty of Economics, Tokyo University: Tokyo

World Bank (1996). *Fiscal Management in Russia*, World Bank: Washington DC.

—— (2000). *Making Transition Work for Everyone: Poverty and Inequality in Europe and Central Asia*, World Bank: Washington DC.

Westlund, H., A. Granberg, and F. Snickars (2000). *Regional Development in Russia*, Edward Elgar: Cheltenham.

Yemtsov, R. (2003). 'Through the Looking Glass: What Can Official Data on Poverty in Russia Tell Us?' (mimeo), World Bank: Washington DC.

Zhuravskaya, F. V. (2000). 'Market-Hampering Federalism: Local Incentives for Reform in Russia' (mimeo), Russian–European Centre for Economic Policy: Moscow.

Author index

Subject index

Page numbers in *italic* relate to figures/tables.